THE
TOP
10
OF EVERYTHING
1999

THE
TOP
10
OF EVERYTHING
1999

— RUSSELL ASH —

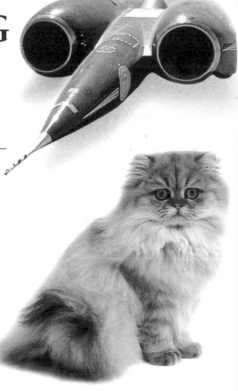
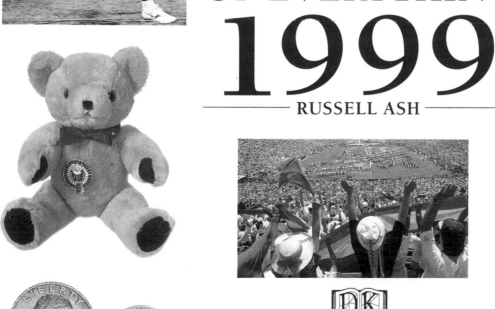

DORLING KINDERSLEY
London • New York • Sydney • Moscow

A DORLING KINDERSLEY BOOK

Production Controller Silvia La Greca
Project Editor Adèle Hayward
Managing Editor Stephanie Jackson
Managing Art Editor Nigel Duffield

Produced by GLS Editorial and Design,
Garden Studios, 11–15 Betterton Street,
London, WC2H 9BP
Designers Donna Askem, Ian Merrill,
Sue Caws, Jamie Hanson, Harvey de Roemer
Editors Claire Calman, Fergus Day, Helen Ridge
Design director Ruth Shane
Editorial director Jane Laing

Published in Great Britain in 1998 by
Dorling Kindersley Limited,
9 Henrietta Street,
London WC2E 8PS

Copyright © 1998
Dorling Kindersley Limited, London
Text copyright © 1998 Russell Ash

A CIP catalogue record of this book is available
from the British Library.

ISBN 0 7513 06096

Reproduction by HBM Print Ltd, Singapore.
Printed and bound in Italy by Eurolitho.

CONTENTS

INTRODUCTION

Welcome to No. 10! This edition of *The Top 10 of Everything* is, appropriately, the 10th. When it was first published in 1988, no one – including me – imagined that it would be published annually, but such has been its success that it has been issued every year since then. It has also appeared in many national editions and in a variety of languages around the world, has given rise to a range of spin-off publications, and has now inspired a television series.

TOP 10 LISTS

For the benefit of newcomers to the book, I should explain that *The Top 10 of Everything* does not contain any "bests" or favourites, but exclusively quantifiable rankings. Some are "worsts", as in the case of murder and disaster victims, which are, sadly, measurable. It focuses on superlatives in numerous categories – tallest, fastest, richest, and so on – but also contains a variety of "firsts" or "latests", which recognize, for instance, the first 10 holders of the Land Speed Record. "Latests", as in the case of award winners, are the most recent 10 achievers in a field of endeavour, and are thus a sort of chronological Top 10.

WHAT'S NEW?

In an attempt to squeeze a quart into a pint pot, and thereby increase the total number of featured lists to over the 1,000 mark for the first time, certain lists have been compacted. Those lists marked with stars are new to this edition, but even those without a star are new in the sense that although the subject may have appeared previously, the entries within the list have been fully updated. Another new feature this year is the introduction of certain "Then & Now" lists, which juxtapose today's listing with that of a decade ago, resulting in often revealing comparisons. Occasional "Snap Facts", another innovation, provide extra snippets of information on the subjects of the adjacent lists.

INFORMATION SOURCES

In response to readers who have asked that sources be included, you will find that these appear adjacent to certain lists. By default, those that do not have credits result from work specially undertaken for the book by myself or by specialists in various fields, using multiple sources of information. Lists on topics ranging from accidents to place names can be compiled only by extensive research in diverse sources, and through constant monitoring for changes. Most lists contain the latest available information, as at the time the book went to press, or, if based on annual statistics, the latest available year. The latter is usually the last calendar year. The exceptions are generally those that are based on "official", or government, figures, which often – despite such technological advances as electronic publishing and the Internet – follow a tortuous route from their source to public availability, and may consequently be a couple of years old. However, without wishing to absolve the sluggards of the statistical world, I would suggest that one of the things *The Top 10 of Everything* attempts to do is to take such figures, which are more often than not issued in dense (and expensive) publications, and present them in a form that is accessible. Regrettably, the demands of our production schedule make it impossible to update certain lists beyond a certain cut-off point – frustratingly, certain sporting and other events, such as soccer World Cups and various annual awards ceremonies, have a habit of taking place while the book is being finalized, so they sometimes don't make it in time.

THANK YOU!

From the very first year, the book has remained a personal endeavour, but one that could not be compiled without the help of the many individuals and organizations who have kindly supplied information, and whose contributions are acknowledged at the end. I would also like to thank those readers who have taken the trouble to write or e-mail me with their helpful comments and suggestions. Whenever possible I have responded to them, but the pressures inherent in producing a book of this kind mean that I have sometimes not had the time to do so, and I hope they will accept this as my special "thank you".

SUGGESTIONS AND CORRECTIONS

If you wish to present either, you can contact me on our World Wide Web site at http://www.dk.com (where you will find more Top 10 lists and information about other Dorling Kindersley books), e-mail me direct at ash@pavilion.co. uk, or write to me c/o the publishers.

Watch out for the next – the millennium – edition of *The Top 10 of Everything*!

SPECIAL FEATURES FOR THIS EDITION

• More than 1,000 lists give you the most comprehensive
Top 10 of Everything ever.

• Stars highlight lists that are new to this edition.

• Then & Now lists pinpoint specific changes over the last decade.

• Snapfact panels supplement the lists on many pages, providing
additional nuggets of intriguing and unusual information.

• Anniversary panels are distributed throughout the book, recalling
fascinating events that occurred 50, 100, or even 200 years ago.

• Caption lists are appended to many pictures to provide extra
snippets of data.

• Sources for many Top 10 lists are displayed adjacent to them.

THE UNIVERSE
& THE EARTH

TOP 10

BRIGHTEST STARS*

	Star	Constellation	Distance[#]	Apparent magnitude
1	Sirius	Canis Major	8.64	−1.46
2	Canopus	Carina	1,200	−0.73
3	Alpha Centauri	Centaurus	4.35	−0.27
4	Arcturus	Boötes	34	−0.04
5	Vega	Lyra	26	+0.03
6	Capella	Auriga	45	+0.08
7	Rigel	Orion	900	+0.12
8	Procyon	Canis Minor	11.4	+0.38
9	Achernar	Eridanus	85	+0.46
10	Beta Centauri	Cantaurus	460	+0.61

* *Excluding the Sun*

\# *From Earth in light years, unless otherwise stated*

Based on apparent visual magnitude as viewed from Earth – the lower the number, the brighter the star. At its brightest, the star Betelgeuse is brighter than some of these, but as it is variable its average brightness disqualifies it from the Top 10.

TOP 10

STARS NEAREST TO THE EARTH*

	Star	Light years[#]	Distance from the Earth km (millions)	miles (millions)
1	Proxima Centauri	4.22	39,923,310	24,792,500
2	Alpha Centauri	4.35	41,153,175	25,556,250
3	Barnard's Star	5.98	56,573,790	35,132,500
4	Wolf 359	7.75	73,318,875	45,531,250
5	Lalande 21185	8.22	77,765,310	48,292,500
6	Luyten 726-8	8.43	79,752,015	49,526,250
7	Sirius	8.64	81,833,325	50,818,750
8	Ross 154	9.45	89,401,725	55,518,750
9	Ross 248	10.40	98,389,200	61,100,000
10	Epsilon Eridani	10.80	102,173,400	63,450,000

* *Excluding the Sun*

\# *One light year = 9,460,528,404,000 km/5,878,812,000 miles*

A spaceship travelling at a speed of 40,237 km/h/ 25,000 mph – which is faster than any human (as opposed to unmanned probes) has yet achieved in space – would take more than 113,200 years to reach Earth's closest star, Proxima Centauri.

THE 10 TYPES OF STAR

Type	Maximum surface temperature °C
1 W	80,000
2 O	40,000
3 B	25,000
4 A	10,000
5 F	7,500
6 G	6,000
7 K	5,000
8 M	3,400
9= C (formerly R & N)	2,600
= S	2,600

Stars are classified by type according to their spectra – the colours by which they appear when viewed with a spectroscope. These vary according to the star's surface temperature. A letter is assigned to each – although there are some variations, Type C sometimes being divided into R and N. Using this code, one mnemonic for remembering the sequence in the correct order takes the initial letters of the words in the phrase "Wow! O Be A Fine Girl Kiss Me Right Now Sweetie". Within these types, there are sub-types, with dwarfs generally hotter than giants. Most stars fall in the mid-range (B to M), with those at the extreme ends being comparatively rare.

- The Andromeda Galaxy is 2,200,000 light years away from the Milky Way, contains 300 billion stars, and is 180,000 light years in diameter. It is the most distant thing in the Universe the unaided human eye can see.
- Andromeda is a rotating spiral nebula 2,309,000 light years from Earth (13 million trillion miles). Its light left there just after the first humans appeared on Earth, and comes from thousands of millions of stars – no individual one can be made out.
- More than half of all stars are binary stars – two or more stars that orbit one another. They range in size from giants up to 40 times the mass of the Sun to dwarfs down to 1/10 the mass of the Sun.

TOP 10 GALAXIES NEAREST TO THE EARTH

Galaxy	Distance light years
1 Large Cloud of Magellan	169,000
2 Small Cloud of Magellan	190,000
3 Ursa Minor dwarf	250,000
4 Draco dwarf	260,000
5 Sculptor dwarf	280,000
6 Fornax dwarf	420,000
7= Leo I dwarf	750,000
= Leo II dwarf	750,000
9 Barnard's Galaxy	1,700,000
10 Andromeda Spiral	2,200,000

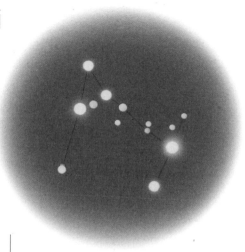

THE MILKY WAY
Often referred to as just "the Galaxy", the Milky Way is a giant spiral made up of several billion stars, including our Sun. Its true nature has been discovered only in the 20th century.

TOP 10 LARGEST REFLECTING TELESCOPES IN THE WORLD

Telescope name	Location	Opened*	Aperture m
1 Keck I and II Telescopes	Mauna Kea Observatory, Hawaii	1992/96	10.82
2 Bolshoi Teleskop Azimutal'ny	Special Astrophysical Observatory of the Russian Academy of Sciences, Mount Pastukhov, Russia	1976	6.0
3 Hale Telescope	Palomar Observatory, California	1948	5.0
4 William Herschel Telescope	Observatorio del Roque de los Muchachos, La Palma, Canary Islands	1987	4.2
5= Mayall Telescope#	Kitt Peak National Observatory, Arizona, USA	1973	4.0
= 4-metre Telescope#	Cerro Tololo Inter-American Observatory, Chile	1976	4.0
7 Anglo-Australian Telescope	Siding Spring Observatory, New South Wales, Australia	1974	3.9
8= ESO 3.6-metre Telescope	European Southern Observatory, La Silla, Chile	1975	3.6
= Canada-France-Hawaii Telescope	Mauna Kea Observatory, Hawaii	1970	3.6
= United Kingdom Infrared Telescope	Mauna Kea Observatory, Hawaii	1979	3.6

* *Dedicated or regular use commenced*

Northern/southern hemisphere "twin" telescopes

THE SOLAR SYSTEM

T O P 1 0

LARGEST PLANETARY MOONS IN THE SOLAR SYSTEM

	Moon	Planet	Diameter km	miles
1	Ganymede	Jupiter	5,269	3,274

Discovered by Galileo in 1609–10, Ganymede is thought to have a surface of thick ice.

2	Titan	Saturn	5,150	3,200

The Dutch astronomer Christian Huygens discovered Titan in 1655. It has a dense atmosphere rich in nitrogen and ethane.

3	Callisto	Jupiter	4,820	2,995

Similar in composition to Ganymede, Callisto is heavily pitted with craters.

4	Io	Jupiter	3,632	2,257

Io has a crust of solid sulphur with volcanic eruptions hurling material far into space.

5	Moon	Earth	3,475	2,159

Our own satellite is a quarter of the size of the Earth and the 5th largest in the Solar System.

6	Europa	Jupiter	3,126	1,942

Europa's ice-covered surface is crossed with mysterious black lines resembling canals.

7	Triton	Neptune	2,750	1,708

Discovered by British amateur astronomer William Lassell in 1846, Triton has nitrogen and methane glaciers on its surface.

8	Titania	Uranus	1,580	982

Titania was discovered by William Herschel in 1787 and has a snowball-like surface of ice.

9	Rhea	Saturn	1,530	951

Saturn's second largest moon was discovered by 17th-century French astronomer Giovanni Cassini. Its icy surface is pitted with craters.

10	Oberon	Uranus	1,516	942

Discovered by Herschel, Oberon was named after the fairy husband of Titania in Shakespeare's A Midsummer Night's Dream.

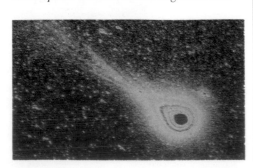

T O P 1 0

LARGEST METEORITES EVER FOUND

	Location	Estimated weight (tonnes)
1	Hoba West, Grootfontein, South Africa	54.4
2	Ahnighito ("The Tent"), Cape York, West Greenland	30.9
3	Bacuberito, Mexico	27.0
4	Mbosi, Tanganyika	26.0
5	Agpalik, Cape York, West Greenland	20.1
6	Armanti, Western Mongolia	20.0
7 =	Willamette, Oregon, USA	14.0
=	Chupaderos, Mexico	14.0
9	Campo del Cielo, Argentina	13.0
10	Mundrabilla, Western Australia	12.0

It is calculated that some 500 meteorites strike the surface of Earth every year, although many fall in the sea and in unpopulated areas. The actual risk of being struck by a falling meteorite has also been estimated, and for citizens of the USA placed at one occurrence every 9,300 years.

T O P 1 0

MOST FREQUENTLY SEEN COMETS

	Comet	Period (years)
1	Encke	3.302
2	Grigg-Skjellerup	4.908
3	Honda-Mrkós-Pajdusáková	5.210
4	Tempel 2	5.259
5	Neujmin 2	5.437
6	Brorsen	5.463
7	Tuttle-Giacobini-Kresák	5.489
8	Tempel-L. Swift	5.681
9	Tempel 1	5.982
10	Pons-Winnecke	6.125

HALLEY'S COMET
Returning every 76 years, its next appearance will be in 2061.

T O P 1 0

BODIES FURTHEST FROM THE SUN*

	Body	Average distance from Sun '000 km	'000 miles
1	Pluto	5,914,000	3,675,000
2	Neptune	4,497,000	2,794,000
3	Uranus	2,871,000	1,784,000
4	Chiron	2,800,000	1,740,000
5	Saturn	1,427,000	887,000
6	Jupiter	778,300	483,600
7	Mars	227,900	141,600
8	Earth	149,600	92,900
9	Venus	108,200	67,200
10	Mercury	57,900	36,000

* In the Solar System, excluding satellites and asteroids

Chiron, a "mystery object" which may be either a comet or an asteroid, was discovered on 1 November 1977 by American astronomer Charles Kowal. It measures 200-300 km/124-186 miles in diameter and orbits between Saturn and Uranus. A so-called "Planet X" is believed by some to orbit beyond Pluto.

T O P 1 0

LONGEST DAYS IN THE SOLAR SYSTEM

	Body	days	Length of day hours	mins
1	Venus	244	0	0
2	Mercury	58	14	0
3	Sun	25#	0	0
4	Pluto	6	9	0
5	Mars		24	37
6	Earth		23	56
7	Uranus		17	14
8	Neptune		16	7
9	Saturn		10	39
10	Jupiter		9	55

* Period of rotation, based on Earth day
\# Variable

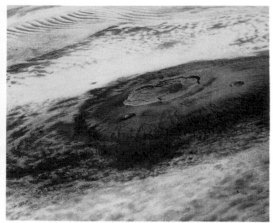

SURFACE OF MARS

TOP 10 LARGEST BODIES IN THE SOLAR SYSTEM
(Diameter)

❶ Sun (1,392,140 km/ 865,036 miles) ❷ Jupiter (142,984 km/ 88,846 miles) ❸ Saturn (120,536 km/ 74,898 miles) ❹ Uranus (51,118 km/ 31,763 miles) ❺ Neptune (49,532 km/30,778 miles) ❻ Earth (12,756 km/7,926 miles) ❼ Venus (12,103 km/7,520 miles) ❽ Mars (6,794 km/4,222 miles) ❾ Ganymede (5,269 km/3,274 miles) ❿ Titan (5,150km/3,200 miles)

TOP 10
LARGEST ASTEROIDS IN THE SOLAR SYSTEM

	Asteroid	Year discovered	Diameter km	miles
1	Ceres	1801	936	582
2	Pallas	1802	607	377
3	Vesta	1807	519	322
4	Hygeia	1849	450	279
5	Euphrosyne	1854	370	229
6	Interamnia	1910	349	217
7	Davida	1903	322	200
8	Cybele	1861	308	192
9	Europa	1858	288	179
10	Patienta	1899	275	171

Asteroids, sometimes known as "minor planets", are fragments of rock orbiting between Mars and Jupiter. There are perhaps 45,000 of them, but fewer than 10 per cent have been named. The first (and largest) to be discovered was Ceres.

TOP 10
LONGEST YEARS IN THE SOLAR SYSTEM

	Body	Length of year* years	days
1	Pluto	247	256
2	Neptune	164	298
3	Uranus	84	4
4	Saturn	29	168
5	Jupiter	11	314
6	Mars		687
7	Earth		365
8	Venus		225
9	Mercury		88
10	Sun		0

* *Period of orbit round Sun, in Earth years/days*

TOP 10
BODIES IN THE SOLAR SYSTEM WITH THE GREATEST ESCAPE VELOCITY*

	Body	Escape velocity (km/s)
1	Sun	617.50
2	Jupiter	60.22
3	Saturn	32.26
4	Neptune	23.90
5	Uranus	22.50
6	Earth	11.18
7	Venus	10.36
8	Mars	5.03
9	Mercury	4.25
10	Pluto	1.18

* *Excluding satellites. Escape velocity is the speed a rocket has to attain to overcome the gravitational pull of the body it is leaving*

TOP 10
BODIES IN THE SOLAR SYSTEM WITH THE GREATEST SURFACE GRAVITY*

	Body	Surface gravity	Weight#		Body	Surface gravity	Weight#
1	Sun	27.90	1,813.50	6	Earth	1.00	65.00
2	Jupiter	2.64	171.60	7	Venus	0.90	58.50
3	Neptune	1.20	78.00	8	Mars	0.38	24.70
4	Uranus	1.17	76.05	9	Mercury	0.38	24.70
5	Saturn	1.16	75.40	10	Pluto	0.06	3.90

* *Excluding satellites*
\# *Of a 65 kg adult on the body's surface*

TOP 10
MOST MASSIVE BODIES IN THE SOLAR SYSTEM

	Name	Mass*		Name	Mass*
1	Sun	332,800.000	6	Earth	1.000#
2	Jupiter	317.828	7	Venus	0.815
3	Saturn	95.161	8	Mars	0.10745
4	Neptune	17.148	9	Mercury	0.05527
5	Uranus	14.536	10	Pluto	0.0022

* *Compared with Earth = 1; excluding satellites*
\# *The mass of Earth is approximately 73,500,000,000,000,000,000,000 tonnes*

SPACE FIRSTS

FIRST UNMANNED MOON LANDINGS

	Spacecraft	Country	Date (launch/impact)
1	Lunik 2	USSR	12/14 Sep 1959
2	Ranger 4*	USA	23/26 Apr 1962
3	Ranger 6	USA	30 Jan/2 Feb 1964
4	Ranger 7	USA	28/31 Jul 1964
5	Ranger 8	USA	17/20 Feb 1965
6	Ranger 9	USA	21/24 Mar 1965
7	Luna 5*	USSR	9/12 May 1965
8	Luna 7*	USSR	4/8 Oct 1965
9	Luna 8*	USSR	3/7 Dec 1965
10	Luna 9	USSR	31 Jan/3 Feb 1966

* Crash landing

THE 10 FIRST PLANETARY PROBES
(Country/planet/arrival date)

❶ Venera 4 (USSR, Venus, 18 Oct 1967) ❷ Venera 5 (USSR, Venus, 16 May 1969) ❸ Venera 6 (USSR, Venus, 17 May 1969) ❹ Venera 7 (USSR, Venus, 15 Dec 1970) ❺ Mariner 9 (USA, Mars, 13 Nov 1971) ❻ Mars 2 (USSR, Mars, 27 Nov 1971) ❼ Mars 3 (USSR, Mars, 2 Dec 1971) ❽ Venera 8 (USSR, Venus, 22 Jul 1972) ❾ Venera 9 (USSR, Venus, 22 Oct 1975) ❿ Venera 10 (USSR, Venus, 25 Oct 1975)

MARS SPACE PROBE

FIRST COUNTRIES TO HAVE ASTRONAUTS OR COSMONAUTS IN SPACE

	Country/name	Date*
1	USSR Yuri Alekseyiviech Gagarin	12 Apr 1961
2	USA John Herschell Glenn	20 Feb 1962
3	Czechoslovakia Vladimir Remek	2 Mar 1978
4	Poland Miroslaw Hermaszewski	27 Jun 1978
5	East Germany Sigmund Jahn	26 Aug 1978
6	Bulgaria, Georgi I. Ivanov	10 Apr 1979
7	Hungary Bertalan Farkas	26 May 1980
8	Vietnam, Pham Tuan	23 Jul 1980
9	Cuba, Arnaldo T. Mendez	18 Sep 1980
10	Mongolia, Jugderdemidiyn Gurragcha	22 Mar 1981

* Of first space entry of a national of that country

FIRST MOONWALKERS

	Name/spacecraft	Mission dates
1	Neil A. Armstrong (Apollo 11)	16–24 Jul 1969
2	Edwin E. ("Buzz") Aldrin (Apollo 11)	16–24 Jul 1969
3	Charles Conrad, Jr. (Apollo 12)	14–24 Nov 1969
4	Alan L. Bean (Apollo 12)	14–24 Nov 1969
5	Alan B. Shepard (Apollo 14)	31 Jan–9 Feb 1971
6	Edgar D. Mitchell (Apollo 14)	31 Jan–9 Feb 1971
7	David R. Scott (Apollo 15)	26 Jul–7 Aug 1971
8	James B. Irwin (Apollo 15)	26 Jul–7 Aug 1971
9	John W. Young (Apollo 16)	16–27 Apr 1972
10	Charles M. Duke (Apollo 16)	16–27 Apr 1972

FIRST BODIES TO HAVE BEEN VISITED BY SPACECRAFT*

	Body	Spacecraft/country	Year
1	Moon	Pioneer 4 (USA)	1959
2	Venus	Mariner 2 (USA)	1962
3	Mars	Mariner 4 (USA)	1965
4	Sun	Pioneer 7 (USA)	1966
5	Jupiter	Pioneer 10 (USA)	1973
6	Mercury	Mariner 10 (USA)	1974
7	Saturn	Pioneer 11 (USA)	1979
8	Comet Giacobini-Zinner	International Sun-Earth Explorer 3 (International Cometary Explorer, USA/Europe)	1985
9	Uranus	Voyager 2 (USA)	1986
10	Halley's Comet	Giotto (Europe)	1986

* Spacecraft did not land

THE 10 FIRST ANIMALS IN SPACE
(Animal/country/date)

❶ Laika (dog, USSR, 3 November 1957)
❷= Laska and Benjy (mice, USA, 13 December 1958) ❹= Able (female rhesus monkey) and Baker (female squirrel monkey, USA, 28 May 1959) ❻= Otvazhnaya (female Samoyed husky) and an unnamed rabbit, (USSR, 2 July 1959) ❽ Sam (male rhesus monkey, USA, 4 December 1959) ❾ Miss Sam (female rhesus monkey, USA, 21 January 1960) ❿= Belka and Strelka (female Samoyed huskies, USSR, 19 August 1960)

FIRST DOG IN SPACE
Launched in Sputnik II, Laika, a female Samoyed, became the first animal in Space. She died when her oxygen supply was exhausted, and her capsule was incinerated on re-entry to the Earth's atmosphere.

THE 10
FIRST PEOPLE TO ORBIT THE EARTH

	Name	Age	Orbits	Duration hr:min	Spacecraft/ country of origin	Date
1	Fl. Major Yuri Alekseyivich Gagarin	27	1	1:48	*Vostok I* USSR	12 Apr 1961
2	Major Gherman Stepanovich Titov	25	17	25:18	*Vostok II* USSR	6–7 Aug 1961
3	Lt.-Col. John Herschel Glenn	40	3	4:56	*Friendship 7* USA	20 Feb 1962
4	Lt.-Col. Malcolm Scott Carpenter	37	3	4:56	*Aurora 7* USA	24 May 1962
5	Major Andrian Grigoryevich Nikolayev	32	64	94:22	*Vostok III* USSR	11–15 Aug 1962
6	Col. Pavel Romanovich Popovich	31	48	70:57	*Vostok IV* USSR	12–15 Aug 1962
7	Cdr. Walter Marty Schirra	39	6	9:13	*Sigma 7* USA	3 Oct 1962
8	Major Leroy Gordon Cooper	36	22	34:19	*Faith 7* USA	15–16 May 1963
9	Lt.-Col. Valeri Fyodorovich Bykovsky	28	81	119:6	*Vostok V* USSR	14–19 Jun 1963
10	Jr. Lt. Valentina Vladimirovna Tereshkova	26	48	70:50	*Vostok VI* USSR	16–19 Jun 1963

THE 10
FIRST WOMEN IN SPACE

	Name/country/ spacecraft/mission	Date
1	Valentina Vladimirovna Tereshkova, USSR, *Vostok 6*	16–19 Jun 1963

Tereshkova (b. 6 Mar 1937) was the first and, at 26, the youngest woman in space.

2	Svetlana Savitskaya, USSR, *Soyuz T7*	19 Aug 1982

On 25 Jul 1984 Savitskaya (b. 4 Aug 1948) also walked in space (from Soyuz T12).

3	Sally K. Ride, USA, *STS-7*	18–24 Jun 1983

Ride (b. 26 May 1951) was the first American woman in space.

4	Judith A. Resnik, USA, *STS-41-D*	30 Aug–5 Sep 1984

Resnik (b. 5 Apr 1949) was later killed in the STS-51-L Shuttle disaster.

5	Kathryn D. Sullivan, USA, *STS-41-G*	5–13 Oct 1984

Sullivan (b. 3 Oct 1951) was the first American woman to walk in space.

6	Anna L. Fisher, USA, *STS-51-A*	8–16 Nov 1984

Fisher (b. 24 Aug 1949) was the first American mother in space.

7	Margaret Rhea Seddon, USA, *STS-51-D*	12–19 Apr 1985

Seddon (b. 8 Nov 1947) flew again in STS-40 (5–14 Jun 1991) and STS-58 (18 Oct–1 Nov 1993).

8	Shannon W. Lucid, USA, *STS-51-G*	17–24 Jun 1985

Lucid (b. 14 Jan 1943) also flew in STS-34 (18–23 Oct 1989), STS-43 (2–11 Aug 1991), STS-58 (18 Oct–1 Nov 1993). From STS-76 she transferred to the Russian Mir space station, then returned to Earth with STS-79 (22 Mar–26 Sep 1996).

9	Bonnie J. Dunbar, USA, *STS-61-A*	30 Oct–6 Nov 1985

Dunbar (b. 3 Mar 1949) also flew in STS-32 (9–20 Jan 1990), STS-50 (25 Jun–9 Jul 1992), and STS-71 (27 Jun–7 Jul 1995).

10	Mary L. Cleave, USA, *STS-61-B*	26 Nov–3 Dec 1985

Cleave (b. 5 Feb 1947) also flew in STS-30 (4–8 May 1989).

ASTRONAUTS & COSMONAUTS

TOP 10

MOST EXPERIENCED SPACEMEN*

	Name	Missions	Total duration of missions			
			day	hr	min	sec
1	Valeri V. Polyakov	2	678	16	33	18
2	Anatoli Y. Solovyov	5	601	15	01	55
3	Musa K. Manarov	2	541	00	29	38
4	Alexander S. Viktorenko	4	489	01	35	17
5	Sergei K. Krikalyov	3#	471	14	18	39
6	Yuri V. Romanenko	3	430	18	21	30
7	Alexander A. Volkov	3	391	11	52	14
8	Vladimir G. Titov	5#	387	00	51	03
9	Vasily V. Tsibliev	2	381	15	53	02
10	Yuri V. Usachyov	2	375	19	34	36

* To 1 January 1998

\# Including flights aboard US Space Shuttles

All the missions listed were undertaken by the USSR (and, latterly, Russia). The new record-holder, Plyakov, gained 241 days' experience as a USSR Mir space station astronaut in 1988, and spent his second – and the longest-ever residence in space – at Mir from 8 January 1994 until 26 March 1995.

TOP 10

LONGEST SPACEWALKS*

	Astronaut	Spacecraft	EVA date	EVA# hr:min
1 =	Thomas D. Akers	STS-49	13 May 1992	8:30
=	Richard J. Hieb	STS-49	13 May 1992	8:30
=	Pierre J. Thuot	STS-49	13 May 1992	8:30
4 =	Jeffrey A. Hoffman	STS-61	4 Dec 1993	7:54
=	F. Story Musgrave	STS-61	4 Dec 1993	7:54
6 =	Thomas D. Akers	STS-49	14 May 1992	7:47
=	Kathryn C. Thornton	STS-49	14 May 1992	7:47
8 =	Takao Doi	STS-87	24 Nov 1997	7:43
=	Winston E. Scott	STS-87	24 Nov 1997	7:43
10 =	Gregory J. Harbaugh	STS-82	15 Feb 1997	7:27
=	Joseph R. Tanner	STS-82	15 Feb 1997	7:27

* To 1 January 1998

\# Extra Vehicular Activity

This Top 10 (which excludes the EVAs of Apollo astronauts on the lunar surface) consists entirely of spacewalks conducted by US astronauts during recent space shuttle missions.

SHANNON W. LUCID
The USA's 6th woman in space, and the most experienced, Shannon Lucid holds the record for time spent in space by a woman. In 1996 she travelled 121 million km/75.2 million miles during 188 days in orbit.

TOP 10

YOUNGEST US ASTRONAUTS*

	Astronaut	First flight	Age#
1	Janice E. Voss	21 Jun 1993	27
2	Kenneth D. Bowersox	25 Jun 1984	28
3	Sally K. Ride	18 Jun 1983	32
4	Tamara E. Jernigan	5 Jun 1991	32
5	Eugene A. Cernan	3 Jun 1966	32
6	Koichi Wakata	11 Jan 1996	32
7	Steven A. Hawley	30 Aug 1984	32
8	Mary E. Weber	13 Jul 1995	32
9	Kathryn D. Sullivan	5 Oct 1984	33
10	Ronald E. McNair†	3 Feb 1984	33

* To 1 January 1998

\# Those of apparently identical age have been ranked according to their precise age in days at the time of their first flight.

† Killed in Challenger disaster, January 1986

TOP 10

OLDEST US ASTRONAUTS*

	Astronaut	Last flight	Age#
1	F. Story Musgrave	7 Dec 1996	61
2	Vance D. Brand	11 Dec 1990	59
3	Karl G. Henize	6 Aug 1985	58
4	Roger K. Crouch	17 Jul 1997	56
5	William E. Thornton	6 May 1985	56
6	Don L. Lind	6 May 1985	54
7	Henry W. Hartsfield	6 Nov 1988	54
8	John E. Blaha	7 Dec 1996	54
9	William G. Gregory	18 Mar 1995	54
10	Robert A. Parker	11 Dec 1990	53

* Including payload specialists, etc; to 1 January 1998

\# Those of apparently identical age have been ranked according to their precise age in days at the time of their last flight.

T O P 1 0
LONGEST SPACE SHUTTLE FLIGHTS*

	Flight	Dates	Duration of flights hr	min	sec
1	STS-80 *Columbia*	19 Nov–7 Dec 1996	423	53	18
2	STS-78 *Columbia*	20 Jun–7 Jul 1996	405	48	30
3	STS-67 *Endeavour*	2–18 Mar 1995	399	9	46
4	STS-73 *Columbia*	20 Oct–5 Nov 1995	381	53	16
5	STS-75 *Columbia*	22 Feb–9 Mar 1996	377	41	25
6	STS-94 *Columbia*	1–17 Jul 1997	376	46	1
7	STS-87 *Atlantis*	25 Sept–6 Oct 1997	376	35	1
8	STS-65 *Columbia*	8–23 Jul 1994	353	55	0
9	STS-58 *Columbia*	18 Oct–1 Nov 1993	336	12	32
10	STS-62 *Columbia*	9–18 Mar 1994	335	16	41

* To 1 January 1998

The acronym STS (Space Transportation System) has been used throughout the Shuttle programme. The first nine flights were simply numbered STS-1 (12–14 April 1981) to STS-9 (28 November – 8 December 1983). Thereafter a more complex system was employed until the ill-fated *Challenger* mission of 28 January 1986, which was designated STS-S1-L. Subsequent launches have reverted to the system of STS plus a number.

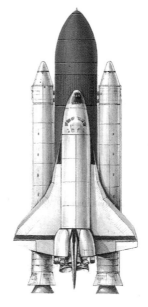

SPACE SHUTTLE
NASA's first space shuttle lifted off on 12 April 1981. The launch system consists of the orbiter, with two solid rocket boosters, and a gigantic external fuel tank weighing 756,441kg/1,667,667 lb when full. The boosters parachute back to Earth and are reused, but the tank disintegrates in the atmosphere.

T O P 1 0
MOST EXPERIENCED SPACEWOMEN*

	Name#	No. of missions	Duration of missions day	hr	min	sec
1	Shannon W. Lucid	5	223	2	52	26
2	Yelena V. Kondakova	2	178	10	41	31
3	Tamara E. Jernigan	4	53	6	12	39
4	Marsha S. Ivins	4	43	0	27	43
5	Bonnie J. Dunbar	4	41	12	37	50
6	Kathryn C. Thornton	4	40	15	15	18
7	Janice E. Voss	4	37	21	10	18
8	Susan J. Helms	3	33	20	16	31
9	Margaret Rhea Seddon	3	30	2	22	15
10	Ellen S. Baker	3	28	14	31	42

* To 1 January 1998
\# All US except No. 2 (Russian)

Already a veteran of four missions, Shannon Lucid became America's most experienced astronaut and the world's most experienced female astronaut in 1996. She took off in US Space Shuttle STS-76 *Atlantis* on 22 March, and transferred to the Russian Mir Space Station, returning on board STS-79 *Atlantis* on 26 September, after travelling 121,000,000 km/75,200,000 miles.

T O P 1 0
COUNTRIES WITH THE MOST SPACEFLIGHT EXPERIENCE*

	Country	No. of astronauts	Duration of missions day	hr	min	sec
1	USSR/Russia#	85	13,094	2	7	17
2	USA	234	5,768	3	44	1
3	Germany	9	298	11	30	13
4	France	7	137	20	8	27
5	Kazakhstan	2	133	21	6	15
6	Canada	6	73	3	0	34
7	Japan	5	55	4	54	50
8	Italy	3	39	10	35	47
9	Switzerland	1	34	12	53	58
10	Ukraine	1	15	16	34	4

* To 1 January 1998
\# Russia became a separate independent state on 25 December 1991

The USSR, and now Russia, has clocked up its considerable lead over the rest of the world (claiming 66 per cent of the total time spent by humans in space) largely through the long-duration stays of its cosmonauts on board the Mir space station, which has been continually occupied since 1986.

WORLD WEATHER

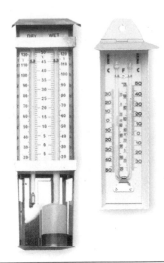

WETTEST YEARS IN ENGLAND AND WALES

	Year	Total rainfall mm	in
1	1872	1,288	50.70
2	1852	1,266	49.84
3	1768	1,192	46.92
4	1960	1,171	46.10
5	1903	1,147	45.15
6	1882	1,135	44.68
7	1877	1,134	44.64
8	1848	1,130	44.48
9	1841	1,120	44.09
10	1912	1,118	44.01

In 1866 the British meteorologist George Symons published a table of rainfall for the period 1726–1865, listing 1852 as the wettest year. In 1872, this was beaten by an average annual rainfall that holds the record to this day. In modern times (1961–90), the annual average for England and Wales was 796 mm/31.33 inches, and for Scotland 1,114 mm/43.86 inches.

TOP 10 HOTTEST YEARS IN THE UK*

(Average temperature)

❶ 1990 (10.63°C/51.13°F) ❷ 1949 (10.62°C/51.12°F) ❸ 1995 (10.55°C/50.99°F), 1997 (10.55°C/50.99°F) ❺ 1989 (10.50°C/50.90°F) ❻ 1959 (10.48°C/50.86°F) ❼ 1733 (10.47°C/50.85°F), 1834 (10.47°C/50.85°F), 1921 (10.47°C/50.85°F) ❿ 1779 (10.40°C/50.72°F)

* Since 1659, based on Central England averages

WARMEST PLACES IN GREAT BRITAIN

	Weather station	Average annual temperature* °C	°F
1	St. Mary's, Isles of Scilly	11.5	52.7
2	Penzance, Cornwall	11.1	52.0
3	Ilfracombe, Devon	11.0	51.8
4=	Central London	10.9	51.6
=	Southampton, Hampshire	10.9	51.6
4=	Southsea (Portsmouth), Hampshire	10.9	51.6
=	Torbay and Teignmouth, Devon	10.9	51.6
8=	Herne Bay, Kent	10.8	51.4
=	Lizard, Cornwall	10.8	51.4
=	Ryde and Sandown, Isle of Wight	10.8	51.4

* Based on The Meteorological Office's 30-year averages for the period 1961–90

COLDEST PLACES IN GREAT BRITAIN

	Weather station	Average annual temperature* °C	°F
1	Dalwhinnie, Highland	6.0	42.8
2=	Leadhills, Strathclyde	6.3	43.3
=	Braemar, Grampian	6.3	43.3
=	Balmoral, Grampian	6.3	43.3
5	Tomatin, Highland	6.4	43.5
6	Granton-on-Spey, Highland	6.5	43.7
7	Lagganlia, nr Kingraig, Highland	6.6	43.9
8	Crawfordjohn, Strathclyde	6.7	44.1
9	Eskdalemuir, Dumfries and Galloway	6.8	44.2
10	Lerwick, Shetland	6.9	44.4

* Based on The Meteorological Office's 30-year averages for the period 1961–90

TOP 10 COLDEST YEARS IN THE UK*

(Average temperature)

❶ 1740 (6.86°C/44.35°F) ❷ 1695 (7.29°C/45.12°F) ❸ 1879 (7.44°C/ 45.39°F) ❹= 1694(7.67°C/45.81°F), 1698 (7.67°C/45.81°F) ❻ 1692 (7.73°C/45.91°F) ❼ 1814 (7.78°C/46.00°F) ❽ 1784 (7.85°C/ 46.13°F) ❾ 1688 (7.86°C/46.15°F) ❿ 1675 (7.88°C/46.18°F)

** Since 1659, based on
Central England averages*

TOP 10 SUNNIEST YEARS IN ENGLAND AND WALES*

(Average daily sunshine hours)

❶ 1995 (4 hrs 51 mins) ❷ 1989 (4 hrs 49.8 mins) ❸ 1990 (4 hrs 43.8 mins) ❹ 1959 (4 hrs 40.2 mins) ❺ 1911 (4 hrs 39 mins) ❻ 1921 (4 hrs 38.4 mins) ❼ 1949 (4 hrs 37.8 mins) ❽ 1997 (4 hrs 28.8 mins) ❾ 1955 (4 hrs 28.2 mins) ❿ 1975 (4 hrs 26.4 mins)

* Since 1909

T O P   1 0

DRIEST INHABITED PLACES IN THE WORLD

	Location	Average annual rainfall	
		mm	in
1	Aswan, Egypt	0.5	0.02
2	Luxor, Egypt	0.7	0.03
3	Arica, Chile	1.1	0.04
4	Ica, Peru	2.3	0.09
5	Antofagasta, Chile	4.9	0.19
6	Minya el Qamn, Egypt	5.1	0.20
7	Asyût, Egypt	5.2	0.20
8	Callao, Peru	12.0	0.47
9	Trujillo, Peru	14.0	0.54
10	Fayyum, Egypt	19.0	0.75

The total annual rainfall of these 10 driest inhabited places, as recorded over extensive periods, is just 64.8 mm/2.5 inches – the average length of an adult's little finger.

T O P   1 0

HOTTEST INHABITED PLACES IN THE WORLD

	Location	Average temperature	
		°C	°F
1	Dijbouti, Dijbouti	30.0	86.0
2 =	Timbuktu, Mali	29.3	84.7
=	Tirunelevi, India	29.3	84.7
=	Tuticorin, India	29.3	84.7
5 =	Nellore, India	29.2	84.6
=	Santa Marta, Colombia	29.2	84.6
7 =	Aden, South Yemen	28.9	84.0
=	Madurai, India	28.9	84.0
=	Niamey, Niger	28.9	84.0
10 =	Hudaydah, North Yemen	28.8	83.8
=	Ouagadougou, Burkina Faso	28.8	83.8
=	Thanjavur, India	28.8	83.8
=	Tiruchirapalli, India	28.8	83.8

T O P   1 0

WETTEST INHABITED PLACES IN THE WORLD

	Location	Average annual rainfall	
		mm	in
1	Buenaventura, Colombia	6,743	265.47
2	Monrovia, Liberia	5,131	202.01
3	Pago Pago, American Samoa	4,990	196.46
4	Moulmein, Myanmar (Burma)	4,852	191.02
5	Lae, Papua New Guinea	4,645	182.87
6	Baguio, Luzon Island, Philippines	4,573	180.04
7	Sylhet, Bangladesh	4,457	175.47
8	Padang, Sumatra Island, Indonesia	4,225	166.34
9	Conakry, Guinea	4,341	170.91
10	Bogor, Java, Indonesia	4,225	166.34

The total annual rainfall of the Top 10 locations is equivalent to more than 26 adults, each measuring 1.83 m/6 ft, standing on top of each other.

SNAP FACTS

- Cilaos, La Réunion, received the most rainfall in 24 hours – 1,870 mm/ 73.62 in, 15–16 March 1952.
- Cherrapunji, Assam, clocked up the most rainfall in a year with 26,461 mm/1,041.8 in from 1 August 1860 to 31 July 1861.

RIVERS & LAKES

18

DEEPEST FRESHWATER LAKES IN THE WORLD

	Lake/location	Greatest depth m	ft
1	Baikal, Russia	1,637	5,371
2	Tanganyika, Burundi/Tanzania/ Dem. Rep. of Congo/ Zambia	1,471	4,825
3	Malawi, Malawi/ Mozambique/Tanzania	706	2,316
4	Great Slave, Canada	614	2,015
5	Matana, Celebes, Indonesia	590	1,936
6	Crater, Oregon, USA	589	1,932
7	Toba, Sumatra, Indonesia	529	1,736
8	Hornindals, Norway	514	1,686
9	Sarez, Tajikistan	505	1,657
10	Tahoe, California/Nevada	501	1,645

LAKE BAIKAL
Four Empire State Buildings stacked on top of one another still would not quite measure up to the depth of Lake Baikal at its deepest point. Because of its depth, Lake Baikal contains more water than any other freshwater lake, despite its small surface area.

LONGEST RIVERS IN THE WORLD

	River/location	Length km	miles
1	Nile, Tanzania/Uganda/ Sudan/Egypt	6,670	4,145
2	Amazon, Peru/Brazil	6,448	4,007
3	Yangtze–Kiang, China	6,300	3,915
4	Mississippi–Missouri– Red Rock, USA	5,971	3,710
5	Yenisey–Angara–Selenga, Mongolia/Russia	5,540	3,442
6	Huang Ho (Yellow River), China	5,464	3,395
7	Ob–Irtysh, Mongolia/ Kazakhstan/Russia	5,410	3,362
8	Congo, Angola/Dem. Rep. of Congo	4,700	2,920
9	Lena–Kirenga, Russia	4,400	2,734
10	Mekong, Tibet/China/ Myanmar (Burma)/Laos/ Cambodia/Vietnam	4,350	2,703

FRESHWATER LAKES WITH THE GREATEST VOLUME OF WATER

	Lake	Location	Volume km³	miles³
1	Baikal	Russia	22,995	5,517
2	Tanganyika	Burundi/Tanzania/ Dem. Rep. of Congo/ Zambia	18,304	4,391
3	Superior	Canada/USA	12,174	2,921
4	Nyasa (Malawi)	Malawi/Mozambique/ Tanzania	6,140	1,473
5	Michigan	USA	4,874	1,169
6	Huron	Canada/USA	3,575	858
7	Victoria	Kenya/Tanzania/Uganda	2,518	604
8	Great Bear	Canada	2,258	542
9	Great Slave	Canada	1,771	425
10	Ontario	Canada/USA	1,539	369

LONGEST GLACIERS IN THE WORLD

	Name	Location	Length km	m
1	Lambert-Fisher	Antarctica	515	320
2	Novaya Zemlya	Russia	418	260
3	Arctic Institute	Antarctica	362	225
4	Nimrod-Lennox-King	Antarctica	290	180
5	Denman	Antarctica	241	150
6=	Beardmore	Antarctica	225	140
=	Recovery	Antarctica	225	140
8	Petermanns	Greenland	200	124
9	Unnamed	Antarctica	193	120
10	Slessor	Antarctica	185	115

Although the longest glacier in the world, the Lambert-Fisher Glacier was only discovered as recently as 1956; it is as much as 3.5 km/2.2 miles deep and 64 km/40 miles wide. The Hubbard Glacier, Alaska, which measures 146 km/91 miles, is the longest in North America, while in Europe, the longest glacier is the Aletsch Glacier, Switzerland, which measures 35 km/22 miles.

TOP 10
GREATEST* WATERFALLS IN THE WORLD

	Waterfall	Location	Average flow (m³/sec)
1	Boyoma (Stanley)	Dem. Rep. of Congo	17,000
2	Khône	Laos	11,500
3	Niagara (Horseshoe)	Canada/USA	5,610
4	Grande	Uruguay	4,500
5	Paulo Afonso	Brazil	2,800
6	Iguaçu	Argentina/Brazil	1,700
7	Maribondo	Brazil	1,500
8	Churchill (Grand)	Canada	1,390
9	Kabalega (Murchison)	Uganda	1,200
10	Victoria	Zimbabwe	1,090

* Based on volume of water

With an average flow rate of 13,000 m³/sec, and a peak of 50,000 m³/sec, the Guaíra between Brazil and Paraguay, once occupied second place in this list, but following the completion of the Itaipú dam in 1982, it is now "lost". At 10.8 km/6.7 miles, the Khône Falls are the widest in the world.

TOP 10
HIGHEST WATERFALLS IN THE WORLD

	Waterfall	Location	Total drop m	ft
1	Angel	Venezuela	979	3,212
2	Tugela	South Africa	948	3,110
3	Utigård	Nesdale, Norway	800	2,625
4	Mongefossen	Mongebekk, Norway	774	2,540
5	Yosemite	California, USA	739	2,425
6	Østre Mardøla Foss	Eikisdal, Norway	657	2,154
7	Tyssestrengane	Hardanger, Norway	646	2,120
8	Cuquenán	Venezuela	610	2,000
9	Sutherland	South Island, New Zealand	580	1,904
10	Kjellfossen	Gudvangen, Norway	561	1,841

TOP 10
RIVERS PRODUCING THE MOST SEDIMENT

	River	Sediment discharged (tonnes per annum)
1	Yellow	1,900,000,000
2	Ganges	1,450,000,000
3	Brahmaputra	725,000,000
4	Yangtze	500,000,000
5	Indus	435,000,000
6	Amazon	360,000,000
7	Mississippi–Missouri	310,000,000
8	Irrawaddy	300,000,000
9	Mekong	170,000,000
10	Colorado	136,000,000

TOP 10
GREATEST RIVERS IN THE WORLD*

	River	Outflow/sea	Average flow(m³/sec)
1	Amazon	Brazil/South Atlantic	175,000
2	Congo	Angola–Dem. Rep. of Congo/South Atlantic	39,000
3	Negro	Brazil/South Atlantic	35,000
4	Yangtze–Kiang	China/Yellow Sea	32,190
5	Orinoco	Venezuela/South Atlantic	25,200
6	Plata–Paraná–Grande	Uruguay/South Atlantic	22,900
7	Madeira–Mamoré–Grande	Brazil/South Atlantic	21,800
8	Brahmaputra	Bangladesh/Bay of Bengal	19,200
9	Yenisey–Angara–Selenga	Russia/Kara Sea	17,600
10	Lena–Kirenga	Russia/Arctic Ocean	16,600

* Based on rate of discharge at mouth

THE AMAZON RIVER
The output of water from the Amazon River into the Atlantic Ocean is so great that if it drained Lake Baikal, the deepest freshwater lake in the world would be empty in 1¹/₂ days.

ISLANDS & SEAS

T O P 1 0

LARGEST ISLANDS IN THE UK

Island	Population	Approx. area sq km	sq miles
1 Lewis and Harris, Outer Hebrides	23,390	2,225.30	859.19
2 Skye, Hebrides	8,139	1,666.08	643.27
3 Mainland, Shetland	22,184	967.00	373.36
4 Mull, Inner Hebrides	2,605	899.25	347.20
5 Ynys Môn (Anglesey), Wales	69,800	713.80	275.60
6 Islay, Inner Hebrides	3,997	638.79	246.64
7 Isle of Man	69,788	571.66	220.72
8 Mainland, Orkney	14,299	536.10	206.99
9 Arran, Inner Hebrides	4,726	435.32	168.08
10 Isle of Wight	126,600	380.99	147.10

T O P 1 0

LARGEST ISLANDS IN EUROPE

Island	Location	Approx. area sq km	sq miles
1 Great Britain	North Atlantic	218,041	84,186
2 Iceland	North Atlantic	103,000	39,769
3 Ireland	North Atlantic	83,766	32,342
4 West Spitsbergen (Vestspitzbergen)	Arctic Ocean	39,368	15,200
5 Sicily	Mediterranean Sea	25,400	9,807
6 Sardinia	Mediterranean Sea	23,800	9,189
7 North East Land	Barents Sea	15,000	5,792
8 Cyprus	Mediterranean Sea	9,251	3,572
9 Corsica	Mediterranean Sea	8,720	3,367
10 Crete	Mediterranean Sea	8,260	3,189

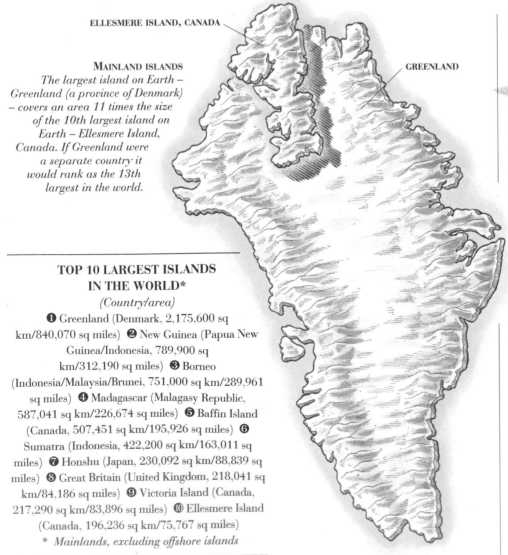

ELLESMERE ISLAND, CANADA

GREENLAND

MAINLAND ISLANDS
The largest island on Earth – Greenland (a province of Denmark) – covers an area 11 times the size of the 10th largest island on Earth – Ellesmere Island, Canada. If Greenland were a separate country it would rank as the 13th largest in the world.

TOP 10 LARGEST ISLANDS IN THE WORLD*
(Country/area)
❶ Greenland (Denmark, 2,175,600 sq km/840,070 sq miles) ❷ New Guinea (Papua New Guinea/Indonesia, 789,900 sq km/312,190 sq miles) ❸ Borneo (Indonesia/Malaysia/Brunei, 751,000 sq km/289,961 sq miles) ❹ Madagascar (Malagasy Republic, 587,041 sq km/226,674 sq miles) ❺ Baffin Island (Canada, 507,451 sq km/195,926 sq miles) ❻ Sumatra (Indonesia, 422,200 sq km/163,011 sq miles) ❼ Honshu (Japan, 230,092 sq km/88,839 sq miles) ❽ Great Britain (United Kingdom, 218,041 sq km/84,186 sq miles) ❾ Victoria Island (Canada, 217,290 sq km/83,896 sq miles) ❿ Ellesmere Island (Canada, 196,236 sq km/75,767 sq miles)
* *Mainlands, excluding offshore islands*

T O P 1 0

MOST HIGHLY POPULATED ISLAND COUNTRIES IN THE WORLD

	Country	Population (1997)
1	Indonesia	203,479,000
2	Japan	125,638,000
3	Philippines	70,724,000
4	Great Britain	57,138,000
5	Malaysia	21,018,000
6	Sri Lanka	18,273,000
7	Madagascar	15,845,000
8	Cuba	11,068,000
9	Dominican Republic	8,097,000
10	Haiti	7,395,000

There are 18 island countries in the world with populations of more than one million, of which these are the Top 10. Australia is regarded as a continental land mass, rather than an island, but if it were included, its population of 18,250,000 would put it in sixth place in the world.

Source: United Nations

TOP 10

LARGEST ISLAND COUNTRIES IN THE WORLD

	Country	Area sq km	sq miles
1	Indonesia	1,904,569	735,358
2	Madagascar	587,041	226,658
3	Papua New Guinea	462,840	178,704
4	Japan	372,801	143,939
5	Malaysia	329,758	127,320
6	Philippines	300,000	115,831
7	New Zealand	269,057	103,883 *
8	Great Britain	229,957	88,786
9	Cuba	110,861	42,804
10	Iceland	103,000	39,769

* Total – South Island 150,449 sq km/
58,093 sq miles, North Island 114,678 sq
km/44,281 sq miles, others 3,527 sq
km/1,362 sq miles

TOP 10

LARGEST ISLANDS IN THE US

	Island	Area sq km	sq miles
1	Hawaii, Hawaii	10,456	4,037
2	Kodiak, Alaska	9,510	3,672
3	Puerto Rico	8,959	3,459
4	Prince of Wales, Alaska	6,700	2,587
5	Chicagof, Alaska	5,400	2,085
6	Saint Lawrence, Alaska	4,430	1,710
7	Admiralty, Alaska	4,270	1,649
8	Nunivak, Alaska	4,210	1,625
9	Unimak, Alaska	4,160	1,606
10	Baranof, Alaska	4,140	1,598

Long Island, New York (3,630 sq km/
1,396 sq miles) falls just outside the Top 10
list. Manhattan, New York, measures just
57 sq km/22 sq miles.

TOP 10

DEEPEST DEEP-SEA TRENCHES IN THE WORLD

	Trench/ocean	Deepest point m	ft
1	Marianas, Pacific	10,924	35,837
2	Tonga*, Pacific	10,800	35,430
3	Philippine, Pacific	10,497	34,436
4	Kermadec*, Pacific	10,047	32,960
5	Bonin, Pacific	9,994	32,786
6	New Britain, Pacific	9,940	32,609
7	Kuril, Pacific	9,750	31,985
8	Izu, Pacific	9,695	31,805
9	Puerto Rico, Atlantic	8,605	28,229
10	Yap, Pacific	8,527	27,973

* Some authorities consider these parts of the
same feature

The eight deepest ocean trenches would be
deep enough to submerge Mount Everest,
which is 8,846 m/29,022 ft above sea level.

TOP 10

LARGEST OCEANS AND SEAS IN THE WORLD

	Island	Approx. area* sq km	sq miles
1	Pacific Ocean	166,240,000	64,185,629
2	Atlantic Ocean	86,560,000	33,421,006
3	Indian Ocean	73,430,000	28,351,484
4	Arctic Ocean	13,230,000	5,108,132
5	South China Sea	2,974,600	1,148,499
6	Caribbean Sea	2,753,000	1,062,939
7	Mediterranean Sea	2,510,000	969,116
8	Bering Sea	2,261,000	872,977
9	Gulf of Mexico	1,542,985	595,749
10	Sea of Okhotsk	1,527,570	589,798

Geographers disagree with one another about whether certain
bodies of water are regarded as seas in their own right or as parts of
larger oceans. The Coral, Weddell, and Tasman Seas, for example,
would be eligible for this list, but most authorities consider them to
be part of the Pacific Ocean, whereas the Bering Sea is more
commonly identified as an independent sea.

TOP 10

DEEPEST OCEANS AND SEAS IN THE WORLD

	Island	Greatest depth m	ft	Approx. depth* m	ft
1	Pacific Ocean	10,924	35,837	4,028	13,215
2	Indian Ocean	7,455	24,460	3,963	13,002
3	Atlantic Ocean	9,219	30,246	3,926	12,880
4	Caribbean Sea	6,946	22,788	2,647	8,685
5	South China Sea	5,016	16,456	1,652	5,419
6	Bering Sea	4,773	15,659	1,547	5,075
7	Gulf of Mexico	3,787	12,425	1,486	4,874
8	Mediterranean Sea	4,632	15,197	1,429	4,688
9	Japan Sea	3,742	12,276	1,350	4,429
10	Arctic Ocean	5,625	18,456	1,205	3,953

The deepest point in the deepest ocean is the Marianas Trench in the
Pacific at a depth of 10,924 m/35,837 ft according to a recent survey,
although the slightly lesser depth of 10,916 m/35,814 was recorded
on 23 January 1960 by Jacques Piccard and Donald Walsh in their
17.7-m/58-ft long bathyscaphe *Trieste 2* during the deepest – ever
ocean descent. Whichever is correct, it is close to 11 km/6.8 miles
down, or almost 29 times the height of the Empire State Building.

ON TOP OF THE WORLD

TOP 10

COUNTRIES WITH THE HIGHEST ELEVATIONS IN THE WORLD

	Country/peak	Height* m	ft
1	Nepal#, Everest	8,846	29,022
2	Pakistan, K2	8,611	28,250
3	India, Kangchenjunga	8,598	28,208
4	Bhutan, Khula Kangri	7,554	24,784
5	Tajikstan, Mt. Garmo (formerly Kommunizma)	7,495	24,590
6	Afghanistan, Noshaq	7,499	24,581
7	Kyrgystan, Pik Pobedy	7,439	24,406
8	Kazakhstan, Khan Tengri	6,995	22,949
9	Argentina, Cerro Aconcagua	6,960	22,834
10	Chile, Ojos del Salado	6,885	22,588

* *Based on the tallest peak in each country*

\# *Everest straddles Nepal and Tibet, which – now known as Xizang – is a province of China.*

NAMING THE HIGHEST
Originally named "Peak XV", the highest mountain was renamed Everest in 1865 after Sir George Everest, Surveyor General of India at the time.

TOP 10

LONGEST MOUNTAIN RANGES IN THE WORLD

	Range/location	Length km	miles
1	Andes, South America	7,242	4,500
2	Rocky Mountains, North America	6,035	3,750
3	Himalayas/Karakoram/ Hindu Kush, Asia	3,862	2,400
4	Great Dividing Range, Australia	3,621	2,250
5	Trans-Antarctic Mountains, Antarctica	3,541	2,200
6	Brazilian East Coast Range, Brazil	3,058	1,900
7	Sumatran/Javan Range, Sumatra, Java	2,897	1,800
8	Tien Shan, China	2,253	1,400
9	Eastern Ghats, India	2,092	1,300
10=	Altai, Asia	2,012	1,250
=	Central New Guinean Range, Papua-New Guinea	2,012	1,250
=	Urals, Russia	2,012	1,250

TOP 10

HIGHEST MOUNTAINS IN AUSTRALIA

	Mountain	Height m	ft
1	Kosciusko	2,229	7,314
2	Townsend	2,209	7,249
3	Clarke	2,200	7,219
4	Twynham	2,195	7,203
5	Carruthers Peak	2,145	7,039
6	Sentinel	2,140	7,022
7	Northcote	2,131	6,992
8=	Gungartan	2,068	6,786
=	Tate	2,068	6,786
10	Jagungal	2,062	6,766

TOP 10 HIGHEST MOUNTAINS IN THE WORLD
(Height)

❶ Everest, Nepal/Tibet (8,846 m/ 29,022 ft) ❷ K2, Kashmir/China (8,611 m/28,250 ft) ❸ Kangchenjunga, Nepal/Sikkim (8,598 m/28,208 ft) ❹ Lhotse, Nepal/Tibet (8,501 m/27,890 ft) ❺ Makalu I, Nepal/Tibet (8,470 m/ 27,790 ft) ❻ Dhaulagiri I, Nepal (8,172 m/26,810 ft) ❼ Manaslu I, Nepal (8,156 m/26,760 ft) ❽ Cho Oyu, Nepal (8,153 m/26,750 ft) ❾ Nanga Parbat, Kashmir (8,126 m/26,660 ft) ❿ Annapurna I, Nepal (8,078 m/26,504 ft)

TOP 10

STATES WITH THE HIGHEST ELEVATIONS IN THE US

State/peak	Height	
	m	ft
1 Alaska, Mount McKinley	6,194	20,320
2 California, Mount Whitney	4,418	14,494
3 Colorado, Mount Elbert	4,399	14,433
4 Washington, Mount Rainier	4,392	14,410
5 Wyoming, Gannett Peak	4,207	13,804
6 Hawaii, Mauna Kea	4,205	13,796
7 Utah, Kings Peak	4,123	13,528
8 New Mexico, Wheeler Peak	4,011	13,161
9 Nevada, Boundary Peak	4,005	13,140
10 Montana, Granite Peak	3,901	12,799

TOP 10

HIGHEST MOUNTAINS IN OCEANIA

Mountain/location	Height	
	m	ft
1 Jaya, Indonesia	5,030	16,503
2 Daam, Indonesia	4,920	16,142
3 Pilimsit, Indonesia	4,801	15,750
4 Trikora, Indonesia	4,749	15,580
5 Mandala, Indonesia	4,700	15,420
6 Wilhelm, Papua New Guinea	4,600	15,092
7 Wisnumurti, Indonesia	4,595	15,075
8 Yamin, Papua New Guinea	4,529	14,860
9 Kubor, Papua New Guinea	4,300	14,108
10 Herbert, Papua New Guinea	4,267	13,999

If the Hawaiian volcano Mauna Kea (4,206m /13,796 ft) is measured from its undersea base, its total height is 10,206 m/33,484 ft.

TOP 10

HIGHEST MOUNTAINS IN EUROPE

Mountain/location	Height*	
	m	ft
1 Mont Blanc, France/Italy	4,807	15,771
2 Monte Rosa, Italy/Switzerland	4,634	15,203
3 Dom, Switzerland	4,545	14,911
4 Liskamm, Italy/Switzerland	4,527	14,853
5 Weisshorn, Switzerland	4,505	14,780
6 Täschorn, Switzerland	4,491	14,734
7 Matterhorn, Italy/Switzerland	4,477	14,688
8 La Dent Blanche, Switzerland	4,357	14,293
9 Nadelhorn, Switzerland	4,327	14,196
10 Le Grand Combin, Switzerland	4,314	14,153

* Height of principal peak; lower peaks of the same mountain are excluded

TOP 10

HIGHEST MOUNTAINS IN AFRICA

Mountain/location	Height	
	m	ft
1 Kibo (Kilimanjaro), Tanganyika/Tanzania	5,895	19,340
2 Batian (Kenya), Kenya	5,199	17,058
3 Ngaliema, Uganda/ Dem. Rep. of Congo	5,109	16,763
4 Duwoni, Uganda	4,896	16,062
5 Baker, Uganda	4,843	15,889
6 Emin, Dem. Rep. of Congo	4,798	15,741
7 Gessi, Uganda	4,715	15,470
8 Sella, Uganda	4,627	15,179
9 Ras Dashen, Ethiopia	4,620	15,158
10 Wasuwameso, Dem. Rep. of Congo	4,581	15,030

TOP 10

HIGHEST MOUNTAINS IN SOUTH AMERICA

Mountain/location	Height	
	m	ft
1 Cerro Aconcagua, Argentina	6,960	22,834
2 Ojos del Salado, Argentina/Chile	6,885	22,588
3 Bonete, Argentina	6,873	22,550
4 Pissis, Argentina/Chile	6,780	22,244
5 Huascarán, Peru	6,768	22,205
6 Llullaillaco, Argentina/Chile	6,723	22,057
7 Libertador, Argentina	6,721	22,050
8 Mercadario, Argentina/Chile	6,670	21,884
9 Yerupajá, Peru	6,634	21,765
10 Tres Cruces, Argentina/Chile	6,620	21,720

TOP 10

HIGHEST MOUNTAINS IN NORTH AMERICA

Mountain/location	Height	
	m	ft
1 McKinley, USA	6,194	20,320
2 Logan, Canada	6,050	19,850
3 Citlaltépetl (Orizaba), Mexico	5,700	18,700
4 St. Elias, USA/Canada	5,489	18,008
5 Popocatépetl, Mexico	5,452	17,887
6 Foraker, USA	5,304	17,400
7 Ixtaccihuatl, Mexico	5,286	17,343
8 Lucania, Canada	5,226	17,147
9 King, Canada	5,173	16,971
10 Steele, Canada	5,073	16,644

THE FACE OF THE EARTH

TOP 10

LONGEST CAVES IN THE WORLD

	Cave	Location	Total known length m	ft
1	Mammoth cave system	Kentucky, USA	560,000	1,837,270
2	Optimisticeskaja	Ukraine	178,000	583,989
3	Hölloch	Switzerland	137,000	449,475
4	Jewel Cave	South Dakota, USA	127,000	416,667
5	Siebenhengsteholensystem	Switzerland	110,000	360,892
6	Ozernaya	Ukraine	107,300	352,034
7	Réseau de la Coume d'Hyouernede	France	90,500	296,916
8	Sistema de Ojo Guarena	Spain	89,100	292,323
9	Wind Cave	South Dakota, USA	88,500	290,354
10	Fisher Ridge cave system	Kentucky, USA	83,000	273,950

TOP 10

DEEPEST CAVES IN THE WORLD

	Cave system	Location	Depth m	ft
1	Réseau Jean Bernard	France	1,602	5,256
2	Lamprechtsofen	Austria	1,535	3,036
3	Gouffre Mirolda	France	1,520	4,987
4	Shakta Pantjukhina	Georgia	1,508	4,947
5	Sistema Huautla	Mexico	1,475	4,839
6	Sistema del Trave	Spain	1,444	4,737
7	Boj Bulok	Ukbekistan	1,415	4,642
8	Illaminako Ateak	Spain	1,408	4,619
9	Lukina Jama	Croatia	1,392	4,567
10	Sistema Cheve	Mexico	1,386	4,547

SNAP FACTS

- The word "meteorite" was first used in 1834.
- No record exists of any human being killed by a meteorite – but Ann Hodges of Sylacauga, Alabama, USA, was slightly injured when a 4-kg/9-lb specimen fell through the roof of her home on 30 November 1954.
- The largest known meteorite is that at Hoba West Grootfontein, South Africa. Discovered in 1920, its estimated weight is 54.4 tonnes.

TOP 10

LARGEST METEORITE CRATERS IN THE WORLD

	Crater/location	Diameter km	miles
1=	Sudbury, Ontario, Canada	140	87
=	Vredefort, South Africa	140	87
3=	Manicouagan, Quebec, Canada	100	62
=	Popigai, Russia	100	62
5	Puchezh-Katunki, Russia	80	50
6	Kara, Russia	60	37
7	Siljan, Sweden	52	32
8	Charlevoix, Quebec, Canada	46	29
9	Araguainha Dome, Brazil	40	25
10	Carswell, Saskatchewan, Canada	37	23

Unlike on the solar system's other planets and moons, many astroblemes (collision sites) on Earth have been weathered over time and obscured, and one of the ongoing debates in geology is thus whether or not certain crater-like structures are of meteoric origin or the remnants of long extinct volcanoes. The Vredefort Ring, for example, long thought to be meteoric, was declared in 1963 to be volcanic, but has since been claimed as a definite meteor crater, as are all the giant meteorite craters in the Top 10 which are listed as such (along with 106 others) by the International Union of Geological Sciences Commission on Comparative Planetology.

TOP 10

COUNTRIES WITH THE LOWEST ELEVATIONS IN THE WORLD

	Country	Highest point	Height m	ft
1	Maldives	Unnamed	3	10
2=	Marshall Islands	Unnamed	6	20
=	Tuvalu	Unnamed	6	20
4	Gambia	Unnamed	43	141
5	Bahamas	Mount Alvernia	63	206
6	Nauru	Unnamed	68	225
7	Quatar	Dukhan Heights	73	240
8	Kiribati	Banaba	81	270
9	Bahrain	Jabal al-Dukhan	134	440
10	Denmark	Yding Skovhøj	173	568

None of these 10 countries possesses a single elevation taller than a medium-sized skyscraper. Compared with these, even the Netherlands' 321m/1,050ft Vaalserberg hill makes the country's appellation as one of the "Low Countries" sound somewhat unfair

DEAD LOW
DEAD LOW
The shore of the Dead Sea is the lowest point on the world's surface. It takes its name from the scarcity of plants and animals in it that results from its high salt content.

T O P 1 0

DEEPEST DEPRESSIONS IN THE WORLD

	Depression/location	Maximum depth below sea level m	ft
1	Dead Sea, Israel/Jordan	400	1,312
2	Turfan Depression, China	154	505
3	Qattâra Depression, Egypt	133	436
4	Poluostrov Mangyshlak, Kazakhstan	132	433
5	Danakil Depression, Ethiopia	117	383
6	Death Valley, USA	86	282
7	Salton Sink, USA	72	235
8	Zapadny Chink Ustyurta, Kazakhstan	70	230
9	Prikaspiyskaya Nizmennost, Kazakhstan/Russia	67	220
10	Ozera Sarykamysh, Turkmenistan/Uzbekistan	45	148

The shore of the Dead Sea, Israel/Jordan is the lowest exposed ground below sea level. However, its bed, at 728 m/2,388 ft below sea level, is only half as deep as that of Lake Baikal, Russia, which is 1,485 m/ 4,872 ft below sea level.

T O P 1 0

LARGEST DESERTS IN THE WORLD

	Desert	Location	Approx. area sq km	sq miles
1	Sahara	North Africa	9,000,000	3,500,000
2	Australian	Australia	3,800,000	1,470,000
3	Arabian	Southwest Asia	1,300,000	502,000
4	Gobi	Central Asia	1,040,000	401,500
5	Kalahari	Southern Africa	520,000	201,000
6	Turkestan	Central Asia	450,000	174,000
7	Takla Makan	China	327,000	125,000
8 =	Namib	Southwest Africa	310,000	120,000
=	Sonoran	USA/Mexico	310,000	120,000
10 =	Somali	Somalia	260,000	100,000
=	Thar	India/Pakistan	260,000	100,000

UNDERGROUND WORLD

According to tradition the world's greatest cave system, the Mammoth Cave, Kentucky, was discovered in 1799 when a hunter who was pursuing a bear stumbled upon what is now called the "Historic Entrance" to the cave. Further exploration showed it to be part of a complex network, with numerous underground streams containing rare fish and other animals. During the war of 1812, the caverns provided a valuable source of saltpetre, an ingredient of gunpowder, and after the war they became a major tourist attraction. Mammoth Cave National Park was established in 1941. In 1972 a connection was discovered between the Mammoth and Flint Ridge caves.

YEARS AGO • YEARS AGO • YEARS AGO • YEARS AGO •
200

This Top 10 presents the approximate areas and ranking of the world's great deserts. These are often broken down into smaller desert regions – the Australian Desert into the Gibson, Simpson, and Great Sandy Desert, for example. Of the total land surface of the Earth, as much as one-quarter may be considered "desert", or land where more water is lost through evaporation than is acquired through precipitation. However, deserts may range from the extremely arid and barren sandy desert, through arid, to semi-arid. Nearly every desert exhibits features that encompass all of these degrees of aridity without a precise line of demarcation between them.

OUT OF THIS WORLD

TOP 10
PRINCIPAL COMPONENTS OF AIR

	Component	Volume per cent
1	Nitrogen	78.110
2	Oxygen	20.953
3	Argon	0.934
4	Carbon dioxide	0.01–0.10
5	Neon	0.001818
6	Helium	0.000524
7	Methane	0.0002
8	Krypton	0.000114
9 =	Hydrogen	0.00005
=	Nitrous oxide	0.00005

Dry air at sea level comprises these 10 basic components plus one further component: xenon (0.0000087 per cent). In addition to these, water vapour, ozone, and various pollutants, such as carbon monoxide from motor vehicle exhausts, are present in the air in variable amounts.

TOP 10
HEAVIEST ELEMENTS

	Element	Year discovered	Density*
1	Osmium	1804	22.59
2	Iridium	1804	22.56
3	Platinum	1748	21.45
4	Rhenium	1925	21.01
5	Neptunium	1940	20.47
6	Plutonium	1940	20.26
7	Gold	Prehistoric	19.29
8	Tungsten	1783	19.26
9	Uranium	1789	19.05
10	Tantalum	1802	16.67

*   *Grams per cm³ at 20°C*

The two heaviest elements were discovered by the British chemist Smithson Tennant (1761–1815), who was also the first to prove that diamonds are made of carbon. A cubic foot (0.028317 m²) of osmium weighs 640 kg/1,410 lb — equivalent to 10 people each weighing 64 kg/141 lb.

TOP 10
ELEMENTS WITH THE LOWEST MELTING POINTS*

	Element	Melting point °C
1	Mercury	-38.9
2	Francium	27.0#
3	Caesium	28.4
4	Gallium	29.8
5	Rubidium	38.9
6	Phosphorus	44.1
7	Potassium	63.3
8	Sodium	97.8
9	Sulphur	112.8
10	Iodine	113.5

*   *Solids only*
\#   *Approximate*

Among other familiar elements that melt at relatively low temperatures are tin (232.0°C) and lead (327.5°C).

TOP 10
LIGHTEST ELEMENTS*

	Element	Year discovered	Density#
1	Lithium	1817	0.533
2	Potassium	1807	0.859
3	Sodium	1807	0.969
4	Calcium	1808	1.526
5	Rubidium	1861	1.534
6	Magnesium	1808	1.737
7	Phosphorus	1669	1.825
8	Beryllium	1798	1.846
9	Caesium	1860	1.896
10	Sulphur	Prehistoric	2.070

*   *Solids only*
\#   *Grams per cm³ at 20°C*

Osmium, the heaviest known element, is more than 42 times heavier than lithium, the lightest known element.

THE 10 DEGREES OF HARDNESS*
❶ Talc ❷ Gypsum
❸ Calcite ❹ Fluorite ❺ Apatite
❻ Orthoclase ❼ Quartz ❽ Topaz
❾ Corundum ❿ Diamond
According to Mohs Scale in which No. 1 is the softest mineral and No. 10 the hardest

TOP 10
ELEMENTS WITH THE HIGHEST MELTING POINTS

	Element	Melting point °C
1	Carbon	3,652
2	Tungsten	3,410
3	Rhenium	3,180
4	Osmium	3,045
5	Tantalum	2,996
6	Molybdenum	2,617
7	Niobium	2,468
8	Iridium	2,410
9	Ruthenium	2,310
10	Hafnium	2,227

Other elements that melt at high temperatures include chromium (1,857°C), iron (1,535°C), and gold (1,064°C). The surface of the Sun attains 5,330°C.

TOP 10
ELEMENTS MOST COMMON IN THE SUN

	Element	Parts per 1,000,000
1	Hydrogen	745,000
2	Helium	237,000
3	Oxygen	8,990
4	Carbon	3,900
5	Iron	1,321
6	Neon	1,200
7	Nitrogen	870
8	Silicon	830
9	Magnesium	720
10	Sulphur	380

Helium was discovered on the Sun before it was detected on Earth, its name deriving from *helios*, the Greek word for Sun. More than 70 elements have been detected in the Sun, the most common of which correspond closely to those found in the Universe as a whole, but with some variations in their ratios, including a greater proportion of the principal element, hydrogen.

TOP 10
ELEMENTS MOST COMMON IN THE EARTH'S CRUST

	Element	Per cent*
1	Oxygen	45.6
2	Silicon	27.3
3	Aluminium	8.4
4	Iron	6.2
5	Calcium	4.7
6	Magnesium	2.8
7	Sodium	2.3
8	Potassium	1.8
9	Hydrogen	1.5
10	Titanium	0.6

* *Totals more than 100% due to rounding*

This is based on the average percentages of the elements in igneous rock. At an atomic level, out of every million atoms, some 205,000 are silicon, 62,600 aluminium, and 29,000 hydrogen.

TOP 10
ELEMENTS MOST COMMON IN THE MOON

	Element	Per cent
1	Oxygen	40.0
2	Silicon	19.2
3	Iron	14.3
4	Calcium	8.0
5	Titanium	5.9
6	Aluminum	5.6
7	Magnesium	4.5
8	Sodium	0.33
9	Potassium	0.14
10	Chromium	0.002

This list is based on the analysis of the 20.77 kg/45.8 lb of rock samples brought back to Earth by the crew of the 1969 *Apollo 11* lunar mission.

TOP 10
ELEMENTS MOST COMMON IN SEAWATER

	Element	Tonnes per km³
1	Water*	991,000,000
2	Chlorine	19,600,000
3	Sodium	10,900,000
4	Magnesium	1,400,000
5	Sulphur	920,000
6	Calcium	420,000
7	Potassium	390,000
8	Bromine	67,000
9	Carbon	29,000
10	Strontium	8,300

* *Composed of two elements, hydrogen and oxygen*

A typical cubic kilometre of seawater is a treasury of often valuable elements, but sodium and chlorine (combined as sodium chloride, or common salt) are the only two that are extracted in substantial quantities. The costs of extracting such elements as gold (approximately four kilos of which are found in the average km³ of seawater) would be prohibitively expensive.

TOP 10
MOST VALUABLE TRADED METALLIC ELEMENTS

	Element*	Price per kg ($)
1	Rhodium	17,040
2	Osmium	12,860
3	Platinum	12,281
4	Iridium	10,931
5	Scandium	10,000
6	Gold	9,460
7	Palladium	7,587
8	Ruthenium	1,222
9	Rhenium	1,100
10	Germanium	1,000

* *Based on 10–100 kg quantities of minimum 99.9% purity; excluding radioactive elements, isotopes, and rare earth elements traded in minute quantities*

The prices of traded metals vary enormously according to their rarity, changes in industrial uses, fashion, and popularity as investments.

Source: London Metal Bulletin 9 March 1998/Lipmann Walton & Co.

TOP 10
ELEMENTS MOST COMMON IN THE UNIVERSE

	Element	Parts per 1,000,000
1	Hydrogen	739,000
2	Helium	240,000
3	Oxygen	10,700
4	Carbon	4,600
5	Neon	1,340
6	Iron	1,090
7	Nitrogen	970
8	Silicon	650
9	Magnesium	580
10	Sulphur	440

LIFE ON EARTH

TOP 10

LARGEST DINOSAURS EVER DISCOVERED

Name/length/estimated weight

1 *Seismosaurus*,
30–36 m/98–119 ft,
50–80 tonnes

A skeleton of this colossal plant-eater was excavated in 1985 near Albuquerque, New Mexico, by US palaeontologist David Gillette.

2 *Supersaurus*,
24–30 m/80–100 ft,
50 tonnes

The remains of Supersaurus *were found in Colorado, USA, in 1972.*

3 *Antarctosaurus*,
18–30 m/60–98 ft,
40–50 tonnes

Named Antarctosaurus *("southern lizard") by Friedrich von Huene in 1929, this creature's thigh bone alone measures 2.3 m/7 ft 6 in.*

4 *Barosaurus*,
23–27.5 m/75–90 ft,
weight uncertain

Barosaurus *("heavy lizard") was so named by US palaeontologist Othniel C. Marsh in 1890.*

5 *Mamenchisaurus*,
27 m/89 ft,
weight uncertain

An almost complete skeleton discovered in 1972 showed it had the longest neck of any known animal, perhaps up to 15 m/49 ft.

Name/length/estimated weight

6 *Diplodocus*,
23–27 m/75–89 ft,
12 tonnes

Diplodocus *was probably one of the most stupid dinosaurs, having the smallest brain in relation to its body size.*

7 *Ultrasauros*,
Over 25 m/82 ft,
50 tonnes

Ultrasauros *was discovered by US palaeontologist James A. Jensen in Colorado in 1979.*

8 *Brachiosaurus*,
25 m/82 ft,
50 tonnes

Some palaeontologists have put the weight of Brachiosaurus *as high as 190 tonnes.*

9 *Pelorosaurus*,
24 m/80 ft,
weight uncertain

The first fragments of Pelorosaurus *("monstrous lizard") were found in Sussex and named by British doctor and geologist Gideon Algernon Mantell as early as 1850.*

10 *Apatosaurus*,
20–21 m/66–70 ft,
20–30 tonnes

Aptosaurus *(meaning "deceptive lizard") is better known by its former name of* Brontosaurus *("thunder reptile"). Its bones were discovered in Colorado in 1879.*

THE 10

FIRST DINOSAURS TO BE NAMED

	Name/meaning/named by	Year
1	*Megalosaurus*, great lizard, William Buckland	1824
2	*Iguanodon*, iguana tooth, Gideon Mantell	1825
3	*Hylaeosaurus*, woodland lizard, Gideon Mantell	1832
4	*Macrodontophion*, large tooth snake, A. Zborzewski	1834
5=	*Thecodontosaurus*, socket-toothed lizard, Samuel Stutchbury and H. Riley	1836
=	*Palaeosaurus*, ancient lizard, Samuel Stutchbury and H. Riley	1836
7	*Plateosaurus*, flat lizard, Hermann von Meyer	1837
8=	*Cladeiodon*, branch tooth, Richard Owen	1841
=	*Cetiosaurus*, whale lizard, Richard Owen	1841
10	*Pelorosaurus*, monstrous lizard, Gideon Mantell	1850

THE FINAL DATES THAT 10 ANIMALS WERE LAST SEEN ALIVE

	Animal	Date
1	Aurochs	1627

This giant wild ox, once described by Julius Caesar, was last recorded in central Europe after the advance of agriculture forced it to retreat from its former territory, which once stretched to the west as far as Britian. It was extensively hunted and the last few specimens died on the Jaktorow Forest in Poland.

	Animal	Date
2	Aepyornis	1649

Also known as the "Elephant bird", the 3-m/10-ft wingless bird was a native of Madagascar.

	Animal	Date
3	Dodo	1681

Discovered by European travellers in 1507, specimens of this curious bird were extensively collected, its lack of flight and tameness making it extremely vulnerable to being caught. Its name comes from the Portuguese for "stupid". The last Dodo seen alive was on the island of Mauritius in 1681.

	Animal	Date
4	Steller's sea cow	1768

This large marine mammal, named after its 1741 discoverer, German naturalist Georg Wilhelm Steller, and one of the creatures that gave rise to the legend of the mermaid, was rapidly hunted to extinction.

	Animal	Date
5	Great auk	1844

The last example in Britain of a breeding Pinguinus impennis – a flightless North Atlantic seabird – was seen nesting in the Orkneys in 1812. The last surviving pair in the world was killed on 4 June 1844 on Eldey island on behalf of an Icelandic collector. There are possibly as many as 80 specimens in natural history collections around the world.

	Animal	Date
6	Tarpan	1851

The Tarpan, a European wild horse, was last seen in the Ukraine. Another wild horse thought extinct, Przewalski's horse, has been rediscovered in Mongolia and new captive-bred stock has been re-introduced into its former territory around the fringes of the Gobi Desert.

	Animal	Date
7	Quagga	1883

This zebra-like creature, found in South Africa and first recorded in 1685, was hunted to such an extent that by 1870 the last wild specimen was killed. The last example, a female in Amsterdam Zoo, died on 12 August 1883.

	Animal	Date
8	Pilori muskrat	1902

The species became extinct following the 8 May 1902 eruption of Mont Pelée, Martinique, which destroyed its habitat.

AS DEAD AS A DODO
The dodo, a flightless member of the dove family, was discovered in 1507, and specimens were taken to Europe where its ungainly appearance was greeted with astonishment. Within 100 years, entirely as a result of human activity in hunting them down, the Dodo had disappeared, its name becoming a synonym for "extinct", as in "dead as a dodo".

	Animal	Date
9	Passenger pigeon	1914

The last moment of this creature can be stated very precisely. At 1.00 pm on Tuesday, 1 September 1914 at Cincinnati Zoo, the very last specimen, a 29-year-old bird named Martha, expired. Once there had been vast flocks of Passenger pigeons, with estimated totals of five to nine billion in the 19th century, but as they were remorselessly killed for food and to protect crops in the USA, and since the bird laid just one egg each season, its decline was inevitable. The last one in the wild was shot on 24 March 1900.

	Animal	Date
10	Heath hen	1932

The prairie chicken known as the Heath hen (Tympanuchus cupido cupido) was extensively hunted until only a few specimens survived, all on the island of Martha's Vineyard, Massachusetts. Many were killed in a forest fire in 1916, and a virus decimated the survivors, the last of them dying on 11 March 1932.

TOP 10

DINOSAUR DISCOVERERS

	Name/country	Period	Dinosaurs named*
1	Friedrich von Huene (Germany)	1902–61	45
2	Othniel C. Marsh (USA)	1870–94	36
3	Harry G. Seeley (UK)	1869–98	29
4	Dong Zhiming (China)	1973–93	24
5	José F. Bonaparte (Argentina)	1969–95	20
6 =	Edward Drinker Cope (USA)	1866–92	18
=	Richard Owen (UK)	1841–84	18
8 =	Henry F. Osborn (USA)	1902–24	17
=	Yang Zhong-Jian ("C.C. Young") (China)	1937–82	17
10	Barnum Brown (USA)	1873–1963	14

* Including joint namings

DIPLODOCUS
This was one of the many dinosaurs identified by US palaeontologist Othniel C. Marsh

ENDANGERED ANIMALS

THE 10
MOST ENDANGERED SPIDERS

	Spider	Country
1	Kauai cave wolf spider	USA
2	Doloff cave spider	USA
3	Empire cave pseudoscorpion	USA
4	Glacier Bay wolf spider	USA
5	Great raft spider	Europe
6	Kocevje subterranean spider (*Troglohyphantes gracilis*)	Slovenia
7	Kocevje subterranean spider (*Troglohyphantes similis*)	Slovenia
8	Kocevje subterranean spider (*Troglohyphantes spinipes*)	Slovenia
9	Lake Placid funnel wolf spider	USA
10	Melones cave harvestman	USA

Source: International Union for the Conservation of Nature

THE 10
COUNTRIES WITH THE MOST THREATENED BIRD SPECIES

	Country	Threatened bird species
1	Indonesia	104
2	Brazil	103
3	China	90
4	Philippines	86
5	India	73
6=	Colombia	64
=	Peru	64
8	Ecuador	53
9	USA	50
10	Vietnam	47

Source: International Union for the Conservation of Nature

PUMA
The Eastern puma is one of the most endangered of all cat species.

FRASER'S DOLPHIN
Discovered as recently as 1956, this previously endangered member of the dolphin family has now increased in numbers.

THE 10
COUNTRIES WITH THE MOST THREATENED REPTILE AND AMPHIBIAN SPECIES

	Country	Total reptiles	Total amphibians
1	Australia	37	25
2	USA	28	24
3	South Africa	19	9
4	Mexico	18	3
5=	Myanmar (Burma)	20	0
=	Brazil	15	5
7=	Indonesia	19	0
=	Madagascar	17	2
=	India	16	3
10	Japan	8	10

Source: International Union for the Conservation of Nature

TOP 10 MOST ENDANGERED BIG CATS*

❶ Amur leopard ❷ Anatolian leopard
❸ Asiatic cheetah ❹ Eastern puma
❺ Florida cougar ❻ North African leopard
❼ Siberian tiger ❽ South Arabian leopard
❾ South China tiger ❿ Sumatran tiger

*Listed alphabetically, all 10 big cats are classed as being "critically endangered".

Source: International Union for the Conservation of Nature

THE 10
COUNTRIES WITH THE MOST THREATENED INVERTEBRATE SPECIES

	Country	Threatened invertebrate species
1	USA	594
2	Australia	281
3	South Africa	101
4	Portugal	67
5	France	61
6	Spain	57
7	Tanzania	46
8=	Congo (Dem. Rep.)	45
=	Japan	45
10=	Austria	41
=	Italy	41

Source: International Union for the Conservation of Nature

THE 10
RAREST NATIVE MAMMALS IN THE UK

	Mammal	Estimated no.
1	Grey long-eared bat	1,000
2	Bechstein's bat	1,500
3	Wildcat	3,500
4	Pine marten	3,650
5	Greater horseshoe bat	4,000
6	Barbastelle bat	5,000
7	Skomer vole	7,000
8	Otter	7,350
9	Leisler's bat	10,000
10=	Lesser-white-toothed shrew	14,000
=	Lesser horseshoe bat	14,000

THE 10

COUNTRIES WITH THE MOST THREATENED MAMMAL SPECIES

	Country	Threatened mammal species
1	Indonesia	128
2 =	China	75
=	India	75
4	Brazil	71
5	Mexico	64
6	Australia	58
7	Papua New Guinea	57
8	Philippines	49
9 =	Madagascar	46
=	Peru	46

Source: International Union for the Conservation of Nature

TOP 10

COUNTRIES WITH THE MOST AFRICAN ELEPHANTS

	Country	Estimated no.
1	Tanzania	73,459 *
2	Congo (Dem. Rep.)	65,974 #
3	Botswana	62,998 *
4	Gabon	61,794 †
5	Zimbabwe	56,297 *
6	Rep. of the Congo	32,563 #
7	Zambia	19,701 *
8	Kenya	13,834 *
9	South Africa	9,990 *
10	Cameroon	8,824 #

* *Definite*
† *Probable*
\# *Possible*

There were once millions of African elephants, but the destruction of natural habitats and extensive poaching have reduced the population. In 1996 the number of African elephants was put at 286,234.

Source: International Union for the Conservation of Nature

THE 10

RAREST BIRDS IN THE WORLD

	Bird/country	Estimated no. *
1 =	Spix's macaw, Brazil	1
=	Cebu flower pecker, Philippines	1
3	Hawaiian crow, Hawaii	5
4	Black stilt, New Zealand	12
5	Echo parakeet, Mauritius	13
6	Imperial Amazon parrot, Dominica	15
7	Magpie robin, Seychelles	20
8	Kakapo, New Zealand	24
9	Pink pigeon, Mauritius	70
10	Mauritius kestrel	100

* *Of breeding pairs reported since 1986*

Several rare bird species are known from old records or from only one specimen but must be assumed to be extinct in the absence of recent sightings or records of breeding pairs. With nowhere to seek refuge, rare birds come under most pressure on islands like Mauritius, where the dodo notoriously met its fate in the seventeenth century.

AFRICAN ELEPHANT
Extensive programmes have been established to rescue the African elephant from its threatened status.

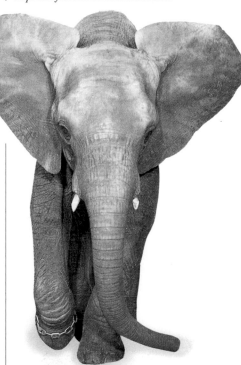

PYGMY HOG
The smallest known pig, the pygmy hog is an increasingly rare inhabitant of the Himalayan foothills. It is estimated that only 150 remain.

THE 10

MOST THREATENED ANIMALS

	Class	Threatened species
1	Birds	1,107
2	Mammals	1,096
3	Gastropods (snails, etc.)	806
4	Actinopterygians (ray-finned fish)	715
5	Insects	537
6	Crustaceans	407
7	Reptiles	253
8	Amphibians	124
9	Bivalves (clams, etc.)	114
10	Elasmobranchii (sharks, etc.)	15

Source: International Union for the Conservation of Nature

TOP 10

COUNTRIES WITH THE MOST ASIAN ELEPHANTS

	Country	Estimated no.
1	India	24,000 *
2	Myanmar (Burma)	6,000
3	Indonesia	4,500
4	Laos	4,000
5	Sri Lanka	3,000
6 =	Thailand	2,000
=	Cambodia	2,000
8 =	Borneo	1,000
=	Malaysia	1,000
10	Vietnam	400

* *Based on maximum estimates*

Source: International Union for the Conservation of Nature

LAND ANIMALS

MAMMALS WITH THE LONGEST GESTATION PERIODS

	Mammal	Average gestation (days)
1	African elephant	660
2	Asiatic elephant	600
3	Baird's beaked whale	520
4	White rhinoceros	490
5	Walrus	480
6	Giraffe	460
7	Tapir	400
8	Arabian camel (dromedary)	390
9	Fin whale	370
10	Llama	360

MAMMALS WITH THE SHORTEST GESTATION PERIODS

	Mammal	Average gestation (days)
1	Short-nosed bandicoot	12
2	Opossum	13
3	Shrew	14
4	Golden hamster	16
5	Lemming	20
6	Mouse	21
7	Rat	22
8	Gerbil	24
9	Rabbit	30
10	Mole	38

The short-nosed bandicoot and the opossum are both marsupial mammals whose new-born young transfer to a pouch to complete their natal development. The babies of marsupials are minute when born: the opossum is smaller than a bee, and the ratio in size between the new-born kangaroo, at under 2.5 cm/1 in long, and the adult, is the greatest of all mammals.

SLOTHFUL SLOTH
One of nature's most somnolent creatures, even the name of the sloth has become a synonym for extreme laziness. The top speed of the three-toed sloth is 0.2 km/h/0.12 mph.

SLEEPIEST ANIMALS

	Animal	Average hours of sleep			Animal	Average hours of sleep
1	Koala	22		6 =	Hamster	14
2	Sloth	20		=	Squirrel	14
3 =	Armadillo	19		8 =	Cat	13
=	Opossum	19		=	Pig	13
5	Lemur	16		10	Spiny anteater	12

This list excludes periods of hibernation, which can last up to several months among creatures such as the ground squirrel. At the other end of the scale comes the frantic shrew, which has to hunt and eat constantly, or else it will perish. This animal literally has no time at all for sleep. Even some of the larger mammals, such as elephants, cows, and horses, generally sleep for periods of less than four hours out of every 24.

MOST PROLIFIC WILD MAMMALS

	Animal	Average litter
1	Malagasy tenrec	25
2	Virginian opossum	22
3	Golden hamster	11
4	Ermine	10
5	Prairie vole	9
6	Coypu	8.5
7 =	European hedgehog	7
=	African hunting dog	7
9 =	Meadow vole	6.5
=	Wild boar	6.5

The prairie vole probably holds the record for the most offspring produced in a season. It has up to 17 litters in rapid succession, bringing up to 150 young into the world.

FASTEST MAMMALS

	Mammal	Maximum recorded speed km/h	mph
1	Cheetah	105	65
2	Pronghorn antelope	89	55
3 =	Mongolian gazelle	80	50
=	Springbok	80	50
5 =	Grant's gazelle	76	47
=	Thomson's gazelle	76	47
7	Brown hare	72	45
8	Horse	69	43
9 =	Greyhound	68	42
=	Red deer	68	42

Although several animals on the list are capable of higher speeds, these figures are based on controlled measurements of average speeds over 0.4 km/¼ mile.

TOP 10

HEAVIEST TERRESTRIAL MAMMALS*

	Mammal	Length m	ft	Weight kg	lb
1	African elephant	7.3	24	7,000	14,432
2	White rhinoceros	4.2	14	3,600	7,937
3	Hippopotamus	4.0	13	2,500	5,512
4	Giraffe	5.8	19	1,600	2,527
5	American bison	3.9	13	1,000	2,205
6	Arabian camel (dromedary)	3.5	12	690	1,521
7	Polar bear	3.0	10	600	1,323
8	Moose	3.0	10	550	1,213
9	Siberian tiger	3.3	11	300	661
10	Gorilla	2.0	7	220	485

* Excluding domesticated cattle and horses

TOP 10

DEADLIEST SNAKES

	Snake	Lethal venom dose (mg)	Maximum venom yield (mg)	Potential deaths per bite	Mortality rate range (per cent)
1	Black mamba	10.0	800	80	95–100
2	Common krait	1.0	50	50	77–93
3	Russell's viper	12.0	270	22	30–65
4	Taipan	3.0	400	130	25–50
5	Indian cobra	20.0	375	18	33
6	Cape cobra	15.0	150	10	25
7	Egyptian cobra	20.0	400	20	Not known
8	Multibanded krait	0.5	22	44	Not known
9	Tropical rattlesnake	7.0	105	15	15–25
10	King cobra	40.0	1,000	20	18

TOP 10

HEAVIEST PRIMATES

	Primate	Length* cm	in	Weight kg	lb
1	Gorilla	200	79	220	485
2	Man	177	70	77	170
3	Orangutan	137	54	75	165
4	Chimpanzee	92	36	50	110
5=	Baboon	100	39	45	99
=	Mandrill	95	37	45	99
7	Gelada baboon	75	30	25	55
8	Proboscis monkey	76	30	24	53
9	Hanuman langur	107	42	20	44
10	Siamung gibbon	90	35	13	29

* Excluding tail

The largest primates (including man) and all the apes are rooted in the Old World (Africa, Asia, and Europe): only one member of a New World species of monkeys (the Guatemalan howler at 91 cm/36 in; 9 kg/20 lb) is a close contender for the Top 10. The difference between the prosimians (primitive primates), great apes, lesser apes, and monkeys is more to do with shape than size, although the great apes mostly top the table anyway.

TOP 10

LARGEST CARNIVORES

	Animal	Length m	ft in	Weight kg	lb
1	Southern elephant seal	6.5	21 4	3,500	7,716
2	Walrus	3.8	12 6	1,200	2,646
3	Steller sea lion	3	9 8	1,100	2,425
4	Grizzly bear	3	9 8	780	1,720
5	Polar bear	2.5	8 2	700	1,543
6	Tiger	2.8	9 2	300	661
7	Lion	1.9	6 3	250	551
8	American black bear	1.8	6 0	227	500
9	Giant panda	1.5	5 0	160	353
10	Spectacled bear	1.8	6 0	140	309

Of the 273 mammal species in the order Carnivora (meat-eaters) many (including its largest representatives on land, the bears) are in fact omnivorous and around 40 specialize in eating fish or insects. All, however, share a common ancestry indicated by the butchers-knife form of their canine teeth. As the Top 10 would otherwise consist exclusively of seals and related marine carnivores, only the first three marine representatives have been included in the list, to enable the terrestrial heavyweight division to make an appearance.

CHEETAH

MARINE ANIMALS

LARGEST SHARKS IN THE WORLD

	Species	Maximum weight kg	lb
1	Whale shark	21,000	46,297
2	Basking shark	14,515	32,000
3	Great white shark	3,314	7,300
4	Greenland shark	1,020	2,250
5	Tiger shark	939	2,070
6	Great hammerhead shark	844	1,860
7	Six-gill shark	590	1,300
8	Grey nurse shark	556	1,225
9	Mako shark	544	1,200
10	Thresher shark	500	1,100

FISHING COUNTRIES IN THE WORLD

	Country	Annual catch (tonnes)
1	China	17,567,907
2	Peru	8,450,600
3	Japan	8,128,121
4	Chile	6,037,985
5	USA	5,939,339
6	Russia	4,461,375
7	India	4,232,060
8	Indonesia	3,637,700
9	Thailand	3,348,149
10	South Korea	2,648,977
	World total	*101,417,500*
	Total caught inland	*17,168,500*

LARGEST TURTLES AND TORTOISES IN THE WORLD

	Turtle/tortoise	Maximum weight kg	lb
1	Pacific leatherback turtle	865	1,908
2	Atlantic leatherback turtle	454	1,000
3=	Green sea turtle	408	900
=	Aldabra giant tortoise	408	900
5	Loggerhead turtle	386	850
6	Galapagos giant or elephant tortoise	385	849
7	Alligator snapping turtle	183	403
8	Black sea turtle	126	278
9	Flatback turtle	84	185
10	Hawksbill turtle	68	150

Both the sizes and the longevity of turtles and tortoises remain hotly debated by zoologists, and although the weights on which this Top 10 are ranked are from corroborated sources, there are many claims of even larger specimens among the 265 species of *Chelonïa* (turtles and tortoises). The largest are marine turtles. The Aldabra giant tortoises, found on an island in the Seychelles, are the largest land-dwellers – and probably the longest-lived land creatures of all, at more than 150 years. The Alligator snapping turtle is the largest freshwater species. All living examples would be dwarfed in size by prehistoric monster turtles such as *Stupendemys geographicus*, which measured up to 3 m/10 ft in length and weighed over 2,040 kg/4,497 lb.

LARGEST MARINE MAMMALS IN THE WORLD

	Mammal	Length m	ft	Weight (tonnes)
1	Blue whale	33.5	110.0	130.0
2	Fin whale	25.0	82.0	45.0
3	Right whale	17.5	57.4	40.0
4	Sperm whale	18.0	59.0	36.0
5	Gray whale	14.0	46.0	32.7
6	Humpback whale	15.0	49.2	26.5
7	Baird's whale	5.5	18.0	11.0
8	Southern elephant seal	6.5	21.3	3.6
9	Northern elephant seal	5.8	19.0	3.4
10	Pilot whale	6.4	21.0	2.9

Probably the largest animal that ever lived, the blue whale dwarfs even the other whales listed here, all but one of which far outweigh the biggest land animal, the elephant.

TOP 10 FASTEST FISH IN THE WORLD
(Maximum recorded speed)

❶ Sailfish (110 km/h/68 mph) ❷ Marlin (80 km/h/50 mph) ❸ Bluefin tuna (74 km/h/46 mph) ❹ Yellowfin tuna (70 km/h/44 mph) ❺ Blue shark (69 km/h/43 mph) ❻ Wahoo (66 km/h/41 mph) ❼= Bonefish, Swordfish (64 km/h/40 mph) ❾ Tarpon (56 km/h/35 mph) ❿ Tiger shark (53 km/h/33 mph)

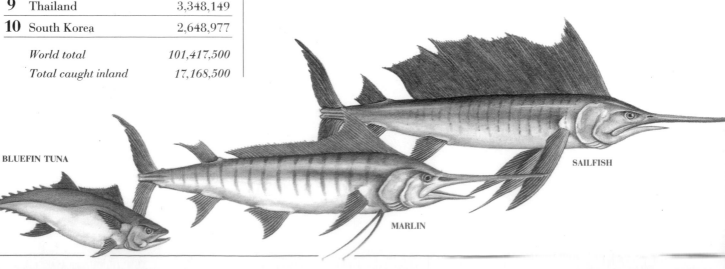

BLUEFIN TUNA

MARLIN

SAILFISH

TOP 10
LARGEST SPECIES OF SALTWATER FISH CAUGHT IN THE WORLD

	Species	Angler/location/date	kg	g	lb	oz
1	Great white shark	Alfred Dean, Ceduna, South Australia, 21 Apr 1959	1,208	39	2,664	0
2	Tiger shark	Walter Maxwell, Cherry Grove, Southern California, USA, 14 Jun 1964	807	41	1,780	0
3	Greenland shark	Terje Nordtvedt, Trondheimsfjord, Norway, 18 Oct 1987	775	0	1,708	9
4	Black marlin	A. C. Glassell, Jr., Cabo Blanco, Peru, 1953	707	62	1,560	0
5	Bluefin tuna	Ken Fraser, Aulds Cove, Nova Scotia, Canada, 26 Oct 1979	678	59	1,496	0
6	Atlantic blue marlin	Paulo Amorim, Vitoria, Brazil, 29 Feb 1992	635	99	1,402	0
7	Pacific blue marlin	Jay W. de Beaubien, Kaaiwi Point, Kona, Honolulu, 31 May 1982	624	15	1,376	0
8	Swordfish	L. Marron, Iquique, Chile, 7 May 1953	536	16	1,182	0
9	Mako shark	Patrick Guillanton, Black River, Mauritius, 16 Nov 1988	505	76	1,115	0
10	Hammerhead shark	Allen Ogle, Sarasota, Florida, USA, 20 May 1982	449	52	991	0

TOP 10
LARGEST SPECIES OF FRESHWATER FISH CAUGHT IN THE WORLD

	Species	Angler/location/date	kg	g	lb	oz
1	White sturgeon	Joey Pallotta III, Benicia, California, USA, 9 Jul 1983	212	28	468	0
2	Alligator gar	Bill Valverde, Rio Grande, Texas, USA, 2 Dec 1951	126	55	279	0
3	Beluga sturgeon	Merete Lehne, Guryev, Kazakhstan, 3 May 1993	101	97	224	13
4	Nile perch	Andy Davison, Lake Victoria, Kenya, 1991	86	86	191	8
5	Blue catfish	George Lijewski, Cooper River, South Carolina, 14 Mar 1991	48	19	109	4
6	Chinook salmon	Les Anderson, Kenai River, Arkansas, USA, 17 May 1985	44	11	97	4
7	Tigerfish	Raymond Houtmans, Zaïre River, Kinshasa, Zaïre, 9 Jul 1988	44	00	97	0
8	Flathead catfish	Mike Rogers, Lake Lewisville, Texas, USA, 28 Mar 1982	41	39	91	4
9	Atlantic salmon	Henrik Henrikson, Tana River, Norway, 1928 (specific date unknown)	35	89	79	2
10	Carp	Leo van der Gugten, Lac de St. Cassien, France, 21 May 1987	34	33	75	11

Source: International Game Fish Association

IN THE CAN
Sardines, along with other species of herring and pilchard, are components of a world fishing industry that in the 1990s first topped 100 million tonnes a year.

TOP 10
SPECIES OF FISH MOST CAUGHT IN THE WORLD

	Species	Tonnes caught per annum
1	Anchoveta	11,896,808
2	Alaska pollock	4,298,619
3	Chilean jack mackerel	4,254,629
4	Silver carp	2,333,669
5	Atlantic herring	1,886,105
6	Grass carp	1,821,606
7	South American pilchard	1,793,425
8	Common carp	1,627,198
9	Chubb mackerel	1,507,497
10	Skipjack tuna	1,462,637

The Food and Agriculture Organization of the United Nations estimates the volume of the world's fishing catch to total almost 110,000,000 tonnes a year, of which about 75,000,000 tonnes is reckoned to be destined for human consumption – equivalent to approximately 13 kg/29 lb a year for every inhabitant. The foremost species, anchoveta, are small anchovies used principally as bait to catch tuna. In recent years, the amount of carp – especially of farmed varieties in China – has increased markedly. Among broader groupings, 3,000,000 tonnes of shrimps and prawns and a similar tonnage of squid, cuttlefish, and octopus is caught annually.

FLYING ANIMALS

TOP 10

SMALLEST BATS IN THE WORLD

Bat/habitat	Weight		Length	
	g	oz	cm	in
1 Kitti's hog-nosed bat (*Craseonycteris thonglongyai*), Thailand	2.0	0.07	2.9	1.10
2 Proboscis bat (*Rhynchonycteris naso*), Central and South America	2.5	0.09	3.8	1.50
3= Banana bat (*Pipistrellus nanus*), Central Africa	3.0	0.11	3.8	1.50
= Smoky bat (*Furiptera horrens*), Central and South America	3.0	0.11	3.8	1.50
5= Little yellow bat (*Rhogeessa mira*), Central America	3.5	0.12	4.0	1.57
= Lesser bamboo bat (*Tylonycteris pachypus*), Southeast Asia	3.5	0.12	4.0	1.57
7 Disc-winged bat (*Thyroptera tricolor*), Central and South America	4.0	0.14	3.6	1.42
8 Lesser horseshoe bat (*Rhynolophus hipposideros*), Europe and Western Asia	5.0	0.18	3.7	1.46
9 California myotis (*Myotis californienses*), North America	5.0	0.18	4.3	1.69
10 Northern blossom bat (*Macroglossus minimus*), Southeast Asia to Australia	15.0	0.53	6.4	2.52

This list focuses on the smallest example of 10 different bat families. The weights shown are typical, rather than extreme. The smallest of all weighs less than a table-tennis ball, and even the heaviest listed here weighs less than an empty aluminium drink can. Length is of head and body only, since tail lengths vary from zero (as in Kitti's hog-nosed bat and the Northern blossom bat) to long, as in the Proboscis bat and Lesser horseshoe bat.

WINGED WONDER
The albatross is among the world's largest birds, with one of the most impressive wingspans. It is compared here with a seagull.

TOP 10

FASTEST BIRDS IN THE WORLD

Bird	Maximum recorded speed	
	km/h	mph
1 Spine-tailed swift	171	106
2 Frigate bird	153	95
3 Spur-winged goose	142	88
4 Red-breasted merganser	129	80
5 White-rumped swift	124	77
6 Canvasback duck	116	72
7 Eider duck	113	70
8 Teal	109	68
9= Mallard	105	65
= Pintail	105	65

Until pilots cracked 306 km/h/190 mph in 1919, birds were the fastest creatures on the Earth: diving peregrine falcons approach 298 km/h/185 mph. However, most comparisons of the air speed of birds rule out diving or wind-assisted flight: most small birds on migration can manage a ground speed (speed relative to ground) of 97 km/h/60 mph to 113 km/h/70 mph. This list therefore picks out star performers among the medium- to large-sized birds that do not need help from wind or gravity to hit their top speed.

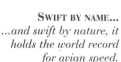

SWIFT BY NAME...
...and swift by nature, it holds the world record for avian speed.

TOP 10

MOST COMMON BIRDS IN THE UK

Species	Estimated number of breeding pairs
1 Wren	7,600,000
2 Chaffinch	5,800,000
3 Blackbird	4,700,000
4 Robin	4,500,000
5 House sparrow	3,850,000
6 Blue tit	3,500,000
7 Willow warbler	2,500,000
8 Wood pigeon	2,450,000
9= Dunnock	2,100,000
= Skylark	2,100,000

Source: Royal Society for the Protection of Birds

FRUIT BAT
Among the most endangered of bats, fruit bats – or flying foxes – are also the largest bats, with wingspans over 10 times that of the smallest species.

TOP 10

BIRDS WITH THE LARGEST WINGSPANS IN THE WORLD

	Bird	Maximum wingspan m	ft
1	Marabou stork	4.0	13
2	Albatross	3.7	12
3	Trumpeter swan	3.4	11
4=	Mute swan	3.1	10
=	Whooper swan	3.1	10
=	Grey pelican	3.1	10
=	Californian condor	3.1	10
=	Black vulture	3.1	10
9=	Great bustard	2.7	9
=	Kori bustard	2.7	9

TOP 10

LARGEST BIRDS OF PREY IN THE WORLD*

	Bird	Length cm	in
1	Californian condor	124	49
2=	Steller's sea eagle	114	45
=	Lammergeier	114	45
4	Bald eagle	109	43
5=	Andean condor	107	42
=	European black vulture	107	42
=	Ruppell's griffon	107	42
8	Griffon vulture	104	41
9	Wedge-tailed eagle	102	40
10	Lappet-faced vulture	100	39

* Diurnal only – hence excluding owls

The entrants in this Top 10 all measure more than 1 m/39 in from beak to tail, but birds of prey generally have smaller body weights than those appearing in the list of 10 largest flighted birds. All of these raptors, or aerial hunters, have remarkable eyesight and can spot their victims from great distances. However, even if they kill animals heavier than themselves, they are generally unable to take wing with them: stories of eagles carrying off lambs and small children are usually fictitious.

TOP 10

LARGEST FLIGHTED BIRDS IN THE WORLD

	Bird	Weight kg	lb	oz
1	Great bustard	20.9	46	1
2	Trumpeter swan	16.8	37	1
3	Mute swan	16.3	35	15
4=	Albatross	15.8	34	13
=	Whooper swan	15.8	34	13
6	Manchurian crane	14.9	32	14
7	Kori bustard	13.6	30	0
8	Grey pelican	13.0	28	11
9	Black vulture	12.5	27	8
10	Griffon vulture	12.0	26	7

Wing size does not necessarily correspond to weight in flighted birds. The 4 m/13 ft wingspan of the marabou stork beats all the birds listed here, yet its body weight is usually no heavier than any of these.

TOP 10

MOST COMMON BREEDING BIRDS IN THE US

1	Red-winged blackbird
2	House sparrow
3	Mourning dove
4	European starling
5	American robin
6	Horned lark
7	Common grackle
8	American crow
9	Western meadowlark
10	Brown-headed cowbird

This list, based on research carried out by the Breeding Bird Survey of the US Fish and Wildlife Service, ranks birds breeding in the US, with the red-winged blackbird (*Agelaius phoeniceus*) heading the list.

TOP 10

LARGEST FLIGHTLESS BIRDS IN THE WORLD

	Bird	Weight kg	lb	oz	Height cm	in
1	Ostrich	156.5	345	0	274.3	108.0
2	Emu	40.0	88	3	152.4	60.0
3	Cassowary	33.5	73	14	152.4	60.0
4	Rhea	25.0	55	2	137.1	54.0
5	Emperor penguin	29.4	64	13	114.0	45.0
6	Flightless cormorant	4.5	9	15	95.0	37.3
7	Flightless steamer	5.5	12	2	84.0	33.0
8	Kakapo	2.5	5	8	66.0	26.0
9	Kagu	5.0	11	0	59.9	23.6
10	Kiwi	3.5	7	12	55.9	22.0

LIVESTOCK

TOP 10

SHEEP COUNTRIES

	Country	Sheep (1997)
1	China	140,150,700
2	Australia	121,900,000
3	Iran	51,499,000
4	New Zealand	47,394,000
5	India	45,653,000
6	UK	41,530,000
7	Turkey	33,791,000
8	Pakistan	31,000,000
9	South Africa	29,016,000
10	Russia	25,800,000
	World total	*1,072,567,000*

This is one of the few world Top 10 lists in which the UK ranks considerably higher than the US, which has only 8,303,000 head of sheep in total. New Zealand's human population is outnumbered by its sheep by a factor of 13:1.

Source: Food and Agriculture Organization of the United Nations

TOP 10

TURKEY COUNTRIES

	Country	Turkeys (1997)
1	USA	88,000,000
2	France	38,000,000
3	Italy	21,500,000
4	UK	12,408,000
5	Germany	6,800,000
6	Brazil	6,000,000
7	Canada	5,800,000
8	Portugal	5,400,000
9	Israel	4,000,000
10	Mexico	3,800,000
	World total	*232,427,000*

Some 82 per cent of the world's turkeys are found in the Top 10 countries listed – with the largest number, appropriately, in North America, their place of origin. The name turkey was applied originally to guinea fowl, since they were brought to the West from Turkish territory; it was then confusingly applied to the birds from the New World. The name is equally misleading in French: in France they are known as *dinde* in the erroneous belief that they originally came from India.

Source: Food and Agriculture Organization of the United Nations

TOP 10

TYPES OF LIVESTOCK

	Animal	World total (1997)
1	Chickens	13,384,560,000
2	Cattle	1,323,962,000
3	Sheep	1,072,567,000
4	Pigs	938,944,200
5	Ducks	735,611,000
6	Goats	703,388,000
7	Rabbits	408,524,000
8	Turkeys	232,427,000
9	Buffaloes	153,078,300
10	Horses	62,129,770

The 19,015,191,270 animals accounted for by the Top 10 outnumber the world's human population by three to one. The world chicken population is more than double the human population, while the cattle population outnumbers the population of China. There are more pigs in the world than the population of India, and almost sufficient turkeys for every citizen of the US to have one each for Thanksgiving.

Source: Food and Agriculture Organization of the United Nations

TOP 10

MILK-PRODUCING COUNTRIES

	Country	Tonnes (1997) *
1	USA	71,072,000
2	India	34,500,000
3	Russia	34,000,000
4	Germany	28,750,000
5	France	24,980,000
6	Brazil	19,100,000
7	Ukraine	15,300,000
8	UK	14,808,300
9	Poland	11,400,000
10	Netherlands	11,188,000
	World total	*471,207,894*

* *Fresh cow milk*

Source: Food and Agriculture Organization of the United Nations

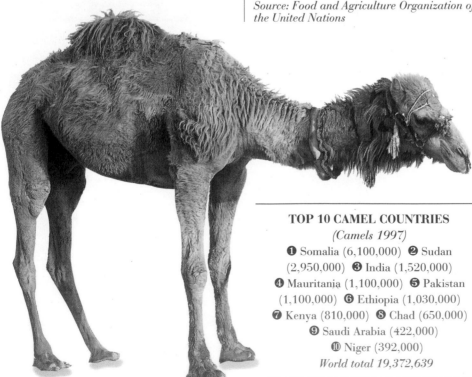

TOP 10 CAMEL COUNTRIES
(Camels 1997)
❶ Somalia (6,100,000) ❷ Sudan
(2,950,000) ❸ India (1,520,000)
❹ Mauritania (1,100,000) ❺ Pakistan
(1,100,000) ❻ Ethiopia (1,030,000)
❼ Kenya (810,000) ❽ Chad (650,000)
❾ Saudi Arabia (422,000)
❿ Niger (392,000)
World total 19,372,639

CHICKEN COUNTRIES

	Country	Chickens (1997)
1	China	3,010,535,000
2	USA	1,553,000,000
3	Indonesia	1,103,310,000
4	Brazil	970,000,000
5	India	570,000,000
6	Russia	415,000,000
7	Mexico	393,000,000
8	Japan	309,000,000
9	France	221,000,000
10	Iran	202,140,000
	World total	13,384,560,000

Source: Food and Agriculture Organization of the United Nations

TOP 10 PIG COUNTRIES
(Pigs 1997)
❶ China (467,828,400)
❷ USA (56,171,000) ❸ Brazil (36,900,000)
❹ Germany (24,144,610) ❺ Russia
(22,631,000) ❻ Spain (18,155,000)
❼ Poland (18,152,000) ❽ Vietnam
(17,500,000) ❾ India (15,419,000)
❿ Mexico (15,020,000)
World total 938,944,200

TOP 10 GOAT COUNTRIES
(Goats 1997)
❶ China (170,993,000) ❷ India
(120,600,000) ❸ Pakistan (47,000,000)
❹ Bangladesh (34,478,000) ❺ Iran
(26,000,000) ❻ Nigeria (24,500,000)
❼ Sudan (16,900,000) ❽ Ethiopia
(16,850,000) ❾ Indonesia (14,400,000)
❿ Somalia (12,500,000)
World total 703,388,000

HORSE COUNTRIES

	Country	Horses (1997)
1	China	10,200,800
2	Brazil	6,394,140
3	Mexico	6,250,000
4	USA	6,150,000
5	Argentina	3,300,000
6	Ethiopia	2,750,000
7	Colombia	2,450,452
8	Mongolia	2,400,000
9	Russia	2,300,000
10	Kazakhstan	1,700,000
	World total	62,129,770

Mongolia makes an appearance in few Top 10 lists – but here it scores doubly as it is also the only country in the world where the horse population is greater than its human population (2,363,000).

Source: Food and Agriculture Organization of the United Nations

EGG-PRODUCING COUNTRIES

	Country	Hen egg production (1997) (tonnes)	(eggs)*
1	China	16,714,530	278,564,356,980
2	USA	4,665,000	77,746,890,000
3	Japan	2,592,000	43,198,272,000
4	Russia	1,747,000	29,115,502,000
5	India	1,622,000	27,032,252,000
6	Brazil	1,415,350	23,588,223,100
7	Mexico	1,290,000	21,499,140,000
8	France	987,000	16,449,342,000
9	Germany	850,340	14,171,766,440
10	Spain	696,000	11,599,536,000
	UK	631,300	10,521,245,800
	World	46,529,020	775,452,647,320

* Based on 1 egg = 60 gm

The world annual total hen egg production would be sufficient for everyone on the planet to eat an egg every three days.

Source: Food and Agriculture Organization of the United Nations

CATTLE COUNTRIES

	Country	Cattle (1997)
1	India	196,702,000
2	Brazil	163,000,000
3	China	116,560,100
4	USA	101,209,000
5	Argentina	51,696,000
6	Russia	39,696,000
7	Ethiopia	29,900,000
8	Mexico	26,900,000
9	Colombia	26,346,000
10	Australia	26,250,000
	UK	11,312,000
	World total	1,277,793,000

Source: Food and Agriculture Organization of the United Nations

CATS, DOGS & OTHER PETS

TOP 10
CRUFT'S DOG SHOW WINNERS

	Breed	Years	Wins
1	Spaniel (Cocker)	1930; 31; 38; 39; 48; 50; 96	7
2	Welsh Terrier	1951; 59; 94; 98	4
3 =	Alsatian	1965; 69; 71	3
=	English Setter	1964; 77; 88	3
=	Fox Terrier (Wire)	1962; 75; 78	3
=	Greyhound	1928; 34; 56	3
=	Irish Setter	1981; 93; 95	3
=	Retriever (Labrador)	1932; 33; 37	3
9 =	Afghan Hound	1983; 87	2
=	Airedale Terrier	1961; 86	2
=	Lakeland Terrier	1963; 67	2
=	Pointer	1935; 58	2
=	Poodle (Standard)	1955; 85	2
=	Poodle (Toy)	1966; 82	2
=	West Highland White Terrier	1976; 90	2

Charles Cruft (1846–1938) held his first dog show in Westminster in 1886. It was called "Cruft's Dog Show" from 1891, and is now held at Olympia under the auspices of the Kennel Club.

TOP 10
FILMS STARRING DOGS

	Film	Year
1	*101 Dalmatians*	1996
2	*One Hundred and One Dalmatians**	1961
3	*Lady and the Tramp**	1955
4	*Oliver and Company*	1988
5	*Turner and Hooch*	1989
6	*The Fox and the Hound**	1981
7	*Beethoven*	1992
8	*Homeward Bound II: Lost in San Francisco*	1996
9	*Beethoven's 2nd*	1993
10	*K-9*	1991

* *Animated*

Man's best friend has been stealing scenes since the earliest years of film-making, with the 1905 low-budget *Rescued by Rover* outstanding as one of the most successful productions of the pioneer period. Since the 1950s, dogs – both real and animated – have been a consistently popular mainstay of the Disney Studios, who were responsible for several films in this Top 10, which includes only films in which a dog or dogs are the principal stars.

LIZARD

TOP 10
CATS' NAMES IN THE UK*

1	Sooty	6	Tom
2	Tigger	7	Fluffy
3	Tiger	8	Lucy
4	Smokey	9	Sam
5	Ginger	10	Lucky

* *Based on a RSPCA survey*

TOP 10
TRICKS PERFORMED BY DOGS IN THE US

	Trick	Percentage of dogs performing
1	Sit	21.0
2	Shake paw	15.0
3	Roll over	11.4
4	"Speak"	10.6
5 =	Lie down	7.4
=	Stand on hind legs	7.4
7	Beg	7.2
8	Dance	6.1
9	"Sing"	3.0
10	Fetch newspaper	1.7

A survey conducted in the US by the Pet Food Institute and Frosty Paws, a pet food manufacturer, concluded that 25,300,500 out of the more than 40,000,000 dogs in the country performed at least one trick, and ranked them by the numbers doing each. Extrapolating from these results, it was claimed that 5,313,105 dogs sit, 3,795,075 shake paw, and so on. Only 1.5 per cent (379,508 dogs) were claimed to "say prayers", and hence are not included.

101 DALMATIANS

TOP 10
TYPES OF PET IN THE UK

	Pet	Percentage of households owning
1	Dog	23.4
2	Cat	21.4
3	Goldfish	9.3
4	Rabbit	3.9
5	Budgerigar	3.6
6	Hamster	3.2
7	Other bird	2.6
8	Tropical fish	2.4
9	Guinea pig	1.6
10	Canary	0.8

Half of the households in the UK own a pet, ranging from dogs, cats, and rabbits to the more exotic snakes, lizards, and spiders.

TOP 10
DOG BREEDS IN THE UK

	Breed	No. registered by Kennel Club
1	Labrador Retriever	34,788
2	German Shepherd (Alsatian)	24,508
3	West Highland White Terrier	16,148
4	Golden Retriever	15,214
5	Cocker Spaniel	14,541
6	English Springer Spaniel	13,869
7	Cavalier King Charles Spaniel	13,022
8	Boxer	10,993
9	Yorkshire Terrier	9,700
10	Staffordshire Bull Terrier	8,699

The list of 10 principal breeds of dogs registered by the Kennel Club in 1997 was identical to that of previous years, and in the same order as 1996, except that Boxers increased in popularity, overtaking Yorkshire Terriers. Independent surveys of dog ownership present a similar picture, though with certain other popular breeds (among them the Jack Russell, Border Collie, and Poodle) making a stronger showing than in the Kennel Club's list.

TOP 10
MOST INTELLIGENT DOG BREEDS

1	Border Collie
2	Poodle
3	German Shepherd (Alsatian)
4	Golden Retriever
5	Doberman Pinscher
6	Shetland Sheepdog
7	Labrador Retriever
8	Papillon
9	Rottweiler
10	Australian Cattle Dog

American psychology professor and pet trainer Stanley Coren devised a ranking of 133 breeds of dogs after studying their responses to a range of IQ tests, as well as the opinions of judges in dog obedience tests. Dog owners who have criticized the results (mostly those whose own pets scored badly) point out that dogs are bred for specialized abilities, such as speed or ferocity, and that the level of obedience to their human masters is only one feature of their "intelligence".

Source: Stanley Coren, The Intelligence of Dogs *(Scribner, 1994)*

THE 10
LEAST INTELLIGENT DOG BREEDS

1	Afghan Hound
2	Basenji
3	Bulldog
4	Chow Chow
5	Borzoi
6	Bloodhound
7	Pekinese
8 =	Beagle
=	Mastiff
10	Bassett Hound

Source: Stanley Coren, The Intelligence of Dogs *(Scribner, 1994)*

TOP 10
DOGS' NAMES IN THE UK

Female		Male
Trixie	1	Sam
Polly	2	Spot
Jessie	3	Pip
Lucy	4	Duke
Bonnie	5	Piper
Cassie	6	Max
Daisy	7	Charlie
Heidi	8	Rocky
Susie	9	Zak
Holly	10	Tiny

TOP 10
PEDIGREE CAT BREEDS IN THE UK

	Breed	No. registered by Cat Fancy, 1997
1	Persian Long Hair	8,418
2	Siamese	4,869
3	British Short Hair	4,286
4	Burmese	3,327
5	Birman	2,214
6	Oriental Short Hair	1,392
7	Maine Coon	1,288
8	Bengal	1,220
9	Ragdoll	933
10	Exotic Short Hair	708

This Top 10 list is based on a total of 32,611 cats registered with the Governing Council of the Cat Fancy in 1997.

PLANTS & FOOD CROPS

T O P 1 0

POTATO-PRODUCING COUNTRIES

	Country	Production 1997 (tonnes)
1	China	48,033,530
2	Russia	40,000,000
3	Poland	27,217,000
4	USA	21,500,000
5	Ukraine	19,000,000
6	India	18,500,000
7	Germany	12,438,000
8	Belarus	11,500,000
9	Netherlands	8,081,000
10	UK	7,219,000
	World	*302,500,700*

Dividing a country's population by the weight of potatoes grown will not reveal who eats the most, since a great deal of the world's potato harvest is used in the manufacture of alcohol and other products. Nonetheless, large populations of the world depend on potatoes for their nutrition.

Source: Food and Agriculture Organization of the United Nations

TOP 10 FRUIT CROPS IN THE WORLD
(*Production 1997 in tonnes*)

❶ Oranges (60,266,130) ❷ Bananas (57,913,410) ❸ Grapes (57,219,190) ❹ Apples (54,686,160)
❺ Watermelons (46,476,680) ❻ Coconuts (46,006,190) ❼ Plantains (29,620,910)
❽ Mangoes (21,964,360) ❾ Tangerines, clementines, satsumas (15,546,200) ❿ Pears (13,069,26)

VEGETABLE CROPS

	Crop	Production 1997 (tonnes)		Crop	Production 1997 (tonnes)
1	Sugar cane	1,215,944,000	6	Sugar beet	274,076,500
2	Rice	571,741,700	7	Cassava	166,464,600
3	Wheat	602,484,000	8	Barley	152,572,600
4	Maize	580,000,100	9	Soybeans	141,527,700
5	Potatoes	302,500,700	10	Sweet potatoes	134,848,300

Source: Food and Agriculture Organization of the United Nations

COTTON-PRODUCING COUNTRIES

	Country	Production 1997 (tonnes)
1	China	4,100,000
2	USA	4,008,000
3	India	2,720,000
4	Pakistan	1,763,000
5	Uzbekistan	1,056,000
6	Turkey	755,000
7	Australia	576,000
8	Mexico	379,000
9	Greece	352,000
10	Argentina	320,000
	World	*19,560,150*

Source: Food and Agriculture Organization of the United Nations

APPLE-PRODUCING COUNTRIES

	Country	Production 1997 (tonnes)		Country	Production 1997 (tonnes)
1	China	8,009,480	7	Poland	1,900,000
2	USA	4,728,000	8	Italy	1,451,575
3	Turkey	2,100,000	9	Germany	1,400,000
4 =	Iran	2,000,000	10 =	Argentina	1,200,000
=	Russia	2,000,000	=	India	1,200,000
6	France	1,918,000		*World total*	*54,686,160*

Source: Food and Agriculture Organization of the United Nations

TOP 10
RICE-PRODUCING COUNTRIES

	Country	Production 1997 (tonnes)
1	China	196,971,300
2	India	121,512,000
3	Indonesia	51,000,000
4	Bangladesh	27,903,000
5	Vietnam	26,396,700
6	Thailand	21,700,000
7	Myanmar	21,200,000
8	Japan	13,000,000
9	Philippines	11,669,000
10	Brazil	9,546,300
	USA	*8,136,700*
	World	*571,741,700*

World production of rice has risen dramatically during this century. It remains the staple diet for a huge proportion of the global population, especially in Asian countries. Relatively small quantities are grown elsewhere.

Source: Food and Agriculture Organization of the United Nations

TOP 10
MOST FORESTED COUNTRIES

	Country	Per cent forest cover
1	Surinam	92
2	Papua New Guinea	91
3	Solomon Islands	85
4	French Guiana	81
5	Guyana	77
6	Gabon	74
7	Finland	69
8 =	Bhutan	66
=	Japan	66
10	North Korea	65

Source: Food and Agriculture Organization of the United Nations

FLOWER POWER
Sunflowers come from North and Central America, but the plant has been successfully introduced into many other parts of the world.

TOP 10
TALLEST TREES IN THE US
(The tallest-known example of each of the 10 tallest species)

	Tree	Location	Height m	ft
1	Coast Douglas fir	Coos County, Oregon	100.3	329
2	Coast redwood	Prairie Creek Redwoods State Park, California	95.4	313
3	General Sherman giant sequoia	Sequoia National Park, California	83.8	275
4	Noble fir	Mount St. Helens National Monument, Washington	82.9	272
5	Grand fir	Redwood National Park, California	78.3	257
6	Western hemlock	Olympic National Park, Washington	73.5	241
7	Sugar pine	Dorrington, California	70.7	232
8	Ponderosa pine	Plumas National Forest, California	68.0	223
9	Port-Orford cedar	Siskiyou National Forest, Oregon	66.8	219
10	Pacific silver fir	Forks, Washington	66.1	217

A coast redwood, which formerly topped this list, fell during 1992. The General Sherman giant sequoia is reckoned to be the planet's most colossal living thing, weighing some 1,400 tonnes, which is equivalent to the weight of nine blue whales or 360 elephants.

Source: American Forests

TOP 10 SUNFLOWER SEED-PRODUCING COUNTRIES
(Production 1997 in tonnes)

❶ Argentina (5,021,000) ❷ Ukraine (2,800,000) ❸ Russia (2,750,000) ❹ France (2,193,000)
❺ USA (1,630,000) ❻ India (1,500,000) ❼ China (1,350,000) ❽ Romania (1,209,311)
❾ Spain (900,000) ❿ Hungary (790,000)

THE HUMAN WORLD

T O P 1 0

LARGEST HUMAN ORGANS

	Organ		Average weight	
			g	oz
1	Liver		1,560	55.0
2	Brain	male	1,408	49.7
		female	1,263	44.6
3	Lungs	right	580	20.5
		left	510	18.0
		total	1,090	38.5
4	Heart	male	315	11.1
		female	265	9.3
5	Kidneys	left	150	5.3
		right	140	4.9
		total	290	10.2
6	Spleen		170	6.0
7	Pancreas		98	3.5
8	Thyroid		35	1.2
9	Prostate	male only	20	0.7
10	Adrenals	left	6	0.2
		right	6	0.2
		total	12	0.4

This list is based on average immediate post-mortem weights, as recorded by St. Bartholemew's Hospital, London, and other sources during a 10-year period.

T H E 1 0

COUNTRIES WITH THE MOST PATIENTS PER HOSPITAL BED

	Country	Patients per hospital bed
1	Bangladesh	5,479
2	Nepal	4,210
3	Benin	4,182
4	Ethiopia	4,141
5	Burkina Faso	3,300
6	Senegal	1,923
7	Pakistan	1,769
8	Guinea	1,712
9	Mexico	1,704
10	Gambia	1,642
	UK	*161*
	USA	*194*

Source: World Bank, World Development Indicators 1997

Data on hospital beds may be misleading in poor countries, where hospital crowding can result in people sleeping on floors in wards and corridors, but there is a huge difference between the countries with the most beds per person and those with the fewest.

T O P 1 0

COUNTRIES WITH THE FEWEST PATIENTS PER HOSPITAL BED

	Country	Patients per hospital bed
1	Slovak Republic	11
2	Japan	64
3	Kazakhstan	75
4	Yugoslavia	73
5=	Russia	77
=	Ukraine	77
7=	Belarus	80
=	Moldova	80
9	Latvia	82
10	Lithuania	84
	UK	*161*
	USA	*194*

Source: World Bank, World Development Indicators 1997

With the exception of Japan, all the countries in the Top 10 are countries of the former Soviet Union and exemplify the extensive nature of the Soviet Union's health care system until recent years.

THE HUMAN BODY & HEALTH

TOP 10
COUNTRIES THAT SPEND THE MOST ON HEALTH CARE

	Country	Total spending as a percentage of GDP*
1	USA	14.3
2	Argentina	10.6
3	Croatia	10.1
4	Czech Republic	9.9
5	Canada	9.8
6=	Austria	9.7
=	France	9.7
8	Switzerland	9.6
9	Germany	9.5
10	Netherlands	8.8
	UK	6.9

* Gross Domestic Product
Source: World Bank, World Development Indicators 1997

THE 10
COUNTRIES THAT SPEND THE LEAST ON HEALTH CARE

	Country	Public spending as a percentage of GDP
1	Georgia	0.3
2=	Gabon	0.5
=	Myanmar (Burma)	0.5
4=	Cambodia	0.7
=	India	0.7
=	Indonesia	0.7
7=	Laos	0.8
=	Pakistan	0.8
9=	Burundi	0.9
=	Guatemala	0.9
=	Guinea	0.9
	UK	6.9
	USA	14.3

Source: World Bank, World Development Indicators 1997

TOP 10
MOST COMMON ELEMENTS IN THE HUMAN BODY

	Element	gm*
1	Oxygen	45,500
2	Carbon	12,600
3	Hydrogen	7,000
4	Nitrogen	2,100
5	Calcium	1,050
6	Phosphorus	700
7	Sulphur	175
8	Potassium	140
9=	Chlorine	105
=	Sodium	105

* Average in 70 kg person

TOP 10
MOST COMMON ALLERGENS
(Substances that cause allergies)

Food allergen		Environmental allergen
Nuts	1	House dust mite
Shellfish/seafood	2	Grass pollens
Milk	3	Tree pollens
Wheat	4	Cats
Eggs	5	Dogs
Fresh fruit (apples, oranges, strawberries, etc.)	6	Horses
Fresh vegetables (potatoes, cucumber, etc.)	7	Moulds (Aspergillus fumigatus, etc.)
Cheese	8	Birch pollen
Yeast	9	Weed pollen
Soya protein	10	Wasp/bee venom

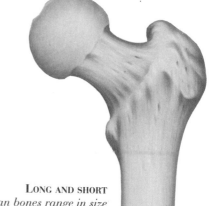

LONG AND SHORT
Human bones range in size from the longest – the femur – at 50.50cm/19.88 in, some 28 per cent of a person's height, to the minute stapes or stirrup bone in the ear, which averages 3.0 mm/0.12 in.

TOP 10 LONGEST BONES IN THE HUMAN BODY
(Length)

❶ Femur/thighbone – upper leg (50.50 cm/19.88 in) ❷ Tibia/shinbone – inner lower leg (43.03 cm/16.94 in) ❸ Fibula/outer lower leg (40.50 cm/15.94 in) ❹ Humerus/upper arm (36.46 cm/14.35 in) ❺ Ulna/inner lower arm (28.20 cm/11.10 in) ❻ Radius/outer lower arm (26.42 cm/10.40 in) ❼ 7th rib (24.00 cm/9.45 in) ❽ 8th rib (23.00 cm/9.06 in) ❾ Innominate bone/hipbone – half pelvis (18.50 cm/7.28 in) ❿ Sternum/breastbone (17.00 cm/6.69 in)

MATTERS OF LIFE & DEATH

COUNTRIES WITH THE MOST CREMATIONS

	Country	Percentage of deaths	Cremations (1996)
1	China	35.20	2,830,000
2	Japan	98.70	938,777
3	USA	21.31	492,434
4	UK	71.28	445,934
5	Germany	37.76	333,373
6	Czech Republic	75.93	85,650
7	Canada	39.58	84,246
8	France	12.73	68,317
9	Australia	54.00	68,208
10	The Netherlands	47.26	65,014

Cremation is least practised in traditionally Roman Catholic countries, such as Spain (5.92 per cent of deaths), Italy (3.27 per cent of deaths), and the Republic of Ireland (3.92 per cent of deaths).

Source: The Cremation Society

MOST COMMON CAUSES OF DEATH IN THE WORLD

	Cause	Approximate deaths per annum
1	Ischaemic heart disease	7,200,000
2	Cerebrovascular disease	4,600,000
3	Acute lower respiratory infection	3,905,000
4	Tuberculosis	3,000,000
5	Chronic obstructive pulmonary disease	2,888,000
6	Diarrhoea, including dysentery	2,473,000
7	Malaria	1,500,000–2,700,000
8	HIV/Aids	1,500,000
9	Hepatitis B	1,156,000
10	Prematurity	1,150,000

If all the different forms of cancer were considered as one, then cancers would fall at No. 2 in the Top 10 with approximately 6,346,000 deaths caused annually.

Source: World Health Organization

MOST COMMON CAUSES OF DEATH CAUSED BY INFECTIOUS AND PARASITIC DISEASES

	Cause	Approximate deaths per annum
1	Acute lower respiratory infection	3,905,000
2	Tuberculosis	3,000,000
3	Diarrhoea (including dysentery)	2,473,000
4	Malaria	1,500,000–2,700,000
5	HIV/AIDS	1,500,000
6	Hepatitis B	1,156,000
7	Measles	1,010,000
8	Whooping cough (pertussis)	355,000
9	Neonatal tetanus	310,000
10	Trypanosomiasis (sleeping sickness)	150,000

Infectious and parasitic diseases account for approximately 17,000,000 of the 52,000,000 annual deaths worldwide.

Source: World Health Organization

COUNTRIES WITH THE MOST SUICIDES

	Country	Suicides per 100,000 population
1	Lithuania	45.8
2	Russia	41.8
3	Estonia	41.0
4	Latvia	40.7
5	Hungary	32.9
6	Slovenia	28.4
7	Belarus	27.9
8	Finland	27.3
9	Kazakhstan	23.8
10	Croatia	22.8
	UK	*8.0*
	USA	*12.0*

COUNTRIES WITH THE HIGHEST DEATH RATE

	Country	Death rate per 1,000
1	Sierra Leone	25.1
2	Afghanistan	21.8
3	Guinea Bissau	21.3
4	Guinea	20.3
5 =	Angola	19.2
=	Uganda	19.2
7	Niger	18.9
8	Gambia	18.8
9 =	Mozambique	18.5
=	Somalia	18.5
	UK	*10.7*
	USA	*8.8*

Source: United Nations

COUNTRIES WITH THE MOST DEATHS FROM LUNG CANCER

	Country	Death rate per 100,000 population
1	Hungary	73.8
2	UK	66.8
3	Belgium	64.5
4	USA	57.7
5	Czech Republic	56.2
6	Netherlands	55.7
7	Italy	54.1
8	Canada	51.8
9	Greece	49.8
10	Poland	49.3

THE 10
COUNTRIES WITH THE MOST CASES OF AIDS

	Country	Number of cases
1	USA	40,051
2	Tanzania	28,341
3	Thailand	17,949
4	Zimbabwe	13,356
5	Brazil	9,695
6	Kenya	8,232
7	Côte d'Ivoire	6,727
8	Spain	6,227
9	Italy	5,476
10	Malawi	5,261
	UK	*1,527*

Two points should be considered in respect of these figures. Firstly, they refer to total numbers of cases, so countries with larger populations are likely to have more cases. Secondly, the accuracy of reporting cases of such a sensitive disease varies markedly between countries – this may be due to failure to diagnose, or reluctance to report cases for social, cultural, or religious reasons. On the basis of the data that exists, 22,600,000 people in the world are now living with the HIV infection or AIDS. In 1996 alone, 3,100,000 new HIV infections were reported, and an estimated 1,500,000 people died.

Source: World Health Organization

THE 10
MOST COMMON CAUSES OF DEATH IN THE UK

	Cause	Deaths (1996)
1	Diseases of the circulatory system	272,216
2	Cancer and other neoplasms	159,254
3	Diseases of the respiratory system	99,828
4	Diseases of the digestive system	22,881
5	Injury and poisoning	19,215
6	Mental disorders	11,049
7	Diseases of the nervous system and sense organs	10,897
8	Endocrine, nutritional, and metabolic diseases, and immunity disorders	8,354
9	Diseases of the genito-urinary system	7,881
10	Infectious and parasitic diseases	4,209
	Total annual deaths from all causes (including some that do not appear in this Top 10)	*638,896*

The 10 principal causes of death remain the same and in approximately the same order from year to year, with only slight fluctuations in total numbers. In 1996, for example, deaths resulting from mental disorders moved up one place. In the same year, in the category of deaths resulting from injury and poisoning, suicide accounted for most fatalities – 4,175 in total.

TOP 10
COUNTRIES WITH THE LOWEST DEATH RATE

	Country	Death rate per 1,000
1	Qatar	1.6
2	Kuwait	2.1
3	United Arab Emirates	2.7
4	Andorra	2.8
5	Belize	3.2
6	Brunei	3.7
7	Marshall Islands	3.9
8	Bahrain	4.0
9	Costa Rica	4.2
10	Tonga	4.2
	UK	*10.7*
	USA	*8.8*

Although it is not an independent country, the lowest death rate in the world is recorded by the island of St. Helena, at 0.6 per 1,000 population per year.

Source: United Nations

THE 10
MOST COMMON CAUSES OF ILLNESS IN THE WORLD

	Cause	New cases annually
1	Diarrhoea (including dysentery)	4,002,000,000
2	Malaria	300,000,000– 500,000,000
3	Acute lower respiratory infections	394,000,000
4	Trichomoniasis	170,000,000
5	Occupational diseases	160,000,000
6	Occupational injuries	125,000,000
7	Mood (affective) disorders	122,865,000
8	Chlamydial infections	89,000,000
9	Alcohol dependence syndrome	75,000,000
10	Gonococcal (bacterial) infections	62,000,000

Source: World Health Organization

PLASTER PIONEER

In 1899, the US pharmaceutical company Johnson & Johnson introduced a new product that we now take entirely for granted. Back in 1876, one of the company's founders, Robert Wood Johnson, had heard an address by English surgeon James Lister on the subject of the prevention of infection in wounds and during surgical operations. Ten years later, in partnership with his two brothers, James Wood and Edward Mead Johnson, he introduced the first ready-made sterile dressings; these were to replace the often contaminated and hence highly dangerous cotton bandages that were then in use. In 1899, the company launched the zinc oxide adhesive plaster. First used by surgeons, in 1921 these sticking plasters were marketed to the general public under the brand name of Band-Aid, and the plaster revolution was born.

YEARS AGO • YEARS AGO • YEARS AGO • YEARS AGO
100

CHARITIES

UK NATIONAL LOTTERY GRANTS TO CHARITABLE ORGANIZATIONS

	Organization/location	Lottery grant (£)
1	Richard House Trust (Greater London)	616,000
2	Family Welfare Association (England)	611,000
3	Horton Housing Association (Yorkshire and Humberside)	610,000
5	Age Concern Liverpool	593,000
6	Ayrshire Hospice	550,000
7	Mental Health Foundation (UK)	543,000
8 =	The Samaritans (UK)	500,000
=	Shree Bharatiya Mandal (North West)	500,000
9	Leonard Cheshire Foundation (UK)	492,000
10	National Schizophrenia Fellowship (Scotland)	488,000

Source: Charities Aid Foundation

TOP 10 ENVIRONMENT CHARITIES IN THE UK

(Voluntary income in £s)
❶ National Trust (77,014,000)
❷ National Trust for Scotland (20,867,000)
❸ Woodland Trust (4,286,000) ❹ Crime Concern Trust (2,148,000) ❺ Council for the Protection of Rural England (1,426,000)
❻ Friends of the Earth Trust (1,290,000)
❼ British Trust for Conservation Volunteers (1,214,000) ❽ Royal Society for Nature Conservation (1,154,000) ❾ Tyne and Wear Foundation (965,000) ❿ Greenpeace Environmental Trust (870,000)

LOGO OF THE GREENPEACE ENVIRONMENTAL TRUST

RELIEF AND DEVELOPMENT CHARITIES IN THE UK

	Charity	Voluntary income (£)
1	Oxfam	92,308,000
2	British Red Cross Society	38,446,000
3	Save the Children Fund	33,075,000
4	ActionAid	26,015,000
5	Christian Aid	22,919,000
6	Tear Fund	20,573,000
7	Charity Projects	16,935,000
8	CAFOD	9,447,000
9	Children's Aid Direct	9,344,000
10	World Vision UK	9,102,000

This list includes a number of charities that have a religious basis (notably Christian Aid, Tear Fund, and CAFOD), but whose work is principally conducted overseas in the area of relief and development.

Source: Charities Aid Foundation

CHARITIES ASSOCIATED WITH DIANA, PRINCESS OF WALES

	Charity	Voluntary income (£)
1	Barnados	47,300,000
2	Help the Aged	43,178,000
3	Red Cross	38,446,000
4	Leprosy Mission	6,811,000
5	Parkinson's Disease Society	4,173,000
6	Malcolm Sargent Cancer Fund for Children	2,006,000
7	Centrepoint	1,647,000
8	Relate	1,274,000
9	British Lung Foundation	1,231,000
10	British Deaf Association	1,196,000

Diana was patron of, or involved with, these charities before resigning from many of her public positions following her divorce.

Source: Charities Aid Foundation

SONG FOR DIANA, PRINCESS OF WALES
Elton John's recorded tribute to Diana, Candle in the Wind, *became the best-selling single ever in the UK. Only five weeks after its release on 13 September 1997, 31.8 million copies had been sold. All royalties from the single are donated to Diana's favourite charities.*

BRITISH COMPANIES DONATING THE MOST TO CHARITIES AND THE VOLUNTARY SECTOR

	Company	Donations (£)
1	British Telecommunications plc	14,869,000
2	GlaxoWellcome plc	10,700,000
3	National Westminster Bank plc	10,561,000
4	Marks and Spencer plc	8,500,000
5	Barclays plc	8,400,000
6	Scottish and Newcastle plc	6,500,000
7	Guinness plc	6,300,000
8	British Petroleum plc	6,100,000
9	Midland Bank plc	5,500,000
10	British Gas plc	5,000,000

Companies donate to charities and other voluntary or community organizations for a number of reasons, which include improving their image, promoting the company name, providing support to the local community, and helping their employees. The amounts given vary considerably from company to company, from small donations of a few hundred pounds to large donations of millions.

Source: Charities Aid Foundation

TOP 10

GRANT-MAKING TRUSTS IN THE UK

	Trust	Grants (£)
1	Wellcome Trust	218,691,000
2	National Lottery Charities Board	158,000,000
3	British Academy	22,505,000
4	Royal Society	21,300,000
5	Garfield Weston Foundation	19,082,000
6	Leverhulme Trust	17,426,000
7	BBC Children in Need	16,238,000
8	Tudor Trust	16,209,000
9	Gatsby Charitable Foundation	16,070,000
10	Henry Smith (Estates Charity)	14,003,000

A grant-making trust is thought of as a charity, independent of government, which has an explicit primary function of making grants to other charities or individuals. However, CAF's figures also include other organizations (such as the National Lottery and the British Academy) that are not independent of government but still have charitable status and make significant grants. The total estimate for grant-making in 1995–96 was £1,854,800,000.

Source: Charities Aid Foundation

TOP 10

MEDICINE AND HEALTH CHARITIES IN THE UK

	Charity	Voluntary income (£)
1	Imperial Cancer Research Fund	70,980,000
2	Cancer Research Campaign	60,211,000
3	British Heart Foundation	57,204,000
4	SCOPE	37,237,000
5	Marie Curie Cancer Care	34,316,000
6	Cancer Relief MacMillan Fund	34,153,000
7	Royal National Institute for the Blind	27,117,000
8	Guide Dogs for the Blind Association	21,554,000
9	Institute of Cancer Research	18,922,000
10	Arthritis and Rheumatism Council	16,025,000

Medicine and health charities account for the largest share of the income of the top 500 charities in England and Wales – over £700,000,000 out of a total £1,984,000,000 in 1996, or more than one third. In a Charities Aid Foundation Survey, people rated medicine and health as the most important area of charitable work.

Source: Charities Aid Foundation

TOP 10

FUND-RAISING CHARITIES IN THE UK

	Charity	Voluntary income (£)
1	Oxfam	92,308,000
2	National Trust	77,014,000
3	Imperial Cancer Research Fund	70,980,000
4	Cancer Research Campaign	60,211,000
5	British Heart Foundation	57,204,000
6	Royal National Lifeboat Institution	55,741,000
7	Barnardos	47,300,000
8	Help the Aged	43,178,000
9	British Red Cross Society	38,446,000
10	SCOPE	37,237,000

In 1996, the year to which these figures relate, there were more than 180,000 registered charities in England and Wales. The order of the Top 10 is for voluntary income only. Most charities also receive income from other sources, such as rents and interest on investments.

Source: Charities Aid Foundation

SUPPORT FOR LANDMINE BAN
In January 1997, Diana, Princess of Wales lent her support to a Red Cross campaign for a worldwide ban on landmines by visiting Luanda, Angola, to talk to victims of the mines.

FOR BETTER OR FOR WORSE

COUNTRIES WITH THE LOWEST DIVORCE RATES

	Country	Divorce rate per 1,000		Country	Divorce rate per 1,000
1	Guatemala	0.15	6	Italy	0.48
2	Macedonia	0.27	7 =	Iran	0.50
3	Mexico	0.35	=	Libya	0.50
4 =	Chile	0.46	9	El Salvador	0.51
=	Turkey	0.46	10	Jamaica	0.54

The UN data on divorce rates omits a number of large countries, and ones that we might expect to have a very low divorce rate, such as Ireland. The data is very difficult to collect, given the different laws relating to divorce in each country.

Source: United Nations

FIRST WEDDING ANNIVERSARY GIFTS

1	Cotton
2	Paper
3	Leather
4	Fruit and flowers
5	Wood
6	Sugar (or iron)
7	Wool (or copper)
8	Bronze (or electrical appliances)
9	Pottery (or willow)
10	Tin (or aluminium)

COUNTRIES WITH THE HIGHEST DIVORCE RATES

	Country	Divorce rate per 1,000		Country	Divorce rate per 1,000
1	Maldives	10.75	6	Belarus	4.26
2	Cuba	5.95	7	Surinam	4.15
3	China	4.63	8	Ukraine	4.00
4	Russia	4.60	9	Estonia	3.74
5	USA	4.57	10	Latvia	3.20
				UK	*3.08*

Source: United Nations

TOP 10 COUNTRIES WITH THE MOST MARRIAGES
(Marriages per annum)

❶ China (9,121,622) ❷ USA (2,362,000)
❸ Bangladesh (1,200,000) ❹ Russia
(1,080,600) ❺ Japan (782,738) ❻ Brazil
(763,129) ❼ Mexico (671,640) ❽ Egypt
(530,746) ❾ Thailand (484,569)
❿ Iran (460,888)
UK (322,251)
Source: United Nations

TOP 10
MONTHS FOR MARRIAGES IN ENGLAND AND WALES

	Month	Marriages
1	July	39,809
2	September	39,348
3	August	39,228
4	June	32,117
5	May	28,410
6	October	24,126
7	April	23,323
8	March	16,256
9	December	14,533
10	November	13,399

The figures are for 1994, when there was a total of 291,069 marriages in England and Wales – a drop of nearly 20 per cent on the 1984 figure of 349,186. The popularity order of the months remains similar from year to year, although as Saturday is the favoured day for weddings, the number of Saturdays in the month can boost the apparent popularity of a particular month (in 1994, January, April, July, and October each had five Saturdays). The least popular months of the year were February (12,013) and January (8,507).

TOP 10
COUNTRIES WITH THE LOWEST MARRIAGE RATE

	Country	Marriages per 1,000 per annum
1	Andorra	2.0
2	Malaysia	3.2
3	South Africa	3.3
4	St. Lucia	3.4
5=	Dominican Republic	3.6
=	Paraguay	3.6
7	Cape Verde	3.8
8=	Bulgaria	4.0
=	United Arab Emirates	4.0
10	El Salvador	4.2

TOP 10
COUNTRIES WITH THE HIGHEST MARRIAGE RATE

	Country	Marriages per 1,000 per annum
1	Maldives	19.7
2	Cuba	17.7
3	Bermuda	14.2
4	Liechtenstein	12.9
5	Seychelles	11.9
6	Barbados	11.2
7	Bangladesh	10.9
8	Tajikistan	9.6
9	Mauritius	9.5
10	Bahamas	9.3
	UK	*5.9*
	USA	*9.1*

THE 10
MOST COMMON CAUSES OF MARITAL DISCORD AND BREAKDOWN

1	Lack of communication		7	Physical or verbal abuse
2	Continual arguments		8	Children (whether to have them; attitudes towards their upbringing)
3	Infidelity		9	Step-parenting
4	Sexual problems		10	Addiction (to drinking, gambling, spending, etc.)
5	Financial problems			
6	Work (usually one partner devoting excessive time to work)			

Source: Relate National Marriage Guidance

WHAT'S IN A NAME?

TOP 10 BOYS' NAMES IN ENGLAND AND WALES

1987		1997
Daniel	**1**	Jack
Christopher	**2**	James
Michael	**3**	Thomas
James	**4**	Daniel
Matthew	**5**	Joshua
Andrew	**6**	Matthew
Adam	**7**	Samuel
Thomas	**8**	Joseph
David	**9**	Ryan
Richard	**10**	Jordan

TOP 10 GIRLS' NAMES IN ENGLAND AND WALES

1987		1997
Rebecca	**1**	Chloe
Sarah	**2**	Emily
Emma	**3**	Sophie
Laura	**4**	Jessica
Rachel	**5**	Megan
Samantha	**6**	Hannah
Charlotte	**7**	Rebecca
Kirsty	**8**	Lauren
Nicola	**9**	Charlotte
Amy	**10**	Georgia

GIRLS' AND BOYS' NAMES IN THE UK 100 YEARS AGO

Girls		Boys
Florence	**1**	William
Mary	**2**	John
Alice	**3**	George
Annie	**4**	Thomas
Elsie	**5**	Charles
Edith	**6**	Frederick
Elizabeth	**7**	Arthur
Doris	**8**	James
Dorothy	**9**	Albert
Ethel	**10**	Ernest

MOST COMMON SURNAMES IN THE MANHATTAN TELEPHONE DIRECTORY

1 Smith/Smyth/Smythe
2 Lee/Lea/Leigh/Ley/Li
3 Brown/Browne
4 Cohen/Coan/Coen/Cohn/Cone/Kohn
5 Johnson/Johnston/Johnsen
6 Rodriguez
7 Miller
8 Williams
9 Jones
10 Davis/Davies

MOST COMMON FEMALE FIRST NAMES IN THE US

	Name	Percentage of all first names
1	Mary	2.629
2	Patricia	1.073
3	Linda	1.035
4	Barbara	0.980
5	Elizabeth	0.937
6	Jennifer	0.932
7	Maria	0.828
8	Susan	0.794
9	Margaret	0.768
10	Dorothy	0.727

Source: US Bureau of the Census

The Top 10 female names according to the latest (1990) US Census account for 10.703 per cent of all names. This list includes females of all age groups.

MOST COMMON PATRONYMS IN THE US

	Name/origin	Percentage of all US names
1	Johnson ("son of John")	0.810
2	Williams ("son of William")	0.699
3	Jones ("son of John")	0.621
4	Davis ("son of Davie/David")	0.480
5	Wilson ("son of Will")	0.339
6 =	Anderson ("son of Andrew")	0.311
=	Thomas ("son of Thomas")	0.311
8	Jackson ("son of Jack")	0.310
9	Harris ("son of Harry")	0.275
10	Martin ("son of Martin")	0.273

Patronyms are names recalling a father or other ancestor. Up to one third of all US surnames may be patronymic in origin. Five US Presidents have borne names within the Top 10, along with possessors of other, less common patronyms, such as Jefferson.

MOST COMMON SURNAMES IN THE UK

1	Smith	6	Davies/Davis
2	Jones	7	Evans
3	Williams	8	Thomas
4	Brown	9	Roberts
5	Taylor	10	Johnson

- French composer Louis Julien (1812–60) had 36 first names.
- Ann Pepper, born in Derby, England, in 1882, was given 26 first names, one for each letter of the alphabet, in alphabetical order.
- O is the world's most common single-letter surname; it is especially common in Korea. However, Social Security records in the US list individuals with one-letter names for the entire alphabet from A to Z.

SNAP FACTS

GIRLS' AND BOYS' NAMES IN THE US 100 YEARS AGO

Girls		Boys
Mary	1	John
Ruth	2	William
Helen	3	Charles
Margaret	4	Robert
Elizabeth	5	Joseph
Dorothy	6	James
Catherine	7	George
Mildred	8	Samuel
Frances	9	Thomas
Alice/Marion	10	Arthur

MOST COMMON MALE FIRST NAMES IN THE US

	Name	Percentage of all first names
1	James	3.318
2	John	3.271
3	Robert	3.143
4	Michael	2.629
5	William	2.451
6	David	2.363
7	Richard	1.703
8	Charles	1.523
9	Joseph	1.404
10	Thomas	1.380

Source: US Bureau of the Census

The Top 10 male names according to the latest (1990) US Census account for 23.185 per cent of all names. It should be noted that this list represents names of people of all age groups enumerated, and not the current popularity of first names.

MOST COMMON SURNAMES IN THE US

	Name	Percentage of all names
1	Smith	1.006
2	Johnson	0.810
3	Williams	0.699
4	Jones	0.621
5	Brown	0.621
6	Davis	0.480
7	Miller	0.424
8	Wilson	0.339
9	Moore	0.312
10 =	Anderson	0.311
=	Taylor	0.311
=	Thomas	0.311

The Top 10 (or, in view of those in equal 10th place, 12) most common US surnames together make up over six per cent of the entire US population. In other words, one American in every 16 bears one of these 12 surnames.

MOST COMMON INITIAL LETTERS OF SURNAMES IN THE US

	Surname initial	Percentage of surnames
1	S	9.8
2	B	7.0
3	M	6.5
4	K	6.4
5	D	5.9
6 =	C	5.5
=	P	5.5
8	G	5.2
9	L	5.0
10	A	4.8

MOST COMMON DESCRIPTIVE SURNAMES IN THE US

	Name/origin	Percentage of all names
1	Brown (brown-haired)	0.621
2	White (light-skinned, or white haired)	0.279
3	Young (youthful, or a younger brother)	0.193
4	Gray (grey-haired)	0.106
5	Long (tall)	0.092
6	Russell (red-haired)	0.085
7	Black (black-haired, or dark-skinned)	0.063
8 =	Little (small)	0.046
=	Reid (red-haired)	0.046
10	Curtis (courteous, or well-educated)	0.040

As many as one in 10 of all US surnames may be derived from a simple physical description that was once applied to an ancestor. The list is headed by the Browns.

MOST COMMON SURNAMES OF LATINO ORIGIN IN THE US

	Name/origin	Percentage of all names
1	Garcia	0.254
2	Martinez	0.234
3	Rodriguez	0.229
4	Hernandez	0.192
5	Lopez	0.187
6	Gonzalez	0.166
7	Perez	0.155
8	Sanchez	0.130
9	Rivera	0.113
10	Torres	0.108

ROYALTY & TITLES

TOP 10 BUSIEST MEMBERS OF THE BRITISH ROYAL FAMILY

1987 Members	Engagements*		1997 Engagements*	Members
The Queen	432	1	498	The Princess Royal
The Princess Royal	367	2	487	The Queen
The Duke of Edinburgh	322	3	339	The Prince of Wales
The Prince of Wales	276	4	284	The Duke of Edinburgh
The Princess of Wales	180	5	168	The Duke of Kent
The Duchess of York	132	6	156	The Duke of York
The Duke of Kent	131	7	153	The Duke of Gloucester
Princess Margaret	129	8	136	Princess Margaret
The Duke of Gloucester	123	9	128	The Duchess of Gloucester
The Duchess of Gloucester	111	10	111	The Princess Alexandra
Total	*2,203*		*2,460*	

* Domestic total, excluding engagements abroad

Source: Tim O'Donovan

BEST-PAID MEMBERS OF THE BRITISH ROYAL FAMILY

	Member	Annual payment (£)
1	The Queen	7,900,000
2	The Queen Mother	643,000
3	The Duke of Edinburgh	359,000
4	The Duke of York	249,000
5	The Duke of Kent	236,000
6	The Princess Royal	228,000
7	Princess Alexandra	225,000
8	Princess Margaret	219,000
9	The Duke of Gloucester	175,500
10	Prince Edward	96,000

The Civil List is not technically the Royal Family's "pay", but the allowance made by the Government for their staff and costs incurred in the course of performing their public duties. The amount of the Civil List was fixed for 10 years from 1 January 1991 and provides a total allocation of £10,417,000. Of that sum, £1,515,000 is refunded to the Treasury. The Prince of Wales receives nothing from the Civil List. His income derives largely from the Duchy of Cornwall.

FIRST IN LINE TO THE BRITISH THRONE

	Title	Date of birth
1	The Prince of Wales *then his elder son:*	14 November 1948
2	Prince William of Wales *then his younger brother:*	21 June 1982
3	Prince Henry of Wales *then his uncle:*	15 September 1984
4	The Duke of York *then his elder daughter:*	19 February 1960
5	Princess Beatrice of York *then her younger sister:*	8 August 1988
6	Princess Eugenie of York *then her uncle:*	23 March 1990
7	Prince Edward *then his sister:*	10 March 1964
8	The Princess Royal *then her son:*	15 August 1950
9	Master Peter Mark Andrew Phillips *then his sister:*	15 November 1977
10	Miss Zara Anne Elizabeth Phillips	15 May 1981

The birth in 1988 of Princess Beatrice ousted David Albert Charles Armstrong-Jones, Viscount Linley (b. 3 November 1961), from the No. 10 position, while the birth in 1990 of her sister, Princess Eugenie, evicted Princess Margaret, Countess of Snowdon (Princess Margaret Rose, b. 21 August 1930) from the Top 10.

LONGEST-REIGNING MONARCHS IN THE WORLD

	Monarch	Country	Reign	Age at accession	Years reigned
1	Louis XIV	France	1643–1715	5	72
2	John II	Liechtenstein	1858–1929	18	71
3	Franz-Josef	Austria–Hungary	1848–1916	18	67
4	Victoria	Great Britain	1837–1901	18	63
5	Hirohito	Japan	1926–89	25	62
6	Kangxi	China	1662–1722	8	61
7	Qianlong	China	1736–96	25	60
8	George III	Great Britain	1760–1820	22	59
9	Louis XV	France	1715–74	5	59
10	Pedro II	Brazil	1831–89	6	58

Some authorities claim a 73-year reign for Alfonso I of Portugal, but he did not assume the title of king until 25 July 1139. He thus ruled as king for 46 years until his death on 6 December 1185.

THE 10
LAST BRITISH MONARCHS TO DIE VIOLENTLY

	Monarch/cause*	Date
1	William III, riding accident	8 Mar 1702
2	Charles I, beheaded	30 Jan 1649
3	Jane, beheaded	12 Feb 1554
4	Richard III, killed in battle	22 Aug 1485
5	Edward V, murdered	1483#
6	Henry VI, murdered	21 May 1471
7	Edward II, murdered	21 Sep 1327
8	Richard I, arrow wound	6 Apr 1199
9	William II, arrow wound	2 Aug 1100
10	William I, riding accident	9 Sep 1087

* Includes illnesses resulting from injuries
\# Precise date unknown

THE 10
SHORTEST-REIGNING BRITISH MONARCHS

	Monarch	Reign	Duration
1	Jane	1553	9 days
2	Edward V	1483	75 days
3	Edward VIII	1936	325 days
4	Richard III	1483–85	2 years
5	James II	1685–88	3 years
6	Mary I	1553–58	5 years
7	Mary II	1689–94	5 years
8	Edward VI	1547–53	6 years
9	William IV	1830–37	7 years
10	Edward VII	1901–10	9 years

Queen Jane, Lady Jane Grey, ruled from 10 to 19 July 1553, before being sent to the Tower of London, where she was executed the following year. Edward V was one of the "Princes in the Tower", allegedly murdered on the orders of their uncle, Richard III. Edward VIII abdicated on 11 December 1936, before his coronation.

QUEEN VICTORIA

TOP 10 LONGEST-LIVED BRITISH MONARCHS
(Age at death)

❶ Victoria (81) ❷ George III (81)
❸ Edward VIII (77) ❹ George II (76)
❺ William IV (71) ❻ George V (70)
❼ Elizabeth I (69) ❽ Edward VII (68)
❾ Edward I (68) ❿ James II (67)

TOP 10
LONGEST-REIGNING LIVING MONARCHS IN THE WORLD*

	Monarch/country	Date of birth	Accession
1	Bhumibol Adulyadej, Thailand	5 Dec 1927	9 Jun 1946
2	Prince Rainier III, Monaco	31 May 1923	9 May 1949
3	Elizabeth II, UK	21 Apr 1926	6 Feb 1952
4	Hussein, Jordan	14 Nov 1935	11 Aug 1952
5	Hassan II, Morocco	9 Jul 1929	26 Feb 1961
6	Isa bin Sulman al-Khalifa, Bahrain	3 Jul 1933	2 Nov 1961
7	Malietoa Tanumafili II, Western Samoa	4 Jan 1913	1 Jan 1962
8	Grand Duke Jean, Luxembourg	5 Jan 1921	12 Nov 1964
9	Taufa'ahau Tupou IV, Tonga	4 Jul 1918	16 Dec 1965
10	Qaboos Bin-Said, Oman	18 Nov 1942	23 Jul 1970

* Including hereditary rulers of principalities, dukedoms, etc

THE 10
LONGEST-REIGNING BRITISH MONARCHS

	Monarch	Reign	Age at accession	Age at death	Years reigned
1	Victoria	1837–1901	18	81	63
2	George III	1760–1820	22	81	59
3	Henry III	1216–72	9	64	56
4	Edward III	1327–77	14	64	50
5	Elizabeth II	1952–	25	–	46
6	Elizabeth I	1558–1603	25	69	44
7	Henry VI	1422–61	8 months	49	38
8	Henry VIII	1509–47	17	55	37
9	Charles II	1649–85	19	54	36
10	Henry I	1100–35	31–32*	66–67*	35

* Henry I's birthdate is unknown, so his age at accession and death are uncertain

This list excludes monarchs before 1066, so omits such rulers as Ethelred II who reigned for 37 years. Queen Elizabeth II overtook her namesake Queen Elizabeth I in June 1996. If she is still on the throne on 11 September 2015, she will have passed Queen Victoria.

US PRESIDENTS

TOP 10
LONGEST-SERVING US PRESIDENTS

	President	Period in office years	days
1	Franklin D. Roosevelt	12	39*
2=	Grover Cleveland	8#	
=	Dwight D. Eisenhower	8#	
=	Ulysses S. Grant	8#	
=	Andrew Jackson	8#	
=	Thomas Jefferson	8#	
=	James Madison	8#	
=	James Monroe	8#	
=	Ronald Reagan	8#	
=	Woodrow Wilson	8#	

* Died in office

\# Two four-year terms – now the maximum any US President may remain in office

THE 10
FIRST PRESIDENTS OF THE USA

	President/dates	Period of office
1	George Washington (1732–99)	1789–97
2	John Adams (1735–1826)	1797–1801
3	Thomas Jefferson (1743–1826)	1801–09
4	James Madison (1751–1836)	1809–17
5	James Monroe (1758–1831)	1817–25
6	John Quincy Adams (1767–1848)	1825–29
7	Andrew Jackson (1767–1845)	1829–37
8	Martin Van Buren (1782–1862)	1837–41
9	William H. Harrison (1773–1841)	1841
10	John Tyler (1790–1862)	1841–45

TOP 10
SHORTEST-SERVING US PRESIDENTS

	President	Period in office years	days
1	William H. Harrison		31*
2	James A. Garfield		199*
3	Zachary Taylor	1	127*
4	Warren G. Harding	2	151*
5	Gerald Ford	2	166
6	Millard Fillmore	2	238
7	John F. Kennedy	2	304*
8	Chester A. Arthur	3	165
9	Andrew Johnson	3	323
10	John Tyler	3	332

* Died in office

TOP 10
LONGEST-LIVED US PRESIDENTS

	President	Age at death years	months
1	John Adams	90	8
2	Herbert Clark Hoover	90	2
3	Harry S. Truman	88	7
4	James Madison	85	3
5	Thomas Jefferson	83	2
6	Richard Nixon	81	3
7	John Quincy Adams	80	7
8	Martin Van Buren	79	7
9	Dwight D. Eisenhower	78	5
10	Andrew Jackson	78	2

TOP 10 YOUNGEST US PRESIDENTS
(Age on taking office)

❶ Theodore Roosevelt (42 yrs/322 days) ❷ John F. Kennedy (43 yrs/236 days) ❸ Bill Clinton (46 yrs/154 days) ❹ Ulysses S. Grant (46 yrs/236 days) ❺ Grover Cleveland (47 yrs/352 days) ❻ Franklin Pierce (48 yrs/101 days) ❼ James A. Garfield (49 yrs/105 days) ❽ James K. Polk (49 yrs/122 days) ❾ Millard Fillmore (50 yrs/184 days) ❿ John Tyler (51 yrs/8 days)

JOHN F. KENNEDY
His dramatic assassination ended the short period in office of America's second-youngest president.

TOP 10

LEAST POPULAR US PRESIDENTS

	President	Survey date	Disapproval rating (%)
1	Richard Nixon	2 Aug 1974	66
2	Harry S. Truman	Jan 1952	62
3	George Bush	31 Jul 1992	60
4	Jimmy Carter	29 Jun 1979	59
5	Ronald Reagan	28 Jan 1983	56
6	Bill Clinton	6–7 Sept 1994	54
7	Lyndon B. Johnson	10 Mar, 7 Aug 1968	52
8=	Franklin D. Roosevelt	Nov 1938	46
=	Gerald Ford	18 Apr, 21 Nov, 12 Dec 1975	46
10	Dwight D. Eisenhower	27 Mar 1958	36

Source: The Gallup Organization

TOP 10

US PRESIDENTS WITH THE GREATEST PERCENTAGE OF THE POPULAR VOTE

	President	Year	Winner's total	Loser's total	Winner's percentage
1	Roosevelt	1904	7,628,834	5,084,491	60.01
2	Reagan	1984	54,281,858	37,457,215	59.17
3	Hoover	1928	21,392,190	15,016,443	58.76
4	Van Buren	1836	762,678	548,007	58.19
5	Buchanan	1856	1,927,995	1,391,555	58.08
6	F.D. Roosevelt	1932	22,821,857	16,646,622	57.82
7	Eisenhower	1956	35,585,316	26,031,322	57.75
8	Jackson	1832	687,502	530,189	56.46
9	Jackson	1828	647,231	509,097	55.97
10	Grant	1872	3,597,070	2,834,079	55.93

Source: World Almanac and Book of Facts

TOP 10

SHORTEST US PRESIDENTS

	President	m	ft	in
1	James Madison	1.63	5	4
2=	Benjamin Harrison	1.68	5	6
=	Martin Van Buren	1.68	5	6
4=	John Adams	1.70	5	7
=	John Quincy Adams	1.70	5	7
=	William McKinley	1.70	5	7
7=	William H. Harrison	1.73	5	8
=	James K. Polk	1.73	5	8
=	Zachary Taylor	1.73	5	8
10=	Ulysses S. Grant	1.74	5	8½
=	Rutherford B. Hayes	1.74	5	8½

(Height in m, ft, in)

TOP 10

TALLEST US PRESIDENTS

	President	m	ft	in
1	Abraham Lincoln	1.93	6	4
2	Lyndon B. Johnson	1.91	6	3
3=	Bill Clinton	1.89	6	2½
=	Thomas Jefferson	1.89	6	2½
5=	Chester A. Arthur	1.88	6	2
=	George Bush	1.88	6	2
=	Franklin D. Roosevelt	1.88	6	2
=	George Washington	1.88	6	2
9=	Andrew Jackson	1.85	6	1
=	Ronald Reagan	1.85	6	1

(Height in m, ft, in)

TOP 10

MOST POPULAR US PRESIDENTS

	President	Survey date	Approval rating per cent
1	George Bush	28 Feb 1991	89
2	Harry S. Truman	May/Jun 1945	87
3	Franklin D. Roosevelt	Jan 1942	84
4	John F. Kennedy	28 Apr 1961	83
5	Dwight D. Eisenhower	14 Dec 1956	79
6	Lyndon B. Johnson	5 Dec 1963	78
7	Jimmy Carter	18 Mar 1977	75
8	Gerald Ford	16 Aug 1974	71
9	Bill Clinton	30 Jan–1 Feb 1998	69
10	Ronald Reagan	8 May, 1981; 16 May 1986	68

The Gallup Organization began surveying ratings of US Presidents in October 1938.

Source: The Gallup Organization

TOP 10

OLDEST US PRESIDENTS

	President	years	days
1	Ronald Reagan	69	349
2	William H. Harrison	68	23
3	James Buchanan	65	315
4	George Bush	64	223
5	Zachary Taylor	64	100
6	Dwight D. Eisenhower	62	98
7	Andrew Jackson	61	354
8	John Adams	61	125
9	Gerald Ford	61	26
10	Harry Truman	60	339

(Age on taking office: years, days)

HUMAN ACHIEVEMENTS

T H E 1 0

FIRST EXPLORERS TO LAND IN THE AMERICAS

	Explorer	Nationality	Place explored	Year
1	Christopher Columbus	Italian	West Indies	1492
2	John Cabot	Italian/English	Nova Scotia/Newfoundland	1497
3	Alonso de Hojeda	Spanish	Brazil	1499
4	Vicente Yañez Pinzón	Spanish	Amazon	1500
5	Pedro Alvarez Cabral	Portuguese	Brazil	1500
6	Gaspar Corte Real	Portuguese	Labrador	1500
7	Rodrigo de Bastidas	Spanish	Central America	1501
8	Vasco Nuñez de Balboa	Spanish	Panama	1513
9	Juan Ponce de León	Spanish	Florida	1513
10	Juan Díaz de Solís	Spanish	Río de la Plata	1515

After his voyage of 1492, Columbus made three subsequent journeys to the West Indies and South America. Other expeditions landing on the same West Indian islands have not been included.

THE 10 FIRST MOUNTAINEERS TO CLIMB EVEREST
(Nationality/date)

❶ Edmund Hillary (New Zealander, 29 May 1953) ❷ Tenzing Norgay (Nepalese, 29 May 1953) ❸ Jürg Marmet (Swiss, 23 May 1956) ❹ Ernst Schmied (Swiss, 23 May 1956) ❺ Hans-Rudolf von Gunten (Swiss, 24 May 1956) ❻ Adolf Reist (Swiss, 24 May 1956) ❼ Wang Fu-chou (Chinese, 25 May 1960) ❽ Chu Ying-hua (Chinese, 25 May 1960) ❾ Konbu (Tibetan, 25 May 1960) ❿= Nawang Gombu (Indian, 1 May 1963), James Whittaker (American, 1 May 1963)

PEAK OF SUCCESS
Edmund Hillary and Sherpa Tenzing Norgay became the first people to conquer Everest on 29 May 1953.

T H E 1 0

FIRST PEOPLE TO GO OVER NIAGARA FALLS AND SURVIVE

	Name	Method	Date
1	Annie Edison Taylor	Barrel	24 Oct 1901
2	Bobby Leach	Steel barrel	25 Jul 1911
3	Jean Lussier	Rubber ball fitted with oxygen cylinders	4 Jul 1928
4	William Fitzgerald (aka Nathan Boya)	Rubber ball	15 Jul 1961
5	Karel Soucek	Barrel	3 Jul 1984
6	Steven Trotter	Barrel	18 Aug 1985
7	Dave Mundy	Barrel	5 Oct 1985
8=	Peter de Bernardi	Metal container	28 Sep 1989
=	Jeffrey Petkovich	Metal container	28 Sep 1989
10	Dave Mundy	Diving bell	26 Sep 1993

Source: Niagara Falls Museum

Captain Matthew Webb, the first person to swim the English Channel, was killed on 24 July 1883 attempting to swim the rapids beneath Niagara Falls, and many people have lost their lives attempting to go over the mighty Falls. They include, in 1901, Maud Willard, who was killed when her dog, which she had cajoled into performing the feat with her, retaliated by pressing its nose against the air vent in the barrel, thus suffocating its owner.

T H E 1 0

FIRST CROSS-CHANNEL SWIMMERS

	Swimmer/nationality	Time hr:min	Date
1	Matthew Webb, British	21:45	24–25 Aug 1875
2	Thomas Burgess, British	22:35	5–6 Sep 1911
3	Henry Sullivan, American	26:50	5–6 Aug 1923
4	Enrico Tiraboschi, Italian	16:33	12 Aug 1923
5	Charles Toth, American	16:58	8–9 Sep 1923
6	Gertrude Ederle, American	14:39	6 Aug 1926
7	Millie Corson, American	15:29	27–28 Aug 1926
8	Arnst Wierkotter, German	12:40	30 Aug 1926
9	Edward Temme, British	14:29	5 Aug 1927
10	Mercedes Gleitze, British	15:15	7 Oct 1927

The first three crossings were from England to France, while the rest were from France to England. Gertrude Ederle was the first woman to swim the Channel, but it was not until 11 September 1951 that American swimmer Florence Chadwick became the first woman to swim from England to France.

THE 10
FIRST PEOPLE TO REACH THE NORTH POLE

Name/nationality	Date
1= Robert Edwin Peary, American	6 Apr 1909
= Matthew Alexander Henson, American	6 Apr 1909
= Ooqueah, Eskimo	6 Apr 1909
= Ootah, Eskimo	6 Apr 1909
= Egingwah, Eskimo	6 Apr 1909
= Seegloo, Eskimo	6 Apr 1909

Name/nationality	Date
7= Pavel Afanaseyevich Geordiyenko, Soviet	23 Apr 1948
= Mikhail Yemel'yenovich Ostrekin, Soviet	23 Apr 1948
= Pavel Kononovich Sen'ko, Soviet	23 Apr 1948
= Mikhail Mikhaylovich Somov, Soviet	23 Apr 1948

THE 10
FIRST PEOPLE TO REACH THE SOUTH POLE

Name/nationality	Date
1= Roald Amundsen*, Norwegian	14 Dec 1911
= Olav Olavsen Bjaaland, Norwegian	14 Dec 1911
= Helmer Julius Hanssen, Norwegian	14 Dec 1911
= Helge Sverre Hassel, Norwegian	14 Dec 1911
= Oscar Wisting Norwegian	14 Dec 1911
6= Robert Falcon Scott*, British	17 Jan 1912
= Henry Robertson Bowers, British	17 Jan 1912
= Edgar Evans, British	17 Jan 1912
= Lawrence Edward Grace Oates, British	17 Jan 1912
= Edward Adrian Wilson, British	17 Jan 1912

* Expedition leader

Scott's British Antarctic Expedition was organized with its avowed goal "to reach the South Pole and to secure for the British Empire the honour of this achievement". Meanwhile, Amundsen also set out for the Pole. When Scott eventually reached his goal, he discovered that the Norwegians had beaten him by 33 days. Scott's entire team died on the return journey.

TOP 10
CELEBRITIES ON *PEOPLE* MAGAZINE COVERS

Celebrity	Covers
1 Diana, Princess of Wales	53
2= Duchess of York (Sarah Ferguson)	14
= Elizabeth Taylor	14
4= Michael Jackson	13
= Jacqueline Kennedy Onassis	13
6 Cher	10
7 John Travolta	8
8= Farrah Fawcett	7
= Olivia Newton-John	7
10= Jane Fonda	6
= John Ritter	6

Source: People magazine

THE 10
LATEST *TIME* MAGAZINE "MEN OF THE YEAR"

Recipient	Year
1 Dr. Andrew S. Grove (1936–), CEO of Intel microchip Co.	1997
2= Dr. David Ho (1952–), AIDS researcher	1996
= Newt Gingrich (1943–), US politician	1995
4 Pope John Paul II (1920–)	1994
5 Yasser Arafat (1929–), F.W. de Klerk (1936–), Nelson Mandela (1918–), Yitzhak Rabin (1922–95), "Peacemakers"	1993
6 Bill Clinton (1946–), US President	1992
7 George Bush (1924–), US President	1991
8 Ted Turner (1938–), US businessman	1990
9 Mikhail Gorbachev (1931–), Soviet leader	1989
10 "Endangered Earth"	1988

Source: Time magazine

Time magazine's "Man of the Year" may be one man, a group of men (such as 15 US scientists in 1960), a couple (General and Madame Chiang Kai-shek in 1937), a woman (as, in 1952, Queen Elizabeth II), a group of women (12 were listed in 1975), a machine (in 1982 a computer), or even (as in 1988) "Endangered Earth".

THE 10
FIRST *TIME* MAGAZINE "MEN OF THE YEAR"

Recipient	Year	Recipient	Year
1 Charles Lindbergh (1902–74), US aviator	1927	**6** Franklin D. Roosevelt (1882–1945), US President	1932
2 Walter P. Chrysler (1875–1940), US businessman	1928	**7** Hugh S. Johnson (1882–1942), US soldier	1933
3 Owen D. Young (1874–1962), US lawyer	1929	**8** Franklin D. Roosevelt, US President	1934
4 Mahatma Gandhi (1869–1948), Indian politician	1930	**9** Haile Salassie (1891–1975), Emperor of Ethiopia	1935
5 Pierre Laval (1883–1945), French President	1931	**10** Wallis Simpson (1896–1986), Duchess of Windsor	1936

NOBEL PRIZE WINNERS

TOP 10

NOBEL PRIZE-WINNING COUNTRIES*

	Country	Phy	Che	Ph/Med	Lit	Pce	Eco	Total
1	USA	65	42	75	10	18	25	235
2	UK	21	24	24	8	11	7	95
3	Germany	19	27	15	6	4	1	72
4	France	12	7	7	12	9	1	48
5	Sweden	4	4	7	7	5	2	29
6	Switzerland	2	5	6	2	3	–	18
7	USSR	7	1	2	3	2	1	16
8	Italy	3	1	3	6	1	–	14
9	Netherlands	6	3	2	–	1	1	13
10	Denmark	3	–	5	3	1	–	12

Phy – Physics; Che – Chemistry; Ph/Med – Physiology or Medicine; Lit – Literature; Pce – Peace; Eco – Economic Sciences. Germany includes the united country before 1948, West Germany to 1990, and the united country since 1990.

* In addition, institutions, such as the Red Cross, have been awarded 16 Nobel Peace Prizes

THE 10

LATEST WOMEN TO WIN A NOBEL PRIZE

	Winner	Country	Prize	Year
1	Jody Williams*	USA	Peace	1997
2	Christiane Nüsslein-Volhard#	Germany	Phys/Med	1995
3	Toni Morrison	USA	Literature	1993
4	Rigoberta Menchu	Guatemala	Peace	1992
5 =	Nadine Gordimer	South Africa	Literature	1991
=	Aung San Suu Kyi	Myanmar	Peace	1991
7	Gertrude B. Ellinson†	USA	Phys/Med	1988
8	Rita Levi-Montalcini★	Italy	Phys/Med	1986
9	Barbara McClintock	USA	Phys/Med	1983
10	Mother Teresa	Macedonia	Peace	1979

* Shared with International Campaign to Ban Landmines
# Shared with Eric F. Wieschaus and Edward B. Lewis
† Shared with Sir James Black and George H. Hitchings
★ Shared with Stanley Cohen

SNAP FACTS

- The youngest-ever Nobel prize winner was Australian-born Lawrence Bragg, who won the Physics Prize jointly with his father in 1915, at the age of 25.
- Rudyard Kipling was 41 when he won the Literature Prize in 1907.
- Linus Pauling uniquely won in two completely different categories at completely different times: the Chemistry Prize in 1954 and the Peace Prize in 1962.
- Joint Peace Prize winner Mairead Corrigan was 32 at the time of receiving her 1976 award.

THE 10

LATEST WINNERS OF THE NOBEL PEACE PRIZE

Prize year	Winner	Country
1997 =	International Campaign to Ban Landmines	
=	Jody Williams (1950–)	USA
1996 =	Carlos Filipe Ximenes Belo (1948–)	East Timor
=	José Ramos-Horta (1949–)	East Timor
1995	Joseph Rotblat (1908–)	UK
1994 =	Yasir Arafat (1929–)	Palestine
=	Shimon Peres (1923–)	Israel
=	Itzhak Rabin (1922–95)	Israel
1993 =	Nelson Rolihlahla Mandela (1918–)	East Timor
=	Frederik Willem de Klerk (1936–)	South Africa

THE 10

LATEST WINNERS OF THE NOBEL PRIZE FOR ECONOMIC SCIENCES

Prize year	Winner	Country
1997 =	Professor Robert C. Merton (1944–)	USA
=	Professor Myron S. Scholes (1941–)	USA
1996 =	James A. Mirrlees (1936–)	UK
=	Professor William Vickrey (1914–)	Canada
1995	Robert E. Lucas (1937–)	USA
1994 =	John C. Harsanyi (1920–)	Hungary/ USA
=	Reinhard Selten (1930–)	Germany
=	John F. Nash (1928–)	USA
1993 =	Robert W. Fogel (1926–)	USA
=	Douglass C. North (1920–)	USA

The Nobel Prize for Economic Sciences is a recent addition to the Nobel prizes, first awarded in 1969. It is presented annually by the Royal Swedish Academy of Sciences.

THE 10

LATEST WINNERS OF THE NOBEL PRIZE FOR PHYSIOLOGY OR MEDICINE

Prize year	Winner	Country
1997	Stanley B. Prusiner (1942–)	USA
1996 =	Peter C. Doherty (1940–)	Australia
=	Rolf M. Zinkernagel (1944–)	Switzerland
1995 =	Christiane Nüsslein-Volhard (1942–)	Germany
=	Eric F. Wieschaus (1947–)	USA
=	Edward B. Lewis (1918–)	USA
1994 =	Alfred G. Gilman (1941–)	USA
=	Martin Rodbell (1925–)	USA
1993 =	Richard J. Roberts (1943–)	USA
=	Phillip A. Sharp (1944–)	USA

THE 10

LATEST WINNERS OF THE NOBEL PRIZE FOR CHEMISTRY

Prize year	Winner	Country
1997 =	Paul D. Boyer (1918–)	USA
=	John E. Walker (1941–)	UK
=	Jens C. Skou (1918–)	Denmark
1996 =	Sir Harold W. Kroto (1939–)	UK
=	Richard E. Smalley (1943–)	USA
1995 =	Paul Crutze (1933–)	Netherlands
=	Mario Molina (1943–)	Mexico
=	Frank Sherwood Rowland (1927–)	USA
1994 =	George A. Olah (1927–)	Hungary/ USA
1993 =	Michael Smith (1932–)	UK/ Canada
=	Kary Banks Mullis (1944–)	USA

THE 10

LATEST WINNERS OF THE NOBEL PRIZE FOR PHYSICS

Prize year	Winner	Country
1997 =	Steven Chu (1948–)	USA
=	William D. Phillips (1948–)	USA
=	Professor Claude Cohen-Tannoudji (1933–)	France
1996 =	David M. Lee (1931–)	USA
=	Douglas D. Osheroff (1945–)	USA
=	Robert C. Richardson (1937–)	USA
1995 =	Martin L. Perl (1927–)	USA
=	Frederick Reines (1918–)	USA
1994 =	Bertram Neville Brockhouse (1918–)	Canada
=	Clifford G. Shull (1915–)	USA

THE 10

LATEST WINNERS OF THE NOBEL PRIZE FOR LITERATURE

Prize year	Winner	Country
1997	Dario Fo (1926–)	Italy
1996	Wislawa Szymborska (1923–)	Poland
1995	Seamus Heaney (1939–)	Ireland
1994	Kenzaburo Oe (1935–)	Japan
1993	Toni Morrison (1931–)	USA
1992	Derek Walcott (1930–)	Saint Lucia
1991	Nadine Gordimer (1923–)	South Africa
1990	Octavio Paz (1914–98)	Mexico
1989	Camilo José Cela (1916–)	Spain
1988	Naguib Mahfouz (1911–)	Egypt

THE 10

FIRST WOMEN TO WIN A NOBEL PRIZE

	Winner	Country	Prize	Year
1	Marie Curie* (1867–1934)	Poland	Physics	1903
2	Bertha von Suttner (1843–1914)	Austria	Peace	1905
3	Selma Lagerlöf (1858–1940)	Sweden	Literature	1909
4	Marie Curie (1867–1934)	Poland	Chemistry	1911
5	Grazia Deledda (1875–1936)	Italy	Literature	1926#
6	Sigrid Undset (1882–1949)	Norway	Literature	1928
7	Jane Addams† (1860–1935)	USA	Peace	1931
8	Irène Joliot-Curie★ (1897–1956)	France	Chemistry	1935
9	Pearl Buck (1892–1973)	USA	Literature	1938
10	Gabriela Mistral (1899–1957)	Chile	Literature	1945

* *Shared half with husband Pierre Curie; other half to Henri Becquerel*

\# *Awarded 1927*

† *Shared with Nicholas Murray Butler*

★ *Shared with husband Frédéric Joliot-Curie*

THE GOOD & THE BAD

T H E   1 0
COUNTRIES WITH THE MOST CAR THEFTS

	Country	Car thefts (1996)		Country	Car thefts (1996)
1	USA	1,395,192	6	Germany	225,787
2	Japan	687,960	7	Canada	178,850
3	UK	536,065	8	Australia	122,931
4	France	344,860	9	Russia	113,916*
5	Italy	317,897	10	Switzerland	83,782

* 1995 figure (latest available)

THE 10 MOST COMMON OFFENCES IN ENGLAND AND WALES
(No. of offenders found guilty)

❶ Motoring offences (658,900) ❷ Summary offences (other than motoring) (488,400) ❸ Theft and handling stolen goods (114,500) ❹ Other offences (43,500) ❺ Drug offences (34,100) ❻ Burglary (32,200) ❼ Violence against the person (30,000) ❽ Fraud and forgery (16,300) ❾ Criminal damage (9,800) ❿ Robbery (5,900)

T H E   1 0
MOST COMMON CRIMES IN ENGLAND AND WALES 100 YEARS AGO

	Offence	No. reported
1	Thefts	63,740
2	Burglary and housebreaking	7,495
3	Frauds	2,628
4	Crimes of violence (other than murder)	1,975
5	Attempted suicide	1,861
6	Crimes against morals	1,736
7	Receiving stolen goods	908
8	Robbery and extortion	375
9	Forgery	343
10	Arson	328

These are the annual averages of indictable crimes reported to the police in England and Wales during the period 1893–97.

THE 10

FBI'S "MOST WANTED" FUGITIVES, 1998

1 Ramon Eduardo Arellano-Felix
(b.31 August 1964)

Drug importation.

2 Harry Joseph Bowman
(b.17 July 1949)

Violent racketeering, murder, bombing, and drug trafficking.

3 Lamen Khalifa Fhimah
(b.4 April 1956, Suk Giuma, Libya)

Blowing up PanAm flight over Lockerbie, 1988. Up to $4,000,000 reward.

4 Victor Manuel Gerena
(b.24 June 1958, New York)

Bank robbery and armed robbery in 1983.

5 Glen Stewart Godwin
(b.26 June 1958, Miami, FL)

Escape from Folsom State Prison (30 June 1987), where he was serving a 25 years sentence for murder.

6 Abdel Basset Ali Al-Megrahi
(b.1 April 1952, Tripoli, Libya)

Blowing up PanAm flight over Lockerbie, 1988. Up to $4,000,000 reward.

7 Eric Robert Rudolph
(b.19 September 1966)

Bombing a clinic in Birmingham, Alabama, on 29 January 1998.

8 Agustin Vasquez-Mendoza
(b.1 October 1969, Mexico)

Murder of Drug Enforcement Administration Special Agent. Total reward of $100,000.

9 Arthur Lee Washington, Jr.
(b.30 November 1949, Neptune, NJ)

Attempted murder of a state trooper.

10 Donald Eugene Webb (b.14 July 1931, Oklahoma City, OK)

Murder in 1980 of police chief.

Since its inception on 14 March 1950 by FBI Director J. Edgar Hoover, the FBI's "10 Most Wanted Fugitives" Program has been used to publicize a wide variety of fugitives sought for many different crimes. When a fugitive is taken off the list, another who fulfils the criteria may be subsequently added. The list is not ranked in any special order (here it is arranged alphabetically). The criteria used for selections are that the individual must have a lengthy record of committing serious crimes and/or be considered a particularly dangerous menace to society, and it must be believed that the nationwide publicity afforded by the program can be of assistance in apprehending the fugitive.

COUNTRIES WITH THE HIGHEST CRIME RATES

Country	Reported crime rate per 100,000 population
1 Surinam	17,819
2 St. Kitts and Nevis	15,468
3 Gibraltar	14,970
4 New Zealand	14,496
5 Sweden	13,750
6 Canada	13,297
7 US Virgin Islands	10,441
8 Denmark	10,399
9 The Netherlands	10,181
10 Guam	10,080
England and Wales	9,395
USA	5,278

COUNTRIES WITH THE LOWEST CRIME RATES

Country	Reported crime rate per 100,000 population
1 Togo	11.0
2 Nepal	13.0
3 Guinea	18.4
4= Dem. Rep. of Congo	32.0
= Niger	32.0
6 Mali	33.0
7 Burkina Faso	41.0
8 Bangladesh	64.0
9 Côte d'Ivoire	67.0
10 Burundi	84.0

There are just 13 countries in the world with reported crime rates of fewer than 100 per 100,000 inhabitants.

COUNTRIES WITH THE MOST BURGLARIES

Country	Burglaries (1996)
1 USA	2,501,524
2 UK	651,444
3 Poland	305,703
4 Australia	269,554
5 Russia	268,000
6 Canada	242,132
7 France	236,272
8 Italy	230,258
9 Japan	223,590
10 Germany	195,801

POLICE & PRISONS

THE 10
COUNTRIES WITH THE MOST PRISONERS

	Country	Prisoners*
1	USA	1,630,940
2	Russia	1,051,515
3	Germany	71,047
4	Poland	57,320
5	England and Wales	55,537
6	France	54,014
7	Italy	48,747
8	Spain	42,105
9	Japan	40,389
10	Canada	33,785

* In latest year for which figures are available

If the list is recast according to the incarceration rate per 1,000 people, the positions of Russia and the US are reversed, with 7.1 and 6.2 incarcerations per 1,000 respectively. The rate among the other countries is little more than one per 1,000.

THE 10
LARGEST PRISONS IN THE UK

	Prison/location	Inmates
1	Walton, Liverpool	1,467
2	Wormwood Scrubs, London	1,360
3	Barlinnie, Glasgow	1,150
4	Armley, Leeds	1,148
5	Doncaster	1,042
6	Winson Green, Birmingham	1,023
7	Strangeways, Manchester	999
8	Holme House, Cleveland	945
9	Pentonville, London	920
10	Durham	916

THE CITY'S FINEST
New York's police force is by far the largest of any US city.

TOP 10
COUNTRIES WITH THE MOST POLICE OFFICERS

	Country	Population per police officer
1	Angola	14*
2	Kuwait	80
3	Nicaragua	90*
4	Brunei	100
5=	Nauru	110
=	Cape Verde	110
7=	Antigua and Barbuda	120
=	Mongolia	120
=	Seychelles	120
10=	Iraq	140
=	United Arab Emirates	140
	USA	318
	UK	420

* Including civilian militia

Police personnel figures generally include only full-time paid officials and exclude clerical and volunteer staff. However, there are variations around the world in the way in which these categories are defined.

THE 10
LARGEST PRISONS IN THE US

	Prison/location	Capacity
1	Mississippi State Penitentiary, Parchman, Mississippi	5,369
2	Louisana State Penitentiary, Angola, Louisiana	5,108
3	Coffield Unit, Tennessee Colony, Texas	4,032
4	Men's Colony, San Luis Obispo, California	3,859
5	Federal Correctional Institution, Fort Dix, New Jersey	3,683
6	Beto Unit, Tennessee Colony, Texas	3,364
7	California State Prison, San Quentin, California	3,286
8	Clements Unit, Amarillo, Texas	3,198
9	Eastern Correctional Institution, Westover, Maryland	3,180
10	Michael Unit, Tennessee Colony, Texas	3,114

Source: American Correctional Association

THE 10
LARGEST FEDERAL CORRECTIONAL INSTITUTIONS IN THE US

	Institution	Location	Rated capacity
1	Federal Correctional Institution	Fort Dix, New Jersey	3,683
2=	Federal Correctional Institution	Beaumont, Texas	1,536
=	Federal Correctional Institution (Medium Security)	Coleman, Florida	1,536
=	Federal Correctional Institution	Elkton, Ohio	1,536
=	Federal Correctional Institution	Forrest City, Arkansas	1,536
=	Federal Correctional Institution	Yazoo City, Mississippi	1,536
7	US Penitentiary	Atlanta, Georgia	1,429
8	Federal Detention Center	Miami, Florida	1,259
9	US Penitentiary	Leavenworth, Kansas	1,197
10	Federal Correctional Institution	Beckley, West Virginia	1,152

Source: Bureau of Federal Prisons

THE 10
COUNTRIES WITH THE FEWEST POLICE OFFICERS

	Country	Population per police officer
1	Maldives	35,710
2	Canada	8,640
3	Rwanda	4,650
4	Côte d'Ivoire	4,640
5	The Gambia	3,310
6	Benin	3,250
7	Madagascar	2,900
8	Central African Republic	2,740
9	Bangladesh	2,560
10	Niger	2,350*

* Including paramilitary forces

The saying "there's never a policeman when you need one" is nowhere truer than in the countries appearing in this list, where the police are remarkably thin on the ground. There are various possible and contradictory explanations for these ratios: countries may be so law-abiding that there is simply no need for large numbers of police officers, or a force may be so underfunded and inefficient as to be completely irrelevant.

TOP 10
US CITIES WITH THE MOST POLICE OFFICERS

	City	Officers
1	New York	37,090
2	Los Angeles	9,148
3	Philadelphia	6,455
4	Houston	5,252
5	Detroit	3,917
6	Washington	3,611
7	Baltimore	3,081
8	Dallas	2,822
9	Phoenix	2,255
10	Boston	2,218

Source: FBI Uniform Crime Reports

THE 10
MOST REPORTED INCIDENTS OF POLICE USE OF FORCE IN THE US

	Force	Rate per 1,000 sworn officers
1	Handcuff/leg restraint	490.4
2	Bodily force (arm, foot, leg)	272.2
3	Come-alongs	226.8
4	Unholstering weapon	129.9
5	Swarm	126.7
6	Twist locks/wrist locks	80.9
7	Firm grip	57.7
8	Chemical agents (mace or cap-stun)	36.2
9	Batons	36.0
10	Flashlights	21.7

Source: Bureau of Justice – National Data Collection of Police Use of Force

THE 10
US STATES WITH THE HIGHEST RATE OF PRISON INCARCERATION

	State	Rate*
1	District of Columbia	1,650
2	Texas	677
3	Louisiana	578
4	Oklahoma	552
5	South Carolina	515
6	Nevada	493
7	Arizona	473
8	Alabama	471
9	Georgia	470
10	Florida	447

* Of sentenced prisoners in State and Federal institutions per 100,000 resident population, as of 31 December 1995

Source: US Department of Justice

THE 10
US STATES WITH THE MOST PRISON INMATES*

	State	Inmates
1	California	153,010
2	Texas	136,599
3	New York	69,530
4	Florida	64,713
5	Ohio	47,248
6	Michigan	43,784
7	Illinois	40,425
8	Georgia	36,329
9	Pennsylvania	34,703
10	North Carolina	32,334

* As of 30 June 1997

Source: Department of Justice

• The first police force was established in Paris in 1667 • Police dogs were first introduced in Scotland in 1816 • The Texas Rangers, established in 1835, were the first US State police force • In 1893 in Detroit, USA, Marie Own became the first policewoman to be appointed • In 1899 in Akron, Ohio, an electric-powered vehicle was the first police car to be used.

SNAP FACTS

MURDER FILE

MOST COMMON MURDER WEAPONS AND METHODS IN THE US

	Weapon/method	Victims (1996)
1	Handguns	8,594
2	Knives or cutting instruments	2,142
3	"Personal weapons" (hands, feet, fists, etc.)	939
4	Firearms (type not stated)	911
5	Blunt objects (hammers, clubs, etc.)	733
6	Shotguns	673
7	Rifles	546
8	Strangulation	243
9	Fire	151
10	Asphyxiation	92

In 1996, "other weapons or weapons not stated" were used in 726 murders. Relatively rare methods included narcotics (32 cases), drowning (24), explosives (14), and poison (8). Total murders amounted to 15,848, as compared with 20,232 the previous year. The proportion involving guns has actually gone down this century – for example, 72 per cent in 1920 as against 68 per cent in 1996.

WORST METROPOLITAN AREAS IN THE US FOR VIOLENT CRIME*

	Metropolitan area	Violent crimes per 1,000 people (1995)
1	Miami-Dade	18.9
2=	Los Angeles-Long Beach	14.2
=	Gainesville	14.2
4=	New York	13.9
=	Baton Rouge	13.9
6	Baltimore	13.4
7=	New Orleans	13.3
=	Lawton, OK	13.3
9	Sioux City	12.7
10	Memphis	12.5

* Murder, rape, aggravated assault, and robbery

THE 10 WORST CITIES IN THE US FOR MURDER

1986 City	Murders		Murders	1996 City
New York	1,582	1	983	New York
Los Angeles	834	2	789	Chicago
Chicago	744	3	709	Los Angeles
Detroit	648	4	428	Detroit
Houston	408	5	414	Philadelphia
Dallas	347	6	397	Washington
Philadelphia	343	7	351	New Orleans
Baltimore	240	8	328	Baltimore
New Orleans	197	9	261	Houston
Washington	194	10	217	Dallas

Source: FBI Uniform Crime Reports

COUNTRIES WITH THE LOWEST MURDER RATES

	Country	Murders p.a. per 100,000 population
1 =	Argentina	0.1
=	Brunei	0.1
3 =	Burkina Faso	0.2
=	Niger	0.2
5 =	Guinea	0.5
=	Guinea-Bissau	0.5
=	Iran	0.5
8 =	Finland	0.6
=	Saudi Arabia	0.6
10 =	Cameroon	0.7
=	Ireland	0.7
=	Mongolia	0.7

WORST STATES FOR MURDER IN THE US

	State	Firearms used	Total murders
1	California	2,061	2,916
2	Texas	962	1,476
3	Illinois*	585	765
4	Louisiana	547	704
5	Michigan	480	695
6	Pennsylvania	493	665
7	North Carolina	397	615
8	Georgia	445	610
9	Maryland	424	578
10	Virginia	322	490

* Provisional figures

Of the 9,514 murders committed in the 10 states above in 1996, firearms were used in 7,616, or 80 per cent of cases.

• The worst murderess and most prolific poisoner of modern times was Susannah Olah, a Hungarian nurse who, in the 1920s, killed as many as 100 people. Captured in 1929, she committed suicide.

• The worst serial killer of the 20th century is believed to be Pedro Alonzo (or Armando) López, who killed more than 300 girls in Colombia, Ecuador, and Peru. Captured in 1980, he was sentenced to life imprisonment.

SNAP FACTS

RELATIONSHIPS OF MURDER VICTIMS TO PRINCIPAL SUSPECTS IN ENGLAND AND WALES

	Relationship	Victims (1995)
1	Male friend or acquaintance	155
2	Male stranger	144
3	Current or former wife, female cohabitant, or lover	93
4	Current or former husband, male cohabitant, or lover	38
5	Female friend or acquaintance	36
6	Son	32
7	Female stranger	25
8	Daughter	21
9	Father	15
10	Mother	10

In addition to these offences, Home Office statistics record that in 1995 14 homicide victims were unspecified males and four were female family members.

COUNTRIES WITH THE HIGHEST MURDER RATES

	Country	Murders p.a. per 100,000 population
1	Swaziland	87.8
2	Bahamas	52.6
3	Monaco	36.0
4	Philippines	30.1
5	Guatemala	27.4
6	Jamaica	20.9
7	Russia	19.9*
8	Botswana	19.5
9	Zimbabwe	17.9
10	Netherlands	14.8
	USA	*8.4*
	England and Wales	*1.2*

* Includes attempted murder

MOST COMMON METHODS OF MURDER IN ENGLAND AND WALES

	Weapon/method	Victims (1996)
1	Sharp instrument	202
2	Hitting and kicking	92
3	Strangulation and asphyxiation	77
4	Blunt instrument	70
5	Shooting	48
6	Poison or drugs	39
7	Burning	27
8	Drowning	11
9	Motor vehicle	4
10	Explosion	2

According to Home Office statistics, there were 627 murders in 1996 throughout England and Wales; 410 of these victims were male and 217 were female.

RELATIONSHIPS OF MURDER VICTIMS TO PRINCIPAL SUSPECTS IN THE US

	Relationship	Victims (1996)
1	Acquaintance	4,797
2	Stranger	2,321
3	Wife	679
4	Friend	478
5	Girlfriend	424
6	Son	261
7	Daughter	207
8	Husband	206
9	Boyfriend	163
10	Neighbour	162

These offences – which remain in similar order from year to year – accounted for 9,698, or over 60 per cent of the 15,848 murders committed in the US in 1996.

WORST YEARS FOR GUN MURDERS IN THE US

	Year	Victims		Year	Victims
1	1993	16,136	6	1990	13,035
2	1994	15,546	7	1981	12,523
3	1992	15,489	8	1974	12,474
4	1991	14,373	9	1975	12,061
5	1980	13,650	10	1989	11,832

BIRTH OF A GANGSTER

The mobster Al Capone, whose name became virtually synonymous with crime in the US in the 1920s, was born in Brooklyn on 17 January 1899. He gained a reputation as a thug, and acquired the nickname "Scarface". He moved to Chicago where he is known to have killed his rival Jim Colosimo, as well as many others as battles were fought between gangs for control of the city, with Capone emerging as the eventual victor. Capone literally got away with murder on numerous occasions, and organized such gangland killings as the legendary St. Valentine's Day Massacre of 14 February 1929. He was finally jailed in 1931 – but for income tax evasion rather than for murder or the many other crimes of which he was guilty. Released in 1939, Al Capone died insane in 1947.

100 YEARS AGO

CAPITAL PUNISHMENT

THE 10

US STATES WITH THE MOST PRISONERS ON DEATH ROW

	State	Prisoners under death sentence*
1	California	454
2	Texas	438
3	Florida	373
4	Pennsylvania	203
5	Ohio	170
6=	Illinois	161
=	North Carolina	161
8	Alabama	151
9	Oklahoma	133
10	Arizona	121

As at 31 December 1996

THE 10

NAZI WAR CRIMINALS HANGED AT NUREMBERG

1	Joachim Von Ribbentrop
2	Field Marshal Wilhelm Von Keitel
3	General Ernst Kaltenbrunner
4	Reichminister Alfred Rosenburg
5	Reichminister Hans Frank
6	Reichminister Wilhelm Frick
7	Gauleiter Julius Streicher
8	Reichminister Fritz Sauckel
9	Colonel-General Alfred Jodl
10	Gauleiter Artur Von Seyss-Inquart

Twelve Nazi war criminals were sentenced to death following the International Military Tribunal trials, but Herman Goering killed himself and Martin Bormann escaped. The other 10 were hanged on 16 October 1946.

THE 10

LAST PEOPLE EXECUTED AT THE TOWER OF LONDON

	Name	Executed
1	Josef Jakobs	15 Aug 1941

A German army sergeant who was caught when he parachuted into England wearing civilian clothes and carrying an identity card in the name of James Rymer. Following General Court Martial, he was shot at 7.15 a.m.– the only spy executed at the Tower during the course of World War II.

	Name	Executed
2	Y.L. Zender-Hurwitz	11 Apr 1916

A spy of Peruvian descent charged with sending information to Germany about British troop movements.

3	Albert Meyer	2 Dec 1915

Like Ries, Meyer was a German spy posing as a commercial traveller.

4	Irving Guy Ries	27 Oct 1915

A German commercial traveller who was sentenced to death on spying charges.

5	Georg T. Breeckow	26 Oct 1915

Posing as an American (Reginald Rowland) with a forged passport, he was caught when he sent a parcel containing secret messages, but addressed in German style, with country and town name preceding that of the street.

6	Fernando Buschman	19 Oct 1915

Posing as a Dutch violinist, he spied while offering entertainment at Royal Navy bases.

7	Agusto Alfredo Roggen	17 Sep 1915

A German who attempted to escape the death penalty by claiming to be Uruguayan. He was found guilty of spying on the trials of a new torpedo at Loch Lomond, then sending the information in invisible ink.

8	Ernst Waldemar Melin	10 Sep 1915

A German spy who was shot after General Court Martial during World War I.

9	Haike Marinus Petrus Janssen	30 Jul 1915

An accomplice of Roos who used the same methods. The two were tried together and executed the same day. Janssen was shot 10 minutes after Roos, at 6.10 a.m.

10	Wilhelm Johannes Roos	30 Jul 1915

Roos was a Dutchman who sent coded messages to a firm in Holland detailing ship movements in British ports. Roos was the 3rd spy of World War I to be executed at the Tower of London. He was shot.

THE 10

LAST MEN HANGED FOR MURDER IN THE UK

	Name	Hanged		Name	Hanged
1	John Robson Welby	13 Aug 1964	6	James Smith	28 Nov 1962
2	Peter Anthony Allen	13 Aug 1964	7	Oswald Grey	20 Nov 1962
3	Dennis Whitty	17 Dec 1963	8	James Hanratty	4 Apr 1962
4	Russell Pascoe	17 Dec 1963	9	Hendryk Niemasz	8 Sep 1961
5	Henry Burnett	15 Aug 1963	10	Samuel McLaughlin	25 Jul 1961

Capital punishment was abolished in the UK on 9 November 1965. Welby and Allen, the last two men to be hanged were executed on the same day but at different prisons after being found guilty of stabbing John Alan West to death during a robbery.

SING SING'S FIRST FEMALE ELECTROCUTION VICTIM

On 20 March 1899 the famous electric chair at Sing Sing prison, Ossining, New York, claimed its 26th victim when 44–year–old Martha M. Place of Brooklyn, New York, was executed. The first female to be electrocuted, she had been convicted of the murder on 7 February 1898 of her step-daughter Ida. It was not until 12 January 1928 that the second female victim, Ruth Snyder, was electrocuted. On 19 June 1953 Ethel Rosenberg, who had been found guilty of spying for the Soviet Union, became the 8th and last woman to be electrocuted at Sing Sing. Her husband, Julius, had been electrocuted in the same chair on the same day.

100 YEARS AGO

T H E   1 0

FIRST COUNTRIES TO ABOLISH CAPITAL PUNISHMENT

	Country	Abolished
1	Russia	1826
2	Venezuela	1863
3	Portugal	1867
4 =	Brazil	1882
=	Costa Rica	1882
6	Ecuador	1897
7	Panama	1903
8	Norway	1905
9	Uruguay	1907
10	Colombia	1910
	UK	*1965*

Some countries abolished capital punishment in peacetime only, or for all crimes except treason, although several countries later reinstated the penalty. Some countries retained capital punishment on their statute books, but effectively abolished it: the last execution in Liechtenstein, for example, took place in 1795, and in Mexico in 1946.

T H E   1 0

US STATES WITH THE MOST WOMEN ON DEATH ROW

	State	No. under death sentence *
1	California	8
2 =	Florida	6
=	Texas	6
4 =	Alabama	4
=	Illinois	4
=	Oklahoma	4
=	Pennsylvania	4
8	North Carolina	3
9	Mississippi	2
10	Missouri	2

* *As at 31 December 1996, when a total of 48 women were on death row*

Source: Department of Justice

T H E   1 0

YEARS WITH THE MOST EXECUTIONS IN THE USA*

	Year	Executions
1	1935	199
2	1936	195
3	1938	190
4	1934	168
5 =	1933	160
=	1939	160
7	1930	155
8 =	1931	153
=	1947	153
10	1937	147

* *All offences, 1930 to 1997*

The total number of executions in the US fell below three figures for the first time this century in 1952, when 82 prisoners were executed, and below double figures in 1965, with seven executions. Only one prisoner was executed in 1966, in 1977 (when Gary Gilmore became the first person for 10 years to receive the death penalty), and in 1981. There were no executions at all between 1968 and 1976, but double figures were recorded again in 1984 (21 executions) and in all subsequent years.

T H E   1 0

FIRST ELECTROCUTIONS AT SING-SING PRISON, NEW YORK

	Name	Electrocuted
1	Harris A. Smiler	7 Jul 1891
2	James Slocum	7 Jul 1891
3	Joseph Wood	7 Jul 1891
4	Schihick Judigo	7 Jul 1891
5	Martin D. Loppy	7 Dec 1891
6	Charles McElvaine	8 Feb 1892
7	Jeremiah Cotte	28 Mar 1892
8	Fred McGuire	19 Dec 1892
9	James L. Hamilton	3 Apr 1893
10	Carlyle Harris	8 May 1893

The electric chair was installed in Sing-Sing Prison, New York, in 1891. By the end of the 19th century, 29 inmates had been executed by this means.

T H E   1 0

FIRST EXECUTIONS BY LETHAL INJECTION IN THE US

	Name	Executed
1	Charles Brooks	7 Dec 1982
2	James Autry	14 Mar 1984
3	Ronald O'Bryan	31 Mar 1984
4	Thomas Barefoot	30 Oct 1984
5	Doyle Skillern	16 Jan 1985
6	Stephen Morin	13 Mar 1985
7	Jesse De La Rosa	15 May 1985
8	Charles Milton	25 Jun 1985
9	Henry Porter	9 Jul 1985
10	Charles Rumbaugh	11 Sep 1985

Although Oklahoma was the first state to legalize execution by lethal injection, this method was not used there until 1990. All of the above prisoners were executed in Texas.

Source: Death Penalty Information Center

BATTLES & MEDALS

THE AMERICAN CIVIL WAR
More than 50,000 died in the Battle of Gettysburg, Pennsylvania, on 1–3 July 1863, the site of which is now preserved as a National Battlefield. The action was the bloodiest of the Civil War, itself the second most devastating in US history.

THE 10

WORST US CIVIL WAR BATTLES

	Battle/dates	Casualties
1	Gettysburg, 1–3 Jul 1863	51,116
2	Seven Day Battles, 25 Jun–1 Jul 1862	36,463
3	Chickamauga, 19–20 Sep 1863	34,624
4	Chancellorsville/ Fredericksburg, 1–4 May 1863	29,609
5	Wilderness, 5–7 May 1862	25,416*
6	Manassas/Chantilly, 27 Aug–2 Sep 1862	25,340
7	Stone's River, 31 Dec 1862–1 Jan 1863	24,645
8	Shiloh, 6–7 Apr 1862	23,741
9	Antietam, 17 Sep 1862	22,726
10	Fredericksburg, 13 Dec 1862	17,962

* *Killed, missing, and wounded*

\# *Confederate totals estimated*

TOP 10

MOST EXPENSIVE MEDALS EVER SOLD AT AUCTION IN THE UK

	Medal/recipient/auction	Price (£)
1	VC Group to Lieutenant W.B. Rhodes Moorhouse, Royal Flying Corps (the first VC ever awarded to an airman), Sotheby's, London, 1990	126,600
2	VC, DFC Group to Wing Commander E.J.B. Nicolson, Royal Air Force (the only VC awarded for service during the Battle of Britain or to a fighter pilot in the Second World War), Glendinning's, London, 1983	110,000
3	VC Group to Captain W. Leefe-Robinson, Royal Flying Corps (the first airman to bring down a Zeppelin over England), Christie's, London, 1988	99,000
4	Imperial Japanese Order of the Chrysanthemum, Grand Cordon Insignia, Christie's, London, 1989	71,500
5=	VC, GCB, OM, GCMG, GCIE, GCVO Group to Field Marshall Sir George White, Gordon Highlanders (VC for Afghanistan Campaign, 1878–80, but recipient best known for his leadership at the defence of Ladysmith during the Boer War, 1899–1900), Sotheby's, London, 1986	60,500
=	VC to Flying Officer Leslie Thomas Manser, Royal Air Force (for bombing raid, 1942, during which 20-year-old Manser died), Christie's, London, 1992	57,200
7=	The Polar Medals to Captain L.E.G. Oates, 6th Inniskilling Dragoons (who sacrificed his life during Scott's Antarctic Expedition, 1910–11), Sotheby's, London, 1984	55,000
=	VC Group to Able Seaman W. Savage, Royal Navy (posthumous award for raid on St. Nazaire, 1942), Sotheby's, London, 1990	55,000
=	Order of the Thistle (KT) gold collar chain (with provenance for the Dukes of Gordon), Sotheby's, London, 1991	55,000
10	DSO (and two bars), DFC Group to Group Captain P.C. "Pick" Pickard, Royal Air Force (leader of Amiens Prison Raid), Sotheby's, London, 1990	50,600

TOP 10

CAMPAIGNS IN WHICH THE MOST VICTORIA CROSSES HAVE BEEN WON

	Campaign	VCs
1	First World War (1914–18)	634
2=	Second World War (1939–45)	182
=	Indian Mutiny (1857–58)	182
4	Crimean War (1854–56)	111
5	Second Boer War (1899–1902)	78
6	Zulu War (1879)	23
7	Second Afghan War (1878–80)	16
8	Waikato-Hauhau Maori War (1863–66)	13
9	Third China War (1860)	7
10=	First Boer War (1880–81)	6
=	Basuto War (1879–82)	6

The Top 10 accounts for all but 92 of the 1,350 Victoria Crosses ever awarded, up to the 1982 Falklands conflict in which two Victoria Crosses were awarded.

20TH-CENTURY WARS WITH THE MOST MILITARY FATALITIES

War/years	Approx. no. of fatalities
1 World War II (1939–45)	15,843,000
2 World War I (1914–18)	8,545,800
3 Korean War (1950–53)	1,893,100
4= Sino-Japanese War (1937–41)	1,000,000
= Biafra–Nigeria Civil War (1967–70)	1,000,000
6 Spanish Civil War (1936–39)	611,000
7 Vietnam War (1961–73)	546,000
8= India–Pakistan War (1947)	200,000
= Soviet invasion of Afghanistan (1979–89)	200,000
= Iran–Iraq War (1980–88)	200,000

The statistics of warfare have always been an imperfect science. Not only are battle deaths seldom recorded accurately, but figures are often deliberately inflated by both sides in a conflict. For political reasons and to maintain morale, each is anxious to enhance reports of its military success and low casualty figures, so that often quite contradictory reports of the same battle may be issued. These figures thus represent military historians' "best guesses", and precise numbers may never actually be known.

BATTLES WITH THE MOST CASUALTIES

Battle	War/date	Casualties*
1 Stalingrad	World War II, 1942–43	2,000,000
2 Somme River I	World War I, 1916	1,000,000
3 Po Valley	World War II, 1945	740,000
4 Moscow	World War II, 1941–42	700,000
5 Gallipoli	World War I, 1915–16	500,000
6 Artois-Loos	World War I, 1915	428,000
7 Berezina	War of 1812	400,000
8 38th Parallel	Korean War, 1951	320,000
9 Somme River II	World War I, 1918	300,000
10 Ypres I	World War I, 1914	250,000

Estimated total of military and civilian dead, wounded, and missing

Total numbers of casualties in the Battle of Stalingrad are at best estimates, but it was undoubtedly one of the longest and almost certainly the bloodiest battles of all time. Fought between German and Soviet forces, it continued from 19 August 1942 to 2 February 1943, with huge losses, especially on the German side, as the Sixth Army was decimated. Of almost 100,000 German troops captured, only about 5,000 were eventually repatriated.

YOUNGEST WINNERS OF THE VICTORIA CROSS

Name	Campaign/action date	Age yrs	mths
1 Andrew Fitzgibbon	Taku Forts, China, 21 Aug 1860	15	3
2 Thomas Flinn	Indian Mutiny, 28 Nov 1857	15	3
3 John Travers Cornwall	Battle of Jutland, 31 May 1916	16	4
4 Arthur Mayo	Indian Mutiny, 22 Nov 1857	17	6
5 George Monger	Indian Mutiny, 18 Nov 1857	17	8
6 Thomas Ricketts	Belgium, 14 Oct 1918	17	9
7 Edward St John Daniel	Crimean War, 5 Nov 1854; 18 Jun 1855*	17	10
8 William McWheeny	Crimean War, 20 Oct 1854; Dec 1854; 18 Jun 1855*	17	?#
9 Basil John Douglas Guy	Boxer Rebellion, 13 Jul 1900	18	2
10 Wilfred St. Aubyn Malleson	Gallipoli, 25 Apr 1915	18	7

VC awarded for actions on more than one date; age based on first date

Precise date of birth unknown; said to have been "aged 17" at the time of his award

Andrew Fitzgibbon beats Thomas Flinn into second place by being just 10 days younger at the time of the action for which he received his Victoria Cross.

WAR WOUNDED
As well as innumerable civilians who were injured and killed, more than 30 million military fatalities have resulted from 20th-century conflicts.

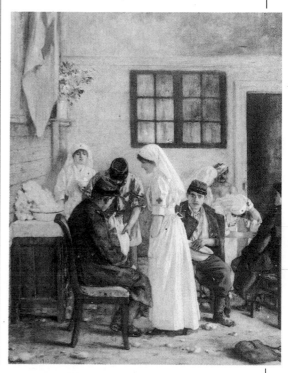

THE WORLD WARS

BRITISH AND COMMONWEALTH AIR ACES OF WORLD WAR I

	Pilot/nationality	Kills claimed
1	Maj. Edward Mannock, British	73*
2	Maj. William Avery Bishop, Canadian	72
3	Maj. Raymond Collishaw, Canadian	62
4	Maj. James Thomas Byford McCudden, British	57
5=	Capt. Anthony Wetherby Beauchamp-Proctor, South African	54
=	Capt. Donald MacLaren, Canadian	54
7=	Maj. William George Barker, Canadian	52
=	Capt. Philip Fletcher Fullard, British	52
9	Maj. R. S. Dallas, Australian	51
10	Capt. George Edward Henry McElroy, Irish	49

COUNTRIES SUFFERING THE GREATEST MERCHANT SHIPPING LOSSES IN WORLD WAR I

		Vessels sunk	
	Country	No.	tonnage
1	UK	2,038	6,797,802
2	Italy	228	720,064
3	France	213	651,583
4	USA	93	372,892
5	Germany	188	319,552
6	Greece	115	304,992
7	Denmark	126	205,002
8	Netherlands	74	194,483
9	Sweden	124	192,807
10	Spain	70	160,383

COUNTRIES WITH THE MOST PRISONERS OF WAR TAKEN, 1914–18

	Country	Prisoners
1	Russia	2,500,000
2	Austria–Hungary	2,200,000
3	Germany	1,152,800
4	Italy	600,000
5	France	537,000
6	Turkey	250,000
7	British Empire	191,652
8	Serbia	152,958
9	Romania	80,000
10	Belgium	34,659

COUNTRIES SUFFERING THE GREATEST MILITARY LOSSES IN WORLD WAR II

	Country	No. killed
1	USSR	13,600,000
2	Germany	3,300,000
3	China	1,324,516
4	Japan	1,140,429
5	British Empire# (UK 264,000)	357,116
6	Romania	350,000
7	Poland	320,000
8	Yugoslavia	305,000
9	USA	292,131
10	Italy	279,800
	Total	*21,268,992*

* Total, of which 7,800,000 battlefield deaths

Including Australia, Canada, India, New Zealand, etc.

COUNTRIES SUFFERING THE GREATEST MERCHANT SHIPPING LOSSES IN WORLD WAR II

		Vessels sunk	
	Country	No.	tonnage
1	UK	4,786	21,194,000
2	Japan	2,346	8,618,109
3	Germany	1,595	7,064,600
4	USA	578	3,524,983
5	Norway	427	1,728,531
6	Netherlands	286	1,195,204
7	Italy	467	1,155,080
8	Greece	262	883,200
9	Panama	107	542,772
10	Sweden	204	481,864

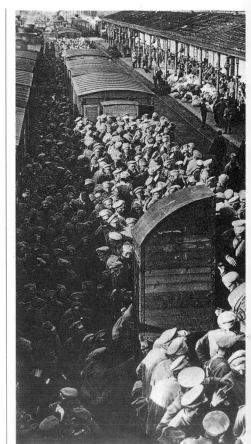

FIGHTING FORCE
More Russian troops served in World War I than those of any other nation, with one in seven killed and one in five taken prisoner.

THE 10 COUNTRIES SUFFERING THE GREATEST MILITARY LOSSES IN WORLD WAR I
(No. killed)

❶ Germany (1,773,700) ❷ Russia (1,700,000) ❸ France (1,357,800) ❹ Austria–Hungary (1,200,000) ❺ British Empire (908,371) ❻ Italy (650,000) ❼ Romania (335,706) ❽ Turkey (325,000) ❾ USA (116,516) ❿ Bulgaria (87,500)

T O P   1 0

BRITISH AND COMMONWEALTH AIR ACES OF WORLD WAR II

	Pilot/nationality	Kills claimed
1	Sqd. Ldr. Marmaduke Thomas St John Pattle, South African	over 40
2	Gp. Capt. James Edgar "Johnny" Johnson, British	33.91
3	Wng. Cdr. Brendan "Paddy" Finucane, Irish	32
4	Flt. Lt. George Frederick Beurling, Canadian	31.33
5	Wng. Cdr. John Randall Daniel Braham, British	29
6	Gp. Capt. Adolf Gysbert "Sailor" Malan, South African	28.66
7	Wng. Cdr. Clive Robert Caldwell, Australian	28.5
8	Sqd. Ldr. James Harry "Ginger" Lacey, British	28
9	Sqd. Ldr. Neville Frederick Duke, British	27.83
10	Wng. Cdr. Colin F. Gray, New Zealander	27.7

THE 10 LARGEST ARMED FORCES OF WORLD WAR I
(Personnel)

❶ Russia (12,000,000) ❷ Germany (11,000,000) ❸ British Empire (8,904,467) ❹ France (8,410,000) ❺ Austria–Hungary (7,800,000) ❻ Italy (5,615,000) ❼ USA (4,355,000) ❽ Turkey (2,850,000) ❾ Bulgaria (1,200,000) ❿ Japan (800,000)

WORLD WAR I CEMETERY

THE 10

SMALLEST ARMED FORCES OF WORLD WAR II

	Country	Personnel*
1	Costa Rica	400
2	Liberia	1,000
3=	El Salvador	3,000
=	Honduras	3,000
=	Nicaragua	3,000
6	Haiti	3,500
7	Dominican Republic	4,000
8	Guatemala	5,000
9=	Bolivia	8,000
=	Paraguay	8,000
=	Uruguay	8,000

* *Total at peak strength*

THE 10

FIRST DECLARATIONS OF WAR IN WORLD WAR II

	Declaration	Date
1=	UK on Germany	3 Sep 1939
=	Australia on Germany	3 Sep 1939
=	New Zealand on Germany	3 Sep 1939
=	France on Germany	3 Sep 1939
5	South Africa on Germany	6 Sep 1939
6	Canada on Germany	10 Sep 1939
7	Italy on UK and France	10 Jun 1940
8	France on Italy	11 Jun 1940
9	UK on Finland, Hungary, Romania	6 Dec 1941
10	Japan on US, UK, Australia, Canada, New Zealand, and South Africa	7 Dec 1941

THE 10

LARGEST ARMED FORCES OF WORLD WAR II

	Country	Personnel*		Country	Personnel*
1	USSR	12,500,000	6	UK	4,683,000
2	USA	12,364,000	7	Italy	4,500,000
3	Germany	10,000,000	8	China	3,800,000
4	Japan	6,095,000	9	India	2,150,000
5	France	5,700,000	10	Poland	1,000,000

* *Total at peak strength*

MODERN MILITARY

NUCLEAR TEST EXPLOSION

THEN & NOW

TOP 10 COUNTRIES WITH THE HIGHEST MILITARY/CIVILIAN RATIO

1987 Country	Ratio*		Ratio*	1997 Country
North Korea	396	1	427	North Korea
Syria	362	2	301	Israel
United Arab Emirates	331	3	250	United Arab Emirates
Israel	317	4	231	Singapore
Jordan	291	5	221	Jordan
Iraq	269	6	209	Syria
Qatar	226	7	208	Qatar
Singapore	213	8	184	Bahrein
Taiwan	208	9	174	Taiwan
Vietnam	204	10	173	Iraq

* *Military personnel per 10,000 population*

TOP 10

LARGEST ARMED FORCES IN THE WORLD

	Country	Army	Navy	Air	Total
1	China	2,090,000	280,000	470,000	2,840,000
2	USA	495,000	395,500	382,200	1,447,600 *
3	Russia	420,000	220,000	130,000	1,240,000 #
4	India	980,000	55,000	110,000	1,145,000
5	North Korea	923,000	47,000	85,000	1,055,000
6	South Korea	560,000	60,000	52,000	672,000
7	Turkey	525,000	51,000	63,000	639,000
8	Pakistan	520,000	22,000	45,000	587,000
9	Iran	350,000	18,000	30,000	518,000†
10	Vietnam	420,000	42,000	15,000	492,000
	UK	*112,200*	*44,900*	*56,700*	*213,800*

Estimated active forces

* *Includes 174,900 Marine Corps*

\# *Includes Strategic Deterrent Forces, Paramilitary, National Guard, etc*

† *Includes 120,000 Revolutionary Guards*

In addition to the active forces listed here, many of the world's foremost countries have substantial reserves on standby; South Korea's has been estimated at some 4,500,000, Vietnam's at 3–4,000,000, and China's at 1,200,000.

THE 10

YEARS WITH THE MOST NUCLEAR EXPLOSIONS

	Year	USA	USSR	UK	France	China	Total
1	1962	96	79	2	1	—	178
2	1958	77	34	5	—	—	116
3	1968	56	17	—	5	1	79
4	1966	48	18	—	7	3	76
5	1961	10	59	—	2	—	71
6	1969	46	19	—	—	2	67
7	1978	19	31	2	11	3	66
8	1967	42	17	—	3	2	64
9	1970	39	16	—	8	1	64
10	1964	45	9	2	3	1	60

Nuclear explosions

TOP 10

DEFENCE COMPANIES IN THE WESTERN WORLD

	Company/country	Annual revenue ($)
1	Lockheed Martin, USA	19,390,000,000
2	Boeing/McDonnell Douglas, USA	17,900,000,000
3	Raytheon/Hughes/Texas Instruments, USA	11,670,000,000
4	British Aerospace, UK	6,470,000,000
5	Northropp Grumman, USA	5,700,000,000
6	Thomson, France	4,680,000,000
7	Aérospatiale/Dassault, France	4,150,000,000
8	GEC, UK	4,120,000,000
9	United Technologies, USA	3,650,000,000
10	Lagardère Group, France	3,290,000,000

TOP 10

COUNTRIES WITH THE LARGEST DEFENCE BUDGETS

	Country	Budget ($)
1	USA	259,400,000,000
2	Japan	43,300,000,000
3	UK	37,100,000,000
4	France	33,100,000,000
5	Russia	32,000,000,000
6	Germany	27,300,000,000
7	Italy	18,300,000,000
8	Saudi Arabia	17,900,000,000
9	South Korea	15,500,000,000
10	Taiwan	11,300,000,000

The so-called "peace dividend" – the savings made as a consequence of the end of the Cold War between the West and the former Soviet Union – means that both the numbers of personnel and the defence budgets of many countries have been cut. The US defence budget has decreased from its 1989 peak of $303.6 billion.

TOP 10

COUNTRIES IMPORTING THE MOST ARMS

	Country	Annual imports ($)
1	Saudi Arabia	9,050,000,000
2	Egypt	2,300,000,000
3	Japan	2,000,000,000
4	China	1,500,000,000
5	Taiwan	1,300,000,000
6	South Korea	1,100,000,000
7	Kuwait	1,036,000,000
8	Turkey	917,000,000
9	Israel	900,000,000
10=	Indonesia	700,000,000
=	Thailand	700,000,000
	UK	undisclosed
	USA (imports from Europe only)	500,000,000

TOP 10

SMALLEST ARMED FORCES IN THE WORLD*

	Country	Estimated total active forces		Country	Estimated total active forces
1	Antigua and Barbuda	200	6	The Bahamas	900
2	Seychelles	300	7=	Belize	1,100
3	Barbados	600	=	Cape Verde	1,100
4=	The Gambia	800	9=	Equatorial Guinea	1,300
=	Luxembourg	800	=	Mauritius	1,300

* Excluding countries not declaring a defence budget

TOP 10

COUNTRIES WITH THE SMALLEST DEFENCE BUDGETS

	Country*	Budget ($)		Country*	Budget ($)
1	Equatorial Guinea	2,300,000	8=	Sierra Leone	11,000,000
2	Antigua and Barbuda	3,200,000	=	Kyrgystan	13,000,000
3	Cape Verde	4,000,000	10=	Barbados	14,000,000
4	Guyana	7,000,000	=	Surinam	14,000,000
5	Guinea-Bissau	8,000,000			
6=	Belize	10,000,000			
=	Seychelles	10,000,000			

* Includes only those countries that declare defence budgets

TOP 10

COUNTRIES WITH THE MOST CONSCRIPTED PERSONNEL

	Country	Conscripts		Country	Conscripts
1	China	1,275,000	6	Italy	163,000
2	Turkey	462,000	7	South Korea	159,000
3	Russia	381,000	8	France	156,950
4	Egypt	320,000	9	Poland	141,600
5	Iran	250,000	10	Israel	138,500

BELL JETRANGER
Expenditure on aircraft and other military equipment is one of the reasons why military budgets worldwide run into billions of dollars.

WORLD RELIGIONS

THEN & NOW

TOP 10 RELIGIONS IN THE UK

1985		
	Religion	Members
1	Anglican	27,100,000
2	Roman Catholic	5,600,000
3	Presbyterian	2,700,000
4	Methodist	1,400,000
5	Muslim	900,000
6	Baptist	600,000
7 =	Orthodox	400,000
=	Hindu	400,000
9 =	Sikh	300,000
=	Church of Scientology	300,000

1995		
	Religion	Members
1	Anglican	26,100,000
2	Roman Catholic	5,700,000
3	Presbyterian	2,600,000
4	Methodist	1,300,000
5	Muslim	1,200,000
6 =	Baptist	600,000
=	Sikh	600,000
8 =	Church of Scientology	500,000
=	Orthodox	500,000
10	Hindu	400,000

THE TORAH
*The sacred Jewish
book of law, containing
the five books of Moses.*

TOP 10

LARGEST CHRISTIAN POPULATIONS IN THE WORLD

	Country	Total Christian population
1	USA	182,674,000
2	Brazil	157,973,000
3	Mexico	88,380,000
4	China	73,300,000
5	Philippines	65,217,000
6	Germany	63,332,000
7	Italy	47,403,000
8	France	45,624,000
9	Nigeria	38,969,000
10	Congo (Dem. Rep.)	37,922,000

TOP 10

LARGEST BUDDHIST POPULATIONS IN THE WORLD

	Country	Total Buddhist population
1	Japan	69,213,191
2	Thailand	59,722,460
3	Myanmar (Burma)	44,354,408
4	Vietnam	42,843,480
5	Sri Lanka	13,457,067
6	South Korea	12,456,290
7	Cambodia	8,740,020
8	India	8,340,240
9	Laos	3,153,303
10	North Korea	2,253,200

Although Christian communities are found in almost every country in the world, it is difficult to put a precise figure on nominal membership (a declared religious persuasion) rather than active participation (regular attendance at a place of worship). For example, the total Christian population of the UK was estimated to be 37,394,000 in 1995, but the population who regularly attend church services (who could be classified as practising Christians) is estimated at just over 6,000,000. Even taking into account other denominations in the UK, there is clearly a wide gulf between thought and deed.

BUDDHA
*Buddhism
originated in
10th-century
India, but
has spread
throughout the
Eastern world.*

TOP 10

CHRISTIAN DENOMINATIONS IN THE WORLD

	Denomination	Adherents
1	Roman Catholic	912,636,000
2	Orthodox	139,544,000
3	Pentecostal	105,756,000
4	Lutheran	84,521,000
5	Baptist	67,146,000
6	Anglican	53,217,000
7	Presbyterian	47,972,000
8	Methodist	25,599,000
9	Seventh Day Adventist	10,650,000
10	Churches of Christ	6,400,000

TOP 10

LARGEST HINDU POPULATIONS IN THE WORLD

	Country	Total Hindu population		Country	Total Hindu population
1	India	814,632,942	6	Pakistan	2,112,071
2	Nepal	21,136,118	7	Malaysia	1,043,500
3	Bangladesh	14,802,899	8	USA	798,582
4	Indonesia	3,974,895	9	South Africa	649,980
5	Sri Lanka	2,713,900	10	Mauritius	587,884
				World	*865,564,992*

TOP 10

LARGEST JEWISH POPULATIONS IN THE WORLD

	Country	Total Jewish population
1	USA	6,122,462
2	Israel	4,354,900
3	France	640,156
4	Russia	460,266
5	Ukraine	424,136
6	UK	345,054
7	Canada	342,096
8	Argentina	253,666
9	Brazil	107,692
10	Belarus	107,350
	World	*14,024,697*

The Diaspora, or scattering of Jewish people, has been in progress for nearly 2,000 years. Today, Jewish communities are found in virtually every country in the world.

BRAHMA THE CREATOR
The supreme being of the Hindu religion is known as Brahma the Creator. Some 99 per cent of the world's Hindu population is in Asia, with 94 per cent located in India, the birthplace of Hinduism.

TOP 10

LARGEST MUSLIM POPULATIONS IN THE WORLD

	Country	Total Muslim population
1	Pakistan	157,349,290
2	Indonesia	156,213,374
3	Bangladesh	133,873,621
4	India	130,316,250
5	Iran	74,087,700
6	Turkey	66,462,107
7	Russia	64,624,770
8	Egypt	57,624,098
9	Nigeria	46,384,120
10	Morocco	33,542,780
	World	*1,340,743,499*

Historically, Islam spread as a result of both missionary activity and through contacts with Muslim traders. In such countries as Indonesia, where Islam was introduced as early as the 14th century, its appeal lay in part to its opposition to Western colonial influences, which, along with the concept of Islamic community and other tenets, has attracted followers worldwide. The global Muslim population is now one in five of the world's population.

TOP 10

CHRISTIAN DENOMINATIONS IN THE UK

	Denomination	Attendance
1	Roman Catholic	1,915,000
2	Anglican	1,785,000
3	Presbyterian	1,100,000
4	Methodist	401,000
5	Orthodox	289,000
6	Baptist	223,000
7	Pentecostal (includes Afro-Caribbean)	197,000
8	New Churches (formerly called house churches)	109,000
9	Christian Brethren	82,000
10	Congregational	74,000

TOP 10

ORGANIZED RELIGIONS IN THE WORLD

	Religion	Followers*		Religion	Followers*
1	Roman Catholic	1,061,896,000	6	Shi'ite Muslim	117,933,000
2	Sunni Muslim	1,061,393,000	7	Anglican	55,077,000
3	Hindu	767,424,000	8	Baptist	54,236,000
4	Buddhist	364,872,000	9	Sikh	22,874,000
5	Orthodox	224,770,000	10	Jewish	15,050,000

* Estimated projections to mid-1998

THE BIBLE

NAMES MOST MENTIONED IN THE BIBLE

	Name	OT*	NT*	Total
1	Jesus (984)/ Christ (576)	0	1,560	1,560
2	David	1,005	59	1,064
3	Moses	767	80	847
4	Jacob	350	27	377
5	Aaron	347	5	352
6	Solomon	293	12	305
7=	Joseph	215	35	250
=	Abraham	176	74	250
9	Ephraim	182	1	183
10	Benjamin	162	2	166

* Occurrences in verses in the King James Bible (Old and New Testaments), including possessive uses, such as "John's"

In addition to these personal names, "God" is referred to on 4,105 occasions (2,749 Old Testament; 1,356 New Testament). The name Judah also appears 816 times, but the total includes references to the territory as well as to the individual with that name. At the other end of the scale, there are many names that appear only once or twice, among them Berodachbaladan and Tilgathpilneser. The most mentioned place names produce few surprises, with Israel heading the list (2,600 references).

LONGEST BOOKS IN THE BIBLE

	Book	Words
1	Psalms	42,732
2	Jeremiah	42,729
3	Ezekiel	39,442
4	Genesis	38,520
5	Isaiah	37,078
6	Numbers	32,943
7	Exodus	32,767
8	Deuteronomy	28,402
9	II Chronicles	26,123
10	Luke	25,986

King James Bible (Old and New Testaments)

ANIMALS MOST MENTIONED IN THE BIBLE

	Animal	OT*	NT*	Total
1	Sheep	155	45	200
2	Lamb	153	35	188
3	Lion	167	9	176
4	Ox	156	10	166
5	Ram	165	0	165
6	Horse	137	27	164
7	Bullock	152	0	152
8	Ass	142	8	150
9	Goat	131	7	138
10	Camel	56	6	62

* Occurrences in verses in the King James Bible (Old and New Testaments), including plurals

The sheep are sorted from the goats in this Top 10, in a menagerie of the animals considered most significant in biblical times, either economically or symbolically (as in the many references to the lion's strength). A number of generic terms are also found in abundance: beast (a total of 337 references), cattle (153), fowl (90), fish (56), and bird (41). Some creatures are mentioned only once, in *Leviticus 11*, which contains a list of animals that are considered "unclean" – the weasel, chameleon, and tortoise, for example – and are never referred to again.

SHORTEST BOOKS IN THE BIBLE

	Book	Words
1	III John	295
2	II John	299
3	Philemon	431
4	Jude	609
5	Obadiah	670
6	Titus	899
7	II Thessalonians	1,023
8	Haggai	1,134
9	Nahum	1,285
10	Jonah	1,323

King James Bible (Old and New Testaments)

LONGEST WORDS IN THE BIBLE

	Word*	Letters
1=	covenantbreakers (NT only)	16
=	evilfavouredness	16
=	lovingkindnesses	16
=	unprofitableness	16
=	unrighteousness (and NT)	16
=	uprighteousness	16
7=	acknowledgement	15
=	administrations (NT only)	15
=	bloodyguiltness	15
=	confectionaries	15
=	fellowdisciples (NT only)	15
=	fellowlabourers (NT only)	15
=	interpretations	15
=	kneadingtroughs	15
=	notwithstanding (and NT)	15
=	prognosticators	15
=	righteousnesses	15
=	stumblingblocks	15
=	threshingfloors	15

* All Old Testament only (King James Bible) unless otherwise stated

TOP 10

LONGEST NAMES OF PEOPLE AND PLACES IN THE BIBLE

	Name	Letters
1	Mahershalalhashbaz (Isaiah's son)	18
2=	Bashanhavothjair (alternative name of Argob)	16
=	Chepharhaammonai (Ammonite settlement)	16
=	Chusharishathaim (king of Mesopotamia)	16
=	Kibrothhattaavah (desert encampment of Israelites)	16
=	Selahammahlekoth (stronghold in Maon)	16
7=	Abelbethmaachah (town near Damascus)	15
=	Almondiblathaim (stopping-place of Israelites)	15
=	Apharsathchites (Assyrian nomadic group)	15
=	Berodachbaladan/Merodachbaladan (king of Babylon)	15
=	Helkathhazzurim (a battlefield)	15
=	Ramathaimzophin (town where Samuel was born)	15
=	Tilgathpilneser (king of Assyria)	15
=	Zaphnathpaaneah (name given to Joseph by Pharaoh)	15

King James Bible (Old Testament)

TOP 10

WORDS MOST MENTIONED IN THE BIBLE

	Word	OT*	NT*	Total
1	The	52,948	10,976	63,924
2	And	40,975	10,721	51,696
3	Of	28,518	6,099	34,617
4	To	10,207	3,355	13,562
5	That	9,152	3,761	12,913
6	In	9,767	2,900	12,667
7	He	7,348	3,072	10,420
8	For	6,690	2,281	8,971
9	I	6,669	2,185	8,854
10	His	7,036	1,437	8,473

* *Occurrences in verses in the King James Bible (Old and New Testaments)*

A century before computers were invented, Thomas Hartwell Horne (1780–1862), a dogged biblical researcher, undertook a manual search of biblical word frequencies and concluded that "and" appeared a total of 35,543 times in the Old Testament and 10,684 times in the New Testament. He was fairly close on the latter – but he clearly missed quite a few in the Old Testament, as a recent computer search of the King James Bible indicates.

THE 10

COMMANDMENTS

1 Thou shalt have no other gods before me.

2 Thou shalt not make unto thee any graven image.

3 Thou shalt not take the name of the Lord thy God in vain.

4 Remember the sabbath day, to keep it holy.

5 Honour thy father and thy mother.

6 Thou shalt not kill.

7 Thou shalt not commit adultery.

8 Thou shalt not steal.

9 Thou shalt not bear false witness against thy neighbour.

10 Thou shalt not covet thy neighbour's house, thou shalt not covet thy neighbour's wife, nor his manservant, nor his maidservant, nor his ox, nor his ass, nor any thing that is thy neighbour's.

Exodus 20.iii (King James Bible)

TOP 10

CROPS MOST MENTIONED IN THE BIBLE

	Crop	OT*	NT*	Total
1	Corn	86	11	97
2	Fig	45	21	66
3	Olive	42	19	61
4	Wheat	40	12	52
5	Grape	46	3	49
6	Barley	43	3	46
7	Pomegranate	33	0	33
8	Raisin	9	7	16
9	Apple	11	0	11
10	Bean	6	0	6

* *Occurrences in verses in the King James Bible (Old and New Testaments), including plurals*

THE PAPACY

THE 10
FIRST POPES

	Pope	Reign
1	St. Peter	c.32–c.64
2	St. Linus	c.66–c.78
3	St. Anacletus (Cletus)	c.79–c.91
4	St. Clement I	c.91–c.101
5	St. Evaristus	c.100–c.109
6	St. Alexander I	c.109–c.116
7	St. Sixtus I	c.116–c.125
8	St. Telesphorus	c.125–c.136
9	St. Hyginus	c.138–c.142
10	St. Pius I	c.142–c.155

The first 10 popes all lived during the first century and a half of the Christian Church. As well as all being revered as Christian martyrs, they have one other striking feature in common, as is indicated by the approximate dating of their reigns: virtually nothing is known about any of them.

ST. PETER'S, ROME
Named after the first Pope, St. Peter's and the Vatican are the focus of the Catholic Church.

LEADING FAITH
With the Pope as its head, the Roman Catholic Church has maintained its position as one of the world's major religions for almost 2,000 years.

THE 10
LATEST POPES

	Pope	Reign
1	John Paul II	16 Oct 1978–
2	John Paul I	26 Aug–28 Sep 1978
3	Paul VI	21 Jun 1963–6 Aug 1978
4	John XXIII	28 Oct 1958–3 Jun 1963
5	Pius XII	2 Mar 1939–9 Oct 1958
6	Pius XI	6 Feb 1922–10 Feb 1939
7	Benedict XV	3 Sep 1914–22 Jan 1922
8	St. Pius X	4 Aug 1903–20 Aug 1914
9	Leo XIII	20 Feb 1878–20 Jul 1903
10	Pius IX	16 Jun 1846–7 Feb 1878

TOP 10
SHORTEST-SERVING POPES

	Pope	Year in office	Duration (days)
1	Urban VII	1590	12
2	Valentine	827	c.14
3	Boniface VI	896	15
4	Celestine IV	1241	16
5	Sisinnius	708	20
6	Sylvester III	1045	21
7	Theodore II	897	c.21
8	Marcellus II	1555	22
9	Damasus II	1048	23
10=	Pius III	1503	26
=	Leo XI	1605	26

Eleven popes have reigned for less than a month. Some authorities give Stephen's two- or three-day reign in March 757 as the shortest, but although he was elected, he died before he was consecrated and is therefore not included in the official list of popes. In fact, his successor was given his title, Stephen II, and reigned for five years – although some call the uncrowned Stephen "Stephen II" and his successors are confusingly known as "Stephen II(III)", and so on. Urban VII thus holds the record for the shortest-serving pope: he was elected on 15 September, caught malaria the following day, and died on 27 September 1590.

TOP 10
MOST COMMON NAMES OF POPES

	Name	Number
1	John	23
2	Gregory	16
3	Benedict	15
4	Clement	14
5=	Innocent	13
=	Leo	13
7	Pius	12
8	Boniface	9
9=	Alexander	8
=	Urban	8

COUNTRIES MOST VISITED BY POPE JOHN PAUL II

	Country	Visits
1 =	Poland	5
=	France	5
=	USA*	5
4 =	Brazil	4
=	Spain	4
6 =	Germany/West Germany	3
=	Kenya	3
=	Mexico	3
=	Ivory Coast	3
10 =	Argentina, Australia, Austria, Belgium, Benin, Cameroon, Canada, Dominican Republic, Guinea Bissau, Papua New Guinea, Peru, Philippines, Portugal, South Korea, Switzerland, Uruguay, Zaïre	2

* Includes 1984 stopover in Fairbanks, Alaska

Soon after taking office as Pope in 1978, John Paul II broke with a long tradition and embarked on an extensive series of travels. Prior to his long trips, only one Pope had ever travelled outside Italy (Paul VI went to Israel in 1964), some never leaving the Vatican. Up to his visit to Cuba in January 1998, John Paul II had visited a total of 117 countries, 28 of them on more than one occasion. Until 1995, the list was headed by Poland, his native country, but his 1995 and 1996 travels to the USA and France made those countries equal first.

SNAP FACTS

- After his death in 896, the body of Pope Formosus was dug up and tried for various crimes.

- John VIII (died 882) was the first Pope to be murdered – he was poisoned and then clubbed to death.

- Stephen VI (897), Leo V (904), John X (929), Stephen VIII (942), and John XIV (984) were among a number of popes who were murdered in prison.

PAPAL TOUR
Pope John Paul II's exhaustive travels have taken him to more than 100 countries in the past 10 years.

NATIONALITIES OF POPES

	Nationality	Number
1	Roman/Italian	208–209*
2	French	15–17#
3	Greek	15–16†
4	Syrian	6
5	German	4–6#
6	Spanish	5
7	African	2–3
8	Galilean	2
9 =	Dutch	1
=	English	1
10 =	Polish	1
=	Portuguese	1

* *Gelasius I was Roman, but of African descent; it is unknown whether Miltiades was African or Roman.*

\# *The Franco-German frontier was variable at the births of two popes, hence their nationalities are uncertain.*

† *Theodore I was of Greek descent, but born in Jerusalem.*

LONGEST-SERVING POPES

	Pope	Period in office	Years
1	Pius IX	16 Jun 1846–7 Feb 1878	31
2	Leo XIII	20 Feb 1878–20 Jul 1903	25
3	Peter	*c.*32–*c.*64	*c.*25
4	Pius VI	15 Feb 1775–29 Aug 1799	24
5	Adrian I	1 Feb 772–25 Dec 795	23
6	Pius VII	14 Mar 1800–20 Aug 1823	23
7	Alexander III	7 Sep 1159–30 Aug 1181	21
8	Sylvester	31 Jan 314–31 Dec 335	21
9	Leo I	29 Sep 440–10 Nov 461	21
10	Urban VIII	6 Aug 1623–29 Jul 1644	20

Popes are usually chosen from the ranks of cardinals, who are customarily men of mature years. As a result, it is unusual for a pope to remain in office for more than 20 years. Although St. Peter is regarded as the first pope, some authorities doubt the historical accuracy of his reign. If he is omitted as unhistorical, Nos. 4–10 all move up one place and Clement XI becomes 10th (23 Sep 1700–19 Mar 1721, a reign of 20 years). Pius IX, the longest-serving pope, was 85 years old at the time of his death. If he is still in office, the present pope, John Paul II, will enter the Top 10 in 1999 and could top it in 2010.

DISASTERS

82 ROAD TRANSPORT DISASTERS **84** RAIL DISASTERS

86 MARINE DISASTERS **88** AIR DISASTERS

90 ACCIDENTS AT WORK & HOME

92 INDUSTRIAL & OTHER DISASTERS

94 NATURAL DISASTERS

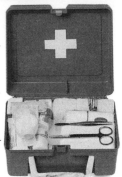

THE 10

MOST ACCIDENT-PRONE CAR COLOURS IN THE UK

	Colour	Accidents per 10,000 cars of each colour
1	Black	179
2	White	160
3	Red	157
4	Blue	149
5	Grey	147
6	Gold	145
7	Silver	142
8	Beige	137
9	Green	134
10=	Brown	133
=	Yellow	133

These statistics were disputed by some car manufacturers, insurance companies, and psychologists who pointed out that the type of vehicle and age and experience of drivers were equally salient factors.

FLAG OF INCONVENIENCE
Until 1896 British drivers had to warn of their presence by having a person precede their car on foot, waving a red flag.

THE 10

WORST YEARS FOR ROAD FATALITIES IN GREAT BRITAIN

	Year	No. killed		Year	No. killed
1	1941	9,169	6	1964	7,820
2	1940	8,609	7	1972	7,763
3	1939	8,272	8	1971	7,699
4	1966	7,985	9	1970	7,499
5	1965	7,952	10	1973	7,406

THE 10

COUNTRIES WITH THE HIGHEST NUMBER OF ROAD DEATHS

	Country	Total deaths *
1	USA	41,907
2	Thailand	15,176
3	Japan	10,649
4	South Korea	10,087
5	Germany	9,814
6	France	8,533
7	Brazil	6,759
8	Poland	6,744
9	Italy	6,578
10	Spain	6,378

* In latest year for which figures are available

ROAD TRANSPORT DISASTERS

WORST MOTOR VEHICLE AND ROAD DISASTERS IN THE WORLD

	Location/date/incident	No. killed
1	Afghanistan, 3 November 1982	2,000+

Following a collision with a Soviet army truck, a petrol tanker exploded in the 2.7-km/1.7-mile long Salang Tunnel. Some authorities estimate that the death toll could have been as high as 3,000.

2	Colombia, 7 August 1956	1,200

Seven army ammunition trucks exploded at night in the centre of the city of Cali, destroying eight city blocks.

3	Thailand, 15 February 1990	150+

A dynamite truck exploded.

4	Nepal, 23 November 1974	148

Hindu pilgrims were killed when a suspension bridge over the River Mahahali collapsed.

5	Egypt, 9 August 1973	127

A bus drove into an irrigation canal.

6	Togo, 6 December 1965	125+

Two lorries collided with a group of dancers during a festival at Sotouboua.

7	Spain, 11 July 1978	120+

A liquid gas tanker exploded in a camping site at San Carlos de la Rapita.

8	South Korea, 28 April 1995	110

An underground explosion destroyed vehicles and caused about 100 cars and buses to plunge into the pit it created.

9	The Gambia, 12 November 1992	c. 100

A bus full of passengers plunged into a river when its brakes failed.

10	Kenya, early December 1992	nearly 100

A bus carrying 112 passengers skidded, hit a bridge, and plunged into a river.

The worst-ever motor racing accident occurred on 13 June 1955, at Le Mans, France, when French driver Pierre Levegh's Mercedes-Benz 300 SLR went out of control, hit a wall, and exploded in mid-air, showering wreckage into the crowd and killing a total of 82 people.

AGE GROUPS MOST VULNERABLE TO ROAD ACCIDENTS IN GREAT BRITAIN

	Age group	Killed or injured (1996)
1	20–24	44,114
2	15–19	41,653
3	25–29	40,333
4	30–34	33,379
5	35–39	24,199
6	10–14	19,603
7	40–44	18,700
8	45–49	17,162
9	5–9	14,320
10	50–54	13,459

The high proportion of accidents among teenagers and people in their early twenties is accounted for partly by inexperience and recklessness in controlling motor cycles and cars. The most vulnerable single age is 18, with 11,135 accidents and fatalities.

COUNTRIES WITH THE MOST DEATHS BY MOTOR ACCIDENTS

	Country	Death rate per 100,000 population
1	South Africa	99.4
2	Latvia	35.3
3	South Korea	33.1
4	Estonia	26.7
5	Russia	23.6
6	Portugal	22.8
7	Lithuania	22.1
8	Greece	21.3
9	Venezuala	20.7
10=	El Salvador	20.3
=	Kuwait	20.3
	UK	*8.1*
	USA	*15.8*

SCENE OF THE ACCIDENT
Car crashes in the US kill more than 40,000 people every year, with people aged under 24 comprising a quarter of all fatalities.

MOST COMMON TYPES OF VEHICLE ACCIDENT IN THE UK*

	Manoeuvre	Accidents
1	Going ahead (various)	184,078
2	Turning right, or waiting to do so	48,257
3	Going ahead on a bend	32,351
4	Held up while waiting to go ahead	32,097
5	Stopping	17,765
6	Parked	15,944
7	Overtaking	15,204
8	Turning left, or waiting to do so	14,025
9	Changing lane	5,670
10	Starting	5,478

* In 1996, by manoeuvre; vehicles other than two-wheel

RAIL DISASTERS

WORST RAIL DISASTERS IN THE UK

Location/date/incident	No. killed
1 Quintinshill near Gretna Green, 22 May 1915	227

A troop train carrying 500 members of the 7th Royal Scots Regiment collided head-on with a passenger train. Barely a minute later, the Scottish express, drawn by two engines and weighing a total of 600 tonnes, ploughed into the wreckage. The gas-lit troop train then caught fire. Since their records were destroyed in the blaze, the actual number of soldiers killed was never established. It was probably 215, as well as two members of the train's crew, eight in the express and two in the local train – a total of 227 killed, and 246 injured, many very seriously. An enquiry established that the accident was caused by the negligence of the signalmen, George Meakin and James Tinsley, who were convicted of manslaughter and jailed.

2 Harrow and Wealdstone Station, 8 October 1952	122

In patchy fog Robert Jones, the relief driver of the Perth to Euston sleeping-car express, pulled by the City of Glasgow, failed to see a series of signal lights warning him of danger, and at 8.19 am collided with the waiting Watford to Euston train. Seconds later, the Euston to Liverpool and Manchester express hit the wreckage of the two trains. The casualties were 112 killed instantly, 10 who died later, and 349 injured.

3 Lewisham, South London, 4 December 1957	90

A steam and an electric train collided in fog. The disaster was made worse by the collapse of a bridge on to the wreckage.

4 Tay Bridge, Scotland, 28 December 1879	80

As the North British mail train passed over it during a storm, the bridge collapsed, killing all 75 passengers and the crew of five. The bridge – the longest in the world at that time – had only been opened on 31 May the previous year, and Queen Victoria had crossed it in a train soon afterwards. The locomotive was salvaged from the bed of the Tay several months later. It had surprisingly little damage, and was repaired. It continued in service until 1919.

Location/date/incident	No. killed
5 Armagh, Northern Ireland, 12 June 1889	78

A Sunday school excursion train with 940 passengers stalled on a hill. When 10 carriages were uncoupled, they ran backwards and collided with a passenger train, killing 78 (claims of 300 deaths have not been substantiated) and leaving 250 injured.

6 Hither Green, South London, 5 November 1967	49

The Hastings to Charing Cross train was derailed by a broken track. As well as those killed, 78 were injured, 27 of them seriously.

7= Bourne End, Hertfordshire, 30 September 1945	43

Travelling at about 50 mph, the Perth to Euston express sped through a crossover with a 20 mph speed restriction imposed during engineering works, and was derailed. Its coaches plunged down an embankment.

7= Moorgate Station, London, 28 February 1975	43

A tube train ran into the wall at the end of the tunnel, killing 43 and injuring 74 in London Transport's worst rail disaster.

9 Castlecary, Scotland, 10 December 1937	35

The Edinburgh to Glasgow train ran into a stationary train and rode over the top of it.

10= Shipton near Oxford, 24 December 1874	34

The Paddington to Birkenhead train plunged over the embankment after a carriage wheel broke, killing 34 and badly injuring 65.

10= Clapham Junction, London, 12 December 1988	34

The 7.18 Basingstoke to Waterloo train, carrying 906 passengers, stopped at signals outside Clapham Junction; the 6.30 train from Bournemouth ran into its rear, and an empty train from Waterloo hit the wreckage, leaving 33 dead (and one who died later) and 111 injured.

WORST UNDERGROUND RAIL DISASTERS IN THE WORLD*

Location/date	No. killed
1 Baku, Azerbaijan, 28 October 1995	over 300
2 Bethnal Green, London, 3 March 1943	173
3 Bank, London, 7 January 1941	111
4 Brooklyn, New York, 1 November 1918,	97
5 Paris, 10 August 1903	84
6 Balham, London, 15 October 1940	68
7 Moorgate, London, 28 February 1975	43
8 Mexico City, 20 October 1975	34
9 King's Cross, London, 18 November 1987	31
10 Berlin, 26 September 1908	21

* Including disasters caused by bombs, fires, and panics in underground stations

---

● The first railway worker fatally injured was John Gillespie, as a result of a boiler explosion on the Stockton and Darlington Railway, on 19 March 1828.

● The first member of the public killed on a public railway was Member of Parliament William Huskisson, run over at the opening ceremony of the Liverpool and Manchester Railway on 15 September 1830.

● The first railroad worker killed in the USA was an unnamed slave working as a fireman on the South Carolina Road (railroad), on 17 June 1831.

SNAP FACTS

THE 10

WORST RAIL DISASTERS IN EUROPE

Location/date/incident	No. killed
1 Chelyabinsk, Russia, 3 June 1989	up to 800

Two passenger trains travelling on the Trans-Siberian railway were destroyed by exploding liquid gas from a nearby pipeline.

2 Modane, France, 12 December 1917	573

A troop-carrying train ran out of control and was derailed. It has been claimed that the train was overloaded and that as many as 1,000 may have died.

3 Balvano, Italy, 2 March 1944	521

A heavily-laden train stalled in the Armi Tunnel, asphyxiating many passengers. The true casualty figure was never published.

4 Torre, Spain, 3 January 1944	over 500

A double collision and fire in a tunnel resulted in many deaths – some have put the total as high as 800. Wartime secrecy prevented full details from being published.

5 Cireau, Romania, 7 January 1917	374

An overcrowded passenger train crashed into a military train and was derailed. As well as the high death toll, 756 were injured.

6 Pomponne near Lagny, France, 23 December 1933	230

France's second-worst rail disaster resulted from a collision in fog between an express and two stationary trains, all laden with passengers travelling in the Christmas season.

7 Quintinshill, Scotland, 22 May 1915	227

Britain's worst rail disaster (see The 10 Worst Rail Disasters in the UK).

8 Nowy Dwor, Poland, 22 October 1949	200

A derailment caused the death of at least 200.

9 Genthin, Germany, 22 December 1939	196

A train was hit in the rear by another in Germany's worst-ever rail accident.

10 Zagreb, Yugoslavia, 3 August 1974	153

A train was derailed on a curve when the driver fell asleep.

THE 10

WORST RAIL DISASTERS IN THE WORLD

Location/date/incident	No. killed
1 Bagmati River, India, 6 June 1981	c. 800

The carriages of a train travelling from Samastipur to Banmukhi in Bihar plunged off a bridge over the river Bagmati near Mansi – when the driver braked, apparently to avoid hitting a sacred cow. Although the official death toll was said to have been 268, many authorities have claimed that the train was so massively overcrowded that the actual figure was in excess of 800, making it probably the worst rail disaster of all time.

2 Chelyabinsk, Russia, 3 June 1989	up to 800

Two Trans-Siberian passenger trains, going to and from the Black Sea, were destroyed when liquid gas from a nearby pipeline exploded.

3 Guadalajara, Mexico, 18 January 1915	over 600

A train derailed on a steep incline, but political strife in the country meant that full details of the disaster were suppressed.

4 Modane, France, 12 December 1917	573

A troop-carrying train ran out of control and was derailed. It was probably overloaded, and as many as 1,000 people may have died.

5 Balvano, Italy, 2 March 1944	521

A heavily-laden train stalled in the Armi Tunnel, and many passengers asphyxiated.

Location/date/incident	No. killed
6 Torre, Spain, 3 January 1944	over 500

A double collision and fire in a tunnel resulted in many deaths. Like the disaster at Balvano two months later, wartime secrecy prevented full details from being published.

7 Awash, Ethiopia, 13 January 1985	428

A derailment hurled a train into a ravine.

8 Cireau, Romania, 7 January 1917	374

An overcrowded passenger train crashed into a military train and was derailed.

9 Quipungo, Angola, 31 May 1993	355

A train was derailed by UNITA guerrilla action.

10 Sangi, Pakistan, 4 January 1990	306

A diverted train resulted in a fatal collision.

Casualty figures for rail accidents are often extremely imprecise, especially during wartime – and half of the 10 worst disasters occurred during the two World Wars.

OVERCROWDING ON INDIA'S TRAINS
The extremely high death-toll in the world's worst rail accident owed much to this fact of Indian life.

MARINE DISASTERS

WORST MARINE DISASTERS OF THE 20TH CENTURY

	Vessel	Date	Approx. no. killed
1	*Wilhelm Gustloff*	30 January 1945	up to 7,800

The German liner, laden with refugees, was torpedoed off Danzig by a Soviet submarine, S-13, 30 January 1945. The precise death toll remains uncertain, but is in the range 5,348 to 7,800.

2	*Goya*	16 April 1945	6,800

A German ship carrying evacuees from Danzig was torpedoed in the Baltic near Cape Rixhöft.

3	Unknown vessel	November 1947	over 6,000

An unidentified Chinese troopship carrying Nationalist soldiers from Manchuria sank off Yingkow. The exact date is unknown.

4	*Cap Arcona*	3 May 1945	5,000

A German ship carrying concentration camp survivors was bombed and sunk by British aircraft in Lübeck harbour.

5	*Lancastria*	17 June 1940	3,050

A British troop ship sank off St. Nazaire.

6	*Steuben*	9 February 1945	3,000

German war-wounded and and refugees were lost when it was torpedoed off Stolpmünde by the same Russian submarine that had sunk the Wilhelm Gustloff.

7	*Dona Paz*	20 December 1987	up to 3,000

The ferry Dona Paz *was struck by oil tanker* MV Victor *in the Tabias Strait, Philippines.*

8	*Kiangya*	3 December 1948	over 2,750

An overloaded steamship carrying refugees struck a Japanese mine off Woosung, China.

9	*Thielbeck*	3 May 1945	2,750

A refugee ship sank during the British bombardment of Lübeck harbour in the closing weeks of World War II.

10	*Laconia*	12 September 1942	2,279

A British passenger vessel carrying Italian prisoners-of-war was sunk by German U-boat U-156.

Recent reassessments of the death tolls in some of the World War II marine disasters mean that the most famous of all, the *Titanic*, the British liner that struck an iceberg in the North Atlantic and sank, 15 April 1912 with the loss of 1,517 lives, no longer ranks in the Top 10. However, the *Titanic* tragedy remains one of the worst-ever peacetime disasters, along with such notable incidents as that involving the *General Slocum*, an excursion liner that caught fire in the port of New York on 15 June 1904 with the loss of 1,021 lives. Among other disasters that occurred during wartime and resulted in losses of more than 1,000 were the explosion of *Mont Blanc*, a French ammunition ship, following its collision with Belgian steamer *Imo* off Halifax, Nova Scotia, on 6 December 1917, with 1,635 lives lost.

WORST SUBMARINE DISASTERS OF ALL TIME

(Excluding those as a result of military action)

	Submarine	Date	No. killed
1	*Le Surcouf*	18 February 1942	159

The French submarine was accidentally rammed by a US merchant ship.

2	*Thresher*	10 April 1963	129

The three-year-old US nuclear submarine, worth $45,000,000, sank in the North Atlantic, 350 km/220 miles east of Boston, USA.

3	*I-12*	January 1945	114

The Japanese submarine sank in the Pacific in unknown circumstances.

4	*I-174*	3 April 1944	107

A Japanese submarine sank in the Pacific in unknown circumstances.

5	*I-26*	October 1944	105

This Japanese submarine sank east of Leyte, cause and date unknown.

6	*I-169*	4 April 1944	103

A Japanese submarine flooded and sank while in harbour at Truk.

7	*I-22*	October 1942	100

A Japanese submarine sank off the Solomon Islands, exact date unknown.

8 =	*Seawolf*	3 October 1944	99

A US submarine was sunk in error by USS Rowell off Morotai.

=	*Thetis*	13 March 1943	99

The British submarine sank on 1 June 1939 during trials in Liverpool Bay, with civilians on board. Her captain and three crew members escaped. Thetis *was later salvaged and renamed* Thunderbolt. *She was sunk by an Italian ship with the loss of 63 lives.*

=	*Scorpion*	21 May 1968	99

This US nuclear submarine was lost in the North Atlantic, south-west of the Azores. The wreck was located on 31 October of that year.

The loss of the *Thresher* is the worst accident ever involving a nuclear submarine. It sank while undertaking tests off the US coast and was located by the bathyscaphe *Trieste*. The remains of the submarine were scattered over the ocean floor at a depth of 2,560 m/8,400 ft. The cause of the disaster remains a military secret.

SNAP FACT

A rare example of a liner destroying a warship occurred on 2 October 1942, when the *Queen Mary*, carrying 10,000 US troops, sliced the British cruiser *Curaçao* in half, killing 338.

CLEANING UP
Around two million tonnes of oil are spilled into the seas every year, damaging the environment. Seabirds suffer because they are unable to clean oil from their feathers.

THE 10

WORST PRE-20TH-CENTURY MARINE DISASTERS

	Location/date/vessel	Approx. no. killed
1	Off British coast, August to October 1588, Spanish Armada	4,000
2 =	Off Egg Island, Labrador, 22 August 1711, British fleet	over 2,000
=	4 December 1811, *St. George*, *Defence*, and *Hero*	over 2,000
4	Near Memphis, USA, 27 April 1865, *Sultana*	1,547
5	Off Florida Coast, 31 July 1715, *Capitanas*	over 1,000
6	Off Spithead, 29 August 1782, *Royal George*	over 900
7	River Thames near Woolwich, 3 September 1878, *Princess Alice*	786
8	Livorno harbour, 17 March 1800, *Queen Charlotte*	over 700
9	Off the Japanese coast, 19 September 1890, *Ertogrul*	587
10	Off Gibraltar, 17 March 1891, *Utopia*	576

THE 10

WORST OIL TANKER SPILLS OF ALL TIME

	Tanker	Location	Date	Approx. spillage (tonnes)
1	*Atlantic Empress* and *Aegean Captain*	Trinidad	19 July 1979	300,000
2	*Castillio de Bellver*	Cape Town, South Africa	6 August 1983	255,000
3	*Olympic Bravery*	Ushant, France	24 January 1976	250,000
4	*Showa-Maru*	Malacca, Malaya	7 June 1975	237,000
5	*Amoco Cadiz*	Finistère, France	16 March 1978	223,000
6	*Odyssey*	Atlantic, off Canada	10 November 1988	140,000
7	*Torrey Canyon*	Scilly Isles, UK	18 March 1967	120,000
8	*Sea Star*	Gulf of Oman	19 December 1972	115,000
9	*Irenes Serenada*	Pilos, Greece	23 February 1980	102,000
10	*Urquiola*	Corunna, Spain	12 May 1976	101,000

The grounding of the *Exxon Valdez* in Prince William Sound, Alaska, USA, on 24 March 1989 ranks outside the 10 worst spills, at about 35,000 tonnes of oil spilled, but resulted in major ecological damage. All the accidents in this Top 10 were caused by collision, grounding, fire, or explosion, but worse oil tanker spills have been caused by military action. Between January and June 1942, for example, German U-boats torpedoed a number of tankers off the east coast of the US with a loss of some 600,000 tonnes of oil, and in June 1991, during the Gulf War, various tankers were sunk in the Persian Gulf, spilling a total of more than 1,000,000 tonnes of oil.

FIRE DESTROYS SHIP ON GREAT LAKES

Canada suffered its greatest ship loss since the *Titanic* 50 years ago when a giant liner, the *Noronic*, burst into flames in the early hours of the morning of 17 September 1949 while docked at the Ontario Pier in Toronto. The cause of the fire has never been established. Most of the passengers and crew aboard the giant liner ran terrified to the starboard side of the ship, causing it to crash into the pier. The fire gutted the ship in 15 minutes, allowing no time to lower the lifeboats, which burned with the ship. Of the 511 on board that night, 207 died. Only four years earlier, the *Noronic*'s sister ship, the *Hamonic*, was also destroyed by fire. However, in that case only one person was killed in the blaze.

50 YEARS AGO

AIR DISASTERS

THE 10 WORST AIR DISASTERS IN EUROPE
(No. killed)

❶ Tenerife, Canary Islands, 27 March 1977 (583) ❷ Paris, France, 3 March 1974 (346) ❸ Off the Irish coast, 23 June 1985 (329) ❹ Lockerbie, Scotland, 21 December 1988 (270) ❺= Barajas Airport, Madrid, Spain, 27 November 1983 (183), Warsaw, Poland, 9 May 1987 (183) ❼= Zagreb, Yugoslavia, 10 September 1976 (176),= Moscow, USSR, 13 October 1972 (176) ❾ Corsica, 1 December 1981 (174) ❿ Over Ukraine, 17 August 1979 (173)

THE 10
WORST AIR COLLISIONS IN THE WORLD

	Location/date/incident	No. killed
1	Charkhi Dadrio, India, 12 November 1996	349

(See The 10 Worst Air Disasters in the World, No. 3.)

| **2** | Near Gaj, Yugoslavia, 10 September 1976 | 177 |

A British Airways Trident and a Yugoslav DC-9 collided.

| **3** | Near Dneprodzerzhinsk, Ukraine, USSR, 11 August 1979 | 173 |

Two Soviet Tupolev-134 Aeroflot airliners collided in mid air.

| **4** | Morioko, Japan, 30 July 1971 | 162 |

An air collision occurred between an All Nippon Boeing 727 and Japanese Air Force F-86F.

| **5** | Near Souq as-Sabt, Libya, 22 December 1992 | 157 |

A Libyan Boeing 747 and a Libyan air force MiG-23 fighter collided.

| **6** | San Diego, California, USA, 25 September 1978 | 144 |

A Pacific Southwest Boeing 727 collided in the air with a Cessna 172 light aircraft with a student pilot, killing 135 in the airliner.

| **7** | New York City, USA, 16 December 1960 | 134 |

A United Airlines DC-8, and a TWA Super Constellation collided.

| **8** | Tehran, Iran, 8 February 1993 | 132 |

As it took off, a passenger aircraft was struck by a military aircraft.

| **9** | Grand Canyon, Arizona, USA, 30 June 1956 | 128 |

A United Airlines DC-7 and a TWA Super Constellation collided.

| **10** | Ankara, Turkey, 1 February 1963 | 104 |

A Middle East Airlines Viscount 754 and a Turkish Air Force C-47 collided.

THE 10
WORST AVIATION DISASTERS WITH GROUND FATALITIES

	Location/date/incident	Ground fatalities
1	Kinshasa, Zaïre, 8 January 1996	300

(See The 10 Worst Air Disasters in the World, No. 7.)

| **2** | Santa Cruz, Bolivia, 13 October 1976 | 110 |

A Lloyd A. Boliviana B-707 crashed on take-off.

| **3** | Dar Nang, South Vietnam, 24 December 1966 | 107 |

A Canadair CL-44 crash-landed onto a village.

| **4** | Ankara, Turkey, 1 February 1963 | 87 |

A Vickers Viscount 754 and a Turkish Air Force Douglas C-47 collided and fell into the city.

| **5** | Maracaibo, Venezuela, 16 March 1969 | 71 |

A DC-9 crashed onto the city after hitting power lines.

| **6** | Ramstein US base, Germany, 28 August 1988 | 67 |

Three fighters in an Italian aerobatic team crashed into a crowd.

| **7** | Irkutsk, Russia, 6 December 1997 | 63 |

An Antonov An-124 cargo aircraft suffered engine failure.

| **8** | Campo de Marte, Bogota, Colombia, 24 July 1938 | 53 |

A low-flying stunt plane crashed into a stand, broke up, and hurled blazing wreckage into the crowd.

| **9** | Freckelton, Lancashire, UK, 23 August 1944 | 51 |

A B-24 bomber crashed onto a school.

| **10** | Mexico City, Mexico, 1 August 1987 | 44 |

An overloaded Belize Air B-377 crashed on takeoff.

THE 10
WORST AIRSHIP DISASTERS IN THE WORLD

	Location/date/incident	No. killed
1	Off the Atlantic coast, USA, 4 April 1933	73

US Navy airship Akron *crashed into the sea in a storm.*

2	Over the Mediterranean, 21 December 1923	52

French airship Dixmude *is assumed to have been struck by lightning.*

3	Near Beauvais, France, 5 October 1930	50

British airship R101 *crashed into a hillside.*

4	Off the coast near Hull, UK, 24 August 1921	44

Airship R38, *broke in two on a training and test flight.*

5	Lakehurst, New Jersey, USA, 6 May 1937	36

German Zeppelin Hindenburg *caught fire when mooring.*

6	Hampton Roads, Virginia, USA, 21 February 1922	34

Roma *crashed, killing all but 11 people on board.*

7	Berlin, Germany, 17 October 1913	28

German airship LZ18 crashed after engine failure during a test flight.

8	Baltic Sea, 30 March 1917	23

German airship SL9 was struck by lightning on a flight.

9	Mouth of the River Elbe, Germany, 3 September 1915	19

German airship L10 was struck by lightning and plunged into the sea.

10 =	Off Heligoland, 9 September 1913	14

German Navy airship L1 crashed into the sea.

10 =	Caldwell, Ohio, USA, 3 September 1925	14

US dirigible Shenandoah *broke up in a storm, scattering sections over many miles of the Ohio countryside.*

THE 10
WORST AIR DISASTERS IN THE WORLD

	Location/date/incident	No. killed
1	Tenerife, Canary Islands, 27 March 1977	583

Two Boeing 747s (Pan Am and KLM, carrying 364 passengers with 16 crew, and 230 passengers with 11 crew, respectively) collided and caught fire on the runway of Los Rodeos airport after the pilots received incorrect control tower instructions.

2	Mt. Ogura, Japan, 12 August 1985	520

A JAL Boeing 747 on an internal flight from Tokyo to Osaka crashed, killing all but four on board in the worst-ever disaster involving a single aircraft.

3	Charkhi Dadrio, India, 12 November 1996	349

Soon after taking off from New Delhi's Indira Gandhi International Airport, a Saudi Airways Boeing 747 collided with a Kazakh Airlines Ilyushin IL-76 cargo aircraft on its descent and exploded, killing all 312 on the Boeing and 37 on the Ilyushin in the world's worst mid-air crash.

4	France, 3 March 1974, Paris	346

A Turkish Airlines DC-10 crashed at Ermenonville, north of Paris, immediately after take-off for London, with many English rugby supporters among the dead.

5	Off the Irish coast, 23 June 1985	329

An Air India Boeing 747, on a flight from Vancouver to Delhi, exploded in mid-air, perhaps as a result of a terrorist bomb.

6	Riyadh, Saudi Arabia, 19 August 1980	301

A Saudia (Saudi Arabian) Airlines Lockheed TriStar caught fire during an emergency landing.

7	Kinshasa, Zaïre, 8 January 1996	300

A Zaïrean Antonov-32 cargo plane crashed shortly after take-off, killing shoppers in a city-centre market in Kinshasa. The final death toll has not yet been officially announced.

8	Off the Iranian coast, 3 July 1988	290

An Iran Air A300 Airbus was shot down in error by a missile fired by the USS Vincennes.

9	Chicago, USA, 25 May 1979	273

The worst air disaster in the US occurred when an engine fell off a DC-10 as it took off from Chicago's O'Hare airport. The aircraft plunged out of control, killing all 271 on board and two on the ground.

10	Lockerbie, Scotland, UK, 21 December 1988	270

Pan Am Flight 103 from London Heathrow to New York exploded in mid-air as a result of a terrorist bomb, killing 243 passengers, 16 crew, and 11 on the ground.

DEADLY HIJACK
On 23 November 1996, an Ethiopian Airlines Boeing 767 was hijacked and ditched in the sea off the Comoros Islands, killing 158 of the 175 on board.

ACCIDENTS AT WORK & HOME

THE 10

MOST COMMON SOURCES OF DOMESTIC FIRES IN THE UK

	Source of ignition	No. of fires		Source of ignition	No. of fires
1	Electric cooker	18,855	6	Candle	1,375
2	Gas cooker	7,839	7	Electric space heater	1,040
3	Smokers' materials	4,881	8	Matches	1,024
4	Washing machine	2,262	9	Gas space heater	861
5	Wire and cable	1,678	10	Blanket, bed warmer	817
				UK total	53,267

THE 10

MOST COMMON CAUSES OF INJURY AT WORK IN THE UK

	Cause	Fatalities	Injuries*
1	Injured while handling, lifting, or carrying		47,889
2	Slip, trip, or fall on same level	3	32,343
3	Struck by moving (including flying or falling) object	43	22,335
4	Fall from height	56	13,220
5	Struck against something fixed or stationary	3	8,713
6	Contact with moving machinery	15	7,266
7	Exposure to or contact with a harmful substance	4	4,641
8	Acts of violence	2	4,374
9	Struck by moving vehicle	32	3,647
10	Injured by an animal	1	901
	Total (including causes not in Top 10)	210	151,741

* Resulting in work absence of more than three days, employees only (excluding self-employed), 1996/97 provisional figures

THE 10

MOST ACCIDENT-PRONE COUNTRIES

	Country	Accidental death rate (per 100,000 population)
1	Estonia	153.5
2	Lithuania	120.7
3	South Africa	99.4
4	Hungary	74.3
5	Moldova	72.1
6	Latvia	71.7
7	Czech Republic	60.7
8	South Korea	59.9
9	Romania	57.1
10	Slovenia	55.2
	UK	21.5
	USA	35.0
	Canada	29.6

THE 10

MOST COMMON CAUSES OF DOMESTIC FIRES IN THE UK

	Cause	Approximate no. of fires*		Cause	Approximate no. of fires*
1	Malicious (or suspected malicious)	15,500	6	Placing articles too close to heat	4,500
2	Misuse of equipment or appliances	15,400	7	Other accidental	4,200
3	Chip/fat pan fires	11,300	8	Faulty fuel supplies	2,000
4	Faulty appliances and leads	8,400	9	Playing with fire	1,000
5	Careless handling of fire or hot substances	5,600	10	Unspecified	800
				UK total	68,800

* National estimates based on actual Home Accident Surveillance System figures for sample population

TOP 10

ARTICLES MOST FREQUENTLY INVOLVED IN ACCIDENTS IN THE HOME IN THE UK

	Article	Accidents per annum
1	Construction feature	775,000
2	Furniture	329,000
3	Person	230,000
4	Outdoor surface	194,000
5	Clothing/footwear	191,000
6	Building/raw materials	159,000
7	Furnishings	145,000
8	Cooking/kitchen equipment	134,000
9	Animal/insect	113,000
10	Food/drink	109,000
	Total	*2,502,000*

* *National estimates based on actual Home Accident Surveillance System figures for sample population*

THE 10

MOST COMMON CAUSES OF FATAL ACCIDENTS AT WORK IN THE UK

	Cause	Fatalities
1	Falls from a height	56
2	Struck by a moving object (including flying/falling)	43
3	Struck by a moving vehicle	32
4 =	Contact with electricity	15
=	Contact with moving machinery	15
6	Trapped by something collapsing/overturning	10
7	Drowning or asphyxiation	7
8	Exposure to an explosion	6
9	Exposure or contact with a harmful substance	4
10 =	Slip, trip, or fall on same level	3
=	Struck against something fixed or stationary	3
	Total (all causes)	*210*

THE 10

MOST DANGEROUS JOBS IN THE UK

1	Formula One Driver
2	Bomb disposal officer
3	Test pilot
4	SAS employee
5	Circus acts
6	Film stuntman
7	Commercial diver
8	Oil rig worker
9	Scaffolder
10 =	Fisherman
=	Miner
=	Dockworker
=	Merchant Navy
=	Linesman (electrical industry)

Life assurance companies carefully base their premiums on actuarial statistics that take into account the likelihood of people in each job being involved in an accident that injures or kills them at work, or as a result of their contact with dangerous substances.

THE 10

MOST COMMON TYPES OF ACCIDENT IN UK HOMES

	Type	Accidents (1995)
1	Unspecified falls	413,000
2	Struck by static object	293,000
3	Fall on same level	284,000
4	Cut/tear by sharp object	280,000
5	Fall on/from stairs	230,000
6	Struck against moving object	140,000
7	Foreign body	121,000
8	Struck (unspecified)	100,000
9	Thermal effect	89,000
10	Pinch/crush by blunt object	80,000

Falls are the leading cause of accidents in the home. Total accidents resulting from falls were estimated to be 960,000 in 1995, including tripping over (284,000), falling on or from stairs (230,000), falling on or from a ladder (24,000), falling from buildings (9,000) and all other types of falls (413,000). Official statistics also list 196,000 accidents of unknown or other causes. Figures cover only non-fatal accidents within homes and gardens.

THE 10

MOST COMMON CAUSES OF FATAL ACCIDENT IN THE HOME IN THE UK

	Cause	Fatalities
1	Unspecified falls	1,261
2	Poisoning/inhalation	512
3	Fall from stairs	490
4	Uncontrolled fire	430
5	Foreign body	243
6	Fall between two levels	139
7	Fall on same level	75
8	Suffocating/choking	71
9	Drowning	61
10	Fall from building	54
	Total (including causes not in Top 10)	*3,569*

INDUSTRIAL & OTHER DISASTERS

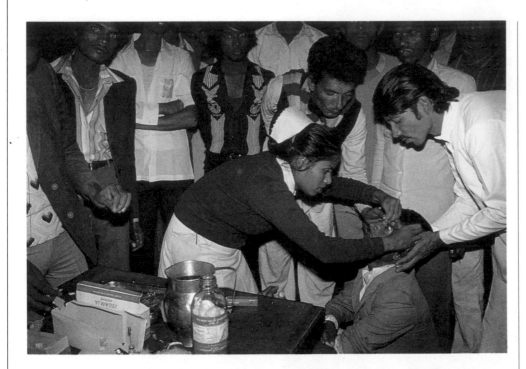

BHOPAL DISASTER
*The leak of toxic gas at a chemical plant
in a heavily populated area of Bhopal,
India resulted in nearly 3,000 deaths,
with up to 200,000 people injured.*

THE 10
WORST MINING DISASTERS

	Location	Date	No. killed
1	Hinkeiko, China	26 Apr 1942	1,549
2	Courrières, France	10 Mar 1906	1,060
3	Omuta, Japan	9 Nov 1963	447
4	Senghenydd, UK	14 Oct 1913	439
5	Coalbrook, South Africa	21 Jan 1960	437
6	Wankie, Rhodesia	6 Jun 1972	427
7	Dharbad, India	28 May 1965	375
8	Chasnala, India	27 Dec 1975	372
9	Monongah, USA	6 Dec 1907	362
10	Barnsley UK	12 Dec 1866	361*

** Including 27 killed the following day while
searching for survivors*

A mine disaster at the Fushun mines,
Manchuria, in February 1931 may have
resulted in up to 3,000 deaths, but
information was suppressed by the Chinese
government. Soviet security was
responsible for obscuring details of an
explosion at the Johanngeorgendstadt
uranium mine in East Germany on 29
November 1949, when as many as 3,700
may have died. Among the most tragic
disasters of this century, that at Aberfan,
Wales, on 20 October 1966, was a mine
disaster that affected the mining
community rather than the miners. Waste
from the local mine had built up for many
years to become a heap some 244 m/800 ft
high. Weakened by the presence of a
spring, a huge volume of slurry suddenly
flowed down and engulfed the local school,
killing 144, of whom 116 were children.

THE 10
WORST DISASTERS AT SPORTS VENUES IN THE 20TH CENTURY

	Location/incident	Date	No. killed
1	Hong Kong Jockey Club (stand collapse and fire)	26 February 1918	604
2	Lenin Stadium, Moscow, USSR (crush in football stadium)	20 October 1982	340
3	Lima, Peru (football stadium riot)	24 May 1964	320
4	Sinceljo, Colombia (bullring stand collapse)	20 January 1980	222
5	Hillsborough, Sheffield, UK (crush in football stadium)	15 April 1989	96
6	Guatemala City, Guatemala (stampede in Mateo Flores National Stadium during World Cup soccer qualifying match, Guatemala *vs.* Costa Rica, with 127 injured)	16 October 1996	83
7	Le Mans, France (racing car crash)	11 June 1955	82
8	Katmandu, Nepal (stampede in football stadium)	12 March 1988	80
9	Buenos Aires, Argentina (riot in football stadium)	23 May 1968	74
10	Ibrox Park, Glasgow, Scotland (barrier collapse in football stadium)	2 January 1971	66

Before the Ibrox Park disaster, the worst accident at a British stadium was caused by the
collapse of a stand at Burnden Park, Bolton, on 9 March 1946, which left 33 dead and 400
injured. If stunt-flying is included as a "sport", the worst airshow disaster of all time
occurred at the Ramstein US base, Germany, on 28 August 1988, when three fighters in an
Italian aerobatic team collided, one of them crashing into the crowd, leaving 70 dead and
150 injured. Such tragedies are not an exclusively modern phenomenon: during the reign of
Roman Emperor Antoninus Pius (AD 138–161), a stand at the Circus Maximus collapsed
during a gladiatorial spectacle and 1,162 spectators were killed.

THE 10

WORST EXPLOSIONS*

	Location/incident	Date	No. killed #
1	Lanchow, China (arsenal)	26 Oct 1935	2,000
2	Halifax, Nova Scotia (ammunition ship *Mont Blanc*)	6 Dec 1917	1,635
3	Memphis, Tennessee (*Sultana* boiler explosion)	27 Apr 1865	1,547
4	Bombay, India (ammunition ship *Fort Stikine*)	14 Apr 1944	1,376
5	Cali, Colombia (ammunition trucks)	7 Aug 1956	1,200
6	Salang Tunnel, Afghanistan (petrol tanker collision)	2 Nov 1982	over 1,100
7	Chelyabinsk, USSR (liquid gas beside railway)	3 Jun 1989	up to 800
8	Texas City, Texas (ammonium nitrate on *Grandcamp* freighter)	16 Apr 1947	752
9	Oppau, Germany (chemical plant)	21 Sep 1921	561
10	Mexico City, Mexico (PEMEX gas plant)	20 Nov 1984	540

* *Excluding mining disasters, and terrorist and military bombs*

All these "best estimate" figures should be treated with caution, since – as with fires and shipwrecks – body counts are notoriously unreliable

THE 10

WORST FIRES OF THE 20TH CENTURY*

	Location/incident	Date	No. killed
1	Kwanto, Japan (following earthquake)	1 Sep 1923	60,000
2	Chungking, China (docks)	2 Sep 1949	1,700
3	Cloquet, Minnesota, USA (forest)	12 Oct 1918	800
4	Mandi Dabwali, India (school tent)	23 Dec 1995	over 500
5	Hoboken, New Jersey, USA (docks)	30 Jun 1900	326
6	Brussels, Belgium (department store)	22 May 1967	322
7	Ohio State Penitentiary, Columbus, Ohio, USA	21 Apr 1930	322
8	London High School, London, Texas, USA	18 Mar 1937	294
9	Guatemala City, Guatemala (mental hospital)	14 Jul 1960	225
10	Sao Paulo, Brazil (city fire)	1 Feb 1974	220

* *Excluding sports and entertainment venues, mining disasters and the results of military action*

THE 10

WORST COMMERCIAL AND INDUSTRIAL DISASTERS*

	Location/incident	Date	No. killed
1	Bhopal, India (methyl isocyante gas escape at Union Carbide plant)	3 Dec 1984	up to 3,000
2	Seoul, Korea (collapse of Sampoong Department Store)	29 Jun 1995	640
3	Oppau, Germany (chemical plant explosion)	21 Sep 1921	561
4	Mexico City, Mexico (explosion at a PEMEX liquified petroleum gas plant)	20 Nov 1984	540
5	Brussels, Belgium (fire in L'Innovation department store)	22 May 1967	322
6	Novosibirsk, USSR (anthrax infection following accident at biological and chemical warfare plant)	Apr 1979	up to 300
7	Guadalajara, Mexico (explosions caused by gas leak into sewers)	22 Apr 1992	230
8	São Paulo, Brazil (fire in Joelma bank and office building)	1 Feb 1974	227
9	Oakdale, Pennsylvania USA, (chemical plant explosion)	18 May 1918	193
10	Bangkok, Thailand (fire engulfed a four-storey doll factory)	10 May 1993	187

* *Including industrial sites, factories, offices and stores; excluding military, mining, marine and other transport disasters*

THE 10

WORST DISASTERS AT THEATRE AND ENTERTAINMENT VENUES*

	Location	Date	No. killed
1	Canton, China (theatre)	25 May 1845	1,670
2	Shanghai, China (theatre)	Jun 1871	900
3	Lehmann Circus, Russia,	14 Feb 1836	800
4	Antoung, China (cinema)	13 Feb 1937	658
5	Ring Theatre, Vienna	8 Dec 1881	620
6	Iroquois Theatre, Chicago	30 Dec 1903	591
7	Cocoanut Grove Night Club, Boston	28 Nov 1942	491
8	Abadan, Iran (theatre)	20 Aug 1978	422
9	Niteroi, Brazil (circus)	17 Dec 1961	323
10	Brooklyn Theatre, New York	5 Dec 1876	295

* *19th and 20th centuries, excluding sports stadiums and race tracks*

NATURAL DISASTERS

T H E   1 0

WORST FLOODS AND STORMS
OF THE 20TH CENTURY

	Location	Date	Estimated no. killed
1	Huang He River, China	Aug 1931	3,700,000
2	Bangladesh	13 Nov 1970	300–500,000
3	Henan, China	1939	over 200,000
4	Chang Jiang River, China	1911	100,000
5	Bengal, India	15–16 Nov 1942	40,000
6	Bangladesh	1–2 Jun 1965	30,000
7	Bangladesh	28–29 May 1963	22,000
8	Bangladesh	11–12 May 1965	17,000
9	Morvi, India	11 Aug 1979	5,000-15,000
10 =	Hong Kong	18 Sep 1906	10,000
=	Bangladesh	25 May 1985	10,000

T H E   1 0

WORST EARTHQUAKES OF THE 20TH CENTURY

	Location	Date	Estimated no. killed
1	Tang-shan, China	28 Jul 1976	242,419
2	Nan-shan, China	22 May 1927	200,000
3	Kansu, China	16 Dec 1920	180,000
4	Messina, Italy	28 Dec 1908	160,000
5	Tokyo/Yokohama, Japan	1 Sep 1923	142,807
6	Kansu, China	25 Dec 1932	70,000
7	Yungay, Peru,	31 May 1970	66,800
8	Quetta, India*	30 May 1935	50–60,000
9	Armenia	7 Dec 1988	over 55,000
10	Iran	21 Jun 1990	over 40,000

* *Now Pakistan*

There are some discrepancies between the "official" death tolls in many of the world's worst earthquakes and the estimates of other authorities: a figure of 750,000 is sometimes quoted for the Tang-shan earthquake of 1976, for example. The earthquake that struck Kobe, Japan (now officially known as the Hyougo-ken Nanbu earthquake) at 5.46 a.m. on 17 January 1995 was exceptionally precisely monitored. It left a total of 3,842 dead and 14,679 injured. A further 114,679 people were immediately evacuated.

T H E   1 0

WORST EPIDEMICS OF ALL TIME

	Epidemic	Location	Date	Estimated no. killed
1	Black Death	Europe/Asia	1347–51	75,000,000
2	Influenza	Worldwide	1918–20	21,640,000
3	AIDS	Worldwide	1981–	6,400,000
4	Plague	India	1896–1907	5,000,000
5 =	"Plague of Justinian"	Rome	541–590	millions
=	Cholera	Worldwide	1846–60	millions
=	Cholera	Europe	1826–37	millions
=	Cholera	Worldwide	1893–94	millions
=	Plague	China, India	1910–13	millions
=	Smallpox	Mexico	1530–45	over 1,000,000

* *No precise figures available*

KOBE EARTHQUAKE DAMAGE
Reaching 7.2 on the Richter scale, the initial shock of the Kobe earthquake completely destroyed 54,949 buildings and damaged a further 31,783.

T H E 1 0

WORST AVALANCHES AND LANDSLIDES
OF THE 20TH CENTURY*

	Location	Incident	Date	Estimated no. killed
1	Yungay, Peru	Landslide	31 May 1970	17,500
2	Italian Alps	Avalanche	13 Dec 1916	10,000
3	Huarás, Peru	Avalanche	13 Dec 1941	5,000
4	Nevada Huascaran, Peru	Avalanche	10 Jan 1962	3,500
5	Medellin, Colombia	Landslide	27 Sep 1987	683
6	Chungar, Peru	Avalanche	19 Mar 1971	600
7	Rio de Janeiro, Brazil	Landslide	11 Jan 1966	550
8=	Northern Assam, India	Landslide	15 Feb 1949	500
=	Grand Riviere du Nord, Haiti	Landslide	13/14 Nov 1963	500
10	Blons, Austria	Avalanche	11 Jan 1954	411

* Excluding those where most deaths resulted from flooding, earthquakes, etc. associated with landslides

The worst incident of all, the destruction of Yungay, Peru, in May 1970, was only part of a much larger cataclysm that left a vast total of up to 70,000 people dead.

THE BLACK RAT
Fleas carried by the black rat (Rattus rattus) from Asia to Europe in 1347 transmitted the Black Death (a form of bubonic plague) to humans. The disease swept through Europe, killing about a quarter of its population.

T H E 1 0

WORST 20TH CENTURY VOLCANIC ERUPTIONS

	Location/date	Estimated no. killed
1	Mt. Pelée, Martinique, 8 May 1902	up to 40,000

After lying dormant for centuries, Mt. Pelée began to erupt in April 1902. When the volcano burst apart at 7.30 a.m. on 8th May, it showered the port with molten lava, ash, and gas, destroying all life and property.

2	Nevado del Ruiz, Colombia, 13 November 1985	22,940

The Andean volcano gave warning signs of erupting, but by the time it was decided to evacuate the local inhabitants, it was too late. The hot steam, rocks, and ash ejected from Nevado del Ruiz melted its icecap, resulting in a mudslide that completely engulfed the town of Armero.

3	Keluit, Java, 19 May 1919	5,110

One of the most remarkable of all volcanic eruptions on record, water pouring from Keluit's crater lake drowned inhabitans on the lower slopes.

4	Santa Maria, Guatemala, 24 October 1902	4,500

Some 1,500 died as a direct consequence of the volcanic eruption, and a further 3,000 as a result of its after effects.

5	Mt. Lamington, New Guinea, 21 January 1951	2,942

Mt. Lamington erupted with hardly any warning, with a huge explosion that was heard up to 320 km/200 miles away.

6	El Chichón, Mexico, 29 March 1982	1,879

Of these, 1,755 people were reported missing and 124 confirmed killed.

7	Lake Nyos, Cameroon, 21 August 1986	more than 1,700

A volcano erupted beneath the lake, and gases killed sleeping villagers.

8	La Soufriere, St. Vincent, 7–8 May 1902	1,565

The day before the cataclysmic eruption of Mt. Pelée (No. 1), La Soufriere erupted and engulfed the local inhabitants in ash flows.

9	Merapi, Java, 18 December 1931	1,369

In addition to the human casualties, 2,140 cattle were killed.

10	Taal, Philippines, 30 January 1911	1,335

Taal has erupted frequently, with the 1911 incident the worst of several during this century.

T H E 1 0

WORST TSUNAMIS OF THE 20TH CENTURY

	Locations affected	Date	Estimated no. killed
1	Agadir, Morocco*	29 Feb 1960	12,000
2=	Philippines	17 Aug 1976	5,000
=	Chile/Pacific islands/Japan	22 May 1960	5,000
4	Japan/Hawaii,	2 Mar 1933	3,000
5	Japan*	21 Dec 1946	1,088
6	Japan	1944	998
7	Colombia	12 Dec 1979	500
8	Lomblem Island, Indonesia	22 Jul 1979	700
9	Hawaii/Aleutians/California,	1 Apr 1946	173
10	Alaska/Aleutians/California*	27 Mar 1964	122

* Combined effect of earthquake and tsunamis

Tsunamis (from the Japanese *tsu* [port] and *nami* [wave]) are powerful waves caused by undersea disturbances such as earthquakes or volcanic eruptions. Tsunamis can be so intense that they frequently cross entire oceans, devastating any islands and coastal regions that lie in their paths.

TOWN & COUNTRY

96 WORLD POPULATION **98** COUNTRIES OF THE WORLD

100 WORLD CITIES **102** COUNTIES OF BRITAIN **104** PLACE NAMES

106 TALLEST INHABITED BUILDINGS **108** TALLEST

UNINHABITED BUILDINGS **110** BRIDGES &

TUNNELS **112** OTHER STRUCTURES

NEW YORK

THE TEN

LEAST POPULATED COUNTRIES IN THE WORLD

	Country	Population
1	San Marino	25,000
2	Monaco	27,000
3	Liechtenstein	28,000
4	Marshall Islands	45,000
5	Dominica	72,000
6	Kiribati	73,000
7	Seychelles	74,000
8	Grenada	89,000
9	Tonga	93,000
10	Micronesia (Fed. States of)	105,000

Source: United Nations

THEN & NOW

THE TEN MOST HIGHLY POPULATED COUNTRIES IN THE WORLD

1987 Population	Country		Country	1997 Population
1,104,193,000	China	1	China	1,243,738,000
783,730,000	India	2	India	960,178,000
242,836,000	USA	3	USA	271,648,000
172,010,000	Indonesia	4	Indonesia	203,479,000
145,386,000	Russia	5	Brazil	163,132,000
137,267,000	Brazil	6	Russia	147,709,000
122,069,000	Japan	7	Pakistan	143,831,000
102,705,000	Pakistan	8	Japan	125,638,000
102,563,000	Bangladesh	9	Bangladesh	122,013,000
101,408,000	Nigeria	10	Nigeria	118,369,000
57,009,000	*UK*		*UK*	*58,201,000*
5,026,319,000	*World*		*World*	*5,847,465,000*

The population of China is now more than 20 times that of the UK and represents a percentage of the total population of the world that proves the commonly-stated statistic that "one person in five is Chinese". The Top 10, which accounts for some 60 per cent of the world's population, remains largely the same from year to year, and contains every country with a population of more than 100,000,000.

Source: United Nations

INDIA'S TEEMING MILLIONS
India's high birth rate has resulted in its population more than tripling during the 20th century. The population is set to exceed one billion by the millennium, closing the gap with China's slower-growing population.

TOP 10

COUNTRIES OF ORIGIN OF US IMMIGRANTS, 1820–1996

	Country of last residence	No. of immigrants
1	Germany	7,142,393
2	Mexico*	5,542,625
3	Italy	5,427,298
4	UK	5,225,701
5	Ireland	4,778,159
6	Canada	4,423,066
7	USSR#	3,752,811
8	Austria†	1,841,068
9	Hungary†	1,673,579
10	Philippines	1,379,403

* *Unreported 1886–93*

\# *Russia before 1917*

† *Unreported before 1861; combined 1861–1905; separately 1905; Austria included with Germany 1938–45*

For many years the United States was the magnet that attracted vast numbers of immigrants: in 1903–15, for example, an average of 982,655 arrived every year. From 1820, when detailed records were first kept, until 1996, the total number of immigrants recorded was 63,140,227.

Source: US Immigration and Naturalization Service

TOP 10

COUNTRIES WITH THE YOUNGEST POPULATIONS

	Country	Percentage of population under 15
1	Côte d'Ivoire	49.1
2	Uganda	48.8
3	Comoros	48.7
4	Niger	48.4
5	Dem. Rep. of Congo	48.0
6	Kenya	47.7
7 =	Oman	47.5
=	Somalia	47.5
9 =	Benin	47.4
=	Mali	47.4
=	Zambia	47.4
	UK	*19.6*

Source: World Health Organization

TOP 10

FASTEST-GROWING COUNTRIES IN THE WORLD

	Country	Population growth rate (per cent per annum)
1	Liberia	8.56
2	Rwanda	7.85
3	Afghanistan	5.27
4	Oman	4.16
5	Bosnia and Herzegovina	3.90
6	Somalia	3.89
7	Yemen	3.74
8	Eritrea	3.66
9	Marshall Islands	3.51
10	Maldives	3.44
	UK	*0.09*

Source: United Nations

TOP 10

FASTEST-SHRINKING COUNTRIES IN THE WORLD

	Country	Population growth rate (per cent per annum)		Country	Population growth rate (per cent per annum)
1	Latvia	-1.13	6	Russia	-0.31
2	Estonia	-0.96	7	Lithuania	-0.25
3	Hungary	-0.59	8	Romania	-0.20
4	Bulgaria	-0.48	9 =	Belarus	-0.13
5	Ukraine	-0.37	=	Czech Republic	-0.13
	Source: United Nations			*UK*	*0.09*

COUNTRIES OF THE WORLD

TOP 10

COUNTRIES WITH THE MOST NEIGHBOURS

	Country/neighbours	No. of neighbours
1	China	15

Afghanistan, Bhutan, India, Kazakhstan, Kyrgyzstan, Laos, Macau, Mongolia, Myanmar (Burma), Nepal, North Korea, Pakistan, Russia, Tajikistan, Vietnam

2	Russia	14

Azerbaijan, Belarus, China, Estonia, Finland, Georgia, Kazakhstan, Latvia, Lithuania, Mongolia, North Korea, Norway, Poland, Ukraine

3	Brazil	10

Argentina, Bolivia, Colombia, French Guiana, Guyana, Paraguay, Peru, Surinam, Uruguay, Venezuela

4=	Germany	9

Austria, Belgium, Czech Republic, Denmark, France, Luxembourg, Netherlands, Poland, Switzerland

4=	Sudan	9

Central African Republic, Chad, Congo (Dem. Rep.), Egypt, Eritrea, Ethiopia, Kenya, Libya, Uganda

4=	Congo (Dem. Rep.)	9

Angola, Burundi, Central African Republic, Rep. of the Congo, Rwanda, Sudan, Tanzania, Uganda, Zambia

7=	Austria	8

Czech Republic, Germany, Hungary, Italy, Liechtenstein, Slovakia, Slovenia, Switzerland

7=	France	8

Andorra, Belgium, Germany, Italy, Luxembourg, Monaco, Spain, Switzerland

7=	Saudi Arabia	8

Iraq, Jordan, Kuwait, Oman, People's Democratic Republic of Yemen, Qatar, United Arab Emirates, Yemen Arab Republic

7=	Tanzania	8

Burundi, Congo (Dem. Rep.), Kenya, Malawi, Mozambique, Rwanda, Uganda, Zambia

7=	Turkey	8

Armenia, Azerbaijan, Bulgaria, Georgia, Greece, Iran, Iraq, Syria

TOP 10

LONGEST BORDERS IN THE WORLD

	Country	Length km	miles
1	China	22,143	13,759
2	Russia	20,139	12,514
3	Brazil	14,691	9,129
4	India	14,103	8,763
5	USA	12,248	7,611
6	Dem. Rep. of Congo	10,271	6,382
7	Argentina	9,665	6,006
8	Canada	8,893	5,526
9	Mongolia	8,114	5,042
10	Sudan	7,697	4,783

This list represents the total length of borders, compiled by adding together the lengths of individual land borders. The 12,248 km/7,611 miles of the US's borders include those shared with Canada (6,416 km/ 3,987 miles of which comprise the longest continuous border in the world), the 2,477km/ 1,539 mile boundary between Canada and Alaska, that with Mexico (3,326 km/ 2,067 miles), and that between the US naval base at Guantánamo and Cuba (29 km/ 18 miles).

VAST CONTINENT This stylized map of Africa depicts the 10 largest countries on the continent.

TOP 10

LARGEST COUNTRIES IN EUROPE

	Country	Area sq km	sq miles
1	Russia (in Europe)	4,710,227	1,818,629
2	Ukraine	603,700	233,090
3	France	547,026	211,208
4	Spain*	504,781	194,897
5	Sweden	449,964	173,732
6	Germany	356,999	137,838
7	Finland	337,007	130,119
8	Norway	324,220	125,182
9	Poland	312,676	120,725
10	Italy	301,226	116,304

* Including offshore islands

The United Kingdom falls just outside the Top 10 with an area of 244,101 sq km/ 94,247 sq miles, excluding the Isle of Man and the Channel Islands.

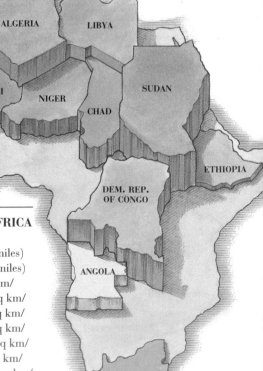

TOP 10 LARGEST COUNTRIES IN AFRICA
(Area)
❶ Sudan (2,505,813 sq km/967,500 sq miles)
❷ Algeria (2,381,741 sq km/919,595 sq miles)
❸ Dem. Rep. of Congo (2,345,409 sq km/ 905,567 sq miles) ❹ Libya (1,759,540 sq km/ 679,362 sq miles) ❺ Chad (1,284,000 sq km/ 495,755 sq miles) ❻ Niger (1,267,080 sq km/ 489,222 sq miles) ❼ Angola (1,246,700 sq km/ 481,354 sq miles) ❽ Mali (1,240,000 sq km/ 478,767 sq miles) ❾ Ethiopia (1,128,121 sq km/ 435,609 sq miles) ❿ South Africa (1,221,031 sq km/471,445 sq miles)

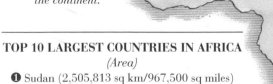

TOP 10 LARGEST COUNTRIES IN THE WORLD
(Area)

❶ Russia (17,070,289 sq km/6,590,876 sq miles) ❷ Canada (9,970,599 sq km/ 3,849,670 sq miles) ❸ China (9,596,961 sq km/3,705,408 sq miles) ❹ USA (9,169,389 sq km/3,540,321 sq miles) ❺ Brazil (8,511,965 sq km/3,286,488 sq miles) ❻ Australia (7,686,848 sq km/2,967,909 sq miles) ❼ India (3,287,590 sq km/ 1,269,346 sq miles) ❽ Argentina (2,780,400 sq km/ 1,073,512 sq miles) ❾ Kazakhstan (2,717,300 sq km/1,049,156 sq miles) ❿ Sudan (2,505,813 sq km/967,500 sq miles)

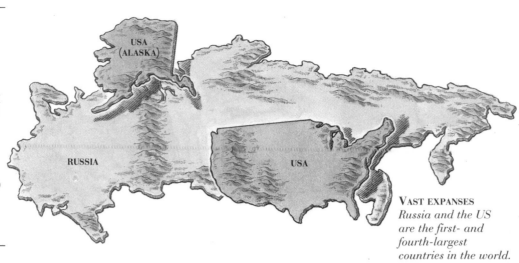

VAST EXPANSES
Russia and the US are the first- and fourth-largest countries in the world.

TOP 10

LARGEST COUNTRIES IN ASIA

	Country	Area sq km	sq miles
1	China	9,596,961	3,705,408
2	India	3,287,590	1,269,346
3	Kazakhstan	2,717,300	1,049,156
4	Saudi Arabia	2,149,640	830,000
5	Indonesia	1,904,569	735,358
6	Iran	1,648,000	636,296
7	Mongolia	1,565,000	604,250
8	Pakistan	803,950	310,407
9	Turkey (in Asia)	790,200	305,098
10	Myanmar (Burma)	676,552	261,218

TOP 10

SMALLEST COUNTRIES IN THE WORLD

	Country	Area sq km	sq miles
1	Vatican City	0.44	0.17
2	Monaco	1.81	0.7
3	Gibraltar	6.47	2.5
4	Macao	16.06	6.2
5	Nauru	21.23	8.2
6	Tuvalu	25.90	10.0
7	Bermuda	53.35	20.6
8	San Marino	59.57	23.0
9	Liechtenstein	157.99	61.0
10	Antigua	279.72	108.0

The "country" status of several of these micro-states is questionable, since their government, defence, currency, and other features are often intricately linked with those of larger countries – the Vatican City with Italy, and Monaco with France, for example, while Gibraltar and Bermuda are dependent territories of the UK.

TOP 10

LARGEST COUNTRIES IN THE AMERICAS

	Country	Area sq km	sq miles
1	Canada	9,970,599	3,849,670
2	USA	9,169,389	3,540,321
3	Brazil	8,511,965	3,286,488
4	Argentina	2,780,400	1,073,512
5	Mexico	1,958,201	756,066
6	Peru	1,285,216	496,225
7	Colombia	1,138,914	439,937
8	Bolivia	1,098,581	428,165
9	Venezuela	912,050	352,145
10	Chile	756,626	292,134

Geographically, Greenland (the largest island in the world) is considered part of the Americas but does not qualify as a country as it is under Danish control.

TOP 10

LARGEST COUNTRIES IN OCEANIA

	Country	Area sq km	sq miles
1	Australia	7,686,848	2,967,909
2	Papua New Guinea	461,691	178,260
3	New Zealand	268,676	103,736
4	Solomon Islands	28,446	10,983
5	New Caledonia	19,058	7,358
6	Fiji	18,274	7,055
7	Vanuatu	12,190	4,706
8	French Polynesia	4,000	1,544
9	Western Samoa	2,842	1,097
10	Kiribati	728	281

Australia is over nine times as large as the combined areas of the rest of the Top 10 Oceanian countries.

SNAP FACT

● Since the independence of Nauru in 1968, the landlocked state of San Marino has lost its status as the smallest republic. However, it remains the world's oldest state, having been founded during the fourth century.

WORLD CITIES

TOP 10

MOST HIGHLY POPULATED CITIES IN SOUTH AMERICA

	City/country	Population*
1	São Paulo, Brazil	18,701,000
2	Rio de Janeiro, Brazil	11,688,000
3	Buenos Aires, Argentina	11,657,000
4	Lima, Peru	6,815,000
5	Bogotá, Colombia	5,913,000
6	Santiago, Chile	5,378,000
7	Belo Horizonte, Brazil	3,812,000
8	Caracas, Venezuela	3,217,000
9	Pôrto Alegre, Brazil	3,114,000
10	Salvador, Brazil	2,298,000

* Of urban agglomeration

TOP 10

HIGHEST TOWNS AND CITIES IN THE WORLD

	City/country	Height m	ft
1	Wenchuan, China	5,099	16,730
2	Potosí, Bolivia	3,976	13,045
3	Oruro, Bolivia	3,702	12,146
4	La Paz, Bolivia	3,632	11,916
5	Lhasa, Tibet	3,684	12,087
6	Cuzco, Peru	3,399	11,152
7	Huancayo, Peru	3,249	10,660
8	Sucre, Bolivia	2,835	9,301
9	Tunja, Colombia	2,820	9,252
10	Quito, Ecuador	2,819	9,249

Lhasa was formerly the highest capital city in the world, a role now occupied by La Paz, the capital of Bolivia. Wenchuan in China is more than half the elevation of Everest.

TOP 10 COUNTRIES WITH THE MOST MILLION-PLUS CITIES

(No. of cities)

❶ China* (48) ❷ USA (35) ❸ India (29)
❹ Germany (16) ❺= Brazil, Russia (13)
❼ Indonesia (9) ❽ Pakistan (8) ❾= Japan, Mexico, South Korea (6)
* Includes Hong Kong

TOP 10

MOST DENSELY POPULATED CITIES IN THE WORLD*

	City/country	Population per sq km	sq mile
1	Hong Kong, China	98,053	253,957
2	Lagos, Nigeria	67,561	174,982
3	Dhaka, Bangladesh	63,900	165,500
4	Jakarta, Indonesia	56,650	146,724
5	Bombay, India	54,997	142,442
6	Ahmadabad, India	50,676	131,250
7	Ho Chi Minh City, Vietnam	50,617	131,097
8	Shenyang, China	44,125	114,282
9	Bangalore, India	43,583	112,880
10	Cairo, Egypt	41,413	107,260

* Includes only cities with populations of over 2,000,000. Figures pertain to urban agglomeration

TOP 10

MOST HIGHLY POPULATED CITIES IN OCEANIA

	City/country	Population*
1	Sydney, Australia	3,656,000
2	Melbourne, Australia	3,080,800
3	Brisbane, Australia	1,310,650
4	Perth, Australia	1,193,130
5	Adelaide, Australia	1,049,875
6	Auckland, New Zealand	885,600
7	Newcastle, Australia	428,760
8	Honolulu, Hawaii	365,272
9	Wellington, New Zealand	325,682
10	Christchurch, New Zealand	307,200

* Of urban agglomeration

TOP 10

MOST HIGHLY POPULATED CITIES IN EUROPE

	City/country	Population*
1	Moscow#, Russia	10,769,000
2	London#, UK	8,897,000
3	Paris#, France	8,764,000
4	Istanbul†, Turkey	7,624,000
5	Essen, Germany	7,364,000
6	Milan, Italy	4,795,000
7	Madrid#, Spain	4,772,000
8	St. Petersburg, Russia	4,694,000
9	Barcelona, Spain	4,492,000
10	Manchester, UK	3,949,000

* Of urban agglomeration

\# Capital city

† Located in the European part of Turkey

The problem of defining a city's boundaries means that population figures generally relate to "urban agglomerations", which often include large suburbs sprawling over enormous areas.

MOST POPULATED CHINESE CITY

China is the most populous country on the Earth, with Shanghai, its foremost port and industrial centre, its largest city, with a total population of 15,082,000.

TOP 10

MOST HIGHLY POPULATED CITIES IN ASIA

	City/country	Population*
1	Tokyo, Japan	26,836,000
2	Bombay, India	15,093,000
3	Shanghai, China	15,082,000
4	Beijing, China	12,362,000
5	Calcutta, India	11,673,000
6	Seoul, South Korea	11,641,000
7	Jakarta, Indonesia	11,500,000
8	Tianjin, China	10,687,000
9	Osaka, Japan	10,601,000
10	Delhi, India	9,882,000

* Of urban agglomeration
Source: United Nations

THE COLOSSEUM, ROME

TOP 10

MOST HIGHLY POPULATED CITIES IN AFRICA

	City/country	Population*		City/country	Population*
1	Lagos, Nigeria	10,287,000	6	Casablanca, Morocco	3,289,000
2	Cairo, Egypt	9,656,000	7	Tripoli, Libya	3,272,000
3	Kinshasa, Congo (Dem. Rep.)	4,214,000	8	Abidjan, Cote d'Ivoire	2,797,000
4	Algiers, Algeria	3,702,000	9	Cape Town, South Africa	2,671,000
5	Alexandria, Egypt	3,577,000	10	Khartoum, Sudan	2,429,000

* Of urban agglomeration   *Source: United Nations*

THE 10 FIRST CITIES WITH POPULATIONS OF MORE THAN ONE MILLION

❶ Rome, Italy ❷ Angkor, Cambodia
❸ Hangchow (Hangzhou), China ❹ London, UK ❺ Paris, France ❻ Peking, China
❼ Canton, China ❽ Berlin, Prussia
❾ New York, USA ❿ Vienna, Austria

TOP 10

MOST HIGHLY POPULATED CITIES IN THE WORLD, 1990/2000*

	City/country	1990 population	2000 population
1	Tokyo-Yokohama, Japan	26,952,000	29,971,000
2	Mexico City, Mexico	20,207,000	27,872,000
3	São Paulo, Brazil	18,052,000	25,354,000
4	Seoul, South Korea	16,268,000	21,976,000
5	Bombay, India	11,777,000	15,357,000
6	New York, USA	14,622,000	14,648,000
7	Osaka-Kobe-Kyoto, Japan	13,826,000	14,287,000
8	Tehran, Iran	9,354,000	14,251,000
9	Rio de Janeiro, Brazil	11,428,000	14,169,000
10	Calcutta, India	11,663,000	14,088,000

* Of urban agglomeration

TOP 10

LARGEST CITIES IN THE US

	City/state	Population*
1	New York, New York	7,380,906
2	Los Angeles, California	3,553,638
3	Chicago, Illinois	2,721,547
4	Houston, Texas	1,744,058
5	Philadelphia, Pennsylvania	1,478,002
6	San Diego, California	1,171,121
7	Phoenix, Arizona	1,159,014
8	San Antonio, Texas	1,067,816
9	Dallas, Texas	1,053,292
10	Detroit, Michigan	1,000,272

* Estimated figures up to 1 July 1996 for central city areas only, not for the total urban agglomeration

Source : US Bureau of the Census

COUNTIES OF BRITAIN

LARGEST COUNTIES AND REGIONS IN THE UK

	County/location	Area sq km	sq miles		County/location	Area sq km	sq miles
1	Highland, Scotland	25,784	9,952	6	Dumfries and Galloway, Scotland	6,439	2,486
2	North Yorkshire, England	8,309	3,208	7	Aberdeenshire, Scotland	6,318	2,439
3	Argyll and Bute, Scotland	6,930	2,676	8	Lincolnshire, England	5,921	2,286
4	Cumbria, England	6,824	2,635	9	Norfolk, Englan d	5,372	2,074
5	Devon, England	6,703	2,588	10	Perth and Kinross, Scotland	5,311	2,051

Under the Local Government Act, new local authorities came into being on 1 April 1974. Some are similar in area to previous counties, but others are entirely new: Cumbria, for example, was created by amalgamating Cumberland and Westmorland and the Furness district of Lancashire, while Dyfed was formed from the former counties of Cardiganshire, Carmarthenshire, and Pembrokeshire.

SMALLEST COUNTIES AND REGIONS IN THE UK

	County/location	Area sq km	sq miles		County/location	Area sq km	sq miles
1	Dundee City, Scotland	65	25	6	Belfast, Northern Ireland	110	42
2=	Carrickfergus, N. Ireland	81	31	7	Merthyr Tydfil, Wales	111	43
=	North Down, N. Ireland	81	31	8	Torfaen, Wales	126	49
4	Castlereagh, N. Ireland	85	33	9	Cardiff, Wales	140	54
5	Blaenau Gwent, Wales	109	42	10	Newtonabbey, N. Ireland	151	58

Following local government reorganization in 1996, "counties" have been replaced by "Council Areas" in Scotland, of which there are a total of 32, and by "Unitary Authorities" in Wales, of which there are a total of 22. These sub-regions are considerably smaller than the old counties, which means that the list of smallest British "counties" is now comprised entirely of areas in Scotland, Wales, and Northern Ireland.

COUNTY BOOKS THAT STARTED WITH VICTORIA

The publication of the *Victoria County Histories* was begun in 1899 – and, remarkably, continues to the present day. Named, with her permission, after Queen Victoria, the series set out to deal with the history and topography of every county of England, with a general history of each county from earliest times and detailed descriptions of every town and village. As the publishing programme nears its third century just 14 counties are "complete", some with several volumes devoted to them (Wiltshire has 15, Oxfordshire 12), while others, such as Devon, have only one and await the millennium for completion.

YEARS AGO • YEARS AGO • 100 • YEARS AGO • YEARS AGO

LEAST DENSELY POPULATED COUNTIES AND REGIONS IN THE UK

	County/location	Population per sq km
1	Highland, Scotland	8
2	Western Isles, Scotland	9
3	Argyll and Bute, Scotland	`13
4	Shetland Islands, Scotland	16
5	Orkney Islands, Scotland	20
6	Scottish Borders, Scotland	22
7	Dumfries and Galloway, Scotland	23
8	Powys, Wales	24
9	Perth and Kinross, Scotland	25
10	Moyle, Northern Ireland	30

Of the present Western Isles, North and South Uist were once included with the closest mainland county of Inverness-shire.

MOST DENSELY POPULATED COUNTIES AND REGIONS IN THE UK

	County/location	Population per sq km
1	Greater London, England	4,440
2	Glasgow City, Scotland	3,522
3	West Midlands, England	2,934
4	Belfast, Northern Ireland	2,707
5	Dundee City, Scotland	2,306
6	Cardiff, Wales	2,209
7	Merseyside, England	2,178
8	Tyne and Wear, England	2,093
9	Greater Manchester, England	2,005
10	Edinburgh City, Scotland	1,711

Since the abolition of the Greater London Council in 1986, local government in the former area is under the control of 32 borough councils. Hence Greater London is in the unique position of being a county in name only, without the centralized power of the other metropolitan counties.

TOP 10

LARGEST NATIONAL PARKS IN ENGLAND AND WALES

	National Park/location	Established	Area sq km	sq miles
1	Lake District, Cumbria	9 May 1951	2,292	885
2	Snowdonia, Gwynedd	18 Oct 1951	2,142	827
3	Yorkshire Dales, North Yorkshire	13 Oct 1954	1,769	683
4	Peak District, Derbyshire	17 Apr 1951	1,438	555
5	North York Moors, North Yorkshire	28 Nov 1952	1,436	554
6	Brecon Beacons, Mid Glamorgan	17 Apr 1957	1,351	522
7	Northumberland	6 Apr 1956	1,049	405
8	Dartmoor, Devon	30 Oct 1951	954	368
9	Exmoor, Somerset	19 Oct 1954	693	268
10	Pembrokeshire Coast	29 Feb 1952	584	225

TOP 10

LARGEST NATURE RESERVES IN SCOTLAND

	Nature Reserve/location	Area hectares	acres
1	Cairngorms, Grampian and Highland Regions	25,949	64,121
2	Inverpolly, Highland Region	10,857	26,828
3	Rum, Highland Region	10,684	26,401
4	Caerlaverock, Dumfries and Galloway Region	7,706	19,042
5	Ben Wyvis, Highland Region	5,673	14,026
6	Beinn Eighe, Highland Region	4,758	11,757
7	Glen Tanar, Grampian Region	4,185	10,341
8	Ben Lawers, Tayside and Central Regions	4,060	10,032
9	Creag Meagaidh, Highland Region	3,948	9,756
10	Gualin, Sutherland	2,522	6,232

TOP 10

LARGEST NATURE RESERVES IN WALES

	Nature Reserve/location	Area hectares	acres
1	Berwyn, Powys	3,238	8,001
2	Dyfi, Dyfed	2,268	5,604
3	Y Wyddfa-Snowdon, Gwynedd	1,677	4,144
4	Newborough Warren, Anglesea	1,452	3,586
5	Morfa Harlech, Gwynedd	884	2,184
6	Cors Caron, Dyfed	816	2,016
7	Claerwen, Powys	789	1,950
8	Whiteford, West Glamorgan	782	1,932
9	Rhinog, Gwynedd	598	1,478
10	Kenfig Pool and Dunes, Mid Glamorgan	518	1,280

TOP 10

BRITISH COUNTIES WITH THE SHORTEST PERIMETERS

	County/location	Total perimeter km	miles
1	South Glamorgan, Wales	115	71
2	Isle of Wight, England	122	76
3	Tyne and Wear, England	170	106
4	Cleveland, England	178	111
5	Mid Glamorgan, Wales	202	126
6	West Glamorgan, Wales	219	136
7	Bedfordshire, England	242	150
8	South Yorkshire, England	246	153
9	West Midlands, England	249	155
10	Greater Manchester, England	251	156

TOP 10

BRITISH COUNTIES WITH THE LONGEST PERIMETERS

	County/location	Total perimeter km	miles
1	Highland Region, Scotland	2,417	1,052
2	Strathclyde Region, Scotland	1,661	1,032
3	N. Yorkshire, England	729	453
4	Dyfed, Wales	728	453
5	Dumfries and Galloway Region, Scotland	709	441
6	Cornwall, England	672	417
7	Devon, England	665	413
8	Essex, England	592	368
9	Lincolnshire, England	572	355
10	Powys, Wales	569	354

- Prior to the 1996 reorganization, the smallest "traditional" county in the UK was Rutland, with an area of just 373 sq km/144 sq miles.

- The smallest county in England is now the Isle of Wight, which measures only 380 sq km/147 sq miles.

- The National Parks of England and Wales cover about nine per cent of the area of the two countries. The total area of the National Parks is 14,011 sq km/5,410 sq miles.

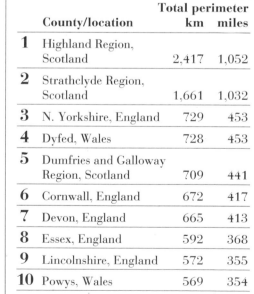

SNAP FACTS

Highland Region, Scotland, the largest British county or region, and the least populated, came into being in 1974 when the counties of Caithness, Sutherland, Ross and Cromarty (except the Isle of Lewis), Inverness-shire (except the Outer Hebrides), Nairnshire, and parts of Moray and North Argyll were amalgamated.

PLACE NAMES

T O P   1 0

MOST COMMON HOUSE NAMES IN THE UK

1	The Cottage
2	The Bungalow
3	Rose Cottage
4	The Lodge
5	The Coach House
6	The School House
7	The White House
8	Woodlands
9	Hill Crest
10	The Gables

When they purchase a house, most people retain its existing name, rather than change it. As a consequence this 1998 survey of the most popular property names in the UK indicates that there have been few changes during the decade. However, The Cottage overtook The Bungalow to take first place, while The Coach House has moved up from its former 9th place to 5th, pointing to the number of former coach houses that have been converted to domestic use in recent years.

T O P   1 0

MOST COMMON PLACE NAMES IN THE UK

	Name	Occurrences
1	Newton	150
2	Blackhill/Black Hill	141
3	Mountpleasant/Mount Pleasant	130
4	Castlehill/Castle Hill	127
5	Woodside/Wood Side	116
6	Newtown/New Town	111
7	Greenhill/Green Hill	108
8	Woodend/Wood End	106
9	Burnside	105
10	Beacon Hill	94

Research undertaken specially for this book by Adrian Room (the author of *A Concise Dictionary of Modern Place-names in Great Britain and Ireland*) reveals the place names most frequently encountered in the UK. These include the names of towns and villages, as well as woods, hills, and other named locations, but exclude combinations of these names with others (Newton Abbot and Newton-le-Willows, for example, are not counted with the Newtons).

T O P   1 0

LONGEST PLACE NAMES IN THE UK*

	Name/location	Letters
1	Gorsafawddachaidraigddanheddo-gleddollônpenrhyn-areurdraeth-ceredigion (*see* The 10 Longest Place Names in the World)	67
2	Llanfairpwllgwyngyllgogerychwy-rndrobwllllantysiliogogogoch(*see* The 10 Longest Place Names in the World)	58
3	Sutton-under-Whitestonecliffe, North Yorkshire	27
4	Llanfihangel-yng-Ngwynfa, Powys	22
5 =	Llanfihangel-y-Creuddyn, Dyfed	21
=	Llanfihangel-y-traethau, Gwynedd	21
7	Cottonshopeburnfoot, Northumberland	19
8 =	Blakehopeburnhaugh, Northumberland	18
=	Coignafeuinternich, Inverness-shire	18
10 =	Claddach-baleshare, North Uist, Outer Hebrides	17
=	Claddach-knockline, North Uist, Outer Hebrides	17

* *Single and hyphenated words only*

T O P   1 0

COUNTRIES WITH THE LONGEST OFFICIAL NAMES

	Official name*	Common English name	Letters
1	Al Jamāhīrīyah al ʿArabīyah al Lībīyah ash Shaʿbīyah al Ishtirakīyah	Libya	56
2	Al Jumhūrīyah al Jazāʾirīyah ad Dīmuqrāṭīyah ash Shaʿbīyah	Algeria	49
3	United Kingdom of Great Britain and Northern Ireland	United Kingdom	45
4	Sri Lankā Prajathanthrika Samajavadi Janarajaya	Sri Lanka	43
5	Jumhūrīyat al-Qumur al-Ittihādīyah al-Islāmīyah	The Comoros	41
6 =	Al Jumhūrīyah al Islāmīyah al Mūrītānīyah	Mauritania	36
=	The Federation of St. Christopher and Nevis	St. Kitts and Nevis	36
8	Jamhuuriyadda Dimuqraadiga Soomaaliya	Somalia	35
9 =	Al-Mamlakah al-Urdunnīyah al-Hāshimīyah	Jordan	34
=	Repoblika Demokratika nʾiʿ Madagasikara	Madagascar	32

* *Some official names have been transliterated from languages that do not use the Roman alphabet; their lengths may vary according to the method of transliteration used*

T O P   1 0

MOST COMMON SOURCES OF PLACE NAMES IN AUSTRALIA

	Source/example	Occurrences (%)
1	Aboriginal (Canberra)	29
2	Australian people (Macquarie River)	28
3	Descriptive (Snowy River)	13
4 =	British people (Darwin)	8
=	British places (Perth)	8
6	Events (Attack Creek)	4
7 =	Other people (Mount Koshiusko)	3
=	Other places (American river)	3
9	Ships (Adventure Bay)	2
10	Miscellaneous (Mount, Sunny)	1

TOP 10

MOST COMMON PLACE NAMES OF BIBLICAL ORIGIN IN THE US

	Name/meaning	Occurrences
1	Bethel (house of God)	141
2	Salem (peace)	134
3	Eden (pleasure)	101
4	Shiloh (peace)	98
5	Paradise (pleasure ground)	94
6	Antioch (named for Antiochus, king of Syria)	83
7	Sharon (plain)	72
8	Jordan (descender)	65
9=	Bethany/Bethania (house of affliction)	59
=	Zion (mount, sunny)	59

This list takes account of all populated places (cities, towns, and villages) in the US and includes compound names, such as Salemville and Salem Heights.

TOP 10

MOST COMMON STREET NAMES IN THE UK

1	High Street	6	Station Approach
2	Station Road	7	Green Lane
3	Church Road	8	The Avenue
4	Park Road	9	London Road
5	The Drive	10	Church Lane

TOP 10

LONGEST PLACE NAMES IN THE WORLD*

	Name	Letters
1	Krung thep mahanakhon bovorn ratanakosin mahintharayutthaya mahadilok pop noparatratchathani burirom udomratchanivetma hasathan amornpiman avatarnsa thit sakkathattiyavisnukarmprasit	167

When the poetic name of Bangkok, capital of Thailand, is used, it is usually abbreviated to "Krung Thep" (City of Angels).

2	Taumatawhakatangihangakoauau-otamateaturipukakapikimaunga-horonukupokaiwhenuakitanatahu	85

This is the longer version (the other has a mere 83 letters) of the Maori name of a hill in New Zealand. It translates as "The place where Tamatea, the man with the big knees, who slid, climbed, and swallowed mountains, known as land-eater, played on the flute to his loved one".

3	Gorsafawddacha'idraigodanhed-dogleddollônpenrhynareur-draethceredigion	67

A name contrived by the Fairbourne Steam Railway, Gwynedd, North Wales, UK, for publicity purposes and in order to out-do its rival, No. 4. It means "The Mawddach station and its dragon teeth at the Northern Penrhyn Road on the golden beach of Cardigan Bay".

4	Llanfairpwllgwyngyllgogerychwyrn-drobwllllantysiliogogogoch	58

This is the place in Gwynedd, UK, famed especially for the length of its railway tickets. It means "St. Mary's Church in the hollow of the white hazel near to the rapid whirlpool of Llantysilio of the Red Cave". Its official name consists of only the first 20 letters.

	Name	Letters
5	El Pueblo de Nuestra Señora la Reina de los Angeles de la Porciuncula	57

The site of a Franciscan mission and the full Spanish name of Los Angeles, USA, it means "the town of Our Lady the Queen of the Angels of the Little Portion".

6	Chargoggagoggmanchauggagogg-chaubunagungamaugg	45

This is a lake near Webster, Massachusetts, USA. Its Native American name loosely means "You fish on your side, I'll fish on mine, and no one fishes in the middle". An invented extension of its real name (Chagungungamaug Pond, or "boundary fishing place"), this name was devised in the 1920s by Larry Daly, editor of the Webster Times.

7=	Lower North Branch Little Southwest Miramichi	40

Canada's longest place name belongs to a short river in New Brunswick.

7=	Villa Real de la Santa Fe de San Francisco de Asis	40

The full Spanish name of Santa Fe, New Mexico, USA, translates as "Royal city of the holy faith of St. Francis of Assisi".

9	Te Whakatakanga-o-te-ngarehu-o-te-ahi-a-Tamatea	38

The Maori name of Hammer Springs, New Zealand, like the 2nd name in this list, refers to a legend of Tamatea, explaining how the springs were warmed by "the falling of the cinders of the fire of Tamatea".

10	Meallan Liath Coire Mhic Dhubhghaill	32

The longest multiple name in Scotland, this is the name of a place near Aultanrynie, Highland, alternatively spelled Meallan Liath Coire Mhic Dhughaill.

* *Including single-word, hyphenated, and multiple names*

THE LONG SIDE OF THE TRACKS
For the benefit of its many visitors, the original 58-letter version of the name of this Welsh village is spelled phonetically on its station signboard. It is of dubious origin, however, the modern invention of local poet John Evans, and today ranks only as the world's second longest railway station name, having been overtaken by a similarly contrived Welsh place name.

TALLEST INHABITED BUILDINGS

TOP 10 TALLEST HABITABLE BUILDINGS IN THE WORLD

1987 Building/location/year	Height m	ft		Height m	ft	1997 Building/location/year
Sears Tower, Chicago, USA (1974)	443	1,454	**1**	452	1,482	Petronas Towers, Kuala Lumpur, Malaysia (1996)
World Trade Center, New York, USA (1973)	417	1,368	**2**	443	1,454	Sears Tower, Chicago, USA (1974)
Empire State Building, New York, USA (1931)	381	1,250	**3**	417	1,368	World Trade Center, New York, USA (1973)
Amoco Building, Chicago, USA (1973)	346	1,136	**4**	382	1,255	Jin Mao Building, Shanghai, China (1997)
John Hancock Center, Chicago, USA (1968)	344	1,127	**5**	381	1,250	Empire State Building, New York, USA (1931)
Chrysler Building, New York, USA (1930)	319	1,046	**6**	348	1,142	T & C Tower, Kao-hsiung, Taiwan (1997)
Texas Commerce Tower, Houston USA (1981)	305	1,002	**7**	346	1,136	Amoco Building, Chicago, USA (1973)
Allied Bank Plaza, Houston, USA (1983)	302	992	**8**	344	1,127	John Hancock Center, Chicago, USA (1968)
First Canadian Place, Toronto, Canada (1975)	290	952	**9**	330	1,082	Shun Hing Square, Shenzen, China (1996)
International Building, New York, USA (1932)	289	950	**10**	323	1,060	Sky Central Plaza, Guangzhou, China (1996)

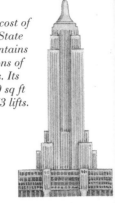

EMPIRE STATE BUILDING
Completed in 1931 at a cost of $25 million, the Empire State Building in New York contains 54,000 tonnes/60,000 tons of steel and 6,500 windows. Its 208,846 sq m/2,248,000 sq ft of offices are served by 73 lifts.

WORLD CITIES WITH MOST SKYSCRAPERS*

	City	Skyscrapers
1	New York City, USA	140
2	Chicago, USA	68
3	Hong Kong, China	36
4	Houston, USA	36
5	Kuala Lumpur, Malaysia	25
6	Los Angeles, USA	24
7	Dallas, USA	22
8=	San Francisco, USA	20
=	Shanghai, China	20
9=	Singapore, Singapore	18
=	Sydney, Australia	18

* Habitable buildings of over 152 m/500 ft

The word "skyscraper" was first used in the 18th century to mean a high-flying flag on a ship, and later to describe a tall horse or person. It was not used to describe buildings until the 1880s, when the first tall office blocks of 10 storeys or more were built in Chicago and New York, with the Eiffel Tower following at the end of the decade. The first modern, steel-framed skyscraper was the Woolworth Building, New York, built in 1913.

REACHING FOR THE SKY

Apart from the Eiffel Tower and the Washington Memorial, most tall buildings erected before the 1890s had been religious structures. The six-storey 40-m/130-ft Equitable Life Building, New York, completed in 1870, the first building with a lift, marked the beginning of the rise of the city's skyline. In 1895, it was taken to 90 m/306 ft by the 21-storey American Surety Building, followed in 1899 by the St. Paul Building on Broadway and Ann Streets, a 16-storey structure measuring 94 m/310 ft, and the Park Row Building, which at 29 storeys and 118 m/386 ft briefly held the record as the tallest building in the world.

SNAP FACTS

- The Woolworth Building cost $13.5 million – which F.W. Woolworth paid in cash.
- A gargoyle on the building depicts its designer, Cass Gilbert.
- Its 29 lifts were the world's fastest.

100 YEARS AGO

T O P 1 0

TALLEST BUILDINGS IN THE WORLD ERECTED MORE THAN 100 YEARS AGO

	Building/location	Year completed	Height m	ft
1	Eiffel Tower, Paris, France	1889	300	984
2	Washington Memorial, Washington, DC, USA	1885	169	555
3	Ulm Cathedral, Ulm, Germany	1890	161	528
4	Lincoln Cathedral, Lincoln, England (destroyed 1548)	c.1307	160	525
5	Cologne Cathedral, Cologne, Germany	1880	156.4	513
6	Rouen Cathedral I, Rouen, France (destroyed 1822)	1530	156	512
7	St. Pierre Church, Beauvais, France (collapsed 1573)	1568	153	502
8	Lin-He Pagoda, Hang Zhoc, China (destroyed 1121)	970	150	492
9	St. Paul's Cathedral, London, England (destroyed 1561)	1315	149	489
10	Rouen Cathedral II, Rouen, France	1876	148	485

T O P 1 0

TALLEST HOTELS IN THE WORLD

	Building/location	Storeys	Height m	ft
1	Baiyoke II Tower, Bangkok, Thailand	89	319	1,046
2	Yu Kyong, Pyong Yang, North Korea	105	300	985
3	Emirates Tower 2, Dubae, UAE	50	262	858
4	Shangri-la, Hong Kong	60	228	748
5	Raffles Western Hotel, Singapore	73	226	742
6	Westin Peachtree, Hotel, Atlanta, USA	71	220	723
7	Westin Hotel, Detroit, USA	71	219	720
8	Four Seasons Hotel, New York City, USA	52	208	682
9	Trump International Hotel, New York City, USA	45	207	679
10	Trump Tower, New York City, USA	68	202	664

T O P 1 0

TALLEST APARTMENT BUILDINGS IN THE WORLD

	Building/location	Storeys	Height m	ft
1	Lake Point Tower, Chicago, USA	70	197	645
2	Central Park Place, New York City, USA	56	191	628
3	Olympic Tower, New York City, USA	51	189	620
4	May Road Apartments, Hong Kong, China	58	180	590
5	Marina City Apartments, Chicago, USA	61	179	588
6	North Pier Apartments, Chicago, USA	61	177	581
7	Onterie Centre, Chicago, USA	58	174	570
8	30 Broad Street, New York City, USA	48	171	562
9	Huron Apartments, Chicago, USA	58	170	560
10	Harbour Point, Chicago, USA	59	170	558

T O P 1 0

TALLEST HABITABLE BUILDINGS IN 2001

	Building/location/year*	Height m	ft
1	Shanghai World, Finance Centre, Shanghai, China, 2001	460	1,508
2	Chongqing Tower, Chongqing, China, 2000	457	1,500
3	Petronas Towers, Kuala Lumpur, Malaysia, 1997	452	1,482
4	Sears Tower, Chicago, USA, 1974	443	1,454
5	Tour Sans Fin, Paris, France, 2000	419	1,377
6	World Trade Center, New York, USA, 1973	417	1.368
7	Daewoo Corporation, Puxi, Shanghai, China, 2000	400	1,310
8	International Finance Tower, Hong Kong, China, 2002	400	1,310
9	Jin Mao Building, Shanghai, China, 1998	382	1,255
10	Empire State Building, New York, USA, 1931	381	1,250

* Opened or expected completion year

CHICAGO SKYLINE

TALLEST UNINHABITED BUILDINGS

COLOGNE CATHEDRAL

TOP 10

TALLEST CHIMNEYS IN THE WORLD

Chimney/location	Height m	ft
1 Ekibastuz power station, Kazakhstan	420	1,377
2 International Nickel Company, Copper Hill, Sudbury, Ontario, Canada	381	1,250
3 Pennsylvania Electric Company, Homer City, Pennsylvania, USA	371	1,216
4 Kennecott Copper Corporation, Magna, Utah, USA	370	1,215
5 Ohio Power Company, Cresap, West Virginia, USA	368	1,206
6 Zasavje power station, Trboulje, Yugoslavia	360	1,181
7 Empresa Nacional de Electricidad SA, Puentes de Garcia Rodriguez, Spain	356	1,169
8 Appalachian Power Company, New Haven, West Virginia, USA	336	1,103
9 Indiana and Michigan Electric Company, Rockport, Indiana, USA	316	1,037
10 West Penn Power Company, Reesedale, Pennsylvania, USA	308	1,012

Numbers 2 to 5 and 7 to 10 in the list were all built by Pullman Power Products Corporation (formerly a division of M. W. Kellogg), an American engineering company that has been in business since 1902 and has built many of the world's tallest chimneys. The largest internal volume is No. 7 – 6,700,000 cubic feet. The diameter of No. 1, completed in 1991, tapers from 44 m/144 ft at the base to 14 m/47 ft at the top; the outside diameter of No. 4, built in 1974 and formerly the world's largest, is 38 m/124 ft at the base, tapering to 12 m/40 ft at the top.

TOP 10

TALLEST TELECOMMUNICATIONS TOWERS IN THE WORLD

Tower/location	Year	Height m	ft
1 CN Tower, Toronto, Canada	1975	555	1,821
2 Ostankino Tower, Moscow, Russia	1967	537	1,762
3 Oriental Pearl Broadcasting Tower, Shanghai, China	1995	468	1,535
4 Telecom Tower, Kuala Lumpur, Malaysia	1995	420	1,380
5 Central Radio and TV Tower, Beijing, China	1994	405	1,328
6 Liberation Tower, Kuwait City, Kuwait	1998	372	1,220
7 Alma-Ata Tower, Kazakhstan	1983	370	1,214
8 TV Tower, Berlin, Germany	1969	365	1,198
9 TV Tower, Tashkent, Uzbekistan	1983	357	1,171
10 Stratosphere Tower, Las Vegas, USA	1996	350	1,149

All the towers listed are self-supporting, rather than masts braced with guy wires, and all have observation facilities. The Menara Jakarta, a tower under construction in Jakarta, Indonesia, scheduled for completion in 2001 but currently "on hold", is intended to be 558 m/1,831 ft tall, making it the tallest tower in the world.

TOP 10

TALLEST MASTS IN THE WORLD

Mast/location	Height m	ft
1 KTHI-TV Mast, Fargo, North Dakota	629	2,063
2 KSLA-TV Mast, Shreveport, Louisiana	579	1,898
3 = WBIR-TV Mast, Knoxville, Tennessee	533	1,749
= WTVM and WRBL Television Mast, Columbus, Georgia	533	1,749
5 KFVS Television Mast, Cape Girardeau, Missouri	511	1,676
6 WPSD-TV Mast, Paducah, Kentucky	499	1,638
7 WGAN Television Mast, Portland, Maine	493	1,619
8 WKY-TV Mast, Oklahoma City, Oklahoma	488	1,600
9 KWTV Television Mast, Oklahoma City, Oklahoma	479	1,572
10 BREN Tower, Nevada	464	1,521

On 10 August 1991, the former No. 1, the Warszawa Radio Mast, Konstantynow, Poland, which measured 646 m/2,120 ft, collapsed during renovation. As a result, the entire Top 10 are in the USA.

TOP 10

HIGHEST PUBLIC OBSERVATORIES IN THE WORLD

	Building/location/observatory	Year	Height m	ft
1	CN Tower, Toronto, Canada (space deck)	1975	447	1,465
2	World Trade Center, New York, USA (roof top Tower B)	1973	415	1,360
3	Sears Tower, Chicago, USA (103rd floor)	1974	412	1,353
4	Empire State Building, New York, USA (102nd floor) (outdoor observatory)	1931	381 320	1,250 1,050
5	Ostankino Tower, Moscow, Russia (5th floor turret)	1967	360	1,181
6	Oriental Pearl Broadcasting Tower, Shanghai (VIP Observation level) (public observation level)	1995	350 263	1,148 863
7	Jin Mao Building, Shanghai, China (88th floor)	1997	340	1,115
8	John Hancock Center, Chicago, USA (94th floor)	1968	314	1,030
9	Sky Central Plaza, Guanghshou, China (90th-floor observatory)	1996	310	1,016
10	KL Tower, Kuala Lumpur, Malaysia (revolving restaurant) (public observation level)	1995	282 276	925 907

The facility to ascend to a great height and look out over vast distances is a feature of towers and buildings the world over. The Eiffel Tower, constructed for this purpose and as a symbol of the technological skills of the French people, was built between 1887 and 1889 as the centrepiece of the Paris Exhibition, providing at 274 m/900 ft the world's highest viewing platform in a man-made structure for 42 years, until the opening of the Empire State Building. From the 1930s onwards, US observatories dominated the world, but have been steadily losing ground to Asian buildings, with the KL Tower, Kuala Lumpur, recently joining the list. For the first time, more than half the Top 10 are outside the USA.

TOP 10

TALLEST CHURCHES IN THE WORLD

	Church	Location	Year completed	Height m	ft
1	Chicago Methodist Temple	Chicago, USA	1924	173	568
2	Ulm Cathedral	Ulm, Germany	1890	161	528
3	Notre Dame de la Paix	Yamoussoukro, Côte d'Ivoire	1989	158	519
4	Cologne Cathedral	Cologne, Germany	1880	156	513
5	Rouen Cathedral	Rouen, France	1876	148	485
6	St. Nicholas	Hamburg, Germany	1847	145	475
7	Notre Dame	Strasbourg, France	1439	142	465
8	St. Peter's	Rome, Italy	1612	140	458
9	St. Stephen's Cathedral	Vienna, Austria	1433	136	446
10 =	Amiens Cathedral	Amiens, France	1260	134	440
=	St. Michael	Hamburg, Germany	1906	134	440

TOP 10

TALLEST LIGHTHOUSES IN THE UK

	Lighthouse/location	Height m	ft
1 =	Bishop Rock, Scilly Isles	49	161
=	Eddystone, English Channel	49	161
3	Skerryvore, Hebrides	48	157
4	Chicken Rock, Calf of Man	44	144
5 =	Beachy Head, East Sussex	43	141
=	Dungeness, Kent	43	141
7	North Ronaldsay, Orkney	42	138
8 =	The Smalls, Dyfed	41	135
=	Tarbat Ness, Ross and Cromarty	41	135
=	Portland Bill, Dorset	41	135
=	Wolf Rock, Cornwall	41	135

THE SEARS TOWER
Chicago's tallest building has one of the highest public observatories in the world on its 103rd floor.

BRIDGES & TUNNELS

T O P 1 0

LONGEST SUSPENSION BRIDGES IN THE WORLD

	Bridge/location	Year completed	Length of main span m	ft
1	AkasHi-Kaiko, Kobe-Naruto, Japan	1998	1,990	6,529
2	Great Belt, Denmark	1997	1,624	5,328
3	Jiangyin, China	1998	1,624	5,328
4	Humber Estuary, UK	1980	1,410	4,626
5	Tsing Ma, Hong Kong, China	1997	1,377	4,518
6	Verrazano Narrows, New York, USA	1964	1,298	4,260
7	Golden Gate, San Francisco, USA	1937	1,280	4,200
8	Höga Kusten, Veda, Sweden	1997	1,210	3,970
9	Mackinac Straits, Michigan, USA	1957	1,158	3,800
10	Minami Bisan-seto, Kojima-Sakaide, Japan	1988	1,100	3,609

T O P 1 0

LONGEST CABLE–STAYED BRIDGES IN THE WORLD

	Bridge/location	Year completed	Length of main span m	ft
1	Pont de Normandie, Le Havre, France	1994	856	2,808
2	Qunghzhou Minjiang, Fozhou, China	1996	605	1,985
3	Yangpu, Shanghai, China	1993	602	1,975
4 =	Meiko-Chuo, Nagoya, Japan	1997	590	1,936
=	Xupu, Shanghai, China	1997	590	1,936
6	Skarnsundet, Trondheim, Fjord, Norway	1991	530	1,739
7	Ikuchi, Onomichi-Imabari, Japan	1994	490	1,608
8	Higashi-Kobe, Kobe, Japan	1992	485	1,591
9	Ying Kau, Hong Kong, China	1997	475	1,558
10	Seohae Grand, Asan Man, South Korea	1997	470	1,542

T O P 1 0

LONGEST RAIL TUNNELS IN THE WORLD

	Tunnel/location	Year completed	Length km	miles
1	Seikan, Japan	1988	53.90	33.49
2	Channel Tunnel, France/England	1994	49.94	31.03
3	Moscow Metro (Medvedkovo/ Belyaevo section), Russia	1979	30.70	19.07
4	London Underground (East Finchley/ Morden Northern Line), UK	1939	27.84	17.30
5	Dai-Shimizu, Japan	1982	22.17	13.78
6	Simplon II, Italy/Switzerland	1922	19.82	12.31
7	Simplon I, Italy/Switzerland	1906	19.80	12.30
8	Shin-Kanmon, Japan	1975	18.68	11.61
9	Apennine, Italy	1934	18.52	11.50
10	Rokko, Japan	1972	16.25	10.10

T O P 1 0

TALLEST RAIL BRIDGES IN THE WORLD

	Bridge/location	Year completed	Height m	ft
1	Mala Reka Viaduct, Yugoslavia	1976	198	650
2	Vresk, Iran	1938	152	500
3	Fades Viaduct, France	1909	133	435
4	Khotur, Iran	1973	131	430
5	Victoria Falls, Zimbabwe	1904	128	420
6	Pfaffenberg-Zwenberg, Austria	1971	120	394
7	Viaur, France	1902	116	381
8	Garabit Viaduct, France	1884	112	367
9	Müngstner, Germany	1897	107	350
10 =	Rio Grande, Costa Rica	1890	105	346
=	Vance Creek, USA	1928	105	346

T O P 1 0

LONGEST CANTILEVER BRIDGES IN THE WORLD

	Bridge/location	Longest span m	ft		Bridge/location	Longest span m	ft
1	Pont de Québec, Canada	549	1,800	=	Greater New Orleans 2, Louisiana, USA	480	1,575
2	Firth of Forth, Scotland	521	1,710	7	Howrah, Calcutta, India	457	1,500
3	Minato, Osaka, Japan	510	1,673	8	Gramercy, Gramercy, Louisiana, USA	445	1,460
4	Commodore John Barry, Pennsylvania, USA	494	1,622	9	Transbay, San Francisco, USA	427	1,400
5 =	Greater New Orleans 1, Louisiana, USA	480	1,575	10	Baton Rouge, Louisiana, USA	376	1,235

T O P 1 0

LONGEST STEEL ARCH BRIDGES IN THE WORLD

	Bridge/location	Year completed	Longest span m	ft
1	New River Gorge, Fayetteville, West Virginia, USA	1977	518	1,700
2	Kill Van Kull, Bayonne, New Jersey/ Staten Island, New York, USA	1931	504	1,654
3	Sydney Harbour, Australia	1932	503	1,650
4	Fremont, Portland, Oregon, USA	1973	383	1,257
5	Port Mann, Vancouver, Canada	1964	366	1,200
6	Thatcher Ferry, Panama Canal	1962	344	1,128
7	Laviolette, Quebec, Canada	1967	335	1,100
8 =	Runcorn-Widnes, UK	1961	330	1,082
=	Zdákov, Lake Orlik, Czech Republic	1967	330	1,082
10 =	Birchenough, Fort Victoria, Zimbabwe	1935	329	1,080
=	Roosevelt Lake, Arizona, USA	1990	329	1,080

T O P 1 0

LONGEST ROAD TUNNELS IN THE WORLD

	Tunnel/location	Year completed	Length km	miles
1	St. Gotthard, Switzerland	1980	16.32	10.14
2	Arlberg, Austria	1978	13.98	8.69
3 =	Fréjus, France/Italy	1980	12.90	8.02
=	Pinglin Highway, Taiwan	u/c*	12.90	8.02
5	Mt. Blanc, France/Italy	1965	11.60	7.21
6	Gudvangen, Norway	1992	11.40	7.08
7	Leirfjord, Norway	u/c*	11.11	6.90
8	Kan–Etsu, Japan	1991	11.01	6.84
9	Kan–Etsu, Japan	1985	10.93	6.79
10	Gran Sasso, Italy	1984	10.17	6.32

* u/c = under construction

TOP 10 LONGEST UNDERWATER TUNNELS IN THE WORLD
(Length)

❶ Seikan, Japan (53.90 km/33.49 miles) ❷ Channel Tunnel, France/England (49.94 km/31.03 miles) ❸ Dai-Shimizu, Japan (22.17 km/13.78 miles) ❹ Shin-Kanmon, Japan (18.68 km/ 11.61 miles) ❺ Great Belt Fixed Link (Eastern Tunnel), Denmark (8.00 km/4.97 miles) ❻ Severn, UK (7.01 km/4.46 miles) ❼ Haneda, Japan (5.98 km/3.72 miles) ❽ BART, San Francisco, USA (5.83 km/3.62 miles) ❾ Kammon, Japan (3.60 km/2.24 miles) ❿ Kammon, Japan (3.46 km/2.15 miles)

T O P 1 0

LONGEST TUNNELS IN THE UK*

	Tunnel/location	Type	Length km	miles
1	Severn, Avon/Gwent	Rail	7.02	4.36
2	Totley, South Yorkshire	Rail	5.70	3.54
3	Standedge, Manchester/West Yorkshire	Canal	5.10	3.17
4 =	Standedge, Manchester/West Yorkshire	Rail	4.89	3.04
=	Woodhead New, South Yorkshire	Rail	4.89	3.04
6	Sodbury, Avon	Rail	4.07	2.53
7	Strood, Kent	Rail#	3.57	2.22
8	Disley, Cheshire	Rail	3.54	2.20
9	Ffestiniog, Gwynedd	Rail	3.52	2.19
10	Sapperton, Gloucestershire	Canal	3.49	2.17

* Excluding underground railways

 # Formerly canal

THE CHANNEL TUNNEL
First proposed almost 200 years ago, the Channel Tunnel was finally opened in 1994. It is Europe's longest and the world's second longest undersea rail tunnel.

OTHER STRUCTURES

HIGHEST DAMS IN THE WORLD

	Dam	Location	Completed	Height m	ft
1	Rogun	Vakhsh, Tajikstan	u/c*	335	1,099
2	Nurek	Vakhsh, Tajikstan	1980	300	984
3	Grand Dixence	Dixence, Switzerland	1961	285	935
4	Inguri	Inguri, Georgia	1980	272	892
5	Chicoasén	Grijalva, Mexico	u/c*	261	856
6	Tehri	Bhagirathi, India	u/c*	261	856
7	Kishau	Tons, India	u/c*	253	830
8	Ertan	Yangtse-kiang, China	u/c*	245	804
9	Sayano-Shushensk	Yeniesei, Russia	u/c*	245	804
10	Guavio	Guavio, Colombia	u/c*	243	797

* *u/c = under construction*

HIGH ASWAN DAM AND LAKE
*Containing 18 times the amount of material used in the
Great Pyramid of Cheops, the High Aswan Dam has
created the third largest artificial lake in the world.*

LARGEST-VOLUME DAMS IN THE WORLD

(*Ranked according to the volume of material used in construction*)

	Dam/location	Completed	Volume (m³)
1	Syncrude Tailings, Alberta, Canada	1992	540,000,000
2	Pati, Paraná, Argentina	1990	230,180,000
3	New Cornelia, Ten Mile Wash, Tailings Arizona, USA	1973	209,500,000
4	Tarbela, Indus, Pakistan	1976	105,922,000
5	Fort Peck, Missouri, Montana, USA	1937	96,050,000
6	Lower Usuma, Usuma, Nigeria	1990	93,000,000
7	Atatürk, Euphrates, Turkey	1990	84,500,000
8	Yacyreta-Apipe, Paraná, Paraguay/Argentina	1991	81,000,000
9	Guri (Raul Leoni), Caroni, Venezuela	1986	77,971,000
10	Rogun, Vakhsh, Tajikstan	1987	75,500,000

Numerous major projects are in development for completion by
the end of the century, by which time this Top 10 will contain
some exciting new entries throughout the world.

LARGEST MAN-MADE LAKES IN THE WORLD*

	Dam/lake	Location	Completed	Volume (m³)
1	Owen Falls	Uganda	1954	204,800,000,000
2	Bratsk	Russia	1964	169,900,000,000
3	High Aswan	Egypt	1970	162,000,000,000
4	Kariba	Zimbabwe	1959	160,368,000,000
5	Akosombo	Ghana	1965	147,960,000,000
6	Daniel Johnson	Canada	1968	141,851,000,000
7	Guri (Raul Leoni)	Venezuela	1986	135,000,000,000
8	Krasnoyarsk	Russia	1967	73,300,000,000
9	W.A.C. Bennett	Canada	1967	70,309,000,000
10	Zeya	Russia	1978	68,400,000,000

* *Includes only those formed as a result of dam construction*

The enlargement of the existing natural lake that resulted from the
construction of the Owen Falls not only created the largest reservoir
in the world, but also the man-made lake with the greatest surface
area: at 69,484 sq km/26,828 sq miles, it is almost as large as the
Republic of Ireland. The building of the Akosombo Dam on the
River Volta, Ghana, created a lake that occupies some four per
cent of the entire area of the country.

TOP 10

LONGEST FLIGHTS OF STAIRS IN THE WORLD

	Stairs/location	Steps
1	Niesenbahn funicular railway, Spiez, Switzerland	11,674
2	T'ai Chan Temple, China	6,600
3	Mår Power Station, Norway	3,875
4	Aura Power Station, Norway	3,715
5	CN Tower, Toronto, Canada	3,642
6	Ostankino Tower, Moscow, Russia	3,544
7	World Trade Centre, New York, USA	3,140
8	Empire State Building, New York, USA	2,908
9	Sears Tower, Chicago, USA	2,906
10	Tokyo Tower, Tokyo, Japan	2,184

TOP 10

LONGEST SEASIDE PIERS IN THE UK

	Pier/location	Length m	ft
1	Southend, Essex	2,158.0	7,080
2	Southport, Merseyside	1,107.3	3,633
3	Walton-on-the-Naze, Essex	792.5	2,600
4	Ryde, Isle of Wight	702.6	2,305
5	Llandudno, Gwynedd	699.5	2,295
6	Ramsey, Isle of Man	683.1	2,241
7	Hythe, Hampshire	640.1	2,100
8	Brighton (Palace Pier), East Sussex	536.5	1,760
9	Bangor (Garth Pier), Gwynedd	472.4	1,550
10	Weston Super Mare (Birnbeck Pier), Avon	411.5	1,350

TOP 10

LARGEST BELLS IN THE WESTERN WORLD

	Bell/location	Year cast	Weight (tonnes)
1	*Tsar Kolokol*, Kremlin, Moscow, Russia	1735	201.90
2	*Voskresenskiy (Resurrection)*, Ivan the Great Bell Tower, Kremlin, Moscow, Russia	1746	65.50
3	*Petersglocke*, Cologne cathedral, Germany	1923	25.40
4	Lisbon cathedral, Portugal	post-1344	24.40
5	St. Stephen's cathedral, Vienna, Austria	1957	21.39
6	Bourdon, Strasbourg cathedral, France	1521	20.00
7	*Savoyarde*, Sacre-Coeur basilica, Paris, France	1891	18.85
8	Bourdon, Riverside Church, New York, USA	1931	18.54
9	Olmütz, Czech Republic	1931	18.19
10	*Campagna gorda*, Toledo cathedral, Spain	1753	17.27

The largest bell in the world is the 6.14-m/20-ft 2-in high 6.6-m/21-ft 8-in diameter *Tsar Kolokol*, cast in Moscow for the Kremlin. It cracked before it had been installed and has remained there, unrung, ever since. New York's Riverside Church bell (the largest ever cast in England) is the bourdon (that sounding the lowest note) of the 74-bell Laura Spelman Rockefeller Memorial Carillon.

TOP 10

LARGEST SPORTS STADIUMS IN THE WORLD

	Stadium	Location	Capacity
1	Strahov Stadium	Prague, Czech Republic	240,000
2	Maracaña Municipa Stadium	Rio de Janeiro, Brazil	205,000
3	Rungnado Stadium	Pyongyang, North Korea	150,000
4	Estadio Maghalaes Pinto	Belo Horizonte, Brazil	125,000
5 =	Estadio Morumbi	São Paulo, Brazil	120,000
=	Estadio da Luz	Lisbon, Portugal	120,000
=	Senayan Main Stadium	Jakarta, Indonesia	120,000
=	Yuba Bharati Krirangan	nr. Calcutta, India	120,000
9	Estadio Castelão	Fortaleza, Brazil	119,000
10 =	Estadio Arrudão	Recife, Brazil	115,000
=	Estadio Azteca	Mexico City, Mexico	115,000
=	Nou Camp	Barcelona, Spain	115,000

The Aztec Stadium, Mexico City, holds 107,000, with most of the seats under cover. The New Orleans Superdome is the largest indoor stadium, with a capacity of 97,365. The largest stadium in the United Kingdom is Wembley Stadium with a capacity of 80,000.

CULTURE & LEARNING

TOP 10

COUNTRIES WITH THE HIGHEST PROPORTION OF WOMEN IN UNIVERSITY EDUCATION

	Country	Percentage of women*
1	United Arab Emirates	78
2	Cyprus	77
3	Qatar	72
4	Mongolia	70
5	Kuwait	66
6	Myanmar (Burma)	64
7	Barbados	63
8	Bulgaria	61
9 =	Cuba	60
=	Panama	60
	UK	*45*
	USA	*53*

* *Percentage of women out of the total number of university students*

TOP 10

COUNTRIES THAT SPEND THE MOST ON EDUCATION

	Country	Annual expenditure (as percentage of GNP)
1	Uzbekistan	11.0
2	Tajikistan	9.5
3	Norway	9.2
4	Namibia	8.7
5 =	Botswana	8.5

	Country	Annual expenditure (as percentage of GNP)
5 =	Denmark	8.5
7 =	Finland	8.4
=	Sweden	8.4
9 =	Congo	8.3
=	Zimbabwe	8.3
	USA	*5.5*
	UK	*5.2*

Since the list ranks countries spending the most on education as a percentage of Gross National Product, it includes several African countries with very small GNPs. Also figuring prominently in this, and just outside the Top 10, are several former Soviet countries that have inherited a relatively highly developed and expensive education system, but whose GNPs have collapsed following the break-up of the Soviet Union. As these countries adapt to their new economic and political situation, their GNP's are likely to increase, and spending on education as a percentage of GNP will shrink, so they may be expected to disappear from the list.

Source: UNESCO

ST. JOHN'S COLLEGE, CAMBRIDGE UNIVERSITY

TOP TEN COUNTRIES WITH THE MOST UNIVERSITY STUDENTS

(No. of students per 100,000 population)

❶ Canada (6,980) ❷ USA (5,546)
❸ Korea (4,756) ❹ New Zealand (4,675)
❺ Norway (4,111) ❻ Finland (3,902)
❼ Spain (3,719) ❽ Armenia (3,711)
❾ France (3,623) ❿ Netherlands (3,352)
UK (2,788)
Source: UNESCO

T O P   1 0

LARGEST UNIVERSITIES IN THE WORLD

	University	Students
1	University of Paris, France	308,904
2	University of Calcutta, India	300,000
3	University of Bombay, India	262,350
4	University of Mexico, Mexico	261,693
5	University of Guadalajara, Mexico	214,986
6	University of Buenos Aires, Argentina	206,658
7	University of Rome, Italy	184,000
8	University of Rajasthan, India	175,000
9	University of Wisconsin	154,620
10	State University of New York, USA	146,873

The huge number of university institutions in India reflects the country's population and the high value placed on education in Indian culture, but also the inclusion of many "Affiliating and Teaching" colleges attached to universities. Several other universities in the US, India, Egypt, and Italy have more than 100,000 students.

T O P   1 0

COUNTRIES WITH THE LONGEST SCHOOL YEARS

	Country	School year (days)
1	China	251
2	Japan	243
3	Korea	220
4	Israel	215
5=	Germany	210
=	Russia	210
7	Switzerland	207
8=	Netherlands	200
=	Scotland	200
=	Thailand	200
	England	*192*
	USA	*180*

T O P   1 0

LARGEST UNIVERSITIES IN THE UK*

	University	Full-time students
1	Manchester Metropolitan	28,433
2	University of Wolverhampton	23,874
3	University of Sheffield	23,625
4	University of Leeds	23,125
5	University of Birmingham	22,567
6	Nottingham Trent University	22,542
7	Victoria University of Manchester	22,282
8	University of Nottingham	22,143
9	De Montfort University	21,242
10	University of Strathclyde	20,378

* Excluding The Open University

T O P   1 0

COUNTRIES WITH THE MOST SECONDARY-SCHOOL STUDENTS

	Country	Secondary-school students		Country	Secondary-school students
1	India	64,115,978	6	Japan	10,202,510
2	China	53,837,300	7	Germany	7,796,256
3	USA	20,578,000	8	Iran	7,652,829
4	Russia	13,732,000	9	Mexico	7,264,650
5	Indonesia	11,360,349	10	Egypt	6,138,263
	Source: UNESCO			*UK*	*4,537,000*

BOOK RECORDS

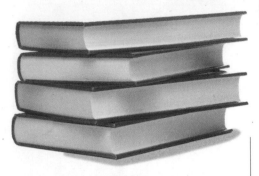

FIRST PENGUIN PAPERBACKS*

Author/book

1 André Maurois, *Ariel*

2 Ernest Hemingway, *A Farewell to Arms*

3 Eric Linklater, *Poet's Pub*

4 Susan Ertz, *Madame Claire*

5 Dorothy L. Sayers, *The Unpleasantness at the Bellona Club*

6 Agatha Christie, *The Mysterious Affair at Styles*

7 Beverley Nichols, *Twenty-five*

8 E. H. Young, *William*

9 Mary Webb, *Gone to Earth*

10 Compton Mackenzie, *Carnival*

* Published 30 July 1935

TYPES OF BOOK PUBLISHED IN THE UK

	Subject	New titles published 1997
1	Fiction	8,965
2	Children's	8,208
3	Economics	4,305
4	Social sciences	4,254
5	History	4,168
6	Religion	4,109
7	Medicine	4,052
8	Biography	3,164
9	Management	3,086
10	School textbooks	3,049

MOST EXPENSIVE BOOKS/MANUSCRIPTS EVER SOLD AT AUCTION

	Book/manuscript/sale	Price (£)*
1	*The Codex Hammer*, Christie's, New York, 11th November 1994 ($30,800,000)	19,230,000

This is one of Leonardo da Vinci's notebooks, which includes many scientific drawings and diagrams. It was purchased by Bill Gates, the billionaire founder of Microsoft.

2	*The Gospels of Henry the Lion*, c.1173-75, Sotheby's, London, 6 December 1983	7,400,000

At the time of its sale, it became the most expensive manuscript, book, or work of art other than a painting ever sold.

3	*The Gutenberg Bible*, 1455, Christie's, New York, 22 October 1987 ($5,390,000)	2,934,131

One of the first books ever printed, by Johann Gutenberg and Johann Fust in 1455, it holds the record for the most expensive printed book.

4	*The Northumberland Bestiary*, c.1250–60, Sotheby's, London, 29 November 1990	2,700,000

The highest price ever paid for an English manuscript.

5	Autograph manuscript of nine symphonies by Wolfgang Amadeus Mozart, c.1773–74, Sotheby's, London, 22 May 1987	2,350,000

The record for a music manuscript.

* Excluding premiums

	Book/manuscript/sale	Price (£)*
6	John James Audubon's *The Birds of America*, 1827–38, Sotheby's, New York, 6 June 1989 ($3,600,000)	2,292,993

The record for any natural history book. Further copies of the same book, a collection of more than 400 large, hand-coloured engravings, have also fetched high prices. A facsimile reprint of Audubon's The Birds of America *published in 1985 by Abbeville Press, New York, is listed at $30,000/£15,000 – the most expensive book ever published.*

7	The Bible in Hebrew, Sotheby's, London, 5 December 1989	1,850,000

A manuscript written in Iraq, Syria, or Babylon in the 9th or 10th century, it holds the record for any Hebrew manuscript.

8	*The Monypenny Breviary*, illuminated manuscript, c.1490–95, Sotheby's, London, 19 June 1989	1,700,000

The record for any French manuscript.

9	*The Hours and Psalter of Elizabeth de Bohun, Countess of Northampton*, c.1340–45, Sotheby's, London, 21 June 1988	1,400,000

10	Schumann's Second Symphony, Sotheby's, London, 1 December 1994	1,350,000

Completed in 1847, this manuscript was lost to scholars for more than 50 years. It achieved the record for a single musical work.

100 YEARS OF BOOK BLURBS

Two New York publishers, Harper and Dodd Mead, first featured brief descriptions on their book jackets in 1899, but it was several years before these descriptions were given a name. At a booksellers' dinner in 1907, as a publicity gimmick, humour author Frank Gelett Burgess (1866–1951) gave away copies of his latest book, entitled *Are You a Bromide?*, with a specially designed cover featuring an imaginary author called "Miss Belinda Blurb", who Burgess claimed had written the "sensation of the year". By doing so, he invented the word "blurb", which is what these often exaggerated summaries have been called ever since.

THE 10
FIRST BOOKS PUBLISHED BY EVERYMAN'S LIBRARY

	Author/book
1	James Boswell, *The Life of Samuel Johnson, Vol. I*
2	James Boswell, *The Life of Samuel Johnson, Vol. II*
3	John Gibson Lockhart, *History of Napoleon Bonaparte*
4	Hans Christian Andersen, *Fairy Tales and Stories*
5	Nathaniel Hawthorne, *A Wonder Book, and Tanglewood Tales*
6	William Henry Kingston, *Peter the Whaler*
7	William Henry Kingston, *The Three Midshipmen*
8	Charles Lamb, *Tales from Shakespeare*
9	Marcus Aurelius, *The Meditations of Marcus Aurelius*
10	Francis Bacon, *Essays*

The first books in British publisher J.M. Dent's Everyman's Library series were issued in 1906. Within 50 years, the number of titles had reached 1,000.

THE 10
FIRST PUBLICATIONS PRINTED IN ENGLAND

	Author/book	Year
1	*Propositio ad Carolum ducem Burgundiae*	1476
2	Cato, *Disticha de Morbidus*	1476-77
3	Geoffrey Chaucer, *The Canterbury Tales*	1476-77
4	*Ordinale seu Pica ad usem Sarum ("Sarum Pie")*	1476-77
5	John Lydgate, *The Temple of Glass*	1476-77
6	John Lydgate, *Stans puer mensam*	1476-77
7	John Lydgate, *The Horse, the Sheep and the Goose*	1476-77
8	John Lydgate, *The Churl and the Bird*	1476-77
9	*Infanta Salvatoris*	1476-77
10	William Caxton, advertisement for *"Sarum Pie"*	1476-77

PRINTING PRESS
The first mechanized printing presses began to be used early in the 17th century.

THE 10
FIRST BOOKS PUBLISHED IN THE US

	Book	Year
1	*Massachusetts Bay Colony: The Oath of a Free-Man*	1638
2	*An Almanack for the Year of our Lord 1639*	1639
3	*An Almanack for the Year of our Lord 1640*	1640
4	*Bay Psalm Book*	1640
5	*An Almanack for the Year of our Lord 1641*	1641
6	*Massachusetts Bay Colony: The Liberties of the Massachusetts Colonie in New England*	1641
7	*A Short Catechism, Agreed Upon by the Elders at the Desire of the General Court*	1641
8	*An Almanack for the Year of our Lord 1642*	1642
9	*Harvard College: Theses Philologicas, Theses Philosophicas*	1642
10	*Massachusetts Bay Colony: By the Court – In the Yeares 1641, 1642. Capital Lawes, Established Within the Jurisdiction of Massachusets. The Oath of a Free-Man*	1642

Source: Charles Evans, The American Bibliography of Charles Evans, 1903–34

WORD POWER

TOP 10
LONGEST WORDS IN THE OXFORD ENGLISH DICTIONARY*

	Word (first used)	Letters
1	Pneumonoultramicroscopicsilico-volcanoconiosis (1936)	45
2	Supercalifragilisticexpialidocious (1964)	34
3	Pseudopseudohypoparathyroidism (1952)	30
4	Floccinaucinihilipilification (1741)	29
5 =	Antidisestablishmentarianism (1923)	28
=	Hepaticocholangiogastrostomy (1933)	28
=	Octamethylcyclotetrasiloxane (1946)	28
=	Tetrachlorodibenzoparadioxin (1959)	28
9 =	Radioimmunoelectrophoresis (1962)	26
=	Radioimmunoelectrophoretic (1962)	26

*Words that are hyphenated, including compound words, have not been included

TOP 10
WORDS WITH THE MOST MEANINGS IN THE OXFORD ENGLISH DICTIONARY

	Word	Meanings
1	Set	464
2	Run	396
3	Go	368
4	Take	343
5	Stand	334
6	Get	289
7	Turn	288
8	Put	268
9	Fall	264
10	Strike	250

TOP 10
MOST STUDIED FOREIGN LANGUAGES IN THE US*

	Language	Registrations
1	Spanish	606,286
2	French	205,351
3	German	96,263
4	Japanese	44,723
5	Italian	43,760
6	Chinese	26,471
7	Latin	25,897
8	Russian	24,729
9	Ancient Greek	16,272
10	Hebrew	13,127#

* In US Institutions of Higher Education
# Comprises 5,648 registrations in Biblical Hebrew and 7,479 in Modern Hebrew

These figures are from the most recent survey conducted every five years, from colleges and universities in the autumn of 1995, which indicated a total of 1,138,772 foreign language registrations.

Source: Modern Language Association of America

TOP 10
MOST COMMONLY MISSPELLED ENGLISH WORDS

1	consensus
2	innovate
3	practice/practise
4	facsimile
5	instalment
6	supersede
7	fulfil
8	withhold
9	occurred
10	possession

This list is based on the mistakes most frequently made by entrants for the Royal Society of Arts Examinations Board's Spelltest for Officeworkers.

TOP 10
MOST WIDELY SPOKEN LANGUAGES IN THE EC

	Language	Approx. no. of speakers*
1	German	86,562,000
2	English	59,735,000
3	French	58,084,000
4	Italian	55,320,000
5	Spanish (Castilian)	31,398,000
6	Dutch	20,711,000
7	Portuguese	10,622,000
8	Greek	10,411,000
9	Swedish	8,207,000
10	Catalan	5,120,000

* As a "first language", including speakers resident in EC countries other than those where it is the main language, such as German-speakers living in France

Sweden's joining the European Union on 1 January 1995 means that Danish has dropped out of this list.

TOP 10
MOST STUDIED FOREIGN LANGUAGES IN THE UK

1	French
2	Spanish
3	Arabic
4	Chinese (Mandarin)
5	German
6	Italian
7	Russian
8	Japanese
9	Dutch
10	Portuguese

This ranking is based on language courses studied at the School of Languages at the University of Westminster, the largest source of language teaching in the state sector in the whole of Europe.

TOP 10
MOST USED LETTERS IN WRITTEN ENGLISH

	i	ii
1	e	e
2	t	t
3	a	a
4	o	i
5	i	n
6	n	o
7	s	s
8	r	h
9	h	r
10	l	d

Column i is the order indicated by a survey across approximately 1,000,000 words appearing in a wide variety of printed texts. Column ii is the order estimated by Samuel Morse, the inventor in the 1830s of Morse Code, based on his calculations of the respective quantities of type used by a printer.

TOP 10
MOST WIDELY SPOKEN LANGUAGES IN THE WORLD

	Language	Approximate no. of speakers
1	Chinese (Mandarin)	1,034,000,000
2	English	500,000,000
3	Hindustani	478,000,000
4	Spanish	413,000,000
5	Russian	280,000,000
6	Arabic	230,000,000
7	Bengali	204,000,000
8	Portuguese	186,000,000
9	Malay-Indonesian	164,000,000
10=	French	126,000,000
=	Japanese	126,000,000

According to 1997 estimates by Sidney S. Culbert of the University of Washington, there are only two other languages spoken by more than 100,000,000 people: German (124,000,000) and Urdu (104,000,000).

TOP 10
MOST WIDELY SPOKEN LANGUAGES IN THE US

	Language	Approximate no. of speakers
1	English	198,601,000
2	Spanish	17,339,172
3	French	1,702,176
4	German	1,547,099
5	Italian	1,308,648
6	Chinese	1,249,213
7	Tagalog	843,251
8	Polish	723,483
9	Korean	626,478
10	Vietnamese	507,069

Source: US Bureau of the Census

TOP 10
MOST COMMON WORDS IN ENGLISH

Spoken English		Written English
the	1	the
and	2	of
I	3	to
to	4	in
of	5	and
a	6	a
you	7	for
that	8	was
in	9	is
it	10	that

Various surveys have been conducted to establish the most common words in spoken English of various types, from telephone conversations to broadcast commentaries. Beyond the Top 10, various other words, such as "yes" and "well", also appear with far greater frequency in everyday speech than in the comparative list of the most common words in written English, which is based on a survey of newspaper usages.

TOP 10
COUNTRIES WITH THE MOST ENGLISH-LANGUAGE SPEAKERS

	Country	Approximate no. of speakers
1	USA	228,770,000
2	UK	57,190,000
3	Canada	18,112,000
4	Australia	15,538,000
5	South Africa	3,800,000
6	Irish Republic	3,540,000
7	New Zealand	3,290,000
8	Jamaica	2,390,000
9	Trinidad and Tobago	1,189,000
10	Guyana	692,000

TOP 10
LANGUAGES OFFICIALLY SPOKEN IN THE MOST COUNTRIES

	Language	Countries
1	English	54
2	French	33
3	Arabic	24
4	Spanish	21
5	Portuguese	8
6	German	5
7=	Malay	4
=	Dutch	4
9	Chinese (Mandarin)	3
10=	Italian	2
=	Russian	2
=	Tamil	2

There are many countries in the world with more than one official language – both English and French are recognized officially in Canada, for example. English is also used in numerous countries as the lingua franca, the common language that enables people who speak mutually unintelligible languages to communicate with each other.

120 LIBRARIES OF THE WORLD

TOP 10

LARGEST REFERENCE LIBRARIES IN THE UK

	Library	Founded	Books
1	British Library, London	1753	13,000,000
2	Bodleian Library, Oxford	1602	6,100,000
3	National Library of Scotland, Edinburgh	1682	6,000,000
4	University Library, Cambridge	c.1400	5,850,000
5	National Library of Wales, Aberystwyth	1907	5,000,000
6	British Library of Political and Economic Science, London School of Economics	1894	4,000,000
7	John Rylands University Library of Manchester	1972*	3,500,000
8	University of Edinburgh	1580	2,600,000
9	University of Leeds	1874	2,500,000
10	University of Birmingham	1880	2,000,000

* *In 1972 the John Rylands Library (founded 1900) was amalgamated with Manchester University Library (founded 1851)*

The top five libraries listed here are "copyright deposit libraries". By law one copy of every book published in the UK must be deposited with each of these libraries within one month of publication. In addition to the books held by these libraries, many have substantial holdings of manuscripts, periodicals, and other printed materials: the Bodleian Library, for example, has almost 1,000,000 maps, and the British Library of Political and Economic Science's total includes periodicals as well as books; its books-only figure is believed to be closer to 2,000,000, placing it in 10= position. Recently, the number of documents held in electronic form or on microfiche has also increased dramatically.

TOP 10

LARGEST LIBRARIES IN THE WORLD

	Library	Location	Founded	Books
1	Library of Congress	Washington DC, USA	1800	23,041,334
2	National Library of China	Beijing, China	1909	15,980,636
3	National Library of Canada	Ottawa, Canada	1953	14,500,000
4	Deutsche Bibliothek*	Frankfurt, Germany	1990	14,350,000
5	British Library#	London, UK	1753	13,000,000
6	Harvard University Library	Cambridge, Massachusetts, USA	1638	12,877,360
7	Russian State Library†	Moscow, Russia	1862	11,750,000
8	National Diet Library	Tokyo, Japan	1948	11,304,139
9	New York Public Library	New York, USA	1895★	10,505,079
10	Yale University Library	New Haven, Conneticut, USA	1701	9,485,823

* *Formed in 1990 through the unification of the Deutsche Bibliothek, Frankfurt (founded 1947) and the Deutsche Bucherei, Leipzig*

\# *Founded as part of the British Museum, 1753, became an independent body in 1973*

† *Founded 1862 as Rumyantsev Library, formerly State V.I. Lenin Library*

★ *Astor Library founded 1848, consolidated with Lenox Library and Tilden Trust to form New York Public Library in 1895*

The figures for books in such vast collections as held by the libraries listed above represent only a fraction of the total collections, which include manuscripts, microfilms, maps, prints, and records. The Library of Congress has perhaps more than 100,000,000 catalogued items and the New York Public Library more than 26,000,000 manuscripts, maps, audio-visual, and other catalogued items in addition to books.

THE NEW BRITISH LIBRARY
After controversy over the expense of the building, the New British Library finally opened in November 1997. It will take until the turn of the century to complete the move of some 13 million books.

TOP 10

MOST BORROWED ADULT AUTHORS IN THE UK, 1996–97

1	Catherine Cookson
2	Danielle Steel
3	Dick Francis
4	Ruth Rendell
5	Agatha Christie
6	Jack Higgins
7	Josephine Cox
8	Terry Pratchett
9	Ellis Peters
10	Virginia Andrews

Source: Public Lending Right

TOP 10

MOST BORROWED CLASSIC AUTHORS IN THE UK, 1996–97

1	Beatrix Potter
2	Daphne Du Maurier
3	Jane Austen
4	A. A. Milne
5	William Shakespeare
6	Thomas Hardy
7	Charles Dickens
8	J. R. R. Tolkien
9	Anthony Trollope
10	E. M. Forster

Source: Public Lending Right

TOP 10

MOST BORROWED CHILDREN'S AUTHORS IN THE UK, 1996–97

1	R. L. Stine
2	Janet and Allan Ahlberg
3	Roald Dahl
4	Ann M. Martin
5	Edith Blyton
6	Dick King-Smith
7	Goscinny
8	Eric Hill
9	John Cunliffe
10	Shirley Hughes

Source: Public Lending Right

THE 10

FIRST PUBLIC LIBRARIES IN THE US

	Library	Founded
1	Peterboro Public Library, Peterboro, New Hampshire	1833
2	New Orleans Public Library, New Orleans, Louisiana	1843
3	Boston Public Library, Boston, Massachusetts	1852
4	Public Library of Cincinnati and Hamilton County, Cincinnati, Ohio	1853
5	Springfield City Library, Springfield, Massachusetts	1857
6	Worcester Public Library, Worcester, Massachusets	1859
7	County Library, Portland, Oregon	1864
8=	Detroit Public Library, Detroit, Michigan	1865
=	St. Louis Public Library, St. Louis, Missouri	1865
10	Atlanta-Fulton Public Library, Atlanta, Georgia	1867

THE 10

FIRST PUBLIC LIBRARIES IN THE UK

	Library	Founded
1	Manchester Free Library	1852
2	Liverpool	1852
3	Sheffield	1856
4	Birmingham	1860
5	Cardiff	1862
6	Nottinghamshire	1868
7	Dundee	1869
8	Glasgow (Mitchell Library)	1874
9	Aberdeen	1884
10	Edinburgh	1890

Various specialist institutions, such as theological libraries, existed in Britain as early as the 17th century, and were joined in the 19th century by others that charged a small fee to borrowers. Following the passing of the 1850 Public Libraries Act, the Manchester Free Library, which opened its doors on 6 September 1852, became the country's first free municipally-supported lending library open to the public.

TOP 10

LARGEST PUBLIC LIBRARIES IN THE UK*

	Library	Founded	Books
1	Hampshire	1974	3,500,000
2	Kent	1921	3,300,000
3	Lancashire	1924	3,189,800
4	Essex	1926	3,006,349
5	Glasgow	1877	2,557,554
6	Manchester	1852	2,430,000
7=	Devon	1974	2,000,000
=	Leeds	1870	2,000,000
=	Liverpool	1852	2,000,000
10	Hertfordshire	1925	1,932,393

* Figures for books held by counties; figures for individual public libraries not available

ENGLISH-LANGUAGE BESTSELLERS

THEN & NOW

TOP 10 FICTION TITLES IN THE UK

1987 Title/author	Sales		Sales	1997 Title/author
A Matter of Honour, Jeffrey Archer	680,000	1	611,000	*Bridget Jones's Diary*, Helen Fielding
The Moth, Catherine Cookson	579,000	2	243,000	*Evening Class*, Maeve Binchy
Act of Will, Barbara Taylor Bradford	541,000	3	231,000	*High Fidelity*, Nick Hornby
Hollywood Husbands, Jackie Collins	490,000	4	223,000	*The Runaway Jury*, John Grisham
A Perfect Spy, John Le Carré	461,000	5	215,000	*The Upstart*, Catherine Cookson,
The Magic Cottage, James Herbert	425,000	6	210,000	*Captain Corelli's Mandolin*, Louis de Bernières
Power of the Sword, Wilbur Smith	357,000	7	193,000	*Appassionata*, Jilly Cooper
Break-In, Dick Francis	341,000	8	185,000	*The Woman Who Walked Into Doors*, Roddy Doyle
Bolt, Dick Francis	327,000	9	173,000	*Cause of Death*, Patricia. D. Cornwell
It, Stephen King	291,000	10	164,000	*Hogfather*, Terry Pratchett

Source: Bookwatch

TOP 10

HARDBACK FICTION TITLES OF 1997 IN THE UK

	Title/author	Sales
1	*Jingo*, Terry Pratchett	124,000
2	*The God of Small Things*, Arundhati Roy	115,000
3	*10-lb Penalty*, Dick Francis	106,000
4	*Unnatural Exposure*, Patricia D. Cornwell	103,000
5	*Remote Control*, Andy McNab	100,000
6	*Birds of Prey*, Wilbur Smith	88,000
7	*The Partner*, John Grisham	79,000
8	*A Certain Justice*, P. D. James	78,000
9	*Road Rage*, Ruth Rendell	45,000
10	*Excalibur*, Bernard Cornwell	43,000

Source: Bookwatch

SNAP FACT

• Although there were bestsellers before 1889, none was so called until Thursday, 25 April of that year, when the US newspaper the *Kansas Times and Star* listed six books as the "best sellers here ever last week" – the first occasion the phrase appeared in print.

TOP 10

CHILDREN'S TITLES OF 1997 IN THE UK

	Title/author	Sales
1	*The Beano Book 1998*	123,000
2	*Teletubbies: The Flying Toast*	84,000
3	*Teletubbies: La Laa's Ball*	70,000
4	*Teletubbies: The Magic Flag*	63,000
5	*Teletubbies: Tinky Winky's Bag*	61,000
6	*Goosebumps: The Headless Ghost*, R. L. Stine	60,000
7	*Matilda*, Roald Dahl	53,000
8	*Goosebumps Flashing Special*, R. L. Stine	52,000
9	*The Teletubbies Play Hide and Seek*	45,000
10	*Totally 100% Unofficial Special Spice Girls*	44,000

Source: Bookwatch

FROM BLANK PAGES TO BESTSELLER

American author Elbert Hubbard (1856–1915) can be credited with writing both the shortest and one of the bestselling books of all time. In 1898 he published his *Essay on Silence*, a book containing only blank pages. Then, in 1899, he turned his essay *A Message to García* into a pamphlet that was to become one of the bestselling works ever. Now largely forgotten, Hubbard's polemic on the subject of labour relations achieved phenomenal sales at the time, primarily because many employers bought bulk supplies to distribute to their employees. The literary career of Elbert Hubbard was cut short on 7 May 1915 when he went down with the British passenger liner *Lusitania*, torpedoed by a German submarine with the loss of 1,198 civilians.

100 YEARS AGO • YEARS AGO • YEARS AGO

T H E N & N O W

TOP 10 GENERAL NON-FICTION TITLES IN THE UK

1987 Title/author	Sales		Sales	1997 Title/author
How to be a Complete Bitch, Pamela Stephenson	250,000	**1**	465,000	*Notes from a Small Island*, Bill Bryson
Wicked Willie's Low Down on Men, Gray Joliffe & Peter Mayle	210,000	**2**	379,000	*Full Circle*, Michael Palin
One Day for Life, Sarah, Duchess of York (intro.)	170,000	**3**	324,000	*The Little Book of Calm*, Paul Wilson
500-Mile Walkies, Mark Wallington	162,000	**4**	322,000	*Diana: Her True Story in Her Own Words*, Andrew Morton
Backcloth, Dirk Bogarde	150,000	**5**	244,000	*Angela's Ashes*, Frank McCourt
Goodbye Soldier, Spike Milligan	148,000	**6**	223,000	*A Walk in the Woods*, Bill Bryson
Cartoons, Giles	143,000	**7**	202,000	*Men are from Mars, Women are from Venus*, John Gray
His Way, Kitty Kelley	111,000	**8**	185,000	*My Autobiography*, "Dickie" Bird
84 Charing Cross Road, Helene Hanff	102,000	**9**	161,000	*Fever Pitch*, Nick Hornby
The Ultimate Alphabet, Mike Wilkes	94,000	**10**	128,000	*Longitude*, Dava Sobel

Source: Bookwatch

T O P 1 0

REFERENCE TITLES OF 1997 IN THE UK

	Title/author	Sales
1	*Delia's Red Nose Collection*, Delia Smith	537,000
2	*The Highway Code*	420,000
3	*Official Theory Test: Cars and Motorcycles* (2nd edition), Driving Standards Agency	148,000
4	*The Guinness Book Of Records 1998*	135,000
5	*Official Theory Test: Cars and Motorcycles* (1st edition), Driving Standards Agency	96,000
6	*BBC Proms* 1997	69,000
7	*Gardens of England and Wales Open to the Public for Charity 1997*	66,000
8	*Two Fat Ladies Ride Again*, Jennifer Paterson and Clarissa Dickson-Wright	64,000
9	*Delia Smith's Complete Cookery Course*, Delia Smith	63,000
10	*Delia Smith's Winter Collection*, Delia Smith	62,000

Source: Bookwatch

MICHAEL CRICHTON
US author Michael Crichton's Jurassic Park *has remained at the top of the list of bestselling novels of the 1990s in the UK.*

T O P 1 0

BESTSELLING BOOKS OF ALL TIME

	Book	Approx. sales
1	*The Bible*	6,000,000,000
2	*Quotations from the Works of Mao Tse-tung*	800,000,000
3	*American Spelling Book*, Noah Webster	100,000,000
4	*The Guinness Book of Records*	80,000,000*
5	*The McGuffey Readers*, William Holmes McGuffey	60,000,000
6	*A Message to García*, Elbert Hubbard	40–50,000,000
7	*World Almanac*	over 40,000,000*
8	*The Common Sense Book of Baby and Child Care*, Benjamin Spock	over 39,200,000
9	*Valley of the Dolls*, Jacqueline Susann	30,000,000
10	*In His Steps: "What Would Jesus Do?"*, Rev. Charles Monroe Sheldon	28,500,000

* *Aggregate sales of annual publication*

It is difficult to establish precise sales even of contemporary books, and virtually impossible to do so with books published long ago. How many copies of the *Complete Works of Shakespeare* have been sold in countless editions? This Top 10 list offers no more than the "best guess" at the great bestsellers of the past.

TOP 10 NOVELS OF THE 1990s IN THE UK
(Author/sales)

❶ *Jurassic Park* (Michael Crichton, 769,981) ❷ *The Chamber* (John Grisham, 760,495) ❸ *The Client* (John Grisham, 722,195) ❹ *Bravo Two Zero* (Andy McNab, 715,406) ❺ *The Glass Lake* (Maeve Binchy, 683,270) ❻ *Schindler's Ark/List* (Thomas Keneally, 601,308) ❼ *Polo* (Jilly Cooper, 597,562) ❽ *The Negotiator* (Frederick Forsyth, 553,380) ❾ *The Man Who Made Husbands Jealous* (Jilly Cooper, 526,591) ❿ *As the Crow Flies* (Jeffrey Archer, 515,867)

LITERARY PRIZES

THE 10

LATEST WINNERS OF THE PULITZER PRIZE FOR FICTION

Year	Author	Novel
1997	Steven Millhauser	*Martin Dressler: The Tale of an American Dreamer*
1996	Richard Ford	*Independence Day*
1995	Carol Shields	*The Stone Diaries*
1994	E. Annie Proulx	*The Shipping News*
1993	Robert Olen Butler	*A Good Scent from a Strange Mountain: Stories*
1992	Jane Smiley	*A Thousand Acres*
1991	John Updike	*Rabbit at Rest*
1990	Oscar Hijuelos	*The Mambo Kings Play*
1989	Anne Tyler	*Breathing Lessons*
1988	Toni Morrison	*Beloved*

THE 10

LATEST BOOKER PRIZE WINNERS

Year	Author	Novel
1997	Arundhati Roy	*The God of Small Things*
1996	Graham Swift	*Last Orders*
1995	Pat Barker	*The Ghost Road*
1994	James Kelman	*How Late It Was, How Late*
1993	Roddy Doyle	*Paddy Clarke Ha Ha Ha*
1992 =	Michael Ondaatje	*The English Patient*
=	Barry Unsworth	*Sacred Hunger*
1991	Ben Okri	*Famished Road*
1990	A.S. Byatt	*Possession: A Romance*
1989	Kazuo Ishiguro	*The Remains of the Day*

TOP 10

LITERARY PRIZES AND AWARDS IN THE UK*

	Prize/award	Category	Total value (£)
1	International IMPAC Award (IR£100,000)	A work of fiction	84,745
2	Orange Prize for Fiction	Best fiction title by a woman	30,000
3	Whitbread Book of the Year	Books by residents of the UK or Ireland	21,000
4	Booker Prize	Best novel in English	20,000
5	Irish Times Literary Prizes (IR£22,500)	Fiction or poetry in English or Irish	19,067
6 =	Commonwealth Writers' Prize	A work of fiction by a Commonwealth citizen	10,000
=	Catherine Cookson Fiction Prize	Romantic or historical novel	10,000
=	Heywood Hill Literary Prize	Distinguished literary career	10,000
=	W. H. Smith Literary Award	Outstanding work of fiction	10,000
=	Steinbeck Award	Young writer working in the spirit of John Steinbeck	10,000

* *Including Irish awards for which UK writers are eligible*

While the Booker Prize attracts the most publicity, there are numerous other valuable literary prizes awarded in the UK. The relatively newly established David Cohen British Literature Prize was first awarded in 1993 (to V. S. Naipaul), but is not annual. In addition, there are many other awards that total more than some of those in the Top 10, but are divided between several recipients, and many others worth less than £10,000 – some as little as £100 or just a certificate or gift, such as the bronze eggs given to winners of the Mother Goose Award or the diamond dagger received by Crime Writers' Association Award winners. Outside the field of fiction, the qualifications for entry for some prizes are very specialized, such as the Calvin and Rose G. Hoffman Prize, worth at least £7,500, which is awarded for the best work on Christopher Marlowe.

THE 10

LATEST WINNERS OF HUGO AWARDS FOR BEST SCIENCE FICTION NOVEL

Year	Author/novel
1997	Kim Stanley Robinson, *Blue Mars*
1996	Neal Stephenson, *The Diamond Age*
1995	Lois McMaster Bujold, *Mirror Dance*
1994	Kim Stanley Robinson, *Green Mars*
1993 =	Vernor Vinge, *A Fire Upon the Deep*
=	Connie Willis, *Doomsday Book*
1992	Lois McMaster Bujold, *Barrayar*
1991	Lois McMaster Bujold, *The Vor Game*
1990	Dan Simmons, *Hyperion*
1989	C.J. Cherryh, *Cyteen*

Hugo Awards for science fiction novels, short stories, and other fiction and non-fiction works are presented by the World Science Fiction Society. They were established in 1953 as "Science Fiction Achievement Awards for the best science fiction writing". The prize in the Awards' inaugural year was presented to Alfred Bester for *The Demolished Man*.

THE 10
LATEST CARNEGIE MEDAL WINNERS

Year	Author	Title
1996	Melvyn Burgess	*Junk*
1995	Philip Pullman	*Northern Lights*
1994	Theresa Breslin	*Whispers in the Graveyard*
1993	Robert Swindells	*Stone Cold*
1992	Anne Fine	*Flour Babies*
1991	Berlie Doherty	*Dear Nobody*
1990	Gillian Cross	*Wolf*
1989	Anne Fine	*Goggle-eyes*
1988	Geraldine McCaughrean	*A Pack of Lies*
1987	Susan Price	*The Ghost Drum*

Established in 1937, the Carnegie Medal is awarded annually by the Library Association for an outstanding English language children's book published during the previous year. It is named in honour of Scots-born millionaire Andrew Carnegie, who was a notable library benefactor. In its early years, winners included Arthur Ransome, Noel Streatfield, Walter de la Mare, and C. S. Lewis.

THE 10
LATEST WINNERS OF THE JOHN NEWBERY MEDAL

Year	Author	Title
1998	Karen Hesse	*Out of the Dust*
1997	E. L. Konigsburg	*The View from Saturday*
1996	Karen Cushman	*The Midwife's Apprentice*
1995	Sharon Creech	*Walk Two Moons*
1994	Lois Lowry	*The Giver*
1993	Cynthia Rylant	*Missing May*
1992	Phyllis Reynolds Naylor	*Shiloh*
1991	Jerry Spinelli	*Maniac Magee*
1990	Lois Lowry	*Number the Stars*
1989 =	Paul Fleischman	*Joyful Noise*
=	Walter Myers	*Scorpions*

The John Newbery Medal is awarded for "the most distinguished contribution to American literature for children". Its first winner in 1923 was Hugh Lofting's *The Voyages of Doctor Dolittle*. The medal is named after John Newbery (1713–67), a London bookseller and publisher who specialized in children's books.

THE 10
LATEST RANDOLPH CALDECOTT MEDAL WINNERS

Year	Author	Title
1998	Paul O. Zelinsky	*Rapunzel*
1997	David Wisniewski	*Golem*
1996	Peggy Rathman	*Officer Buckle and Gloria*
1995	Eve Bunting (illustrated by David Diaz)	*Smoky Night*
1994	Allen Say	*Grandfather's Journey*
1993	Emily McCully Honor	*Mirette on High Wire*
1992	David Weisner	*Tuesday*
1991	David Macauley	*Black and White*
1990	Ed Young	*Lon Po Po*
1989	Stephen Gammell	*Song and Dance Man*

The Randolph Caldecott Medal, named after the English illustrator (1846–86), has been awarded annually since 1938 "to the artist of the most distinguished American picture book for children published in the United States during the preceding year". The winner in the debut year was Helen Dean Fish's *Animals of the Bible*, illustrated by Dorothy P. Lethrop. In subsequent years many books have been honoured that have gone on to be regarded as modern classics, among them Maurice Sendak's *Where the Wild Things Are*, the Medal winner in 1964.

THE 10
LATEST KATE GREENAWAY MEDAL WINNERS

Year	Illustrator	Title
1996	Helen Cooper	*The Baby Who Wouldn't Go to Bed*
1995	P. J. Lynch (text Susan Wojciechowski)	*The Christmas Miracle of Jonathan Toomey*
1994	Gregory Rogers (text Libby Hathorn)	*The Way Home*
1993	Alan Lee (text Rosemary Sutcliff)	*Black Ships Before Troy*
1992	Anthony Browne	*Zoo*
1991	Janet Ahlberg (text Allan Ahlberg)	*The Jolly Christmas Postman*
1990	Gary Blythe (text Dyan Sheldon)	*The Whales' Song*
1989	Michael Foreman	*War Boy: A Country Childhood*
1988	Barbara Firth (text Martin Waddell)	*Can't You Sleep, Little Bear?*
1987	Adrienne Kennaway (text Mwenye Hadithi)	*Crafty Chameleon*

The Kate Greenaway Medal, named after the English illustrator of children's books (1846–1901), has been awarded annually since 1956 for the most distinguished work in the illustration of children's books published in the United Kingdom.

THE PRESS

OLDEST NATIONAL NEWSPAPERS PUBLISHED IN THE UK

Newspaper	First published
1 *London Gazette*	16 Nov 1665

Originally published as the Oxford Gazette *when the royal court resided in Oxford during a plague outbreak. After 23 issues, it moved to London with the court and changed its name.*

2 *Lloyds List*	1726

Providing shipping news, originally on a weekly basis, but since 1734 Britain's oldest daily.

3 *The Times*	1 Jan 1785

First published as the Daily Universal Register, *it changed to* The Times *on 1 March 1788.*

4 *Observer*	4 Dec 1791

Britain's first Sunday paper was Johnson's British Gazette and Sunday Monitor, *published on 2 March 1780. It closed in 1829, thus making the* Observer *the longest-running Sunday paper.*

5 *Licensee*	8 Feb 1794

Britain's oldest trade paper (started by the Licensed Victuallers Association), and the first national paper on Fleet Street, the Morning Advertiser *changed its name to the* Licensee *and went twice-weekly in 1994.*

6 *Scotsman*	25 Jan 1817

First published weekly, the Daily Scotsman *was published from July 1855 to December 1859, and re-titled the* Scotsman *in January 1860.*

7 *Sunday Times*	Feb 1821

Issued as the New Observer *until March 1821 and the* Independent Observer *from then until 22 October 1822, when it changed to the* Sunday Times. *On 4 February 1962 it became the first British paper to issue a colour supplement.*

8 *Guardian*	5 May 1821

A weekly until 1855 (and called the Manchester Guardian *until 1959).*

9 *News of the World*	1 Oct 1843

The first issue of the national Sunday paper aimed "To give to the poorer classes… a paper that would suit their means, and to the middle… a journal which, from its immense circulation, should command their attention…" In April 1951, sales peaked at 8,480,878 copies, the highest-ever circulation of a British paper.

10 *Daily Telegraph*	29 Jun 1855

The first issues were published as the Daily Telegraph and Courier, *but from 10 August 1855,* Courier *was dropped from the title.*

THE FIRST OCEAN NEWSPAPER

The first newspaper published at sea, using messages transmitted by the latest wireless technology pioneered by Guglielmo Marconi, was published by Marconi himself. On 15 November 1899, on board the 11,600-ton American liner S.S. *St. Paul*, he set up a receiver on which he picked up news transmitted from a station on the Isle of Wight. This was then printed in a four-page newspaper called the *Transatlantic Times*, which was sold to passengers for the then enormous price of one dollar (although the proceeds from its sales were donated to the Seaman's Fund). The first daily ocean newspaper was the *Cunard Daily Bulletin*, published in October 1902 on board the S.S. *Campania* and S.S. *Lucania*, then the two largest liners afloat, receiving wireless news from stations in England and Canada.

100 YEARS AGO • YEARS AGO • YEARS AGO • YEARS AGO

BRITISH NATIONAL SUNDAY NEWSPAPERS

	Newspaper	Average sales per issue*
1	*News of the World*	4,435,267
2	*Sunday Mirror*	2,252,460
3	*Mail on Sunday*	2,232,009
4	*People*	1,875,716
5	*Sunday Times*	1,358,526
6	*Express on Sunday*	1,145,386
7	*Sunday Telegraph*	886,554
8	*Sunday Mail* (Scotland)	818,081
9	*Observer*	437,171
10	*Sunday Sport*	272,377

* Based on average sales August 1997 to January 1998

BRITISH NATIONAL DAILY NEWSPAPERS

	Newspaper	Average daily sales*
1	*Sun*	3,767,941
2	*Mirror*	2,321,608
3	*Daily Mail*	2,247,298
4	*Daily Express*	1,199,392
5	*Daily Telegraph*	1,096,583
6	*The Times*	805,602
7	*Daily Record* (Scotland)	685,039
8	*Daily Star*	609,412
9	*Guardian*	404,616
10	*Financial Times*	329,871

* Based on average daily sales August 1997–January 1998

The 11th bestselling daily newspaper in Great Britain is the *Independent*, with total average daily sales during this period of 255,324 copies. The tabloid papers in the UK still sell many more copies than all the "quality" daily newspapers. For example the combined sales of the *Daily Telegraph*, *The Times*, the *Guardian*, the *Financial Times*, and the *Independent* is only 2,891,996, compared to the average daily sales of the *Sun* alone, which is 3,767,941. The *Evening Standard* sells 454,016 copies a day, but as it does not have national coverage, it does not appear in this Top 10 list. The *Daily Record* (Scotland) is included however, as it has national circulation in Scotland.

TOP 10
CONSUMERS OF NEWSPRINT

	Country	Annual consumption per inhabitant (kg)
1	Finland	67.362
2	Austria	55.697
3	Norway	50.743
4	Denmark	50.064
5	USA	49.915
6	New Zealand	46.783
7	Singapore	46.646
8	Sweden	42.897
9	UK	38.947
10	Australia	37.725

National consumption of newsprint – the cheap wood-pulp paper used for printing newspapers – provides a measure of the extent of newspaper sales in the Top 10 countries, as well as the thickness of certain publications.

Source: UNCESCO

TOP 10
CONSUMER MAGAZINES IN THE UK

	Magazine	Average circulation per issue
1	*What's on TV*	1,694,276
2	*Reader's Digest*	1,493,312
3	*Radio Times*	1,406,152
4	*Cable Guide*	1,258,536
5	*TV Times*	883,281
6	*Woman*	731,754
7	*Woman's Own*	702,765
8	*FHM*	664,110
9	*Woman's Weekly*	638,306
10	*Hello!*	574,585

In addition to the magazines in the Top 10, the fastest-growing magazines are *Official PlayStation Magazine* (circulation 205,619, 156.4 per cent up on the previous year), and *Nintendo Magazine* (circulation 63,173, up 108.7 per cent on the previous year).

MODERN PRINTING PRESS

TOP 10 PRODUCERS OF NEWSPRINT
(Tonnes)

❶ Canada (9,251,000) ❷ USA (7,002,000)
❸ Japan (3,098,000) ❹ Sweden (2,345,000)
❺ Germany (1,726,000) ❻ Russia (1,457,000) ❼ Finland (1,425,000)
❽ Norway (973,000) ❾ South Korea (948,000) ❿ France (890,000)
Source: UNESCO

TOP 10
DAILY NEWSPAPERS IN THE WORLD

	Newspaper	Country	Average daily circulation
1	*Yomiuri Shimbun**	Japan	10,000,000
2	*Asahi Shimbun**	Japan	8,500,000
3	*Sichuan Ribao*	China	8,000,000
4	*Bild-Zeitung*	Germany	4,892,000
5	*Mainichi Shimbun**	Japan	4,500,000
6	*Sun*	UK	3,767,941
7	*Argumenty y Fakty*	Russia	3,600,000
8	*Nihon Keizai Shimbun**	Japan	3,000,000
9	*Chunichi Shimbun**	Japan	2,900,000
10	*Gongren Ribao*	China	2,500,000

* *Morning edition*

TOP 10
COUNTRIES WITH THE MOST DAILY NEWSPAPERS

	Country	No. of daily newspapers
1	India	1,802
2	USA	1,533
3	Germany	406
4	Turkey	400
5	Brazil	320
6	Mexico	310
7	Russia	292
8	Pakistan	223
9	Argentina	190
10	Greece	168

If the list is ranked according to the total daily sales of newspapers per 1,000 inhabitants, the result is very different, with India and the US not even appearing.

Source: UNESCO

TOP 10
ENGLISH-LANGUAGE DAILY NEWSPAPERS IN THE WORLD

	Newspaper/country	Circulation
1	*Sun*, UK	3,767,941
2	*Mirror*, UK	2,321,608
3	*Daily Mail*, UK	2,247,298
4	*Wall Street Journal*, USA	1,783,500
5	*USA Today*, USA	1,591,600
6	*Daily Express*, UK	1,199,392
7	*Daily Telegraph*, UK	1,096,583
8	*New York Times*, USA	1,071,100
9	*Los Angeles Times*, USA	1,029,100
10	*The Times*, UK	805,602

The *New York Post*, formerly called the *New York Evening Post* and first published on 16 November 1801, holds the record as America's longest-running daily.

ART AT AUCTION

RISING SUN
The sale of van Gogh's Sunflowers
*in 1987 established a new world
record price for a painting.*

TOP 10
MOST EXPENSIVE OLD MASTER PAINTINGS EVER SOLD AT AUCTION

Work/artist/sale	Price (£)
1 *Portrait of Duke Cosimo I de Medici*, Jacopo da Carucci (Pontormo) (Italian; 1493–1558), Christie's, New York, 31 May 1989	20,253,164 ($32,000,000)
2 *The Old Horse Guards, London, from St James's Park*, Canaletto (Italian; 1697–1768), Christie's, London, 15 April 1992	9,200,000
3 *View of the Giudecca and the Zattere, Venice*, Francesco Guardi (Italian; 1712–93), Sotheby's, Monaco, 1 December 1989	8,937,960 (F.FR85,000,0000)
4 *Le Retour du Bucentaure le Jour de l'Ascension*, Canaletto, (Italian; 1697–1768), Ader Tajan, Paris, 15 December 1993	7,594,937 (F.FR66,000,000)
5 *Adoration of the Magi*, Andrea Mantegna (Italian; 1431–1606), Christie's, London, 18 April 1985	7,500,000
6 *Venus and Adonis*, Titian (Italian c.1488–1576), Christie's, London, 13 December 1991	6,800,000
7 *Portrait of a Girl Wearing a Gold-trimmed Cloak*, Rembrandt (Dutch; 1606–69), Sotheby's, London, 10 December 1986	6,600,000
8 *View of Molo from Bacino di San Marco, Venice* and *View of the Grand Canal Facing East from Campo di Santi, Venice* (pair), Canaletto, (Italian; 1697–1768), Sotheby's, New York, 1 June 1990	5,988,024 ($10,000,000)
9 *Portrait of Bearded Man in Red Coat*, Rembrandt, (Dutch; 1606–69), Sotheby's, New York, 30 January 1998	5,061,350 ($8,250,000)
10 *Study for Head and Hand of an Apostle*, Raphael (Italian; 1483–1520), Christie's, London, 13 December 1996	4,800,000

TOP 10
MOST EXPENSIVE PAINTINGS BY WOMEN ARTISTS EVER SOLD AT AUCTION

Work/artist/sale	Price (£)
1 *In the Box*, Mary Cassatt (American; 1844–1926), Christie's, New York, 23 May 1988	2,450,331 ($3,700,000)
2 *The Conversation*, Mary Cassatt, Christie's, New York, 11 May 1988	2,180,850 ($4,100,000)
3 *Mother, Sara, and the Baby*, Mary Cassatt, Christie's, New York, 10 May 1989	2,147,239 ($3,500,000)
4 *From the Plains*, Georgia O'Keeffe (American; 1887–1986), Sotheby's, New York, 3 December 1997	2,000,000 ($3,300,000)
5 *Après le déjeuner*, Berthe Morisot (French; 1841–1895), Christie's, New York, 14 May 1997	1,993,865 ($3,250,000)
6 *Autoretrato con chango y loro*, Frida Kahlo (Mexican; 1907–54), Sotheby's, New York, 17 May 1995	1,847,134 ($2,900,000)
7 *Augusta Reading to her Daughter*, Mary Cassatt, Sotheby's, New York, 9 May 1989	1,717,790 ($2,800,000)
8 *Young Lady in a Loge, Gazing to the Right*, Mary Cassatt, Sotheby's, New York, 10 November 1992	1,523,179 ($2,300,000)
9 *Sara Holding her Dog*, Mary Cassatt, Sotheby's, New York, 11 November 1988	1,461,988 ($2,500,000)
10 *Adam et Eve*, Tamara de Lempicka (Polish; 1898–1980), Christie's, New York, 3 March 1994	1,208,054 ($1,800,000)

TOP 10

MOST EXPENSIVE PAINTINGS EVER SOLD AT AUCTION

Work/artist/sale	Price (£)
1 *Portrait of Dr. Gachet,* Vincent van Gogh (Dutch; 1853–80), Christie's, New York, 15 May 1990	44,378,696 ($75,000,000)

Both this painting and the one in the No. 2 position were bought by Ryoei Saito, head of Japanese Daishowa Paper Manufacturing.

2 *Au Moulin de la Galette,* Pierre-Auguste Renoir (French; 1841–1919), Sotheby's, New York, 17 May 1990	42,011,832 ($71,000,000)

3 *Les Noces de Pierrette,* Pablo Picasso (Spanish; 1881–1973), Binoche et Godeau, Paris, 30 Nov 1989	33,123,028 (F.Fr315,000,000)

The painting was sold by Swedish financier Fredrik Roos to Tomonori Tsurumaki, a property developer, who bid for it by telephone from Tokyo.

4 *Irises,* Vincent van Gogh, Sotheby's, New York, 11 Nov 1987	28,000,000 ($49,000,000)

After much speculation, its purchaser was confirmed as businessman Alan Bond. However, he was unable to pay for it in full, so its former status as the world's most expensive work of art has been disputed.

5 *Self Portrait: Yo Picasso,* Pablo Picasso, Sotheby's, New York, 9 May 1989	26,687,116 ($43,500,000)

Work/artist/sale	Price (£)
6 *Le Rêve,* Pablo Picasso, Christie's, New York, 10 Nov 1997	26,035,502 ($44,000,000)

Picasso's Le Rêve (The Dream), a portrait of Marie Thérèsa Walter from the Ganz collection, is the highest-priced painting sold since 1990. Victor and Sally Ganz had paid $7,000 for the painting in 1941.

7 *Au Lapin Agile,* Pablo Picasso, Sotheby's, New York, 15 Nov 1989	23,870,968 ($37,000,000)

The painting depicts Picasso as a harlequin at the bar of the café Lapin.

8 *Sunflowers,* Vincent van Gogh, Christie's, London, 30 March 1987	22,500,000

At the time, this was the most expensive picture ever sold.

9 *Portrait of Duke Cosimo I de Medici,* Jacopo da Carucci (Pontormo) (Italian; 1494–1556/7), Christie's, New York, 31 May 1989	20,253,164 ($32,000,000)

This is the record price paid for an Old Master – and the only one in this Top 10. It was bought by the J. Paul Getty Museum, Malibu, USA.

10 *Acrobate et Jeune Arlequin,* Pablo Picasso, Christie's, London, 28 November 1988	19,000,000

Until the sale of Yo Picasso, this held the world record for a 20th-century painting. It was bought by Mitsukoshi, a Japanese department store.

TOP 10 ARTISTS WITH THE MOST WORKS SOLD FOR MORE THAN ONE MILLION POUNDS

(Number of works sold)

❶ Pablo Picasso (143) ❷ Claude Monet (120) ❸ Pierre Auguste Renoir (92) ❹ Edgar Degas (49) ❺ Paul Cézanne (41) ❻= Henri Matisse (36), Amedeo Modigliani (36) ❽ Vincent van Gogh (34) ❾ Camille Pissaro (29) ❿ Paul Gauguin (26)

TOP 10

MOST EXPENSIVE PAINTINGS EVER SOLD IN THE UK

Work/artist/sale	Price (£)
1 *Acrobate et Jeune Arlequin,* Pablo Picasso (Spanish; 1881–1973), Christie's, London, 28 November 1988	19,000,000
2 *Schloss Kammer am Attersee II,* Gustav Klimt (Austrian; 1862–1918), Christie's, London, 9 October 1997	13,200,000
3 *Dans la Prairie,* Claude Monet (French; 1840–1926), Sotheby's, London, 28 June 1988	13,000,000
4 *Les Tuileries,* Pablo Picasso, Christie's, London, 25 June 1990	12,500,000
5 *Pommes et Serviette,* Paul Cézanne (French; 1839–1906), Christie's, London, 27 November 1989	10,000,000
6 *The Lock,* John Constable (British; 1776–1837), Sotheby's, London, 14 Nov 1990	9,800,000
7 *La Promenade,* Pierre Auguste Renoir (French; 1841–1919), Sotheby's, London, 4 April 1989	9,400,000
8 *The Old Horse Guards, London, from St James's Park,* Canaletto (Italian; 1697–1768), Christie's, London, 15 April 1992	9,200,000
9 *Contrastes de Formes,* Fernand Léger (French; 1881–1955), Christie's, London, 27 November 1989	8,500,000
10 *La Moisson en Provence,* Vincent van Gogh (Dutch; 1853–1890), Sotheby's, London 24 June 1997	8,000,000

20TH-CENTURY ARTISTS

DAVID HOCKNEY
Although a British artist, many of his works depict scenes in California, where he lives, and have achieved high prices among American collectors.

TOP 10 MOST EXPENSIVE PAINTINGS BY DAVID HOCKNEY
(Prices in $)

❶ *Grand procession of Dignitaries in the semi-Egyptian style* (2,000,000) ❷ *Deep and wet water* (1,300,000) ❸ *Henry Geldzahler and Christopher Scott* (1,000,000) ❹ *California art collector* (925,000) ❺ *The Room, Manchester Street* (800,000) ❻ *A neat lawn* (598,400) ❼ *Berlin, a souvenir* (575,000) ❽ *Different kinds of water pouring into swimming pool, Santa Monica* (460,000) ❾ *The Room, Tarzana* (447,200) ❿ *The Actor* (386,400)

T O P   1 0
MOST EXPENSIVE PAINTINGS BY WASSILY KANDINSKY

	Work/sale	Price (£)
1	*Fugue* Sotheby's, New York, 17 May 1990	11,242,604 ($19,000,000)
2	*Sketch for Composition VII – Entwurf I zu Komposition VII* Sotheby's, London, 1 Dec 1992	5,000,000
3	*Dans le cercle noir* Guy Loudmer, Paris, 22 Nov 1993	4,114,286 (F.FR36,000,000)
4	*Das jungste Gericht* Sotheby's, New York, 8 Nov 1995	3,025,478 ($4,750,000)
5	*Milieu accompagné* Sotheby's, London, 22 Jun 1993	2,750,000
6	*Engel des jungsten Gerichts* Christie's, New York, 10 May 1989	2,576,687 ($4,200,000)
7	*Skizze fur Improvisation 4* Sotheby's, London, 27 Jun 1995	2,500,000
8	*Herbstlandschaft* Sotheby's, New York, 9 May 1989	2,208,589 ($3,600,000)
9	*Herbstlandschaft mit Booten* Christie's, New York, 13 Nov 1996	2,108,434 ($3,500,000)
10	*Murnau - Landschaft mit Kirche I* Christie's, New York, 2 Nov 1993	1,689,189 ($2,500,000)

T O P   1 0
MOST EXPENSIVE PAINTINGS BY JASPER JOHNS

	Work/sale	Price (£)
1	*False start* Sotheby's, New York, 10 Nov 1988	8,611,112 ($15,500,000)
2	*Two flags* Sotheby's, New York, 8 Nov 1989	6,962,025 ($11,000,000)
3	*Corpse and Mirror* Christie's, New York, 10 Nov 1997	4,497,042 ($7,600,000)
4	*White Numbers* Christie's, New York, 10 Nov 1997	4,260,355 ($7,200,000)
5	*White flag* Christie's, New York, 9 Nov 1988	3,555,556 ($6,400,000)
6	*Jubilee* Sotheby's, New York, 13 Nov 1991	2,513,967 ($4,500,000)
7	*Decoy* Christie's, New York, 10 Nov 1997	2,366,864 ($4,000,000)
8	*Small false start* Christie's, New York, 7 Nov 1989	2,341,772 ($3,700,000)
9	*Out of the window* Sotheby's, New York, 10 Nov 1986	2,307,693 ($3,300,000)
10	*Device circle* Christie's, New York, 12 Nov 1991	2,234,037 ($4,000,000)

TOP 10

MOST EXPENSIVE PAINTINGS BY ANDY WARHOL

	Work/sale	Price (£)
1	*Marilyn X 100* Sotheby's, New York, 17 Nov 1992	2,251,656 ($3,400,000)
2	*Shot Red Marilyn* Sotheby's, New York, 3 May 1989	2,228,916 ($3,700,000)
3	*Shot Red Marilyn* Sotheby's, New York, 2 Nov 1994	2,062,500 ($3,300,000)
4	*Marilyn Monroe, twenty times* Sotheby's, New York, 10 Nov 1988	2,000,000 ($3,600,000)
5	*Big torn Campbell's soup can* Christie's, New York, 7 May 1997	1,987,578 ($3,200,000)
6	*Liz* Christie's, New York, 7 Nov 1989	1,297,468 ($2,050,000)
7	*Triple Elvis* Sotheby's, New York, 8 Nov 1989	1,265,823 ($2,000,000)
8	*210 Coca-Cola bottles* Christie's, New York, 5 May 1992	1,061,453 ($1,900,000)
9	*Ladies and Gentlemen, 1975* Binoche et Godeau, Paris, 30 Nov 1989	1,030,397 (F.FR9,799,080)
10	*Race Riot* Christie's, New York, 7 Nov 1989	1,012,658 ($1,600,000)

TOP 10

MOST EXPENSIVE PAINTINGS BY JACKSON POLLOCK

	Work/sale	Price (£)
1	*Number 8, 1950* Sotheby's, New York, 2 May 1989	6,325,302 ($10,500,000)
2	*Frieze* Christie's, New York, 9 Nov 1988	2,888,889 ($5,200,000)
3	*Search* Sotheby's, New York, 2 May 1988	2,352,940 ($4,400,000)
4	*Number 19, 1949* Sotheby's, New York, 2 May 1989	2,168,675 ($3,600,000)
5	*Number 31, 1949* Christie's, New York, 3 May 1988	1,711,230 ($3,200,000)
6	*Number 26, 1950* Sotheby's, New York, 4 May 1987	1,506,025 ($2,500,000)
7	*Something of the past* Christie's, New York, 7 May 1996	1,447,369 ($2,200,000)
8	*Number 19, 1948* Christie's, New York, 4 May 1993	1,437,909 ($2,200,000)
9	*Number 13* Christie's, New York, 7 Nov 1990	1,428,570 ($2,800,000)
10	*Number 20* Sotheby's, New York, 8 May 1990	1,309,524 ($2,200,000)

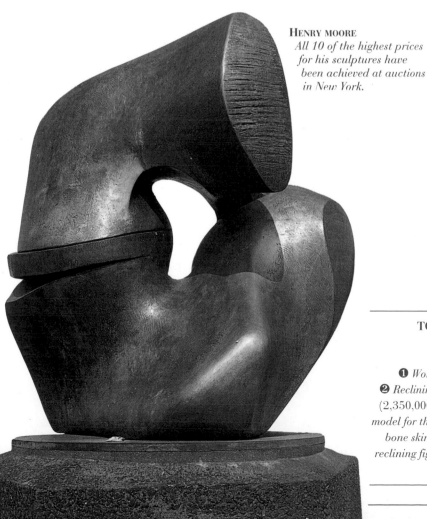

HENRY MOORE
All 10 of the highest prices for his sculptures have been achieved at auctions in New York.

TOP 10 MOST EXPENSIVE SCULPTURES BY HENRY MOORE
(Prices in $)

❶ *Working Model for UNESCO Reclining Figure* (3,700,000)
❷ *Reclining Figure, Angles* (2,400,000) ❸ *Draped reclining woman* (2,350,000) ❹ *Reclining connected forms* (2,200,000) ❺= *Working model for three-way piece no.3 vertebrae* (2,000,000), *Reclining figure, bone skirt* (2,000,000) ❼= *Reclining figure* (1,850,000), *Festival reclining figure* (1,850,000) ❾ *Reclining figure – Festival* (1,750,000)
❿ *Reclining figure – Festival* (1,600,000)

MUSIC

T O P 1 0

SINGLES OF THE 1950s IN THE UK*

	Title/artist	Year
1	*Rock Around the Clock*, Bill Haley and His Comets	1955
2	*Diana*, Paul Anka	1957
3	*Mary's Boy Child*, Harry Belafonte	1957
4	*The Harry Lime Theme (The Third Man)*, Anton Karas	1950
5	*Living Doll*, Cliff Richard	1959
6	*Jailhouse Rock*, Elvis Presley	1958
7	*What Do You Want to Make Those Eyes at Me For?*, Emile Ford	1958
8	*All I Have to Do is Dream/ Claudette*, Everly Brothers	1958
9	*What Do You Want?*, Adam Faith	1959
10	*All Shook Up*, Elvis Presley	1957

* By sales over the decade

T O P 1 0

SINGLES OF THE 1960s IN THE UK*

	Title/artist	Year
1	*She Loves You*, Beatles	1963
2	*I Want to Hold Your Hand*, Beatles	1963
3	*Tears*, Ken Dodd	1965
4	*Can't Buy Me Love*, Beatles	1964
5	*I Feel Fine*, Beatles	1964
6	*We can Work it Out/ Day Tripper*, Beatles	1965
7	*The Carnival is Over*, Seekers	1965
8	*Release Me*, Engelbert Humperdinck	1967
9	*It's Now or Never*, Elvis Presley	1960
10	*Green, Green Grass of Home*, Tom Jones	1966

* By sales over the decade

T O P 1 0

SINGLES OF THE 1970s IN THE UK*

Year	Title	Artist
1970	*The Wonder of You*	Elvis Presley
1971	*My Sweet Lord*	George Harrison
1972	*I'd Like to Teach the World to Sing*	New Seekers
1973	*I Love You Love Me Love*	Gary Glitter
1974	*You Won't Find Another Fool like Me*	New Seekers
1975	*Bohemian Rhapsody*	Queen
1976	*Save Your Kisses for Me*	Brotherhood of Man
1977	*Mull of Kintyre*	Wings
1978	*Rivers of Babylon/ Brown Girl in the Ring*	Boney M
1979	*Y.M.C.A.*	Village People

* By sales over each year

TOP 10

SINGLES OF THE 1980s IN THE UK*

Year	Title	Artist
1980	*Don't Stand so Close to Me*	Police
1981	*Don't You Want Me*	Human League
1982	*Come on Eileen*	Dexy's Midnight Runners
1983	*Karma Chameleon*	Culture Club
1984	*Do They Know it's Christmas?*	Band Aid
1985	*The Power of Love*	Jennifer Rush
1986	*Every Loser Wins*	Nick Berry
1987	*Never Gonna Give You Up*	Rick Astley
1988	*Mistletoe and Wine*	Cliff Richard
1989	*Ride on Time*	Black Box

* By sales over each year

The Band Aid single was not only the No. 1 of 1984, but remained the UK's bestseller of all time until 1997.

TOP 10 GROUPS OF THE 1960S IN THE UK

❶ Beatles ❷ Rolling Stones
❸ Shadows ❹ Hollies
❺ Beach Boys ❻ Kinks ❼ Four Tops
❽ Manfred Mann
❾ Seekers ❿ Bachelors

THE BEACH BOYS

TOP 10

ALBUMS OF THE 1970s IN THE UK*

Year	Title	Artist
1970	*Bridge over Troubled Water*	Simon and Garfunkel
1971	*Bridge over Troubled Water*	Simon and Garfunkel
1972	*20 Dynamic Hits*	Various
1973	*Don't Shoot Me, I'm Only the Piano Player*	Elton John
1974	*The Singles, 1969–1973*	Carpenters
1975	*The Best of the Stylistics*	Stylistics
1976	*Greatest Hits*	Abba
1977	*Arrival*	Abba
1978	*Saturday Night Fever*	Soundtrack
1979	*Parallel Lines*	Blondie

* By sales over each year

TOP 10 JUKEBOX SINGLES OF ALL TIME

(Title/year)

❶ Patsy Cline (*Crazy*, 1962) ❷ Bob Seger (*Old Time Rock 'n' Roll*, 1979) ❸ Elvis Presley (*Hound Dog/Don't Be Cruel*, 1956) ❹ Marvin Gaye (*I Heard it Through the Grapevine*, 1968) ❺ Bobby Darin (*Mack The Knife*, 1959) ❻ Bill Haley and His Comets (*Rock Around the Clock*, 1955) ❼ Doors (*Light My Fire*, 1967) ❽ Otis Redding *(Sittin' On the Dock of the Bay*, 1968) ❾ Temptations (*My Girl*, 1965) ❿ Frank Sinatra (*New York, New York*, 1980)

Source: Amusement and Music Operators Association

TOP 10

ALBUMS OF THE 1980s IN THE UK*

Year	Title	Artist
1980	*Super Trouper*	Abba
1981	*Kings of the Wild Frontier*	Adam and The Ants
1982	*Love Songs*	Barbra Streisand
1983	*Thriller*	Michael Jackson
1984	*Can't Slow Down*	Lionel Richie
1985	*Brothers In Arms*	Dire Straits
1986	*True Blue*	Madonna
1987	*Bad*	Michael Jackson
1988	*Kylie*	Kylie Minogue
1989	*Ten Good Reasons*	Jason Donovan

* By sales over each year

Abba opened the decade by adding a further No.1 album of the year to the two they had achieved in the 1970s. *Brothers In Arms* remains the top-selling UK album ever.

TOP 10

GROUPS OF THE 70s IN THE UK

1	Abba
2	Slade
3	T. Rex
4	Bay City Rollers
5	Sweet
6	Showaddywaddy
7	Mud
8	Wings
9	Electric Light Orchestra
10	Osmonds

CHART HITS – THE RECORD BREAKERS

LOUIS ARMSTRONG

TOP 10 OLDEST SINGERS TO HAVE A CHART HIT IN THE UK
(Title/age)

❶ Frank Sinatra (*New York, New York*, 70 yrs 4 mths) ❷ Louis Armstrong (*What a Wonderful World*, 68 yrs) ❸ Honor Blackman (*Kinky Boots*, 64 yrs) ❹ James Brown (*Living in America*, 56 yrs 10 mths) ❺ Ted Heath (*Swingin' Shepherd Blues*, 56 yrs 2 mths) ❻ Petula Clark (*Downtown '88 Remix*, 56 yrs) ❼ Bobby Vinton, (*Blue Velvet*, 55 yrs 6 mths) ❽ Nina Simone (*My Baby Just Cares for Me*, 54 yrs 10 mths) ❾ Bing Crosby (*Around the World*, 54 yrs 2 mths) ❿ Cliff Richard (*I Still Believe in You*, 52 yrs 2 mths)
Source: MRIB

TOP 10 SINGLES OF ALL TIME IN THE UK

	Artist/title/year	Est. UK sales
1	Elton John, *Candle in the Wind* (1997)/*Something About the Way You Look Tonight* (1997)	4,800,000
2	Band Aid, *Do They Know it's Christmas?* (1984)	3,510,000
3	Queen, *Bohemian Rhapsody* (1975/91)	2,130,000
4	Wings, *Mull of Kintyre* (1977)	2,050,000
5	Boney M, *Rivers of Babylon/Brown Girl in the Ring* (1978)	1,995,000
6	Frankie Goes to Hollywood, *Relax* (1984)	1,910,000
7	Beatles, *She Loves You* (1963)	1,890,000
8	John Travolta and Olivia Newton-John, *You're the One that I Want* (1978)	1,870,000
9	Robson Green and Jerome Flynn, *Unchained Melody* (1995)	1,820,000
10	Boney M, *Mary's Boy Child/Oh My Lord* (1978)	1,790,000

Source: BPI

TOP 10 SINGLES OF ALL TIME WORLDWIDE

	Artist/title	Sales exceed
1	Elton John, *Candle in the Wind*, 1997	35,000,000
2	Bing Crosby, *White Christmas*	30,000,000
3	Bill Haley and His Comets, *Rock Around the Clock*	17,000,000
4	Beatles, *I Want to Hold Your Hand*	12,000,000
5=	Elvis Presley, *It's Now or Never*	10,000,000
=	Whitney Houston, *I Will Always Love You*	10,000,000
7=	Elvis Presley, *Hound Dog/Don't Be Cruel*	9,000,000
=	Paul Anka, *Diana*	9,000,000
9=	Beatles, *Hey Jude*	8,000,000
=	Monkees, *I'm a Believer*	8,000,000
=	Bryan Adams, *(Everything I Do) I Do it for You*	8,000,000

TOP 10 ALBUMS OF ALL TIME WORLDWIDE

	Artist/title	Est. sales
1	Michael Jackson, *Thriller*	40,000,000
2	Pink Floyd, *Dark Side of the Moon*	28,000,000
3	Meat Loaf, *Bat Out of Hell*	27,000,000
4	Soundtrack, *The Bodyguard*	26,000,000
5	Soundtrack, *Saturday Night Fever*	25,000,000
6=	Beatles, *Sgt. Pepper's Lonely Hearts Club Band*	24,000,000
=	Eagles, *Their Greatest Hits 1971–1975*	24,000,000
8	Mariah Carey, *Music Box*	23,000,000
9=	Carole King, *Tapestry*	22,000,000
=	Simon and Garfunkel, *Bridge Over Troubled Water*	22,000,000
=	Soundtrack, *Grease*	22,000,000
=	Michael Jackson, *Dangerous*	22,000,000

TOP 10
ARTISTS WITH THE MOST WEEKS IN THE UK SINGLES CHARTS*

Artist	Total no. of weeks	Artist	Total no. of weeks
1 Elvis Presley	1,155	6 Beatles	456
2 Cliff Richard	1,114	7 Madonna	448
3 Elton John	541	8 Frank Sinatra	439
4 Michael Jackson	480	9 David Bowie	432
5 Rod Stewart	458	10 Diana Ross	430

Up to 31 December 1997
Source: The Popular Music Database

TOP 10
ARTISTS WITH THE MOST WEEKS IN THE UK ALBUM CHARTS

Artist	Total no. of weeks	Artist	Total no. of weeks
1 Beatles	1,207	6 David Bowie	916
2 Queen	1,152	7 U2	907
3 Elvis Presley	1,113	8 Pink Floyd	871
4 Dire Straits	1,103	9 Michael Jackson	853
5 Simon and Garfunkel	1,094	10 Elton John	851

Source: The Popular Music Database

TOP 10
YOUNGEST SINGERS OF ALL TIME IN THE UK SINGLES CHARTS

Artist/title	Year	Age years	mths
1 Microbe (Ian Doody), *Groovy Baby*	1969	3	0
2 Natalie Casey, *Chick Chick Chicken*	1984	3	0
3 Little Jimmy Osmond, *Long Haired Lover from Liverpool*	1974	9	7
4 Lena Zavaroni, *Ma He's Making Eyes at Me*	1974	10	4
5 Neil Reid, *Mother of Mine*	1972	11	0
6 Michael Jackson, *Got to Be There*	1972	13	5
7 Laurie London, *He's Got the Whole World in His Hands*	1957	13	9
8 Jimmy Boyd, *I Saw Mommy Kissing Santa Claus*	1953	13	10
9 Marie Osmond, *Paper Roses*	1973	14	1
10 Helen Shapiro, *Don't Treat Me Like a Child*	1961	14	5

TOP 10
ARTISTS WITH THE MOST WEEKS IN THE US ALBUM CHARTS

Artist	Total no. of weeks
1 Frank Sinatra	2,238
2 Johnny Mathis	2,222
3 Beatles	1,955
4 Elvis Presley	1,858
5 Barbra Streisand	1,702
6 Rolling Stones	1,598
7 Mitch Miller	1,347
8 Elton John	1,337
9 Pink Floyd	1,309
10 Kingston Trio	1,262

Frank Sinatra's prodigious recordings began in the 1940s when he was in the Harry James band. Peaking in the 1950s and 60s, his long career lasted over 60 years.

Source: The Popular Music Database

TOP 10 ARTISTS WITH THE MOST WEEKS IN THE US SINGLES CHARTS
(Total no. of weeks)
❶ Elvis Presley (1,586) ❷ Elton John (956) ❸ Stevie Wonder (770)
❹ Rod Stewart (724) ❺ James Brown (706) ❻ Pat Boone (697)
❼ Madonna (673) ❽ Michael Jackson (661) ❾ Beatles (629)
❿ Fats Domino (604)
Source: The Popular Music Database

STEVIE WONDER
A recording artist since the age of 13, Stevie Wonder's hit singles include Living in the City *and* I Just Called to Say I Love You.

RECORD FIRSTS

BILL HALEY AND HIS COMETS
This US group personifies the birth of the rock era. Its Rock Around
the Clock *was the first single ever by a US group to reach No. 1 in
the UK, and the first UK record to sell a million copies.*

THE 10
FIRST MILLION-SELLING UK SINGLES

	Artist	Title	Year
1	Bill Haley and his Comets	*Rock Around the Clock*	1954
2	Harry Belafonte	*Mary's Boy Child*	1957
3	Paul Anka	*Diana*	1957
4	Elvis Presley	*It's Now or Never*	1960
5	Cliff Richard	*The Young Ones*	1962
6	Mr. Acker Bilk	*Stranger on the Shore*	1961
7	Frank Ifield	*I Remember You*	1962
8	Beatles	*She Loves You*	1963
9	Beatles	*I Want to Hold Your Hand*	1963
10	Beatles	*Can't Buy Me Love*	1964

The Beatles are the all-time platinum singles sales kings: they
amassed five million-selling UK singles in the 1960s, while John
Lennon added one with *Imagine* and McCartney another with
Wings' *Mull of Kintyre/Girls School* in 1978.

THE 10
FIRST UK CHART ALBUMS

	Artist	Title
1	Soundtrack	*South Pacific*
2	Frank Sinatra	*Come Fly With Me*
3	Elvis Presley	*Elvis' Golden Records*
4	Elvis Presley	*King Creole*
5	Broadway Cast	*My Fair Lady*
6	Johnny Mathis	*Warm*
7	Soundtrack	*The King and I*
8	Perry Como	*Dear Perry*
9	Soundtrack	*Oklahoma!*
10	Tom Lehrer	*Songs by Tom Lehrer*

The first album chart was printed in
Melody Maker for the week ending
8 November 1958 and represents a time
capsule of the popular music of the era; a
transitional period when crooners, comedy
singers, and musical singers rubbed
shoulders with up-and-coming rock artistes,
such as 23-year old Elvis Presley.

Source: Melody Maker

THE 10
FIRST UK CHART SINGLES

	Artist	Title
1	Al Martino	*Here in my Heart*
2	Jo Stafford	*You Belong to Me*
3	Nat "King" Cole	*Somewhere along the Way*
4	Bing Crosby	*Isle of Innisfree*
5	Guy Mitchell	*Feet Up*
6	Rosemary Clooney	*Half as Much*
7=	Frankie Laine	*High Noon*
=	Vera Lynn	*Forget Me Not*
9=	Doris Day and Frankie Laine	*Sugarbush*
=	Ray Martin	*Blue Tango*

The first UK singles chart was published in
the *New Musical Express* for the week
ending 15 November 1952. Curiously, the
Top 10 contained 12 entries because those
of equal rank shared the same placing.

Source: New Musical Express

THE 10
FIRST FEMALE SINGERS TO HAVE A NO. 1 HIT IN THE UK

	Artist/title	Date at No. 1
1	Jo Stafford, *You Belong to Me*	16 Jan 1953
2	Kay Starr, *Comes A-Long A-Love*	23 Jan 1953
3	Lita Roza, *(How Much is that) Doggie in the Window?*	17 Apr 1953
4	Doris Day, *Secret Love*	16 Apr 1954
5	Kitty Kallen, *Little Things Mean a Lot*	10 Sep 1954
6	Vera Lynn, *My Son, My Son*	5 Nov 1954
7	Rosemary Clooney, *This Ole House*	26 Nov 1954
8	Ruby Murray, *Softly Softly*	18 Feb 1955
9	Alma Cogan, *Dreamboat*	15 Jul 1955
10	Anne Shelton, *Lay Down Your Arms*	21 Sep 1956

Source: The Popular Music Database

THE 10

FIRST BRITISH SOLO ARTISTS TO HAVE A NO. 1 HIT IN THE US

	Artist	Title	Date at No. 1
1	Mr. Acker Bilk	*Stranger on the Shore*	26 May 1962
2	Petula Clark	*Downtown*	23 Jan 1965
3	Donovan	*Sunshine Superman*	3 Sep 1966
4	Lulu	*To Sir with Love*	21 Oct 1967
5	George Harrison	*My Sweet Lord*	26 Dec 1970
6	Rod Stewart	*Maggie May*	2 Oct 1971
7	Gilbert O'Sullivan	*Alone Again Naturally*	29 Jul 1972
8	Elton John	*Crocodile Rock*	3 Feb 1973
9	Ringo Starr	*Photograph*	24 Nov 1973
10	Eric Clapton	*I Shot the Sheriff*	14 Sep 1974

The majority of British acts that topped the US chart in the 1960s were groups. Prior to the rock era, the first British No. 1 in the US was Vera Lynn's *Auf Wiedersehen (Sweetheart)* in 1952.

Source: The Popular Music Database

THE 10

FIRST AMERICAN SOLO ARTISTS TO HAVE A NO. 1 HIT IN THE UK

	Artist	Title	Date at No. 1
1	Al Martino	*Here in my Heart*	14 Nov 1952
2	Jo Stafford	*You Belong to Me*	16 Jan 1953
3	Kay Starr	*Comes A-Long A-Love*	23 Jan 1953
4	Eddie Fisher	*Outside of Heaven*	30 Jan 1953
5	Perry Como	*Don't Let the Stars Get in your Eyes*	6 Feb 1953
6	Guy Mitchell	*She Wears Red Feathers*	13 Mar 1953
7	Frankie Laine	*I Believe*	24 Apr 1953
8	Doris Day	*Secret Love*	16 Apr 1954
9	Johnnie Ray	*Such a Night*	30 Apr 1954
10	Kitty Kallen	*Little Things Mean a Lot*	10 Sep 1954

In the 1950s it was clearly a great deal easier for American solo artists to top the UK chart than it was for British artists to compete in the US market.

Source: The Popular Music Database

THE 10

FIRST BRITISH GROUPS TO HAVE A NO. 1 HIT IN THE US

	Artist/title	Date at No. 1
1	Tornados, *Telstar*	22 Dec 1962
2	Beatles, *I Want to Hold Your Hand*	1 Feb 1964
3	Animals, *House of the Rising Sun*	5 Sep 1964
4	Manfred Mann, *Do Wah Diddy Diddy*	17 Oct 1964
5	Freddie and the Dreamers, *I'm Telling You Now*	10 Apr 1965
6	Wayne Fontana and the Mindbenders, *The Game of Love*	24 Apr 1965
7	Herman's Hermits, *Mrs. Brown You've Got a Lovely Daughter*	1 May 1965
8	Rolling Stones, *(I Can't Get No) Satisfaction*	10 Jul 1965
9	Dave Clark Five, *Over and Over*	25 Dec 1965
10	Troggs, *Wild Thing*	30 Jul 1966

Source: The Popular Music Database

TORNADOS
Telstar *sold over five million copies and was the first single by a UK group to reach No. 1 in the US.*

THE 10

FIRST AMERICAN GROUPS TO HAVE A NO. 1 HIT IN THE UK

	Artist/title	Date at No. 1
1	Bill Haley and his Comets, *Rock Around the Clock*	25 Nov 1955
2	Dream Weavers, *It's Almost Tomorrow*	16 Mar 1956
3	Teenagers featuring Frankie Lymon, *Why Do Fools Fall in Love?*	20 Jul 1956
4	Crickets, *That'll Be the Day*	1 Nov 1957
5	Platters, *Smoke Gets in Your Eyes*	20 Mar 1959
6	Marcels, *Blue Moon*	4 May 1961
7	Highwaymen, *Michael*	12 Oct 1961
8	B. Bumble and the Stingers, *Nut Rocker*	17 May 1962
9	Supremes, *Baby Love*	19 Nov 1964
10	Byrds, *Mr. Tambourine Man*	22 Jul 1965

Source: The Popular Music Database

CHART TOPPERS

TOP 10

SINGLES WITH MOST WEEKS AT NO. 1 IN THE UK

	Artist/title/year	Weeks at No. 1
1	Frankie Laine, *I Believe*, 1953	18
2	Bryan Adams, *(Everything I Do) I Do it for You*, 1991	16
3	Wet Wet Wet, *Love is all Around*, 1994	15
4	Queen, *Bohemian Rhapsody*, 1975 and 1991	14
5	Slim Whitman, *Rose Marie*, 1955	11
6=	David Whitfield, *Cara Mia*, 1954	10
=	Whitney Houston, *I Will Always Love You*, 1993	10
8=	Paul Anka, *Diana*, 1957	9
=	Al Martino, *Here in My Heart*, 1952	9
=	Wings, *Mull of Kintyre*, 1977	9
=	Eddie Calvert, *Oh Mein Papa*, 1954	9
=	Doris Day, *Secret Love*, 1954	9
=	Frankie Goes to Hollywood, *Two Tribes*, 1984	9
=	John Travolta and Olivia Newton-John, *You're the One that I Want*, 1978	9

The totals for *I Believe* and *Bohemian Rhapsody* are cumulative of more than one run at the top. All other totals are for consecutive chart-topping weeks, which means Bryan Adams is the champion in terms of an unbroken No. 1 run.

Source: The Popular Music Database

TOP 10

OLDEST ARTISTS TO HAVE A NO. 1 SINGLE IN THE UK*

	Artist	Title	Age yrs	mths
1	Louis Armstrong	*What a Wonderful World*	67	10
2	Frank Sinatra	*Somethin' Stupid*	51	4
3	Telly Savalas	*If*	51	1
4	Cliff Richard	*Saviour's Day*	50	2
5	Righteous Brothers	*Unchained Melody*	50/50	2/1
6	Charles Aznavour	*She*	50	1
7	Clive Dunn	*Grandad*	49	0
8	Ben E. King	*Stand by Me*	48	5
9	Gene Pitney	*Something's Gotten Hold of My Heart*	48	0
10	Mantovani	*Theme from "Moulin Rouge"*	47	9

* To 31 March 1997

The ages listed are those of the artists during the final week of their last (to date) No. 1 hit. Gene Pitney was just a day over 48 as his 1989 duet success with Marc Almond finished its chart-topping run. Seven of the 10 are still alive, so there is room for improvement.

Source: The Popular Music Database

TOP 10

ALBUMS WITH THE MOST CONSECUTIVE WEEKS AT NO. 1 IN THE UK

	Artist/title	Consecutive weeks at No. 1
1	Soundtrack, *South Pacific*	70
2	Beatles, *Please Please Me*	30
3	Beatles, *Sgt. Pepper's Lonely Hearts Club Band*	23
4=	Beatles, *With the Beatles*	21
=	Beatles, *A Hard Day's Night*	21
6	Soundtrack, *South Pacific*	19
7=	Soundtrack, *The Sound of Music*	18
=	Soundtrack, *Saturday Night Fever*	18
9	Elvis Presley, *Blue Hawaii*	17
10	Cliff Richard and the Shadows, *Summer Holiday*	14

Source: The Popular Music Database

TOP 10

LONGEST GAPS BETWEEN NO. 1 HIT SINGLES IN THE UK

	Artist	Period	Gap years	months
1	Righteous Brothers	11 Feb 1965–28 Oct 1990	25	8
2	Hollies	15 July 1965–18 Sept 1988	23	2
3	Queen	24 Jan 1976–20 Jan 1991	15	0
4	Diana Ross	11 Sept 1971–2 Mar 1986	14	6
5	Frank Sinatra	1 Oct 1954–27 May 1966	11	7
6	Cliff Richard	17 Apr 1968–19 Aug 1979	11	4
7	Bee Gees	4 Sept 1968–23 Apr 1978	9	7
8	Cliff Richard	15 Sept 1979–4 Dec 1988	9	3
9	Bee Gees	10 Mar 1979–11 Oct 1987	8	7
10	Don McLean	21 June 1972–13 June 1980	8	0

Source: The Popular Music Database

TOP 10

YOUNGEST ARTISTS TO HAVE A NO. 1 SINGLE IN THE UK*

	Artist/title/year	Age# yrs	mths
1	Little Jimmy Osmond, *Long Haired Lover From Liverpool*, 1972	9	8
2	Donny Osmond, *Puppy Love*, 1972	14	6
3	Helen Shapiro, *You Don't Know*, 1961	14	10
4	Paul Anka, *Diana*, 1957	16	0
5	Tiffany, *I Think We're Alone Now*, 1988	16	3
6	Nicole, *A Little Peace*, 1982	17	0
7	Glenn Medeiros, *Nothing's Gonna Change My Love*, 1988	18	0
8	Mary Hopkin, *Those Were the Days*, 1968	18	4
9	Cliff Richard, *Living Doll*, 1958	18	8
10	Adam Faith, *What Do You Want*, 1959	19	5

* *To 31 December 1997*

\# *During first week of debut No.1 UK single*

Source: The Popular Music Database

TOP 10

ARTISTS WITH THE MOST NO. 1 SINGLES IN THE UK

	Artist	No. 1 singles
1 =	Beatles	17
=	Elvis Presley	17
3	Cliff Richard	13
4	Abba	9
5 =	Rolling Stones	8
=	Take That	8
7 =	Madonna	7
=	George Michael	7
9 =	Slade	6
=	Rod Stewart	6
=	Spice Girls	6

Source: The Popular Music Database

TOP 10

ALBUMS LONGEST AT NO. 1 IN THE UK

	Artist/title	Weeks at No. 1
1	Soundtrack, *South Pacific*	115
2	Soundtrack, *The Sound of Music*	70
3	Simon and Garfunkel, *Bridge Over Troubled Water*	41
4	Beatles, *Please Please Me*	30
5	Beatles, *Sgt. Pepper's Lonely Hearts Club Band*	27
6	Elvis Presley/Soundtrack, *G.I. Blues*	22
7 =	Beatles, *With the Beatles*	21
=	Beatles/Soundtrack, *A Hard Day's Night*	21
9 =	Elvis Presley/Soundtrack, *Blue Hawaii*	18
=	Soundtrack, *Saturday Night Fever*	18

Source: The Popular Music Database

ELVIS PRESLEY
No artist has matched his record number of weeks at the top of the UK, as well as the US, singles chart.

TOP 10

ARTISTS WITH THE MOST WEEKS AT NO. 1 IN THE UK

	Artist	Weeks at No. 1
1	Elvis Presley	73
2	Beatles	69
3	Cliff Richard	44*
4	Frankie Laine	32
5	Abba	31
6	Wet Wet Wet	23
7	Take That	21
8 =	Queen	20#
=	Slade	20
10	Everly Brothers	19

* *Including three weeks with the Young Ones*

\# *Including two weeks with David Bowie and three with George Michael and Lisa Stansfield*

Source: The Popular Music Database

TOP 10

ALBUMS OF ALL TIME IN THE UK

	Artist/title	Year
1	Beatles, *Sgt. Pepper's Lonely Hearts Club Band*	1967
2	Oasis, *(What's the Story) Morning Glory*	1996
3	Michael Jackson, *Bad*	1987
4	Dire Straits, *Brothers in Arms*	1985
5	Simply Red, *Stars*	1991
6	Michael Jackson, *Thriller*	1982
7	Queen, *Greatest Hits*	1991
8	Spice Girls, *Spice*	1996
9	Madonna, *The Immaculate Collection*	1990
10	Elton John, *The Very Best of Elton John*	1980

Source: BPI

STAR SINGLES & ALBUMS

TOP 10

ROLLING STONES SINGLES IN THE UK

	Single	Year
1	The Last Time	1965
2	(I Can't Get No) Satisfaction	1965
3	Honky Tonk Women	1969
4	It's All Over Now	1964
5	Get Off of My Cloud	1965
6	Paint It Black	1966
7	Jumpin' Jack Flash	1968
8	Little Red Rooster	1964
9	Miss You	1978
10	Brown Sugar	1971

The Stones had their singles-selling heyday during the mid-1960s, when the first eight of these titles reached No. 1 in the UK.

Source: MRIB

TOP 10

ELVIS PRESLEY SINGLES IN THE UK

	Single	Year
1	It's Now or Never	1960
2	Jailhouse Rock	1958
3	Are You Lonesome Tonight	1961
4	Wooden Heart	1961
5	Return to Sender	1962
6	Can't Help Falling In Love	1962
7	The Wonder of You	1970
8	Surrender	1961
9	Way Down	1977
10	All Shook Up	1957

Elvis was at his sales peak in the UK, shortly after he left the army in the early 1960s. *It's Now or Never* was his only million-seller on UK sales alone, though all the records in this list registered sales in excess of 600,000, and these 10 singles accounted for a total of 46 weeks at the top of the UK chart.

Source: MRIB

THE ROLLING STONES

TOP 10

ROLLING STONES ALBUMS IN THE UK

	Album	Year		Album	Year
1	The Rolling Stones No. 2	1965	6	Some Girls	1978
2	Aftermath	1966	7	Emotional Rescue	1980
3	Rolled Gold – The Very Best of the Rolling Stones	1975	8	Exile on Main Street	1972
4	Let It Bleed	1969	9	The Rolling Stones	1964
5	Sticky Fingers	1971	10	Tattoo You	1981

Source: MRIB

TOP 10

MADONNA SINGLES IN THE UK

	Single	Year
1	Like a Virgin	1984
2	Into the Groove	1985
3	Papa Don't Preach	1986
4	Crazy for You	1985
5	Holiday	1984
6	True Blue	1986
7	Vogue	1990
8	La Isla Bonita	1987
9	Like a Prayer	1989
10	Who's That Girl?	1987

Source: MRIB

TOP 10

JOHN LENNON ALBUMS IN THE UK

	Album	Year
1	Imagine	1971
2	The John Lennon Collection	1982
3	Double Fantasy	1980
4	Shaved Fish	1975
5	Rock 'n' Roll	1975
6	Milk and Honey	1984
7	Walls and Bridges	1974
8	Mind Games	1973
9	John Lennon and the Plastic Ono Band	1971
10	Lennon Legend – The Very Best of John Lennon	1997

Source: The Popular Music Database

TOP 10
MICHAEL JACKSON SINGLES IN THE UK

	Single	Year
1	*Earth Song*	1995
2	*You are not Alone*	1995
3	*One Day in Your Life*	1981
4	*Billie Jean*	1983
5	*Say Say Say* (with Paul McCartney)	1983
6	*Don't Stop Till You Get Enough*	1979
7	*Beat It*	1983
8	*Rockin' Robin*	1972
9	*Black and White*	1991
10	*Ben*	1972

His lengthy career notwithstanding, Michael Jackson's two most successful singles in this country are among his most recent recordings, with *Earth Song* topping the million sales mark in the UK.

Source: MRIB

TOP 10
ELTON JOHN SINGLES IN THE UK

	Single	Year
1	*Candle in the Wind 1997*	1997
2	*Don't Go Breaking My Heart* (with Kiki Dee)	1976
3	*Sacrifice*	1990
4	*Rocket Man*	1972
5	*Nikita*	1985
6	*Crocodile Rock*	1972
7	*Daniel*	1973
8	*Song for Guy*	1978
9	*I Guess That's Why They Call it the Blues*	1983
10	*I'm Still Standing*	1983

During the 1970s, Elton John's popularity in America exceeded that at home. His US million-sellers like *Bennie and the Jets*, *Philadelphia Freedom*, and *Island Girl* do not, however, qualify for this Top 10.

Source: MRIB

TOP 10
DAVID BOWIE SINGLES IN THE UK

	Single	Year
1	*Space Oddity*	1969/75
2	*Let's Dance*	1983
3	*Dancing in the Street* (with Mick Jagger)	1985
4	*Ashes to Ashes*	1981
5	*Under Pressure* (with Queen)	1981
6	*The Jean Genie*	1972
7	*Life on Mars*	1973
8	*Sorrow*	1973
9	*China Girl*	1983
10	*The Laughing Gnome*	1973

Bowie's *Space Oddity* was a Top 5 success when first released, and an even bigger seller, reaching No. 1, on its reissue in 1975.

Source: MRIB

TOP 10
MICHAEL JACKSON ALBUMS IN THE UK

	Album	Year
1	*Bad*	1987
2	*Thriller*	1982
3	*Dangerous*	1991
4	*Off the Wall*	1979
5	*History – Past Present and Future Book 1*	1995
6	*Blood on the Dance Floor*	1997
7	*The Best of Michael Jackson*	1981
8	*The Michael Jackson Mix*	1987
9	*Farewell My Summer Love*	1984
10	*Ben*	1973

Britain is one of the few countries where *Bad* has outsold the all-time global bestselling album, *Thriller*.

Source: MRIB

TOP 10
BOB DYLAN ALBUMS IN THE UK

	Album	Year
1	*Blonde on Blonde*	1966
2	*Bringing it All Back Home*	1965
3	*Bob Dylan's Greatest Hits*	1967
4	*Nashville Skyline*	1969
5	*John Wesley Harding*	1968
6	*Highway 61 Revisited*	1965
7	*Street Legal*	1978
8	*The Freewheelin' Bob Dylan*	1963
9	*Desire*	1976
10	*New Morning*	1970

Bob Dylan's sales peak in Britain was in the mid- and late 1960s, when he was one of the first artists to sell large quantities of albums rather than singles.

Source: MRIB

TOP 10
DAVID BOWIE ALBUMS IN THE UK

	Album	Year
1	*The Rise and Fall of Ziggy Stardust and the Spiders from Mars*	1972
2	*Hunky Dory*	1972
3	*Aladdin Sane*	1973
4	*Let's Dance*	1983
5	*Pinups*	1973
6	*Scary Monsters and Super Creeps*	1980
7	*Changesbowie*	1990
8	*Changesonébowie*	1976
9	*Diamond Dogs*	1974
10	*The Very Best of David Bowie*	1981

Although it never made the top spot, the No. 1 entry in this list spent 176 weeks in the UK album chart, from 1972–74, in 1981, and upon its CD release in 1990.

Source: The Popular Music Database

THE BEATLES

MCCARTNEY AND HARRISON
Although Paul McCartney enjoyed by far the most successful solo career post-Beatles, George Harrison was the first ex-Beatle to secure a chart-topping single with his debut solo, My Sweet Lord (1970).

THE 10
FIRST BEATLES SINGLES RELEASED IN THE UK

	Title	Label	Release date
1	*My Bonnie/The Saints**	Polydor	Jan 1962
2	*Love Me Do/P.S. I Love You*	Parlophone	Oct 1962
3	*Please Please Me/Ask Me Why*	Parlophone	Jan 1963
4	*From Me to You/Thank You Girl*	Parlophone	April 1963
5	*She Loves You/I'll Get You*	Parlophone	Aug 1963
6	*I Want to Hold Your Hand/ This Boy*	Parlophone	Nov 1963
7	*Why/Cry for a Shadow*	Polydor	Feb 1964
8	*Can't Buy Me Love/You Can't Do That*	Parlophone	March 1964
9	*Ain't She Sweet/If You Love Me Baby*	Polydor	May 1964
10	*A Hard Day's Night/Things We Said Today*	Parlophone	July 1964

* *Credited to Tony Sheridan and the Beatles, released in Germany in June 1961 and in the UK in January 1962*

The three singles on Polydor originated from the group's pre-Parlophone days. The songs were recorded in Hamburg in 1961–62 with orchestra leader Bert Kaempfert, and later officially released in the UK.

Source: The Popular Music Database

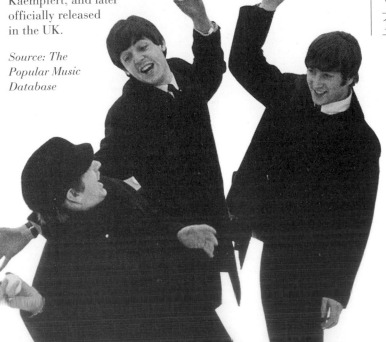

TOP 10
MOST VALUABLE BEATLES ALBUMS IN THE UK

	Title	Special feature	Year	Est. value (£)
1	*The Beatles (White Album)*	Nos. 1–10	1968	3–5,000
2	*Please Please Me*	First UK stereo album with gold/black label	1963	1,250
3	*Abbey Road*	Export	1969	1,000
4	*Yellow Submarine*	Odeon UK	1969	1,000
5	*Beatles VI*	Export – Parlophone yellow/black label	1965	700
6	*Revolver*	Including remix 11 of *Tomorrow Never Knows*	1966	200
7	*From Then to You*	Fan club album compiling Xmas flexis	1970	250
8	*Let it Be*	Box set with *Get Back* book	1970	200
9	*Yellow Submarine*	Mono	1969	150
10	*The Beatles First*	Polydor	1964	60

Source: Record Collector

BEATLEMANIA
The Beatles' first tour of the US in 1964 took the country by storm. In April of that year, they unprecedentedly held all five top slots on the Billboard chart.

TOP 10

MOST COVERED BEATLES SONGS

	Title	Year written
1	*Yesterday*	1965
2	*Something*	1969
3	*Eleanor Rigby*	1966
4	*Let it Be*	1969
5	*Hey Jude*	1968
6	*The Fool on the Hill*	1967
7	*The Long and Winding Road*	1969
8	*Michelle*	1965
9	*With a Little Help from My Friends*	1967
10	*Day Tripper*	1965

Yesterday is one of the most covered songs of all time, with the number of recorded versions now in four figures. Although most of these songs are Lennon/McCartney compositions, the No. 2 entry, *Something*, was written by George Harrison.

Source: MRIB

TOP 10

BEATLES SINGLES THAT STAYED LONGEST IN THE UK CHARTS

	Title	Year	Weeks in Charts
1	*She Loves You*	1963–64	33
2	*I Want to Hold Your Hand*	1963–64	22
3	*From Me to You*	1963	21
4=	*Love Me Do*	1962–63	18
=	*Please Please Me*	1963	18
6	*Get Back*	1969	17
7	*Hey Jude*	1968	16
8	*Can't Buy Me Love*	1964	15
9=	*Help!*	1965	14
=	*The Ballad of John and Yoko*	1969	14

Source: The Popular Music Database

TOP 10

LONGEST BEATLES TRACKS

	Title	Duration min	sec
1	*Revolution No. 9*	8	15
2	*I Want You (She's So Heavy)*	7	49
3	*Hey Jude*	7	11
4	*It's All Too Much*	6	27
5	*You Know My Name (Look Up the Number)*	5	41
6=	*A Day in the Life*	5	3
=	*Within You Without You*	5	3
8	*While My Guitar Gently Weeps*	4	46
9	*I am the Walrus*	4	35
10	*Helter Skelter*	4	30

Most of the Beatles' lengthy tracks come from their later recording days; in the earlier 1960s, most of their songs lasted between two and three minutes. Apart from *Hey Jude* (still the longest No. 1 single ever) and *You Know My Name* (the B side of *Let It Be*), the tracks listed here are found on the albums from *Sgt. Pepper* onwards.

Source: MRIB

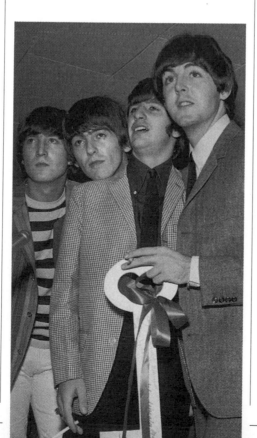

TOP 10

MOST VALUABLE BEATLES SINGLES IN THE UK

	Title/ special feature	Year	Est. value (£)
1	*That'll Be the Day/ In Spite of All the Danger*, (Quarrymen) 78 rpm acetate	1958	100,000
2	*Love Me Do,* Demo	1962	1,200
3	*Our First Four,* Presentation pack including *Hey Jude*	1968	1,000
4	*Something,* Demo	1969	700
5	*Across the Universe,* World Wildlife Fund demo	1968	350
6	*Medley,* Demo for Rock 'n' Roll Music album	1976	250
7	*Michelle,* Export		100
8	*The Beatles Christmas Record,* Fan club flexidisc	1963	80
9	*Love Me Do,* Black label	1962	60
10	*My Bonnie,* Orange label	1963	50

Source: Record Collector

TOP 10 BEATLES ALBUMS THAT STAYED LONGEST IN THE UK CHARTS

(Weeks in Charts)

❶ *Sgt. Pepper's Lonely Hearts Club Band* (181) ❷ *The Beatles, 1962–1966* (172) ❸ *The Beatles, 1967–1970* (136) ❹ *Abbey Road* (89) ❺ *Please Please Me* (74) ❻ *Let It Be* (60) ❼ *With The Beatles* (54) ❽ *Beatles for Sale* (48) ❾ *Rubber Soul* (46) ❿ *A Hard Day's Night* (42)

Source: The Popular Music Database

MUSICAL HERITAGE
In the eight years from 1962 to 1970, the Beatles established themselves as a musical legend.

SINGLES & ALBUMS

TOP 10

ONE-HIT WONDERS IN THE UK

	Artist/title	Year
1	Simon Park Orchestra, *Eye Level*	1973
2	Archies, *Sugar Sugar*	1969
3	Clive Dunn, *Grandad*	1971
4	Joe Dolce Music Theatre, *Shaddup You Face*	1981
5	St. Winifred's School Choir, *There's No One Quite Like Grandma*	1980
6	Phyllis Nelson, *Move Closer*	1985
7	Fern Kinney, *Together We are Beautiful*	1980
8	Lee Marvin, *Wand'rin' Star*	1970
9	Kalin Twins, *When*	1958
10	Ricky Valance *Tell Laura I Love Her*	1960

Source: MRIB

TOP 10

INSTRUMENTAL SINGLES OF ALL TIME IN THE UK

	Artist/title	Year
1	Mr. Acker Bilk, *Stranger on the Shore*	1961
2	Simon Park Orchestra, *Eye Level*	1972
3	Tornados, *Telstar*	1962
4	Anton Karas, *The Harry Lime Theme (The Third Man)*	1950
5	Royal Scots Dragoon Guards Band, *Amazing Grace*	1972
6	Ennio Morricone, *Chi Mai*	1981
7	Shadows, *Wonderful Land*	1962
8	Shadows, *Apache*	1960
9	Fleetwood Mac, *Albatross*	1968
10	Lieutenant Pigeon, *Mouldy Old Dough*	1972

This Top 10 reveals that non-vocal hits are more likely to be found in the "middle-of-the-road" sector than in Rock 'n' Roll. Nos. 1 and 2 were both UK million-sellers.

Source: MRIB

TOP 10

"GREATEST HITS" ALBUMS OF ALL TIME IN THE UK

	Artist/title	Year
1	Queen, *Greatest Hits*	1981
2	Madonna, *The Immaculate Collection*	1990
3	Simon and Garfunkel, *Simon and Garfunkel's Greatest Hits*	1972
4	Elton John, *The Very Best of Elton John*	1990
5	Bob Marley and the Wailers, *Legend*	1984
6	Queen, *Greatest Hits II*	1991
7	Beautiful South, *Carry on Up the Charts – The Best of*	1994
8	Rod Stewart, *The Best of Rod Stewart*	1989
9	Dire Straits, *Money for Nothing*	1989
10	Abba, *Abba's Greatest Hits*	1976

Source: MRIB

TOP 10

JAZZ ALBUMS OF ALL TIME IN THE UK

	Artist/title	Year
1	Harry Connick Jr., *We are in Love*	1990
2	Harry Connick Jr., *Blue Light, Red Light*	1991
3	Various Artists, *Jazz on a Summer's Day*	1992
4	Spyro Gyra, *Morning Dance*	1979
5	George Benson, *In Flight*	1977
6	Kenny G, *Duotones*	1987
7	Kenny Ball, Chris Barber, and Acker Bilk, *Best of Ball, Barber and Bilk*	1962
8	Frank Sinatra and Count Basie, *Sinatra/Basie*	1963
9	Kenny Ball, *Kenny Ball's Golden Hits*	1963
10	Dave Brubeck Quartet, *Time Out Featuring Take Five*	1960

TOP 10

HEAVY METAL SINGLES OF ALL TIME IN THE UK

	Artist/title	Year
1	Meat Loaf, *I'll Do Anything for Love (But I Won't Do That)*	1993
2	Survivor, *Eye of the Tiger*	1982
3	Europe, *The Final Countdown*	1986
4	Foreigner, *I Want to Know What Love Is*	1984
5	Free, *All Right Now*	1970
6	Black Sabbath, *Paranoid*	1970
7	Alice Cooper, *School's Out*	1972
8	Status Quo, *Down Down*	1974
9	Deep Purple, *Black Night*	1970
10	Jimi Hendrix Experience, *Voodoo Chile*	1970

Meat Loaf's comeback single was the biggest seller (from the biggest album) of 1993 and sold over 800,000 copies in the UK.

Source: MRIB

TOP 10

HEAVY METAL ALBUMS OF ALL TIME IN THE UK

	Artist/title	Year
1	Meat Loaf, *Bat Out of Hell*	1978
2	Meat Loaf, *Bat Out of Hell II - Back to Hell*	1993
3	Led Zeppelin, *Led Zeppelin II*	1969
4	Def Leppard, *Hysteria*	1987
5	Led Zeppelin, *Led Zeppelin IV*	1971
6	Bon Jovi, *Cross Road – The Best of Bon Jovi*	1994
7	Bryan Adams, *So Far So Good*	1993
8	ZZ Top, *Eliminator*	1983
9	Guns N' Roses, *Appetite for Destruction*	1987
10	Bon Jovi, *Slippery When Wet*	1986

Source: MRIB

TOP 10

COUNTRY SINGLES OF ALL TIME IN THE UK

	Artist/title	Year
1	Jim Reeves, *I Love You Because*	1964
2	Jim Reeves, *I Won't Forget You*	1964
3	Kenny Rogers, *Ruby (Don't Take Your Love to Town)*	1969
4	Roger Miller, *King of the Road*	1965
5	Kenny Rogers, *Lucille*	1977
6	Tammy Wynette, *Stand by Your Man*	1975
7	Kenny Rogers, *Coward of the County*	1980
8	Jim Reeves, *Distant Drums*	1966
9	Slim Whitman, *Rose Marie*	1955
10	Tennessee Ernie Ford, *Give Me Your Word*	1955

Even though *I Love You Because* made only UK No. 5, it is still the bestselling Country single ever in Britain, shifting over 750,000 copies in 1964 alone.

Source: MRIB

TOP 10

FOREIGN-LANGUAGE SINGLES IN THE UK

	Artist/title	Language
1	Jane Birkin and Serge Gainsbourg, *Je T'aime...Moi Non Plus*	French
2	Falco, *Rock Me Amadeus*	German
3	Julio Iglesias, *Begin the Beguine*	Spanish
4	Manhattan Transfer, *Chanson d'Amour*	French
5	Los Lobos, *La Bamba*	Spanish
6	Marino Marini, *Come Prima/Volare*	Italian
7	Luciano Pavarotti, *Nessun Dorma*	Italian
8	Vanessa Paradis, *Joe le Taxi*	French
9	Kaoma, *Lambada*	Portuguese
10	Singing Nun, *Dominique*	French

Source: MRIB

TOP 10

SINGLES ON THE MOTOWN LABEL IN THE UK

	Artist/title	Year
1	Stevie Wonder, *I Just Called to Say I Love You*	1984
2	Lionel Richie, *Hello*	1984
3	Commodores, *Three Times a Lady*	1978
4	Marvin Gaye, *I Heard It Through The Grapevine*	1969
5	Michael Jackson, *One Day In Your Life*	1981
6	Smokey Robinson, *Being with You*	1981
7	Lionel Richie, *All Night Long (All Night)*	1983
8	Four Tops, *Reach Out, I'll be There*	1966
9	Diana Ross, *I'm Still Waiting*	1971
10	Smokey Robinson and the Miracles, *Tears of a Clown*	1970

Source: MRIB

TOP 10

ORIGINAL CAST RECORDING ALBUMS OF ALL TIME IN THE UK

	Title/venue	Year
1	*Phantom of the Opera*, London	1987
2	*Hair*, London	1968
3	*Joseph and the Amazing Technicolor Dreamcoat*, London	1991
4	*My Fair Lady*, Broadway	1958
5	*The Sound of Music*, London	1961
6	*Oliver*, London	1960
7	*Evita**	1977
8	*Cats*, London	1981
9	*Fiddler on the Roof*, London	1967
10	*Jesus Christ Superstar#*	1972

* *A studio cast recording which outperformed the actual stage show album version released a year later*

\# *A studio cast recording based on the successful musical, although an original cast recording never charted*

Source: MRIB

BOYZ II MEN
Boyz II Men, a Philadelphia R&B vocal quartet, are Motown's biggest-selling act of the 1990s by far, scoring three platinum singles within a period of 18 months.

TOP 10

POSTHUMOUS SINGLES IN THE UK

	Artist/title	Died	Hit year
1	John Lennon, *Imagine*	1980	1981
2	Jackie Wilson, *Reet Petite*	1984	1986
3	Buddy Holly, *It Doesn't Matter Anymore*	1959	1959
4	John Lennon, *Woman*	1980	1981
5	Elvis Presley, *Way Down*	1977	1977
6	Jim Reeves, *I Won't Forget You*	1964	1964
7	Jim Reeves, *Distant Drums*	1964	1966
8	Eddie Cochran, *Three Steps to Heaven*	1960	1960
9	Jimi Hendrix, *Voodoo Chile*	1970	1970
10	Laurel and Hardy, *The Trail of the Lonesome Pine*	1965/ 1975	1975

Jackie Wilson's *Reet Petite* had been a chart hit during the 1950s, but it was the 1986 UK reissue which saw the greater success.

Source: MRIB

GOLD & PLATINUM DISCS

MALE ARTISTS WITH THE MOST PLATINUM ALBUMS IN THE US

	Artist	Platinum albums
1	Billy Joel	69
2	Garth Brooks	68
3	Michael Jackson	51
4	Bruce Springsteen	48
5	Elton John	47
6	Kenny Rogers	45
7	Elvis Presley	42
8	Kenny G	37
9	Neil Diamond	35
10=	George Strait	34
=	Eric Clapton	33

The award of a platinum album, made by the Recording Industry Association of America (RIAA), the trade association of record companies in the US, confirms a minimum sale of 1,000,000 copies of an album. For each additional 1,000,000 copies of an album sold, another platinum album is awarded.

Source: The Popular Music Database

FEMALE ARTISTS WITH THE MOST PLATINUM ALBUMS IN THE US

	Artist	Platinum albums
1	Barbra Streisand	47
2	Madonna	46
3	Whitney Houston	42
4	Mariah Carey	41
5	Celine Dion	24
6	Linda Ronstadt	23
7	Reba McEntire	22
8	Janet Jackson	19
9=	Gloria Estefan	18
=	Sade	18

Source: The Popular Music Database

ALBUM SALES TAKE OFF

Prior to 1948, records were 78-rpm, restricting the length of records to four minutes. In that year, Columbia Records broke through this barrier with the launch of its 12-inch micro-groove disc of non-breakable Vinylite, played at 33⅓ revolutions per minute and offering 23 minutes per side. The company's range of "Long Players" was released on 18 September. By 18 June 1949, Columbia was able to announce sales of 3.5 million LPs in its first year. Now that the new format was an obvious success, Capital and Decca began producing albums. Decca's cast recording of *Oklahoma* became the first-ever multi-million selling LP. It was to take a further 40 years, until 1989, before sales of compact discs overtook those of vinyl LPs.

50 YEARS AGO

MALE ARTISTS WITH THE MOST PLATINUM ALBUMS IN THE UK

	Artist	Platinum albums
1	Michael Jackson	38
2	Phil Collins	27
3	Elton John	19
4	Meat Loaf	16
5 =	George Michael	14
=	Rod Stewart	14
=	Chris Rea	14
8 =	Cliff Richard	13
=	Michael Bolton	13
10 =	Bryan Adams	11
=	Lionel Richie	11

Platinum albums in the UK are those that have achieved sales of 300,000. For every 300,000 copies of an album sold another platinum album is awarded. This represents approximately one sale per 195 inhabitants, – a greater attainment than a US platinum award, where the ratio is one per 266.

Source: BPI

SNAP FACT

• The first gold disc awarded for sales of a million singles went to bandleader Glenn Miller for *Chattanooga Choo Choo*. It was presented to him during a live broadcast on 10 February 1942.

GROUPS WITH THE MOST GOLD ALBUMS IN THE UK

	Group	Gold albums
1	Queen	21
2	Status Quo	19
3	The Rolling Stones	18
4=	Abba	14
=	Genesis	14
6=	The Beatles	13
=	Roxy Music	13
8	UB40	12
9=	Pink Floyd	11
=	10cc	11

Gold discs have been awarded since 1 April 1973 in the UK. They are presented for sales of 400,000 singles or 100,000 albums, cassettes, and CDs (200,000 for budget-priced products). For every 400,000 copies of a single or 100,000 copies of an album sold, another gold single or gold album is awarded. Although neither "groups" nor "solo artists", there are a number of duos who have received multiple gold albums – two with sufficient to qualify them for a place in this list are the Carpenters (14), and Foster and Allen (12).

Source: BPI

TOP 10

FEMALE ARTISTS WITH THE MOST GOLD ALBUMS IN THE UK

	Artist	Gold albums
1	Diana Ross	17
2	Barbra Streisand	12
3	Madonna	11
4	Donna Summer	9
5 =	Kate Bush	7
=	Tina Turner	7
=	Mariah Carey	7
8 =	Joan Armatrading	6
=	Janet Jackson	6
10 =	Gloria Estefan	5
=	Sade	5
=	Shirley Bassey	5
=	Elkie Brooks	5
=	Belinda Carlisle	5
=	Cher	5
=	Barbara Dickson	5
=	Lena Martell	5

Source: BPI

TOP 10

GROUPS WITH THE MOST PLATINUM ALBUMS IN THE UK

	Group	Platinum albums
1	Simply Red	34
2	Queen	29
3	Dire Straits	27
4	Oasis	25
5	U2	23
6	Fleetwood Mac	19
7	Wet Wet Wet	17
8 =	R. E. M.	16
=	UB40	16
10 =	Eurythmics	15
=	Spice Girls	15

Source: BPI

TOP 10

FEMALE ARTISTS WITH THE MOST PLATINUM ALBUMS IN THE UK

	Artist	Platinum albums
1	Madonna	31
2	Whitney Houston	18
3 =	Celine Dion	17
=	Tina Turner	17
5 =	Enya	12
=	Gloria Estefan	12
7	Kylie Minogue	10
8 =	Kate Bush	9
=	Mariah Carey	9
9 =	Diana Ross	8
=	Sade	8

Source: BPI

TOP 10

GROUPS WITH THE MOST GOLD ALBUMS IN THE US

	Group	Gold albums
1	Rolling Stones	37
2	Beatles	29
3	Kiss	22
4 =	Rush	21
=	Alabama	21
6 =	Chicago	20
=	Aerosmith	20
8 =	Beach Boys	17
=	Jefferson Airplane/Starship	17
10 =	AC/DC	16
=	Santana	16
=	Pink Floyd	16
=	Doors	16

The RIAA introduced its gold certificate for albums in 1958. The criteria changed with inflation, and gold awards are now made in recognition of half a million dollars' worth of an album's sales and multiples thereof.

Source: The Popular Music Database

ELTON JOHN
Britain's most successful solo artist ever in the US, Elton had his first US Top 10 hit in 1970 and followed it with numerous No. 1s and bestselling albums.

TOP 10 MALE ARTISTS WITH THE MOST GOLD ALBUMS IN THE UK
(Gold albums)
❶= Elton John (20), Cliff Richard (20)
❸ Rod Stewart (19) ❹= Neil Diamond (17),
James Last (17), Paul McCartney* (17)
❼= David Bowie (15), Mike Oldfield (15),
Elvis Presley (15) ❿ Prince (13)
* Including gold albums with Wings
Source: BPI

TOP 10

GROUPS WITH THE MOST PLATINUM ALBUMS IN THE US

	Group	Platinum albums
1 =	Beatles	80
=	Led Zeppelin	80
3	Pink Floyd	62
4	Eagles	60
5	Aerosmith	49
6	Van Halen	47
7	Fleetwood Mac	45
8	AC/DC	42
9	Alabama	41
10	U2	40

Source: The Popular Music Database

MOVIE MUSIC

SAMMY CAHN
In the 33 years from 1942 to 1970, prolific lyricist Sammy Cahn (1913–93) was nominated for 26 "Best Song" Oscars, winning on four occasions.

TOP 10 ARTISTS WITH MOST "BEST SONG" OSCAR NOMINATIONS
(Nominations)
❶ Sammy Cahn (26) ❷ Johnny Mercer (18)
❸= Paul Francis Webster (16), Alan and Marilyn Bergman (16)
❺ James Van Heusen (14) ❻= Henry Warren (11), Henry Mancini (11), Ned Washington (11) ❾= Alan Menken (10), Sammy Fain (10), Leo Robin (10), Jule Styne (10)

TOP 10
ELVIS PRESLEY FILM SONGS IN THE UK*

	Title	Film	Year
1	Jailhouse Rock	Jailhouse Rock	1957
2	Wooden Heart	G.I. Blues	1960
3	Return to Sender	Girls! Girls! Girls!	1962
4	Can't Help Falling in Love	Blue Hawaii	1961
5	Teddy Bear	Loving You	1957
6	King Creole	King Creole	1958
7	Let's Have a Party	Loving You	1957
8	Hard Headed Woman	King Creole	1958
9	I Just Can't Help Believing	Elvis – That's The Way It Is	1970
10	Always on My Mind	Elvis On Tour	1972

* Based on UK sales

Elvis' film-extracted singles from 1963–69, which actually formed the bulk of his releases during this period, sold much less well than those from the 1950s, when his recording career was at its peak, or from the 1970s, when he was concentrating on live performance. The title song from his first film, *Love Me Tender*, though a multi-million seller in the US, was a much smaller hit in Britain, and would fall to No. 14 if this list were extended.

Source: MRIB

TOP 10
JAMES BOND FILM THEMES IN THE UK

	Artist	Title	Year
1	Duran Duran	A View to a Kill	1985
2	Louis Armstrong	We Have all the Time in the World (from On Her Majesty's Secret Service)	1994
3	A-Ha	The Living Daylights	1987
4	Gladys Knight	Licence to Kill	1989
5	Carly Simon	Nobody Does it Better (from The Spy Who Loved Me)	1977
6	Sheena Easton	For Your Eyes Only	1981
7	Paul McCartney and Wings	Live and Let Die	1973
8	Tina Turner	Goldeneye	1995
9	Nancy Sinatra	You Only Live Twice	1967
10	Sheryl Crow	Tomorrow Never Dies	1997

TOP 10
"BEST SONG" OSCAR-WINNING SINGLES IN THE UK

	Artist	Title	Year
1	Stevie Wonder	I Just Called to Say I Love You	1984
2	Irene Cara	Fame	1980
3	Berlin	Take My Breath Away	1986
4	Celine Dion	My Heart will Go on	1997
5	Irene Cara	Flashdance...What a Feeling	1983
6	Barbra Streisand	Evergreen	1976
7	Bruce Springsteen	Streets of Philadelphia	1994
8	Danny Williams	Moon River	1961
9	Doris Day	Whatever will Be, will Be	1956
10	Sacha Distel	Raindrops Keep Fallin' on My Head	1969

Source: The Popular Music Database

STEVE McQUEEN
The Windmills of Your Mind *from his* The Thomas Crown Affair *won the 1969 "Best Song" Oscar.*

THE 10
"BEST SONG" OSCAR WINNERS OF THE 1940s

Year	Song	Film
1940	*When You Wish upon a Star*	*Pinocchio*
1941	*The Last Time I Saw Paris*	*Lady Be Good*
1942	*White Christmas*	*Holiday Inn*
1943	*You'll Never Know*	*Hello, Frisco, Hello*
1944	*Swinging on a Star*	*Going My Way*
1945	*It Might as Well be Spring*	*State Fair*
1946	*On the Atchison, Topeka and Santa Fe*	*The Harvey Girls*
1947	*Zip-A-Dee-Doo-Dah*	*Song of the South*
1948	*Buttons and Bows*	*The Paleface*
1949	*Baby, It's Cold Outside*	*Neptune's Daughter*

The first "Best Song" Oscar was won in 1934 by *The Continental* from the film *The Gay Divorcée*.

THE 10 "BEST SONG" OSCAR WINNERS OF THE 1960s
(Film)

1960 *Never on Sunday (Never on Sunday)*
1961 *Moon River (Breakfast at Tiffany's)*
1962 *Days of Wine and Roses (Days of Wine and Roses)* **1963** *Call Me Irresponsible (Papa's Delicate Condition)* **1964** *Chim Chim Cheree (Mary Poppins)* **1965** *The Shadow of Your Smile (The Sandpiper)* **1966** *Born Free (Born Free)*
1967 *Talk to the Animals (Dr. Doolittle)*
1968 *The Windmills of Your Mind (The Thomas Crown Affair)* **1969** *Raindrops Keep Fallin' on My Head (Butch Cassidy and the Sundance Kid)*

AUDREY HEPBURN IN *BREAKFAST AT TIFFANY'S*

THE 10
"BEST SONG" OSCAR WINNERS OF THE 1950s

Year	Song	Film	Year	Song	Film
1950	*Mona Lisa*	*Captain Carey*	1955	*Love is a Many-splendored Thing*	*Love is a Many-splendored Thing*
1951	*In the Cool, Cool, Cool of the Evening*	*Here Comes the Groom*	1956	*Whatever Will Be, Will Be (Que Sera, Sera)*	*The Man Who Knew too Much*
1952	*High Noon (Do Not Forsake Me, Oh My Darling)*	*High Noon*	1957	*All the Way*	*The Joker is Wild*
1953	*Secret Love*	*Calamity Jane*	1958	*Gigi*	*Gigi*
1954	*Three Coins in the Fountain*	*Three Coins in the Fountain*	1959	*High Hopes*	*A Hole in the Head*

THE 10
"BEST SONG" OSCAR WINNERS OF THE 1970s

Year	Song	Film
1970	*For All We Know*	*Lovers and Other Strangers*
1971	*Theme from "Shaft"*	*Shaft*
1972	*The Morning After*	*The Poseidon Adventure*
1973	*The Way We Were*	*The Way We Were*
1974	*We May Never Love Like This Again*	*The Towering Inferno*
1975	*I'm Easy*	*Nashville*
1976	*Evergreen*	*A Star is Born*
1977	*You Light up My Life*	*You Light up My Life*
1978	*Last Dance*	*Thank God it's Friday*
1979	*It Goes Like it Goes*	*Norma Rae*

The Way We Were and *Evergreen* were both sung by Barbra Streisand, who became the first artist since Frank Sinatra to win two Oscar song awards in the same decade.

THE 10
"BEST SONG" OSCAR WINNERS OF THE 1980s

Year	Song	Film
1980	*Fame*	*Fame*
1981	*Up Where We Belong*	*An Officer and a Gentleman*
1982	*Arthur's Theme (Best that You Can Do)*	*Arthur*
1983	*Flashdance*	*Flashdance*
1984	*I Just Called to Say I Love You*	*The Woman in Red*
1985	*Say You, Say Me*	*White Nights*
1986	*Take My Breath Away*	*Top Gun*
1987	*(I've Had) The Time of My Life*	*Dirty Dancing*
1988	*Let the River Run*	*Working Girl*
1989	*Under the Sea*	*The Little Mermaid*

MUSIC AWARDS

TOP 10

COUNTRIES WITH THE MOST WINS AT THE EUROVISION SONG CONTEST

	Country	Years	Wins
1	Ireland	1970, 1980, 1987, 1992, 1993, 1994, 1996	7
2=	France	1958, 1960, 1962, 1969*, 1977	5
=	Luxembourg	1961, 1965, 1972, 1973, 1983	5
=	UK	1967, 1969*, 1976, 1981, 1997	5
5	Netherlands	1957, 1959, 1969*, 1975	4
6=	Sweden	1974, 1984, 1991	3
=	Israel	1978, 1979, 1998	3
8=	Italy	1964, 1990	2
=	Spain	1968, 1969*	2
=	Switzerland	1956, 1988	2

* All four countries tied as winners in 1969

The Eurovision Song Contest has been an annual event since its 25 May 1956 debut. Johnny Logan completed a hat-trick for Ireland (even though he is Australian by birth). Having won as a performer in 1980 and 1987, he wrote the Irish entry *Why Me?* for the 1992 winner, Linda Martin.

TOP 10

ARTISTS WITH THE MOST GRAMMY AWARDS

	Artist	Awards
1	Sir George Solti	31
2	Quincy Jones	26
3	Vladimir Horowitz	25
4=	Pierre Boulez	20
=	Henry Mancini	20
6	Stevie Wonder	19
7=	Leonard Bernstein	16
=	John Williams	16
=	Paul Simon	16
10=	Aretha Franklin	15
=	Itzhak Perlman	15

Source: NARAS

TOP 10

NON-CLASSICAL ARTISTS WITH THE MOST GRAMMY AWARDS

	Artist	Awards
1	Quincy Jones	26
2	Henry Mancini	20
3	Stevie Wonder	19
4=	Paul Simon	16
=	John Williams	16
6	Aretha Franklin	15
7=	Chet Atkins	14
=	David Foster	14
9=	Ella Fitzgerald	13
=	Michael Jackson	13
=	Paul McCartney	13

TOP 10

ARTISTS WITH THE MOST BRIT AWARDS

	Artist	Awards		Artist	Awards
1	Annie Lennox	7	6=	Blur	4
2=	Phil Collins	6	=	Oasis	4
=	Prince	6	=	Take That	4
4=	Michael Jackson	5	=	U2	4
=	George Michael	5	=	Bjork	4

THE 10

FIRST GRAMMY RECORDS OF THE YEAR

Year	Record	Artist
1958	*Nel Blu Dipinto di Blu (Volare)*	Domenico Modugno
1959	*Mack the Knife*	Bobby Darin
1960	*Theme From a Summer Place*	Percy Faith
1961	*Moon River*	Henry Mancini
1962	*I Left My Heart in San Francisco*	Tony Bennett
1963	*The Days of Wine and Roses*	Henry Mancini
1964	*The Girl from Ipanema*	Stan Getz & Astrud Gilberto
1965	*A Taste of Honey*	Herb Alpert & the Tijuana Brass
1966	*Strangers in the Night*	Frank Sinatra
1967	*Up Up and Away*	5th Dimension

Source: NARAS

THE 10

LATEST GRAMMY RECORDS OF THE YEAR

Year	Record	Artist
1998	*Sunny Come Home*	Shawn Colvin
1997	*Change the World*	Eric Clapton
1996	*Kiss from a Rose*	Seal
1995	*All I Wanna Do*	Sheryl Crow
1994	*I Will Always Love You*	Whitney Houston
1993	*Tears in Heaven*	Eric Clapton
1992	*Unforgettable*	Natalie Cole with Nat "King" Cole
1991	*Another Day in Paradise*	Phil Collins
1990	*The Wind Beneath My Wings*	Bette Midler
1989	*Don't Worry Be Happy*	Bobby McFerrin

Source: NARAS

TOP 10

ARTISTS WITH THE MOST GRAMMY AWARDS IN A YEAR

	Artist	Year	Grammys
1	Michael Jackson	1984	7
2=	Roger Miller	1966	6
=	Quincy Jones	1991	6
=	Eric Clapton	1993	6
5=	Henry Mancini	1962	5
=	Roger Miller	1965	5
=	Simon & Garfunkel	1971	5
=	Stevie Wonder	1977	5
=	Bee Gees	1979	5
=	Christopher Cross	1981	5
=	Quincy Jones	1982	5
=	Toto	1983	5

Source: The Popular Music Database

THE 10

FIRST RECIPIENTS OF THE GRAMMYS' LIFETIME ACHIEVEMENT AWARD

Year	Artist
1962	Bing Crosby, vocalist
1965	Frank Sinatra, vocalist
1966	Duke Ellington, jazz musician
1967	Ella Fitzgerald, jazz vocalist
1968	Irving Berlin, composer
1971	Elvis Presley, vocalist
1972	Louis Armstrong*, jazz musician
1972	Mahalia Jackson*, gospel vocalist
1984	Chuck Berry, composer/performer
1984	Charlie Parker*, jazz musician

* Presented posthumously

The Lifetime Achievement Award is the most prestigious of Grammy Awards. An ebony and gold plaque, it is not awarded annually but is presented as and when appropriate to artists who have made "creative contributions of outstanding significance to the field of recordings".

THE 10

LATEST WINNERS OF THE BRIT AWARD FOR BEST BRITISH MALE SOLO ARTIST

Year	Artist
1998	Finley Quaye
1997	George Michael
1996	Paul Weller
1995	Paul Weller
1994	Sting
1993	Mick Hucknall
1992	Seal
1991	Elton John
1990	Phil Collins
1989	Phil Collins

THE 10

LATEST WINNERS OF THE BRIT AWARD FOR BEST BRITISH VIDEO*

Year	Video	Artist
1998	*Never Ever*	All Saints
1997	*Say You'll Be There*	Spice Girls
1996	*Wonderwall*	Oasis
1995	*Parklife*	Blur
1994	*Pray*	Take That
1993	*Stay*	Shakespears Sister
1992	*Killer*	Seal
1991	*A Little Time*	The Beautiful South
1990	*Lullaby*	The Cure
1989	*Smooth Criminal*	Michael Jackson

* Formerly "Best Video", hence open to international acts

THE 10

LATEST WINNERS OF THE BRIT AWARD FOR BEST BRITISH FEMALE SOLO ARTIST

Year	Artist
1998	Shola Ama
1997	Gabrielle
1996	Annie Lennox
1995	Eddie Reader
1994	Dina Carroll
1993	Annie Lennox
1992	Lisa Stansfield
1991	Lisa Stansfield
1990	Annie Lennox
1989	Annie Lennox

THE 10

LATEST WINNERS OF THE BRIT AWARD FOR OUTSTANDING CONTRIBUTION TO THE BRITISH RECORD INDUSTRY

Year	Artist
1998	Fleetwood Mac
1997	Bee Gees
1996	David Bowie
1995	Elton John
1994	Van Morrison
1993	Rod Stewart
1992	Freddie Mercury
1991	Status Quo
1990	Queen
1989	Cliff Richard

- The first ever winner of the BRIT "Outstanding Contribution" award was John Lennon, on 24 February 1982. The award was posthumous, however, since Lennon had been murdered in 1980.

- The Beatles, who won the same award in 1983, had ceased to exist as a group more than 12 years previously.

- The BRIT award for "Best International Group" has been awarded on 13 occasions. U2 have won it four times and REM three.

SNAP FACTS

CLASSICAL & OPERA

WOLFGANG AMADEUS MOZART
Considered by many the greatest musical genius of all time, Mozart died at the age of just 35, after a lifetime devoted to composing and performing.

TOP 10

MOST PROLIFIC CLASSICAL COMPOSERS*

	Composer/nationality	Hours of music
1	Joseph Haydn (1732–1809), Austrian	340
2	George Handel (1685–1759), German/English	303
3	Wolfgang Amadeus Mozart (1756–91), Austrian	202
4	Johann Sebastian Bach (1685–1750), German	175
5	Franz Schubert (1797–1828), German	134
6	Ludwig van Beethoven (1770–1827), German	120
7	Henry Purcell (1659–95), English	116
8	Giuseppe Verdi (1813–1901), Italian	87
9	Antonín Dvořák (1841–1904), Czechoslovakian	79
10 =	Franz Liszt (1811–86), Hungarian	76
=	Peter Tchaikovsky (1840–93), Russian	76

* *Based on a survey conducted by* Classical Music *magazine*

TOP 10

LARGEST OPERA HOUSES IN THE WORLD

	Opera house	Location	seating	Capacity standing	total
1	The Metropolitan Opera	New York, USA	3,800	265	4,065
2	Cincinnati Opera	Cincinnati, USA	3,630	–	3,630
3	Lyric Opera of Chicago	Chicago, USA	3,563	–	3,563
4	San Francisco Opera	San Francisco, USA	3,176	300	3,476
5	The Dallas Opera	Dallas, USA	3,420	–	3,420
6	Canadian Opera Company	Toronto, Canada	3,167	–	3,167
7	Los Angeles Music Center Opera	Los Angeles, USA	3,098	–	3,098
8	San Diego Opera	San Diego, USA	2,992	84	3,076
9	Seattle Opera	Seattle, USA	3,017	–	3,017
10	L'Opéra de Montréal	Montreal, Canada	2,874	–	2,874

TOP 10

OPERAS MOST FREQUENTLY PERFORMED AT THE ROYAL OPERA HOUSE, COVENT GARDEN, 1833–1997

	Opera	Composer	First performance	Total
1	*La Bohème*	Giacomo Puccini	2 October 1897	526
2	*Carmen*	Georges Bizet	27 May 1882	495
3	*Aïda*	Giuseppe Verdi	22 June 1876	471
4	*Rigoletto*	Giuseppi Verdi	14 May 1853	429
5	*Faust*	Charles Gounod	18 July 1863	428
6	*Tosca*	Giacomo Puccini	12 July 1900	388
7	*Don Giovanni*	Wolfgang Amadeus Mozart	17 April 1834	386
8	*La Traviata*	Giuseppe Verdi	25 May 1858	369
9	*Norma*	Vincenzo Bellini	12 July 1833	353
10	*Madama Butterfly*	Giacomo Puccini	10 July 1905	342

DEATH OF THE WALTZ KING

The most remarkable member of an extraordinary musical dynasty died on 3 June 1899. Born in 1825, Johann Strauss Jr. had earned the nickname "the Waltz King" for his output of over 400 waltzes, including his legendary work *The Blue Danube* (1867). He was one of three musical brothers, all of whom composed waltzes. Ironically, their father, Johann Strauss Sr. (1804-49), had forbidden any of his children to take up music, insisting that they pursue careers in business. He was known as "the Father of the Waltz", although his output of 152 waltzes was puny in comparison with his most famous son. His grandson, the third Johann, carried on this waltz tradition until his death in 1939.

100 YEARS AGO

TOP 10

LONGEST OPERAS PERFORMED AT THE ROYAL OPERA HOUSE, COVENT GARDEN

	Opera	Composer	Running time* hr:min
1	Götterdämmerung	Richard Wagner	6:00
2	Die Meistersinger von Nürnberg	Richard Wagner	5:40
3	Siegfried	Richard Wagner	5:25
4	Tristan und Isolde	Richard Wagner	5:19
5	Die Walküre	Richard Wagner	5:15
6	Parsifal	Richard Wagner	5:09
7	Donnerstag aus Licht	Karlheinz Stockhausen	4:42
8	Lohengrin	Richard Wagner	4:26
9	Der Rosenkavalier	Richard Strauss	4:25
10	Don Carlo	Giuseppe Verdi	4:19

* Including intervals

THE 10

LATEST WINNERS OF THE "BEST CLASSICAL ALBUM" GRAMMY AWARD

Year	Composer/title	Artist
1998	Danielpour, Kirchner, Rouse, Premieres – Cello Concertos	Yo–Yo Ma, David Zinman, Philadelphia Orchestra
1997	Corigliano, Of Rage And Remembrance	Leonard Slatkin, National Symphony Orchestra
1996	Claude Debussy, La Mer	Pierre Boulez, Cleveland Orchestra
1995	Béla Bartók, Concerto for Orchestra; Four Orchestral Pieces, Op. 12	Pierre Boulez, Chicago Symphony Orchestra
1994	Béla Bartók, The Wooden Prince	Pierre Boulez, Chicago Symphony Orchestra and Chorus
1993	Gustav Mahler, Symphony No. 9	Leonard Bernstein, Berlin Philharmonic Orchestra
1992	Leonard Bernstein, Candide	Leonard Bernstein, London Symphony Orchestra
1991	Charles Ives, Symphony No. 2 (And Three Short Works)	Leonard Bernstein, New York Philharmonic Orchestra
1990	Béla Bartók, Six String Quartets	Emerson String Quartet
1989	Giuseppi Verdi, Requiem And Operatic Choruses	Robert Shaw, Atlanta Symphony Orchestra

Source: NARAS

THE 10

LATEST WINNERS OF THE "BEST OPERA RECORDING" GRAMMY AWARD

Year	Composer/title	Principal soloists/orchestra
1998	Richard Wagner, Die Meistersinger von Nürnberg	Sir Georg Solti, Ben Heppner, Herbert Lippert, Karita Mattila, Alan Opie, Rene Pape, Jose van Dam, Iris Vermillion, Chicago Symphony Chorus, Chicago Symphony Orchestra
1997	Benjamin Britten, Peter Grimes	Philip Langridge, Alan Opie, Janice Watson, Opera London, London Symphony Chorus, City of London Sinfonia
1996	Hector Berlioz, Les Troyens	Charles Dutoit, Orchestre Symphonique de Montréal
1995	Carlisle Floyd, Susannah	Jerry Hadley, Samuel Ramey, Cheryl Studer, Kenn Chester
1994	George Handel, Semele	Kathleen Battle, Marilyn Horne, Samuel Ramey, Sylvia McNair, Michael Chance
1993	Richard Strauss, Die Frau ohne Schatten	Placido Domingo, Jose Van Dam, Hildegard Behrens
1992	Richard Wagner, Götterdämmerung	Hildegard Behrens, Ekkehard Wlashiha
1991	Richard Wagner, Das Rheingold	James Morris, Kurt Moll, Christa Ludwig
1990	Richard Wagner, Die Walküre	Gary Lakes, Jessye Norman, Kurt Moll
1989	Richard Wagner, Lohengrin	Placido Domingo, Jessye Norman, Eva Randova

Source: NARAS

STAGE, SCREEN & BROADCASTING

TOP 10

LONGEST-RUNNING NON-MUSICALS ON BROADWAY

	Show	Performances
1	*Oh! Calcutta!* (1976–89)	5,959
2	*Life with Father* (1939–47)	3,224
3	*Tobacco Road* (1933–41)	3,182
4	*Abie's Irish Rose* (1922–27)	2,327
5	*Deathtrap* (1978–82)	1,792
6	*Gemini* (1977–81)	1,788
7	*Harvey* (1944–49)	1,775
8	*Born Yesterday* (1946–49)	1,642
9	*Mary, Mary* (1961–64)	1,572
10	*Voice of the Turtle* (1943–48)	1,558

Source: Theatre World

TOP 10

LONGEST-RUNNING THRILLERS ON BROADWAY

	Show	Performances
1	*Deathtrap* (1978–82)	1,793
2	*Arsenic and Old Lace* (1941–44)	1,444
3	*Angel Street* (1941–1944)	1,295
4	*Sleuth* (1970–73)	1,222
5	*Dracula* (1977–80)	925
6	*Witness for the Prosecution* (1954–56)	644
7	*Dial M for Murder* (1952–54)	552
8	*Sherlock Holmes* (1975–76)	479
9	*An Inspector Calls* (1994–95)	454
10	*Ten Little Indians* (1944–45)	424

Source: Theatre World

TOP 10

LONGEST-RUNNING COMEDIES ON BROADWAY

	Show	Performances
1	*Life with Father* (1939–47)	3,224
2	*Abie's Irish Rose* (1922–27)	2,327
3	*Gemini* (1977–81)	1,788
4	*Harvey* (1944–49)	1,775
5	*Born Yesterday* (1946–49)	1,642
6	*Mary, Mary* (1961–64)	1,572
7	*Voice of the Turtle* (1943–48)	1,558
8	*Barefoot in the Park* (1963–67)	1,532
9	*Same Time Next Year* (1975–78)	1,444
10	*Brighton Beach Memoirs* (1983–86)	1,299

Source: Theatre World

TOP 10

LONGEST-RUNNING MUSICALS ON BROADWAY

	Show	Performances
1	Cats (1982–)	6,463*
2	A Chorus Line (1975–90)	6,137
3	Les Misérables (1987–)	4,545*
4	The Phantom of the Opera (1988–)	4,263*
5	42nd Street (1980–89)	3,486
6	Grease (1972–80)	3,388
7	Fiddler on the Roof (1964–72)	3,242
8	Miss Saigon (1991–)	2,910*
9	Hello Dolly! (1964–71)	2,844
10	My Fair Lady (1956–62)	2,717

* Still running; total as of 31 March 1998

Off Broadway, the musical show *The Fantasticks* by Tom Jones and Harvey Schmidt has been performed 15,653 times.

Source: Playbill

LONGEST-RUNNING MUSICALS IN THE UK
(Dates/no. of performances)

❶ *Cats* (1981–, 7,242*) ❷ *Starlight Express* (1984–, 5,846*) ❸ *Les Misérables* (1985–, 5,109*) ❹ *The Phantom of the Opera* (1986–, 4,763*) ❺ *Oliver!* (1960–69, 4,125) ❻ *Miss Saigon* (1989–, 3,737*) ❼ *Jesus Christ, Superstar* (1972–80, 3,357) ❽ *Evita* (1978–86, 2,900) ❾ *The Sound of Music* (1961–67, 2,386) ❿ *Salad Days* (1954–60, 2,283)
* Still running; total as of 31 March 1998

TOP 10

LONGEST-RUNNING SHOWS IN THE UK

	Show	Performances
1	The Mousetrap (1952–)	18,872*
2	Cats (1981–)	7,242*
3	No Sex, Please – We're British (1971–81; 1982–86; 1986–87)	6,761
4	Starlight Express (1984–)	5,846*
5	Les Misérables (1985–)	5,109*
6	The Phantom of the Opera (1986–)	4,763*
7	Oliver! (1960–69)	4,125
8	Oh! Calcutta! (1970–74; 1974–80)	3,918
9	Miss Saigon (1989–)	3,737*
10	Jesus Christ, Superstar (1972–80)	3,357

* Still running; total as of 31 March 1998

TOP 10

LONGEST-RUNNING NON-MUSICALS IN THE UK

	Show	Performances
1	The Mousetrap (1952–)	18,872*
2	No Sex, Please – We're British (1971–81; 1982–86; 1986–87)	6,761
3	Oh! Calcutta! (1970–74; 1974–80)	3,918
4	Run for Your Wife (1983–91)	2,638
5	There's a Girl in My Soup (1966–69; 1969–72)	2,547
6	Pyjama Tops (1969–75)	2,498
7	Sleuth (1970; 1972; 1973–75)	2,359
8	Worm's Eye View (1945–51)	2,245
9	Boeing Boeing (1962–65; 1965–67)	2,035
10	Blithe Spirit (1941–42; 1942; 1942–46)	1,997

* Still running; total as of 31 March 1998

ANDREW LLOYD WEBBER
In a 30-year career, originally in partnership with lyricist Tim Rice, Andrew Lloyd Webber has composed the music for and produced some of the most successful shows in theatre history.

TOP 10

LONGEST-RUNNING SHOWS ON BROADWAY

	Show	Performances
1	Cats (1982–)	6,463*
2	A Chorus Line (1975–90)	6,137
3	Oh! Calcutta! (1976–89)	5,959
4	Les Misérables (1987–)	4,545*
5	The Phantom of the Opera (1988–)	4,263*
6	42nd Street (1980–89)	3,486
7	Grease (1972–80)	3,388
8	Fiddler on the Roof (1964–72)	3,242
9	Life with Father (1939–47)	3,224
10	Tobacco Road (1933–41)	3,182

* Still running; total as of 31 March 1998

Cats became the longest running show of all-time on 19 June 1997 when it notched up its 6,138th performance.

Source: Playbill

TOP 10

LONGEST-RUNNING COMEDIES IN THE UK

	Show	Performances
1	No Sex, Please – We're British (1971–81; 1982–86; 1986–87)	6,761
2	Run for Your Wife (1983–91)	2,638
3	There's a Girl in My Soup (1966–69; 1969–72)	2,547
4	Pyjama Tops (1969–75)	2,498
5	Worm's Eye View (1945–51)	2,245
6	Boeing Boeing (1962–65; 1965–67)	2,035
7	Blithe Spirit (1941–42; 1942; 1942–46)	1,997
8	Dirty Linen (1976–80)	1,667
9	Reluctant Heroes (1950–54)	1,610
10	Seagulls over Sorrento (1950–54; 1954)	1,551

No Sex Please – We're British is the longest-running comedy in the world. It opened on 3 June 1971 and, after changing theatres, finally closed on 5 September 1987.

ALL THE WORLD'S A STAGE

THE 10

LATEST WINNERS OF THE AMERICAN EXPRESS AWARD FOR BEST NEW MUSICAL*

Year	Musical
1998	Beauty and the Beast
1997	Martin Guerre
1996	Jolson
1995	Once on this Island
1994	City of Angels
1993	Crazy for You
1992	Carmen Jones
1991	Sunday in the Park with George
1989/90	Return to the Forbidden Planet
1988	Candide

* Sponsored by American Express since 1991

The first recipient, in 1976, was A Chorus Line. In addition to the 1986 win for The Phantom of the Opera, musicals by Andrew Lloyd Webber have won on two further occasions: Evita (1978) and Cats (1981). Stephen Sondheim has had a similar rate of success with Sweeney Todd, Follies, and Sunday in the Park with George.

THE 10

LATEST WINNERS OF THE LAURENCE OLIVIER AWARD FOR BEST ACTRESS

Year	Actress/play
1998	Zöe Wanamaker, Electra
1997	Janet McTeer, A Doll's House
1996	Judi Dench, Absolute Hell
1995	Clare Higgins, Sweet Bird of Youth
1994	Fiona Shaw, Machinal
1993	Alison Steadman, The Rise and Fall of Little Voice
1992	Juliet Stevenson, Death and the Maiden
1991	Kathryn Hunter, The Visit
1989/90	Fiona Shaw, Electra; As You Like It; The Good Person of Sichuan
1987	Judi Dench, Antony and Cleopatra

TOP 10

MOST DEMANDING SHAKESPEAREAN ROLES

	Role	Play	Lines
1	Hamlet	Hamlet	1,422
2	Falstaff	Henry IV, Parts I and II	1,178
3	Richard III	Richard III	1,124
4	Iago	Othello	1,097
5	Henry V	Henry V	1,025
6	Othello	Othello	860
7	Vincentio	Measure for Measure	820
8	Coriolanus	Coriolanus	809
9	Timon	Timon of Athens	795
10	Antony	Antony and Cleopatra	766

Hamlet's role comprises 11,610 words – over 36 per cent of the total number of lines spoken in the play, but if multiple plays are considered he is beaten by Falstaff who, as well as appearing in Henry IV, Parts I and II, also appears in The Merry Wives of Windsor in which he has 436 lines.

THE 10

LATEST WINNERS OF THE LAURENCE OLIVIER AWARD FOR BEST PLAY*

Year	Play/playwright
1998	Closer by Patrick Marber
1997	Stanley by Pam Gems
1996	Skylight by David Hare
1995	Broken Glass by Arthur Miller
1994	Arcadia by Tom Stoppard
1993	Six Degrees of Separation by John Guare
1992	Death and the Maiden by Ariel Dorfman
1991	Dancing at Lughansa by Brian Friel
1989/90	Racing Demon by David Hare
1988	Our Country's Good by Timberlake Wertenbaker

* "BBC Award for Best Play" until 1996; "Best New Play" thereafter

THE 10

LATEST WINNERS OF THE LAURENCE OLIVIER AWARD FOR BEST ACTOR

Year	Actor/play
1998	Ian Holm, King Lear
1997	Anthony Sher, Stanley
1996	Alex Jennings, Peer Gynt
1995	David Bamber, My Night with Reg
1994	Mark Rylance, Much Ado About Nothing
1993	Robert Stephens, Henry IV, Parts 1 and II
1992	Nigel Hawthorne, The Madness of George III
1991	Ian McKellen, Richard III
1989/90	Oliver Ford Davies, Racing Demon
1987	Michael Gambon, A View from the Bridge

The awards are presented retrospectively, thus the 1998 awards are for performances during 1997, and so on.

TOP 10

MOST PRODUCED PLAYS BY SHAKESPEARE

	Play	Productions
1	Twelfth Night	75
2	Hamlet	74
3 =	As You Like It	72
=	The Taming of the Shrew	72
5 =	Much Ado about Nothing	68
=	The Merchant of Venice	68
7	A Midsummer Night's Dream	66
8	Macbeth	60
9	The Merry Wives of Windsor	58
10	Romeo and Juliet	56

This list is based on an analysis of Shakespearean plays produced between 31 December 1878 and 30 April 1998 at Stratford-upon-Avon, and by the Royal Shakespeare Company elsewhere.

THE RECONSTRUCTED GLOBE THEATRE, LONDON

TOP 10
OLDEST LONDON THEATRES

	Theatre	Date opened
1	Theatre Royal, Drury Lane	7 May 1663
2	Sadler's Wells, Rosebery Avenue	3 June 1683
3	The Haymarket (Theatre Royal), Haymarket	29 December 1720
4	Royal Opera House, Covent Garden	7 December 1732
5	The Adelphi (originally Sans Pareil), Strand	27 November 1806
6	The Old Vic (originally Royal Coburg), Waterloo Road	11 May 1818
7	The Vaudeville, Strand	16 April 1870
8	The Criterion, Piccadilly Circus	21 March 1874
9	The Savoy, Strand	10 October 1881
10	The Comedy, Panton Street	15 October 1881

These are London's 10 oldest theatres still operating on their original sites – although most of them have been rebuilt.

TOP 10
LARGEST THEATRES IN LONDON

	Theatre	Seats
1	Labatt's Apollo	3,483
2	Apollo Victoria	2,572*
3	London Coliseum	2,358
4	London Palladium	2,298
5	Theatre Royal	2,237
6	Royal Opera House	2,098
7	Dominion	2,007
8	Prince Edward	1,666
9	Victoria Palace	1,565
10	Adelphi	1,500

* *Official capacity; reduced to 1,524 for current production of* Starlight Express.

Labatt's Apollo has 3,483 seats, but is used only for rock concerts and other non-theatrical events. Among London's newest theatres, neither the Olivier at the National Theatre (1,160 seats) nor the Barbican (1,166 seats) rank in the Top 10. London also boasts several large concert halls, including the Royal Festival Hall (3,111 seats), Barbican Hall (2,047 seats), and the Royal Albert Hall, which can accommodate up to 7,000 people depending on the nature of the performance.

TOP 10
NATIONALITIES OF VISITORS TO SHAKESPEARE'S BIRTHPLACE

	Country	Number
1	USA	19,510
2	UK	15,107
3	Japan	5,462
4	Australia	3,800
5	France	3,027
6	Germany	3,009
7	Italy	2,465
8	Spain	2,302
9	Canada	2,105
10	Korea	1,538

Over 80,000 people a year visit Shakespeare's birthplace in Stratford-on-Avon.

SNAP FACTS

- Shakespeare used a total vocabulary of 29,066 different words (the average is about 8,000).
- He used the word "America" just once, in *The Comedy of Errors*.
- Shakespeare was the first to use certain words that are now common, including "hurry", "bump", "eyeball", and "anchovy".

TOP 10
THEATRE-GOING COUNTRIES IN THE WORLD

	Country	Annual theatre attendance per 1,000 population
1	Cuba	2,559
2	Mongolia	1,700
3	Vietnam	1,000
4	UK	720
5	Iceland	658
6	Bulgaria	650
7	Luxembourg	613
8	Albania	590
9	Romania	578
10	Netherlands	575
	USA	170

FILM HITS & MISSES

In earlier editions of *The Top 10 of Everything*, the rentals earned by the US and Canadian distributors were used to measure the relative success of the films of various artists. However, while this remains a valid way of comparing the success of films over long periods, film has become an international medium and nowadays many Hollywood films earn more outside the US than within it: this is true of most of the James Bond films, for example. Film lists are therefore now based on total worldwide box-office income. When compared with rental-based lists, this revision means that the ranking of certain films of particular stars or genres that achieved greater global than domestic success will appear to have gained ground.

THEN & NOW

TOP 10 FILMS

1987		1997
Fatal Attraction	**1**	*Titanic*
Beverly Hills Cop II	**2**	*The Lost World: Jurassic Park*
The Living Daylights	**3**	*Men in Black*
The Untouchables	**4**	*Air Force One*
Dirty Dancing	**5**	*Liar Liar*
Three Men and a Baby	**6**	*Tomorrow Never Dies*
Good Morning, Vietnam	**7**	*My Best Friend's Wedding*
Moonstruck	**8**	*The Fifth Element*
The Secret of My Success	**9**	*Hercules*
Stakeout	**10**	*Batman and Robin*

TOP 10

BIGGEST FILM FLOPS OF ALL TIME

	Film/year	Estimated loss ($)		Film/year	Estimated loss ($)
1	*Cutthroat Island* (1995)	81,000,000	**6**	*The Cotton Club* (1984)	38,100,000
2	*The Adventures of Baron Munchausen* (1988)	48,100,000	**7**	*Santa Claus – The Movie* (1985)	37,000,000
3	*Ishtar* (1987)	47,300,000	**8**	*Heaven's Gate* (1980)	34,200,000
4	*Hudson Hawk* (1991)	47,000,000	**9**	*Billy Bathgate* (1991)	33,000,000
5	*Inchon* (1981)	44,100,000	**10**	*Pirates* (1986)	30,300,000

As the figures shown here are based upon North American rental earnings balanced against the films' original production cost, some entries in the list may eventually recoup a proportion of their losses via overseas earnings, video, and TV revenue. For others, such as *Inchon* and *Pirates*, time has already run out.

TOP 10

HIGHEST-GROSSING FILMS OF ALL TIME IN THE UK

	Film	Year	Gross (£)
1	*Titanic*	1998	58,508,000
2	*The Full Monty*	1997	51,992,000
3	*Jurassic Park*	1993	47,140,000
4	*Independence Day*	1996	36,800,000
5	*Men in Black*	1997	35,400,000
6	*Four Weddings and a Funeral*	1994	27,800,000
7	*The Lost World: Jurassic Park*	1997	25,300,000
8	*Ghost*	1990	23,300,000
9	*The Lion King*	1994	23,100,000
10	*Toy Story*	1996	22,100,000

Inevitably, bearing inflation in mind, the top-grossing films of all time are releases from the 1990s, although it is also true that UK cinema admissions have risen sharply in recent years. From the nadir of the late 1960s and 1970s, today's films are both more widely viewed (even excluding video) than those of 15 to 25 years ago, as well as grossing considerably more at the box office.

JURASSIC PARK
After a four-year run, its status as "highest grossing film of all time" worldwide was finally eclipsed by the mega-blockbuster Titanic in 1997.

STAR WARS
Although made over 20 years ago, Star Wars remains one of the highest-earning films – second-highest in the US, and fourth-highest worldwide. With the follow-ups The Empire Strikes Back *and* Return of the Jedi, *it is also first among sequels.*

TOP 10 FILM SEQUELS OF ALL TIME

❶ *Star Wars/The Empire Strikes Back/Return of the Jedi* ❷ *Jurassic Park/The Lost World: Jurassic Park* ❸ *Batman/Batman Returns/Batman Forever/Batman and Robin* ❹ *Raiders of the Lost Ark/Indiana Jones and the Temple of Doom/Indiana Jones and the Last Crusade* ❺ *Star Trek I–VI/Generations/First Contact* ❻ *Home Alone 1–2* ❼ *Back to the Future I–II* ❽ *Die Hard 1–2/Die Hard: With a Vengeance* ❾ *Jaws I–IV* ❿ *Rocky I–V*

TOP 10
MOST EXPENSIVE FILMS EVER MADE

	Film*/year	Estimated cost ($)
1	*Titanic* (1997)	200,000,000
2	*Waterworld* (1995)	175,000,000
3	*Dante's Peak* (1997)	116,000,000
4=	*Batman and Robin* (1997)	110,000,000
=	*Tomorrow Never Dies,* (1997)	110,000,000
=	*True Lies* (1994)	110,000,000
=	*Speed 2: Cruise Control* (1997)	110,000,000
8	*Inchon* (USA/Korea), (1981)	102,000,000
9=	*Batman Forever* (1995)	100,000,000
=	*War and Peace* (USSR, 1967)	100,000,000

* All US-made unless otherwise stated

This is the first time that all those in the list exceed $100,000,000, with half the entrants being films released in 1997.

TOP 10
HIGHEST-GROSSING FILMS OF ALL TIME

	Film/year	Gross income ($) US	World total
1	*Titanic* (1997)	565,700,000	1,619,700,000
2	*Jurassic Park* (1993)	357,100,000	920,100,000
3	*Independence Day* (1996)	306,200,000	811,200,000
4	*Star Wars* (1977/97)	461,000,000	780,100,000
5	*The Lion King* (1994)	312,900,000	766,900,000
6	*E.T.: The Extra-Terrestrial* (1982)	399,800,000	704,800,000
7	*Forrest Gump* (1994)	329,700,000	679,700,000
8	*Lost World: Jurassic Park* (1997)	229,100,000	614,100,000
9	*Men in Black* (1997)	250,100,000	586,100,000
10	*The Empire Strikes Back* (1980/97)	290,200,000	533,900,000

TOP 10
FILM OPENINGS OF ALL TIME IN THE US

	Film	Release date	Opening weekend gross ($)
1	*The Lost World: Jurassic Park**	23 May 1997	92,729,064
2	*Mission: Impossible**	22 May 1996	56,811,602
3	*Batman Forever*	16 Jun 1995	52,784,433
4	*Men in Black*	2 Jul 1997	51,068,455
5	*Independence Day*	3 Jul 1996	50,228,264
6	*Jurassic Park*	11 Jun 1993	50,159,460
7	*Batman Returns*	19 Jun 1992	45,687,711
8	*Batman and Robin*	20 Jun 1996	42,872,606
9	*Batman*	22 Jun 1989	42,705,884
10	*Twister*	10 May 1996	41,059,405

* Estimate based on four-day holiday weekend

A film may start its run relatively quietly then gather momentum: for example, *Titanic* earned $28,638,131 in its opening weekend, which would not even rank it in the top 20, but has gone on to become the highest-earning film of all time.

YESTERDAY'S STARS & DIRECTORS

TOP 10
MARILYN MONROE FILMS

Film	Year
1 Some Like It Hot	1959
2 How to Marry a Millionaire	1953
3 The Seven Year Itch	1955
4 Gentlemen Prefer Blondes	1953
5 There's No Business like Show Business	1954
6 Bus Stop	1956
7 The Misfits	1961
8 River of No Return	1954
9 All About Eve	1950
10 Let's Make Love	1960

INGRID BERGMAN
In a career spanning 44 years, the Swedish–born actress (1915–82) appeared in 40 films, including such acclaimed classics as Casablanca and Notorious.

TOP 10 INGRID BERGMAN FILMS
(Year)
❶ *Murder on the Orient Express** (1974)
❷ *Cactus Flower* (1969) ❸ *The Bells of St. Mary's* (1945) ❹ *For Whom the Bell Tolls* (1943) ❺ *Spellbound* (1945) ❻ *Notorious* (1946) ❼ *Casablanca* (1942) ❽ *The Yellow Rolls Royce* (1964) ❾ *The Inn of the Sixth Happiness* (1958) ❿ *Anastasia*# (1956)
* Academy Award for "Best Supporting Actress"
# Academy Award for "Best Actress"

TOP 10
FILMS DIRECTED BY BILLY WILDER

Film	Year	Film	Year
1 Irma La Douce	1963	6= The Lost Weekend	1945
2 Some Like It Hot	1959	= The Emperor Waltz	1948
3 The Front Page	1974	8 Sabrina	1954
4 The Apartment	1960	9 Witness for the Prosecution	1957
5 The Seven Year Itch	1955	10 Stalag 17	1953

TOP 10
PETER SELLERS FILMS

Film	Year
1 The Revenge of the Pink Panther	1978
2 The Return of the Pink Panther	1974
3 The Pink Panther Strikes Again	1976
4 Murder by Death	1976
5 Being There	1979
6 Casino Royale	1967
7 What's New Pussycat?	1965
8 A Shot in the Dark	1964
9 The Pink Panther	1963
10= Dr. Strangelove	1963
= The Fiendish Plot of Dr. Fu Manchu	1980

TOP 10
FILMS DIRECTED BY JOHN HUSTON

Film	Year
1 Annie	1982
2 The Bible	1966
3 Prizzi's Honor	1985
4 The Man Who Would Be King	1975
5 Casino Royale	1967
6 The Life and Times of Judge Roy Bean	1972
7 Moby Dick	1956
8 Night of the Iguana	1964
9 Moulin Rouge	1952
10= Heaven Knows, Mr. Allison	1957
= Victory (or Escape to Victory)	1981

TOP 10
JOHN WAYNE FILMS

	Film	Year
1	How the West was Won	1962
2	The Longest Day	1962
3	True Grit*	1969
4	The Green Berets	1968
5	The Alamo	1960
6=	The Cowboys	1972
=	Big Jake	1971
8	Rooster Cogburn	1975
9	Hatari!	1962
10	The Greatest Story Ever Told	1965

* *Academy Award for "Best Actor"*

John Wayne (born Marion Michael Morrison) was one of Hollywood's most prolific actors, making more than 150 films during a career that spanned 48 years. He is chiefly remembered for his tough-guy roles as a soldier or cowboy – often, curiously, with a Scottish name, such as his title roles in *Big Jim McLain* (1952) *McLintock* (1963) and *McQ* (1974). Occasionally he found himself miscast, for example, as Genghis Khan in *The Conqueror* (1955), and in the 10th film on this list, where he appeared, mercifully briefly, as the Roman centurion who gazes at the crucified Jesus and, in a Western drawl, recites his single memorable line, "Truly, this man was the son of God."

TOP 10
AUDREY HEPBURN FILMS

	Film	Year
1	My Fair Lady	1964
2	Always	1989
3	Wait until Dark	1967
4	Charade	1963
5	War and Peace	1956
6	The Nun's Story	1959
7	Bloodline	1979
8	How to Steal a Million	1966
9	Breakfast at Tiffany's	1961
10=	Sabrina	1954
=	Robin and Marian	1976

Audrey Hepburn (born Edda van Heemstra Hepburn-Ruston, 4 May 1929, Brussels, Belgium; died 20 January 1993) had a British father and a Dutch mother. She began as a dancer and stage actress and appeared in minor parts before achieving acclaim and a "Best Actress" Oscar for *Roman Holiday* (1954). After 1967 her roles were few, and her last years were devoted to charity work with UNICEF.

TOP 10
HUMPHREY BOGART FILMS

	Film	Year
1	The Caine Mutiny	1954
2	Casablanca	1942
3	The African Queen*	1951
4=	Sabrina	1954
=	The Left Hand of God	1955
6	To Have and Have Not	1945
7=	Key Largo	1948
=	The Barefoot Contessa	1954
9=	Dark Passage	1947
=	The Big Sleep	1946

* *Academy Award for "Best Actor"*

TOP 10
FILMS DIRECTED BY ALFRED HITCHCOCK

	Film	Year
1	Psycho	1960
2	Rear Window	1954
3	North by Northwest	1959
4	Family Plot	1976
5	Torn Curtain	1966
6	Frenzy	1972
7	Vertigo	1958
8	The Man Who Knew Too Much	1956
9	The Birds	1963
10	Spellbound	1945

ALFRED HITCHCOCK
British director of more than 50 movies, Hitchcock (1899–1980) is considered the "master of suspense", often filming plots in which ordinary people become entangled in sinister events.

FILMS OF THE DECADES

ALMOST A VICTORY
The colossal success of Independence Day, *in which the Earth's conquest by aliens is averted, makes it a close rival to the 1990s' top two money earners.*

T O P 1 0

FILMS OF THE 1990s

	Film	Year
1	*Titanic**	1997
2	*Jurassic Park*	1993
3	*Independence Day*	1996
4	*The Lion King*	1994
5	*Forrest Gump**	1994
6	*The Lost World: Jurassic Park*	1997
7	*Men in Black*	1997
8	*Home Alone*	1990
9	*Ghost*	1990
10	*Terminator 2: Judgment Day*	1991

* *Academy Award for "Best Picture"*

Each of the Top 10 films of the present decade has earned more than $500,000,000 around the world, a total of more than $7 billion between them.

T O P 1 0

FILMS OF THE 1980s

	Film	Year
1	*E.T.: the Extra-Terrestrial*	1982
2	*Indiana Jones and the Last Crusade*	1989
3	*Batman*	1989
4	*Rain Man*	1988
5	*Return of the Jedi*	1983
6	*Raiders of the Lost Ark*	1981
7	*The Empire Strikes Back*	1980
8	*Who Framed Roger Rabbit?*	1988
9	*Back to the Future*	1985
10	*Top Gun*	1986

The 1980s was clearly the decade of the adventure film, with George Lucas and Steven Spielberg continuing to assert their control of Hollywood, carving up the Top 10 between them, with Lucas as producer of 5 and 7 and Spielberg director of 1, 2, 6, 8 and 9. The 10 highest-earning films scooped in more than $4 billion between them at the global box office.

T O P 1 0

FILMS OF THE 1970s

	Film	Year
1	*Star Wars*	1977/97
2	*Jaws*	1975
3	*Close Encounters of the Third Kind*	1977/80
4	*Moonraker*	1979
5	*The Spy Who Loved Me*	1977
6	*The Exorcist*	1973
7	*The Sting**	1973
8	*Grease*	1978
9	*The Godfather**	1972
10	*Saturday Night Fever*	1977

* *Academy Award for "Best Picture"*

In the 1970s the arrival of the two prodigies, Steven Spielberg and George Lucas, set the scene for the high adventure blockbusters whose domination has continued ever since. Lucas wrote and directed *Star Wars*, formerly the highest-earning film of all time. Spielberg directed *Jaws* and wrote and directed *Close Encounters of the Third Kind.*

T O P 1 0

FILMS OF THE 1960s

	Film	Year
1	*101 Dalmatians*	1961
2	*The Jungle Book*	1967
3	*The Sound of Music**	1965
4	*Thunderball*	1965
5	*Goldfinger*	1964
6	*Doctor Zhivago*	1965
7	*You Only Live Twice*	1967
8	*The Graduate*	1968
9	*Mary Poppins*	1964
10	*Butch Cassidy and the Sundance Kid*	1969

* *Academy Award for "Best Picture"*

Many of the top-earning films of the 1960s were musicals, with *The Sound of Music* producing the fastest-selling album ever, while *Mary Poppins* and those featuring the music from *The Jungle Book* and *Doctor Zhivago* were all No. 1 albums.

T O P 1 0

FILMS OF THE 1950s

	Film	Year
1	*Lady and the Tramp*	1955
2	*Peter Pan*	1953
3	*Ben-Hur**	1959
4	*The Ten Commandments*	1956
5	*Sleeping Beauty*	1959
6	*Around the World in 80 Days**	1956
7=	*The Robe*	1953
=	*The Greatest Show on Earth**	1952
9	*The Bridge on the River Kwai**	1957
10	*Peyton Place*	1957

* *Academy Award for "Best Picture"*

While the popularity of animated films continued with *Lady and the Tramp*, *Peter Pan*, and *Sleeping Beauty*, the 1950s was outstanding as the decade of the "big" picture in terms of cast and scale, and also in terms of the magnitude of the subjects they tackled, such as the biblical epic.

T O P 1 0

FILMS OF THE 1940s

	Film	Year
1	*Bambi*	1942
2	*Pinocchio*	1940
3	*Fantasia*	1940
4	*Cinderella*	1949
5	*Song of the South*	1946
6	*The Best Years of Our Lives**	1946
7	*The Bells of St. Mary's*	1945
8	*Duel in the Sun*	1946
9	*Mom and Dad*	1944
10	*Samson and Delilah*	1949

* *Academy Award for "Best Picture"*

With the top four films of the decade classic Disney cartoons, the drab 1940s may truly be regarded as the "golden age" of the colourful animated film.

T O P 1 0

FILMS OF THE 1930s

	Film	Year
1	*Gone with the Wind**	1939
2	*Snow White and the Seven Dwarfs*	1937
3	*The Wizard of Oz*	1939
4	*The Woman in Red*	1935
5	*King Kong*	1933
6	*San Francisco*	1936
7=	*Hell's Angels*	1930
=	*Lost Horizon*	1937
=	*Mr. Smith Goes to Washington*	1939
10	*Maytime*	1937

* *Academy Award for "Best Picture"*

Gone with the Wind and *Snow White and the Seven Dwarfs* have generated more income than any other pre-war film. However, if the income of *Gone with the Wind* was adjusted to allow for inflation in the period since its release, it could be regarded as the most successful film ever.

THE WONDERFUL WIZARD OF OZ
Although held to an honorable third place by blockbusters Gone with the Wind *and* Snow White and the Seven Dwarfs, The Wizard of Oz *was one of the most popular films of the 1930s.*

164 FILM GENRES

INTERVIEW WITH THE VAMPIRE

TOP 10 VAMPIRE FILMS
(Year)

❶ *Interview with the Vampire* (1994) ❷ *Bram Stoker's Dracula* (1992) ❸ *Love at First Bite* (1979) ❹ *The Lost Boys* (1987) ❺ *Dracula* (1979) ❻ *Fright Night* (1985) ❼ *Vampire in Brooklyn* (1995) ❽ *Buffy the Vampire Slayer* (1992) ❾ *Dracula: Dead and Loving It* (1995) ❿ *Transylvania 6-5000* (1985)

T O P 1 0
COP FILMS

	Film	Year
1	*Die Hard with a Vengeance*	1995
2	*The Fugitive*	1993
3	*Basic Instinct*	1992
4	*Seven*	1995
5	*Lethal Weapon 3*	1993
6	*Beverly Hills Cop*	1984
7	*Beverly Hills Cop II*	1987
8	*Speed*	1994
9	*Lethal Weapon 2*	1989
10	*Kindergarten Cop*	1990

Although films in which one of the central characters is a policeman have never been among the most successful films of all time, many have earned respectable amounts at the box office. Both within and outside the Top 10, they are divided between those with a comic slant, such as the two *Beverly Hills Cop* films, and darker police thrillers, such as *Basic Instinct*. Films featuring FBI and CIA agents have been excluded from the reckoning, hence eliminating blockbusters such as *Mission: Impossible*, and *The Silence of the Lambs*.

T O P 1 0
WAR FILMS

	Film	Year
1	*Platoon*	1986
2	*Good Morning, Vietnam*	1987
3	*Apocalypse Now*	1979
4	*M*A*S*H*	1970
5	*Patton*	1970
6	*The Deer Hunter*	1978
7	*Full Metal Jacket*	1987
8	*Midway*	1976
9	*The Dirty Dozen*	1967
10	*A Bridge Too Far*	1977

This list excludes films with military, rather than war, themes, such as *A Few Good Men* (1992), *The Hunt for Red October* (1990), *Crimson Tide* (1995), and *An Officer and a Gentleman* (1982), which would have been in the top five; and *Top Gun* (1986), which would top the list, just beating *Rambo: First Blood 2* (1985), a post-Vietnam action film.

T O P 1 0
COMEDY FILMS

	Film	Year
1	*Forrest Gump*	1994
2	*Home Alone*	1990
3	*Ghost*	1990
4	*Pretty Woman*	1990
5	*Mrs. Doubtfire*	1993
6	*Flintstones*	1995
7	*Who Framed Roger Rabbit*	1988
8	*The Mask*	1994
9	*Beverly Hills Cop*	1984
10	*Liar, Liar*	1997

T O P 1 0
GHOST FILMS

	Film	Year		Film	Year
1	*Ghost*	1990	6	*Scrooged*	1988
2	*Ghostbusters*	1984	7	*The Frighteners*	1996
3	*Casper*	1995	8	*Ghost Dad*	1990
4	*Ghostbusters II*	1989	9	*The Sixth Man*	1997
5	*Beetlejuice*	1988	10	*High Spirits*	1988

TOP 10
JAMES BOND FILMS

	Film/year	Bond actor
1	*Goldeneye* (1995)	Pierce Brosnan
2	*Tomorrow Never Dies* (1997)	Pierce Brosnan
3	*Moonraker* (1979)	Roger Moore
4	*Never Say Never Again* (1983)	Sean Connery
5	*For Your Eyes Only* (1981)	Roger Moore
6	*The Living Daylights* (1987)	Timothy Dalton
7	*The Spy Who Loved Me* (1977)	Roger Moore
8	*Octopussy* (1983)	Roger Moore
9	*Licence to Kill* (1990)	Timothy Dalton
10	*A View to a Kill* (1985)	Roger Moore

TOP 10
ANIMATED FILMS

	Film	Year
1	*The Lion King*	1994
2	*Aladdin*	1992
3	*Toy Story*	1995
4	*Beauty and the Beast*	1991
5	*Who Framed Roger Rabbit**	1988
6	*Pocahontas*	1995
7	*The Hunchback of Notre Dame*	1996
8	*Casper**	1995
9	*Hercules*	1997
10	*Bambi*	1942

* Part animated, part live action

TOP 10
DISASTER FILMS

	Film	Year
1	*Titanic*	1997
2	*Twister*	1996
3	*Die Hard with a Vengeance*	1995
4	*Apollo 13*	1995
5	*Outbreak*	1995
6	*Dante's Peak*	1997
7	*Daylight*	1996
8	*Die Hard*	1988
9	*Volcano*	1997
10	*Die Hard 2*	1990

TOP 10
FILMS FEATURING DINOSAURS

	Film	Year
1	*Jurassic Park*	1993
2	*The Lost World: Jurassic Park*	1997
3	*Fantasia**	1940
4	*The Land Before Time**	1988
5	*Baby...Secret of the Lost Legend*	1985
6	*One of Our Dinosaurs is Missing*	1975
7	*Journey to the Centre of the Earth*	1959
8	*We're Back: A Dinosaur's Story**	1993
9	*King Kong*	1933
10	*At the Earth's Core*	1976

* Animated

TOP 10
BIBLICAL FILMS

	Film	Year
1	*Ben Hur*	1959
2	*The Ten Commandments*	1956
3	*The Robe*	1953
4	*Jesus Christ Superstar*	1973
5	*Quo Vadis*	1951
6	*Samson and Delilah*	1949
7	*Jesus*	1979
8	*The Greatest Story Ever Told*	1965
9	*King of Kings*	1961
10	*Solomon and Sheba*	1959

TOP 10
SCIENCE-FICTION FILMS

	Film	Year
1	*Jurassic Park*	1993
2	*Independence Day*	1996
3	*Star Wars*	1977
4	*E.T.: The Extra-Terrestrial*	1982
5	*The Lost World: Jurassic Park*	1997
6	*The Empire Strikes Back*	1980
7	*Men in Black*	1997
8	*Terminator 2: Judgement Day*	1991
9	*Return of the Jedi*	1983
10	*Batman*	1989

The first seven films in this list are also in the all-time Top 10, and all 10 are among the 23 most successful films ever, having earned over $400,000,000 each from worldwide box office income. Three further films in this genre have each earned more than $300,000,000 globally: *Back to the Future* (1985), *Batman Forever* (1995), and *Close Encounters of the Third Kind* (1977/80).

TOP 10 WESTERN FILMS
(Year)
❶ *Dances with Wolves* (1990) ❷ *Maverick* (1994) ❸ *Unforgiven* (1992) ❹ *Butch Cassidy and the Sundance Kid* (1969) ❺ *Jeremiah Johnson* (1972) ❻ *How the West Was Won* (1962) ❼ *Young Guns* (1988) ❽ *Young Guns II* (1990) ❾ *Pale Rider* (1985) ❿= *Bronco Billy* (1980), *Little Big Man* (1970)

166 OSCAR WINNERS – FILMS

FILMS NOMINATED FOR THE MOST OSCARS*

	Film	Year	Awards	Nominations
1=	All About Eve	1950	6	14
=	Titanic	1997	11	14
3=	Gone With the Wind	1939	8#	13
=	From Here to Eternity	1953	8	13
=	Mary Poppins	1964	5	13
=	Who's Afraid of Virginia Woolf?	1966	5	13
=	Forrest Gump	1994	6	13
8=	Mrs. Miniver	1942	6	12
=	The Song of Bernadette	1943	4	12
=	Johnny Belinda	1948	1	12
=	A Streetcar Named Desire	1951	4	12
=	On the Waterfront	1954	8	12
=	Ben-Hur	1959	11	12
=	Becket	1964	1	12
=	My Fair Lady	1964	8	12
=	Reds	1981	3	12
=	Dances With Wolves	1990	7	12
=	Schindler's List	1993	7	12
=	The English Patient	1996	9	12

* Oscar® is a registered trade mark of the Academy of Motion Picture Arts and Sciences

Plus two special awards

FILMS TO WIN THE MOST OSCARS

	Film	Year	Nominations	Awards
1=	Ben-Hur	1959	12	11
=	Titanic	1997	14	11
3	West Side Story	1961	11	10
4=	Gigi	1958	9	9
=	The Last Emperor	1987	9	9
=	The English Patient	1996	12	9
7=	Gone With the Wind	1939	13	8*
=	From Here to Eternity	1953	13	8
=	On the Waterfront	1954	12	8
=	My Fair Lady	1964	12	8
=	Cabaret	1972	10	8
=	Gandhi	1982	11	8
=	Amadeus	1984	11	8

* Plus two special awards

Nine other films have won seven Oscars each: *Going My Way* (1944), *The Best Years of Our Lives* (1946), *The Bridge on the River Kwai* (1957), *Lawrence of Arabia* (1962), *Patton* (1970), *The Sting* (1973), *Out of Africa* (1985), *Dances with Wolves* (1991), and *Schindler's List* (1993), each of the last two films being nominated for 12 Awards. *Titanic* (1997) matched the 14 nominations of *All About Eve* (1950), but outshone it by winning 11, compared with the latter's six.

HIGHEST-EARNING "BEST PICTURE" OSCAR WINNERS

	Film	Year
1	Titanic	1997
2	Forrest Gump	1994
3	Dances With Wolves	1990
4	Rain Man	1988
5	Schindler's List	1993
6	The English Patient	1996
7	Braveheart	1995
8	Gone With the Wind	1939
9	The Sound of Music	1965
10	The Sting	1973

STUDIOS WITH THE MOST "BEST PICTURE" OSCARS

	Studio	Awards
1	United Artists	13
2	Columbia	12
3	Paramount	11
4	MGM	9
5	Twentieth Century Fox	7
6	Warner Bros	6
7	Universal	5
8	Orion	4
9	RKO	2
10	Miramax	1

"BEST PICTURE" OSCAR WINNERS OF THE 1930s

1930	All Quiet on the Western Front
1931	Cimarron
1932	Grand Hotel
1933	Cavalcade
1934	It Happened One Night*
1935	Mutiny on the Bounty
1936	The Great Ziegfeld
1937	The Life of Emile Zola
1938	You Can't Take It with You
1939	Gone with the Wind

* Winner of Oscars for "Best Director", "Best Actor", "Best Actress", and "Best Screenplay"

GOLDEN IDOL
Standing 34-cm (13½-in) high, the gold-plated "Oscar" was reputedly named for his resemblance to a film librarian's Uncle Oscar.

THE 10
"BEST PICTURE" OSCAR WINNERS OF THE 1940s

1940	*Rebecca*
1941	*How Green Was My Valley*
1942	*Mrs. Miniver*
1943	*Casablanca*
1944	*Going My Way*
1945	*The Lost Weekend*
1946	*The Best Years of Our Lives*
1947	*Gentleman's Agreement*
1948	*Hamlet*
1949	*All the King's Men*

Several of these "Best Picture" winners are now regarded as film classics, many critics numbering *Casablanca* among the greatest films of all time. *Mrs. Miniver* (which won a total of six Oscars) and *The Best Years of Our Lives* (seven Oscars) were both directed by William Wyler and reflected the concerns of wartime and post-war life respectively. *How Green Was My Valley* and *Going My Way* each won five Oscars. *Rebecca* and *Hamlet* both starred Laurence Olivier, who also directed the latter, winning not only the "Best Picture" award but also that for "Best Actor".

THE 10
"BEST PICTURE" OSCAR WINNERS OF THE 1950s

1950	*All about Eve*
1951	*An American in Paris*
1952	*The Greatest Show on Earth*
1953	*From Here to Eternity*
1954	*On the Waterfront*
1955	*Marty*
1956	*Around the World in 80 Days*
1957	*The Bridge on the River Kwai*
1958	*Gigi*
1959	*Ben-Hur*

The first film of the 1950s, *All about Eve*, received the most nominations (14), while the last, *Ben-Hur*, won the most (11).

THE 10
"BEST PICTURE" OSCAR WINNERS OF THE 1980s

1980	*Ordinary People*
1981	*Chariots of Fire*
1982	*Gandhi*
1983	*Terms of Endearment*
1984	*Amadeus*
1985	*Out of Africa*
1986	*Platoon*
1987	*The Last Emperor*
1988	*Rain Man*
1989	*Driving Miss Daisy*

The winners of "Best Picture" Oscars during the 1990s are: 1990 *Dances With Wolves*; 1991 *The Silence of the Lambs* – which also won Oscars for "Best Director", "Best Actor", "Best Actress", and "Best Screenplay"; 1992 *Unforgiven*; 1993 *Schindler's List* – which won a total of seven awards; 1994 *Forrest Gump*, which also won Oscars in a total of five other categories; 1995 *Braveheart*; 1996 *The English Patient*; and 1997 *Titanic*.

THE 10
"BEST PICTURE" OSCAR WINNERS OF THE 1960s

1960	*The Apartment*
1961	*West Side Story*
1962	*Lawrence of Arabia*
1963	*Tom Jones*
1964	*My Fair Lady*
1965	*The Sound of Music*
1966	*A Man for All Seasons*
1967	*In the Heat of the Night*
1968	*Oliver!*
1969	*Midnight Cowboy*

The Apartment (1960) was the last black-and-white film to receive a "Best Picture" Oscar until Steven Spielberg's *Schindler's List* in 1993, which won seven Oscars.

THE 10
"BEST PICTURE" OSCAR WINNERS OF THE 1970s

1970	*Patton*
1971	*The French Connection*
1972	*The Godfather*
1973	*The Sting*
1974	*The Godfather, Part II*
1975	*One Flew over the Cuckoo's Nest**
1976	*Rocky*
1977	*Annie Hall*
1978	*The Deer Hunter*
1979	*Kramer vs. Kramer*

* *Winner of Oscars for "Best Director", "Best Actor", "Best Actress", and "Best Screenplay"*

OSCAR WINNERS – STARS

RAIN MAN
Dustin Hoffman researched autism for a year before his Oscar-winning performance as Raymond Babbitt in Rain Man.

THE 10

"BEST ACTOR IN A SUPPORTING ROLE" OSCAR WINNERS OF THE 1980s

Year	Actor	Film
1980	Timothy Hutton	*Ordinary People*
1981	John Gielgud	*Arthur*
1982	Louis Gossett, Jr.	*An Officer and a Gentleman*
1983	Jack Nicholson	*Terms of Endearment*
1984	Haing S. Ngor	*The Killing Fields*
1985	Don Ameche	*Cocoon*
1986	Michael Caine	*Hannah and Her Sisters*
1987	Sean Connery	*The Untouchables*
1988	Kevin Kline	*A Fish Called Wanda*
1989	Denzel Washington	*Glory*

THE 10

"BEST ACTRESS IN A SUPPORTING ROLE" OSCAR WINNERS OF THE 1980s

Year	Actress	Film
1980	Mary Steenburgen	*Melvin and Howard*
1981	Maureen Stapleton	*Reds*
1982	Jessica Lange	*Tootsie*
1983	Linda Hunt	*The Year of Living Dangerously*
1984	Peggy Ashcroft	*A Passage to India*
1985	Anjelica Huston	*Prizzi's Honor*
1986	Dianne Wiest	*Hannah and Her Sisters*
1987	Olympia Dukakis	*Moonstruck*
1988	Geena Davis	*The Accidental Tourist*
1989	Brenda Fricker	*My Left Foot*

The same film has received three nominations for "Best Supporting Actress" only once – Diane Cilento, Dame Edith Evans and Joyce Redman for *Tom Jones*.

THE 10 "BEST ACTOR" OSCAR WINNERS OF THE 1980s
(Film/year)

❶ Robert De Niro (*Raging Bull*, 1980)
❷ Henry Fonda (*On Golden Pond*, 1981)
❸ Ben Kingsley (*Gandhi*, 1982) ❹ Robert Duvall (*Tender Mercies*, 1983) ❺ F. Murray Abraham (*Amadeus*, 1984) ❻ William Hurt (*Kiss of the Spider Woman*, 1985) ❼ Paul Newman (*The Color of Money*, 1986)
❽ Michael Douglas (*Wall Street*, 1987)
❾ Dustin Hoffman (*Rain Man*, 1988)
❿ Daniel Day-Lewis (*My Left Foot*, 1989)

TOP 10

YOUNGEST OSCAR WINNERS

	Actor/actress	Award/film (where specified)	Award year	Age
1	Shirley Temple	Special Award – outstanding contribution during 1934	1934	6
2	Margaret O'Brien	Special Award (*Meet Me in St. Louis*, etc)	1944	8
3	Vincent Winter	Special Award (*The Little Kidnappers*)	1954	8
4	Ivan Jandl	Special Award (*The Search*)	1948	9
5	Jon Whiteley	Special Award (*The Little Kidnappers*)	1954	10
6	Tatum O'Neal	Best Supporting Actress (*Paper Moon*)	1973	10
7	Anna Paquin	Best Supporting Actress (*The Piano*)	1993	11
8	Claude Jarman Jr.	Special Award (*The Yearling*)	1946	12
9	Bobby Driscoll	Special Award (*The Window*)	1949	13
10	Hayley Mills	Special Award (*Pollyanna*)	1960	13

* At time of Award ceremony; those of apparently identical age have been ranked according to their precise age in days at the time of the ceremony

THE 10

"BEST ACTOR" OSCAR WINNERS OF THE 1930s

Year	Actor	Film	Year	Actor	Film
1930	George Arliss	*Disraeli*	1935	Victor McLaglen	*The Informer*
1931	Lionel Barrymore	*A Free Soul*	1936	Paul Muni	*The Story of Louis Pasteur*
1932	Wallace Beery	*The Champ*			
1933	Charles Laughton	*The Private Life of Henry VIII*	1937	Spencer Tracy	*Captains Courageous*
			1938	Spencer Tracy	*Boys' Town*
1934	Clark Gable	*It Happened One Night*	1939	Robert Donat	*Goodbye Mr. Chips*

TOP 10

OLDEST OSCAR-WINNING ACTORS

	Actor/actress	Award/film	Year	Age*
1	Jessica Tandy	"Best Actress" (*Driving Miss Daisy*)	1989	80
2	George Burns	"Best Supporting Actor" (*The Sunshine Boys*)	1975	80
3	Melvyn Douglas	"Best Supporting Actor" (*Being There*)	1979	79
4	John Gielgud	"Best Supporting Actor" (*Arthur*)	1981	77
5	Don Ameche	"Best Supporting Actor" (*Cocoon*)	1985	77
6	Peggy Ashcroft	"Best Supporting Actress" (*A Passage to India*)	1984	77
7	Henry Fonda	"Best Actor" (*On Golden Pond*)	1981	76
8	Katharine Hepburn	"Best Actress" (*On Golden Pond*)	1981	74
9	Edmund Gwenn	"Best Supporting Actor" (*Miracle on 34th Street*)	1947	72
10	Ruth Gordon	"Best Supporting Actress" (*Rosemary's Baby*)	1968	72

* *At time of Award ceremony; those of apparently identical age have been ranked according to their precise age in days at the time of the ceremony*

Among those senior citizens who received nominations but did not win Oscars is Ralph Richardson, who was nominated as "Best Supporting Actor" for his role in *Greystoke: The Legend of Tarzan* (1984) at the age of 82. Eva Le Gallienne was the same age when she was nominated as "Best Supporting Actress" for her part in *Resurrection* (1980). Outside the four acting categories, the oldest director to be nominated for a "Best Director" Oscar was John Huston, aged 79 at the time of his nomination for *Prizzi's Honor* (1985), and the oldest winner was George Cukor for *My Fair Lady* (1964), when he was aged 65.

THE 10 "BEST ACTRESS" OSCAR WINNERS OF THE 1980s
(Film/year)

❶ Sissy Spacek (*The Coal Miner's Daughter*, 1980) ❷ Katharine Hepburn (*On Golden Pond*, 1981) ❸ Meryl Streep (*Sophie's Choice*, 1982) ❹ Shirley MacLaine (*Terms of Endearment*, 1983) ❺ Sally Field (*Places in the Heart*, 1984) ❻ Geraldine Page (*The Trip to Bountiful*, 1985) ❼ Marlée Matlin (*Children of a Lesser God*, 1986) ❽ Cher (*Moonstruck*, 1987) ❾ Jodie Foster (*The Accused*, 1988) ❿ Jessica Tandy (*Driving Miss Daisy*, 1989)

TOP 10

"BEST ACTRESS" OSCAR-WINNERS OF THE 1930s

Year	Actress	Film
1930	Norma Shearer	*The Divorcee*
1931	Marie Dressler	*Min and Bill*
1932	Helen Hayes	*The Sin of Madelon Claudet*
1933	Katharine Hepburn	*Morning Glory*
1934	Claudette Colbert	*It Happened One Night*
1935	Bette Davis	*Dangerous*
1936	Luise Rainer	*The Great Ziegfeld*
1937	Luise Rainer	*The Good Earth*
1938	Bette Davis	*Jezebel*
1939	Vivien Leigh	*Gone With The Wind*

PLAYING MISS DAISY
Jessica Tandy was aged 80 years 9 months when she won an Oscar for Driving Miss Daisy.

AND THE WINNER IS . . .

THE 10

FIRST WINNERS OF THE BAFTA BEST FILM AWARD

Year	Film	Country of origin
1947	*The Best Years of Our Lives*	USA
1948	*Hamlet*	UK
1949	*Bicycle Thieves*	Italy
1950	*All About Eve*	USA
1951	*La Ronde*	France
1952	*The Sound Barrier*	UK
1953	*Jeux Interdits*	France
1954	*Le Salaire de la Peur*	France
1955	*Richard III*	UK
1956	*Gervaise*	France

THE 10

LATEST WINNERS OF THE BAFTA BEST FILM AWARD

Year	Film	Country of origin
1997	*The Full Monty*	UK
1996	*The English Patient*	UK
1995	*Sense and Sensibility*	UK
1994	*Four Weddings and a Funeral*	UK
1993	*Schindler's List*	USA
1992	*Howards End*	UK
1991	*The Commitments*	USA/UK
1990	*Goodfellas*	USA
1989	*Dead Poets Society*	USA
1988	*The Last Emperor*	Italy/UK/China

THE 10

FIRST WINNERS OF THE CANNES BEST FILM AWARD

Year	Director/film	Country of origin
1949	Carol Reed, *The Third Man*	UK
1951*	Vittoria De Sica, *Miracle in Milan*	Italy
	and Alf Sjoberg, *Miss Julie*	Sweden
1952*	Orson Welles, *Othello*	Morocco
	and Renato Castellani, *Two Cents Worth of Hope*	Italy
1953	Henri-Georges Clouzot, *Wages of Fear*	France
1954	Teinosuke Kinugasa, *Gates of Hell*	Japan
1955	Delbert Mann, *Marty*	USA
1956	Louis Malle and Jacques-Yves Cousteau, *World of Silence*	France
1957	William Wyler, *Friendly Persuasion*	USA
1958	Mikhail Kalatozov, *The Cranes Are Flying*	USSR
1959	Marcel Camus, *Orfeu Negro*	France

* Prize shared

THE 10

LATEST WINNERS OF THE CANNES *PALME D'OR* FOR BEST FILM

Year	Film	Country of origin
1998	*Eternity and a Day*	Greece
1997	*The Eel/ The Taste of Cherries*	Japan / Iran
1996	*Secrets and Lies*	UK
1995	*Underground*	Yugoslavia
1994	*Pulp Fiction*	USA

Year	Film	Country of origin
1993	*Farewell My Concubine/ The Piano*	China / Australia
1992	*Best Intentions*	Sweden
1991	*Barton Fink*	USA
1990	*Wild at Heart*	USA
1989	*Sex, Lies, and Videotape*	USA

THE 10

FIRST WINNERS OF THE BAFTA BEST DIRECTOR AWARD

Year	Director	Film	Country of origin
1968	Mike Nichols	*The Graduate*	USA
1969	John Schlesinger	*Midnight Cowboy*	USA
1970	George Roy Hill	*Butch Cassidy and the Sundance Kid*	USA
1971	John Schlesinger	*Sunday, Bloody Sunday*	UK
1972	Bob Fosse	*Cabaret*	USA
1973	François Truffaut	*Day for Night*	France
1974	Roman Polanski	*Chinatown*	USA
1975	Stanley Kubrick	*Barry Lyndon*	UK
1976	Milos Forman	*One Flew over the Cuckoo's Nest*	USA
1977	Woody Allen	*Annie Hall*	USA

THE 10

LATEST WINNERS OF THE BAFTA BEST DIRECTOR AWARD

Year	Director	Film	Country of origin
1997	Baz Luhrmann	*William Shakespeare's Romeo and Juliet*	USA
1996	Joel Cohen	*Fargo*	USA
1995	Michael Radford	*Il Postino*	Italy
1994	Mike Newell	*Four Weddings and a Funeral*	UK
1993	Steven Spielberg	*Schindler's List*	USA
1992	Robert Altman	*The Player*	USA
1991	Alan Parker	*The Commitments*	USA/UK
1990	Martin Scorsese	*Goodfellas*	USA
1989	Kenneth Branagh	*Henry V*	UK
1988	Louis Malle	*Au Revoir les Enfants*	France

THE 10

FIRST WINNERS OF THE BAFTA BEST ACTOR AWARD

Year	Actor	Film	Country of origin
1968	Spencer Tracy	*Guess Who's Coming to Dinner*	USA
1969	Dustin Hoffman	*Midnight Cowboy/ John and Mary*	USA USA
1970	Robert Redford	*Tell Them Willie Boy Is Here/ Butch Cassidy and the Sundance Kid/Downhill Racer*	USA USA
1971	Peter Finch	*Sunday, Bloody Sunday*	UK
1972	Gene Hackman	*The French Connection/ The Poseidon Adventure*	USA USA
1973	Walter Matthau	*Pete 'n Tillie/ Charley Varrick*	USA USA
1974	Jack Nicholson	*The Last Detail/ Chinatown*	USA
1975	Al Pacino	*The Godfather Part II/ Dog Day Afternoon*	USA USA
1976	Jack Nicholson	*One Flew Over the Cuckoo's Nest*	USA
1977	Peter Finch	*Network*	USA

THE 10

FIRST WINNERS OF THE BAFTA BEST ACTRESS AWARD

Year	Actress	Film	Country of origin
1968	Katharine Hepburn	*Guess Who's Coming to Dinner/ The Lion in Winter*	USA UK
1969	Maggie Smith	*The Prime of Miss Jean Brodie*	UK
1970	Katharine Ross	*Tell Them Willie Boy Is Here/ Butch Cassidy and the Sundance Kid*	USA USA
1971	Glenda Jackson	*Sunday, Bloody Sunday*	UK
1972	Liza Minnelli	*Cabaret*	USA
1973	Stephane Audrane	*The Discreet Charm of the Bourgeoisie/ Just Before Nightfall*	France/ Spain/Italy France
1974	Joanne Woodward	*Summer Wishes, Winter Dreams*	USA
1975	Ellen Burstyn	*Alice Doesn't Live Here Anymore*	USA
1976	Louise Fletcher	*One Flew over the Cuckoo's Nest*	USA
1977	Diane Keaton	*Annie Hall*	USA

THE 10

LATEST WINNERS OF THE BAFTA BEST ACTOR AWARD

Year	Actor	Film	Country of origin
1997	Robert Carlyle	*The Full Monty*	UK
1996	Geoffrey Rush	*Shine*	Australia
1995	Nigel Hawthorne	*The Madness of King George*	UK
1994	Hugh Grant	*Four Weddings and a Funeral*	UK
1993	Anthony Hopkins	*The Remains of the Day*	US
1992	Robert Downey, Jr.	*Chaplin*	UK
1991	Anthony Hopkins	*The Silence of the Lambs*	USA
1990	Philippe Noiret	*Cinema Paradiso*	Italy/France
1989	Daniel Day Lewis	*My Left Foot*	UK
1988	John Cleese	*A Fish Called Wanda*	USA

THE 10

LATEST WINNERS OF THE BAFTA BEST ACTRESS AWARD

Year	Actress	Film	Country of origin
1997	Judi Dench	*Mrs. Brown*	UK
1996	Brenda Blethyn	*Secrets and Lies*	UK
1995	Emma Thompson	*Sense and Sensibility*	UK
1994	Susan Sarandon	*The Client*	USA
1993	Holly Hunter	*The Piano*	Australia
1992	Emma Thompson	*Howards End*	UK
1991	Jodie Foster	*The Silence of the Lambs*	USA
1990	Jessica Tandy	*Driving Miss Daisy*	USA
1989	Pauline Collins	*Shirley Valentine*	USA/UK
1988	Maggie Smith	*The Lonely Passion of Judith Hearne*	UK

THE 10

LATEST GOLDEN GLOBE AWARDS FOR "BEST MOTION PICTURE – DRAMA"

Year	Film	Year	Film
1997	*Titanic*	1992	*Scent of a Woman*
1996	*The English Patient*	1991	*Bugsy*
1995	*Sense and Sensibility*	1990	*Dances with Wolves*
1994	*Forrest Gump*	1989	*Born on the Fourth of July*
1993	*Schindler's List*	1988	*Rain Man*

FILM STARS – ACTORS

TOP 10
CLINT EASTWOOD FILMS

1	In the Line of Fire	1993
2	The Bridges of Madison County	1995
3	Unforgiven*	1992
4	A Perfect World	1993
5	Every Which Way But Loose	1978
6	Absolute Power	1997
7	Any Which Way You Can	1980
8	Sudden Impact	1983
9	The Enforcer	1976
10	Firefox	1982

* Academy Award for "Best Director"

TOP 10
ROBERT DE NIRO FILMS

1	Heat	1995
2	The Untouchables	1987
3	Cape Fear	1991
4	Sleepers	1996
5	Backdraft	1991
6	The Godfather, Part II*	1974
7	Casino	1995
8	Mary Shelley's Frankenstein	1994
9	Awakenings	1990
10	Goodfellas	1990

* Academy Award for "Best Supporting Actor"

TOP 10
JOHN TRAVOLTA FILMS

1	Grease	1978
2	Look Who's Talking	1989
3	Saturday Night Fever	1977
4	Face/Off	1997
5	Pulp Fiction	1994
6	Phenomenon	1996
7	Broken Arrow	1996
8	Staying Alive	1983
9	Get Shorty	1995
10	Michael	1996

TOP 10 MEL GIBSON FILMS

❶ *Lethal Weapon 3* (1992) ❷ *Ransom* (1996) ❸ *Lethal Weapon 2* (1989) ❹ *Braveheart** (1995) ❺ *Maverick* (1994) ❻ *Conspiracy Theory* (1987) ❼ *Forever Young* (1992) ❽ *Bird on a Wire* (1990) ❾ *Lethal Weapon* (1987) ❿ *Tequila Sunrise* (1988)
* *Academy Award for "Best Director"*

TOP 10
HARRISON FORD FILMS

1	Star Wars	1977
2	Indiana Jones and the Last Crusade	1989
3	Return of the Jedi	1983
4	Raiders of the Lost Ark	1981
5	The Empire Strikes Back	1980
6	The Fugitive	1993
7	Indiana Jones and the Temple of Doom	1984
8	Air Force One	1997
9	Presumed Innocent	1990
10	Clear and Present Danger	1994

Uniquely in Hollywood history, every single one of Harrison Ford's Top 10 films has earned more than $200,000,000 at the world box office – in fact, the cumulative earnings of his Top 10 films alone are in excess of $3.5 billion.

TOP 10
TOM CRUISE FILMS

1	Mission: Impossible	1996
2	Rain Man	1988
3	Top Gun	1986
4	Jerry Maguire	1996
5	The Firm	1993
6	A Few Good Men	1992
7	Interview with the Vampire	1994
8	Days of Thunder	1990
9	Cocktail	1988
10	Born on the Fourth of July	1989

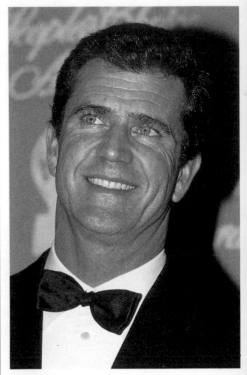

MEL GIBSON

TOP 10
DANNY DEVITO FILMS

1	Batman Returns	1992
2	Get Shorty	1995
3	Romancing the Stone	1984
4	One Flew Over the Cuckoo's Nest	1975
5	Twins	1988
6	Terms of Endearment	1983
7	Mars Attacks!	1996
8	Junior	1994
9	The War of the Roses*	1989
10	Ruthless People	1986

* *Also director*

Danny DeVito had a relatively minor role in *One Flew Over the Cuckoo's Nest*. If this is discounted from the reckoning, his 10th most successful film becomes *L.A. Confidential* (1997). He provided the voices of Whiskers in *Last Action Hero* (1993), Rocks in *Look Who's Talking Now* (1993), and Swackhammer in *Space Jam* (1996), and directed, appeared in, and narrated *Matilda* (1996), which just fails to make his personal Top 10.

TOP 10

TOM HANKS FILMS

1	Forrest Gump*	1994
2	Apollo 13	1995
3	Sleepless in Seattle	1993
4	Philadelphia*	1993
5	Big	1988
6	A League of Their Own	1992
7	Turner & Hooch	1989
8	Splash!	1984
9	Dragnet	1987
10	Joe Versus the Volcano	1990

* Academy Award for "Best Actor"

TOP 10

SYLVESTER STALLONE FILMS

1	Rambo: First Blood Part Two	1985
2	Cliffhanger	1993
3	The Specialist	1994
4	Daylight	1996
5	Rocky IV	1985
6	Rocky III	1982
7	Rocky	1976
8	Judge Dredd	1995
9	Daylight	1996
10	Assassins	1995

TOP 10

ARNOLD SCHWARZENEGGER FILMS

1	Terminator 2: Judgment Day	1991
2	True Lies	1994
3	Total Recall	1990
4	Eraser	1996
5	Twins	1988
6	Kindergarten Cop	1990
7	Jingle All the Way	1996
8	Last Action Hero	1993
9	Junior	1994
10	The Terminator	1984

TOP 10

ROBIN WILLIAMS FILMS

1	Mrs. Doubtfire	1993	6	Good Will Hunting*	1997
2	Hook	1991	7	Nine Months	1995
3	Jumanji	1995	8	Good Morning, Vietnam	1987
4	Dead Poets Society	1989	9	Jack	1996
5	The Birdcage	1996	10	Flubber	1997

* Academy Award for "Best Supporting Actor"

Robin Williams' voice appears as that of the genie in the 1992 animated blockbuster *Aladdin*. If this were included, its earnings would easily place it at the head of the list. His voice also appears in *Ferngully: The Last Rainforest* (1992).

TOP 10

JIM CARREY FILMS

1	Batman Forever	1995
2	The Mask	1994
3	Liar Liar	1997
4	Dumb & Dumber	1994
5	Ace Ventura: When Nature Calls	1995
6	The Cable Guy	1996
7	Ace Ventura: Pet Detective	1994
8	Peggy Sue Got Married	1986
9	The Dead Pool	1988
10	Pink Cadillac	1989

TOP 10

GENE HACKMAN FILMS

1	The Firm	1993
2	The Birdcage	1996
3	Unforgiven*	1992
4	Crimson Tide	1995
5	Superman	1978
6	Get Shorty	1995
7	Superman II	1980
8	The Poseidon Adventure	1972
9	Young Frankenstein	1974
10	Absolute Power	1997

* Academy Award for "Best Supporting Actor"

TOP 10

BRUCE WILLIS FILMS

1	Die Hard: With a Vengeance	1995
2	The Fifth Element	1997
3	Die Hard 2	1990
4	Pulp Fiction	1994
5	Twelve Monkeys	1995
6	Death Becomes Her	1992
7	Die Hard	1988
8	The Jackal	1997
9	The Last Boy Scout	1991
10	Last Man Standing	1996

TOP 10

JACK NICHOLSON FILMS

1	Batman	1989
2	A Few Good Men	1992
3	As Good As It Gets#	1997
4	Terms of Endearment*	1983
5	Wolf	1994
6	One Flew Over the Cuckoo's Nest#	1975
7	Mars Attacks!	1996
8	The Witches of Eastwick	1987
9	The Shining	1980
10	Broadcast News	1987

* Academy Award for "Best Supporting Actor"

Academy Award for "Best Actor"

FILM STARS – ACTRESSES

TOP 10
NICOLE KIDMAN FILMS

1	*Batman Forever*	1995
2	*Days of Thunder*	1990
3	*The Peacemaker*	1997
4	*Far and Away*	1992
5	*Malice*	1993
6	*My Life*	1993
7	*To Die For*	1995
8	*Billy Bathgate*	1991
9	*Dead Calm*	1989
10	*Portrait of a Lady*	1996

TOP 10 WHOOPI GOLDBERG FILMS

❶ *Ghost** (1990) ❷ *Sister Act* (1992) ❸ *The Color Purple* (1985) ❹ *Star Trek: Generations* (1994) ❺ *Made in America* (1993) ❻ *In & Out* (1997) ❼ *Sister Act 2: Back in the Habit* (1993) ❽ *The Little Rascals* (1994) ❾ *Eddie* (1996) ❿ *Soapdish* (1991)
* Academy Award for "Best Supporting Actress"

WHOOPI GOLDBERG

TOP 10
SHARON STONE FILMS

1	*Basic Instinct*	1992
2	*Total Recall*	1990
3	*The Specialist*	1995
4	*Last Action Hero*	1993
5	*Sliver*	1993
6	*Casino*	1995
7	*Diabolique*	1996
8	*Police Academy 4: Citizens on Patrol*	1987
9	*Intersection*	1994
10	*Action Jackson*	1988

Sharon Stone's part in *Last Action Hero* amounted to no more than a brief cameo. If discounted, *Above the Law* (1988) would occupy 10th place.

TOP 10
BETTE MIDLER FILMS

1	*The First Wives Club*	1996
2	*Get Shorty*	1995
3	*Ruthless People*	1986
4	*Down and Out in Beverly Hills*	1986
5	*Beaches**	1988
6	*Outrageous Fortune*	1987
7	*The Rose*	1979
8	*Big Business*	1988
9	*Hocus Pocus*	1993
10	*Hawaii*	1966

* Also producer

Bette Midler's role in *Get Shorty* is no more than a cameo, and that in *Hawaii*, her first film part, is as an extra. If excluded, *Stella* (1990) and *For the Boys* (1991), which she also produced and for which she received an Academy Award nomination for "Best Actress", would join the list. Her voice appears as that of the character Georgette in the animated film *Oliver and Company* (1988). If included, based on its earnings, it would be in third position.

TOP 10
JULIA ROBERTS FILMS

1	*Pretty Woman*	1990
2	*My Best Friend's Wedding*	1997
3	*The Pelican Brief*	1993
4	*Sleeping with the Enemy*	1991
5	*Conspiracy Theory*	1997
6	*Hook*	1991
7	*Steel Magnolias*	1989
8	*Flatliners*	1990
9	*Something to Talk About*	1995
10	*Everyone Says I Love You*	1996

Julia Roberts also appeared in a cameo role as herself in *The Player* (1992), which, along with *Dying Young* (1991), *I Love Trouble* (1994), and *Michael Collins* (1996), just fail to make her personal Top 10.

TOP 10
DEMI MOORE FILMS

1	*Ghost*	1990
2	*Indecent Proposal*	1993
3	*A Few Good Men*	1992
4	*Disclosure*	1995
5	*Striptease*	1996
6	*G.I. Jane*	1997
7	*The Juror*	1996
8	*About Last Night*	1986
9	*St. Elmo's Fire*	1985
10	*Young Doctors in Love*	1982

Demi Moore provided the voice of Esmeralda in the animated film, *The Hunchback of Notre Dame* (1996). If included in her Top 10, it would be in second place. Although uncredited, her voice also appears in *Beavis and Butt-head Do America* (1996).

T O P   1 0
EMMA THOMPSON FILMS

1=	Sense and Sensibility*	1995
=	Junior	1994
3	Dead Again	1991
4	Howards End#	1992
5	In the Name of the Father	1993
6	The Remains of the Day	1993
7	Much Ado About Nothing	1993
8	Henry V	1989
9=	Impromptu	1991
=	Peter's Friends	1992

* Academy Award for "Best Adapted
   Screenplay"

Academy Award for "Best Actress"

SIGOURNEY WEAVER

T O P   1 0
GLENN CLOSE FILMS

1	Fatal Attraction	1987
2	101 Dalmatians	1996
3	Hook	1991
4	Air Force One	1997
5	Mars Attacks!	1996
6	The Big Chill	1983
7	The Natural	1984
8	The Paper	1994
9	Dangerous Liaisons	1988
10	The World According to Garp	1982

Glenn Close appeared as herself in
In & Out (1997), and provided the voice
of Jane Porter in Greystoke: The Legend
of Tarzan, Lord of the Apes (1984),
both of which would merit places in her
personal Top 10 films.

T O P   1 0
JODIE FOSTER FILMS

1	The Silence of the Lambs*	1990
2	Maverick	1994
3	Sommersby	1993
4	Nell	1994
5	The Accused*	1988
6	Taxi Driver	1976
7	Freaky Friday	1976
8	Little Man Tate	1991
9	Home for the Holidays#	1995
10	Alice Doesn't Live Here Any More	1975

* Academy Award for "Best Actress"
# Directed only

TOP 10 SIGOURNEY WEAVER FILMS

❶ Ghostbusters (1984) ❷ Ghostbusters II
(1989) ❸ Aliens (1986) ❹ Alien (1979)
❺ Working Girl (1988) ❻ Dave (1993)
❼= Alien Resurrection (1997), Alien³ (1992)
❽ Copycat (1995) ❾ Gorillas in the Mist
(1988) ❿ 1492: Conquest of Paradise (1992)

T O P   1 0
GOLDIE HAWN FILMS

1	The First Wives Club	1996
2	Death Becomes Her	1992
3	Bird on a Wire	1990
4	Private Benjamin	1980
5	Housesitter	1992
6	Foul Play	1978
7	Shampoo	1975
8	Seems Like Old Times	1980
9	Best Friends	1982
10	Everyone Says I Love You	1996

T O P   1 0
MERYL STREEP FILMS

1	The Bridges of Madison County	1995
2	Kramer vs. Kramer*	1979
3	Out of Africa	1985
4	Death Becomes Her	1992
5	The Deer Hunter	1978
6	Manhattan	1979
7	Postcards from the Edge	1990
8	Silkwood	1983
9	Sophie's Choice#	1982
10	Julia	1982

* Academy Award for "Best Supporting Actress"
# Academy Award for "Best Actress"

It is perhaps surprising that Sophie's
Choice, the film for which Meryl Streep won
an Oscar, scores so far down this list, while
one of her most celebrated films, The
French Lieutenant's Woman (1981), does
not make her personal Top 10 at all.

SNAP FACTS

● In 1915, Mary Pickford, the most prolific actress of all time (in the period
1908–42 she made at least 238 films), was one of the first to be identified as
a major box-office draw.

● Surveys of the most commercially important actresses during the past 65
years place Doris Day as the all-time leader.

● During the 1990s, Julia Roberts has been the most consistently nominated actress in
audience appeal listings, followed by such stars as Sandra Bullock, Demi Moore, Jodie Foster,
and Whoopi Goldberg.

THE STUDIOS

TOP 10
UNITED ARTISTS FILMS OF ALL TIME*

1	*Moonraker*	1979
2	*The Spy Who Loved Me*	1977
3	*Thunderball*	1965
4	*Live and Let Die*	1973
5	*Goldfinger*	1964
6	*Rocky*	1976
7	*Diamonds are Forever*	1971
8	*One Flew Over the Cuckoo's Nest*	1975
9	*You Only Live Twice*	1967
10	*The Man with the Golden Gun*	1974

* Excluding films made since MGM takeover

United Artists was formed in 1919 by actors, including Charlie Chaplin and Douglas Fairbanks, and director D. W. Griffith to provide an independent means of producing and distributing their films. It never actually owned a studio, but rented production facilities. After many vicissitudes, and a successful run in the 1970s with the consistently successful James Bond films, it merged with MGM in 1981.

TOP 10
PARAMOUNT FILMS OF ALL TIME

1	*Titanic*	1997
2	*Forrest Gump*	1994
3	*Terminator 2: Judgment Day*	1991
4	*Ghost*	1990
5	*Indiana Jones and the Last Crusade*	1989
6	*Mission: Impossible*	1996
7	*Raiders of the Lost Ark*	1981
8	*Top Gun*	1986
9	*Grease*	1978
10	*Indiana Jones and the Temple of Doom*	1984

Paramount owes its origin in 1912 to Adolph Zukor's Famous Players Film Company. Following a series of company mergers and name changes in the 1920s, Paramount Pictures eventually emerged and became one of the most commercially successful Hollywood studios. With stars such as the Marx Brothers, Mae West, and Bing Crosby and Bob Hope, and directors including Cecil B. De Mille, Paramount entered a golden age in the 1930s and 1940s.

TOP 10
WALT DISNEY/BUENA VISTA FILMS OF ALL TIME

1	*The Lion King*	1994
2	*Aladdin*	1992
3	*Pretty Woman*	1990
4	*Toy Story*	1995
5	*Beauty and the Beast*	1991
6	*Who Framed Roger Rabbit?*	1988
7	*Pocahontas*	1995
8	*The Rock*	1996
9	*The Hunchback of Notre Dame*	1996
10	*101 Dalmatians*	1996

In 1923, having started his business in Kansas City, Walt Disney moved to California where he experienced modest success with his animated films until the advent of sound made a notable commercial success of *Steamboat Willie* (1928), Mickey Mouse's first starring vehicle. Distribution deals with major studios enabled the Disney Studio to capitalize on such blockbusters as *Snow White and the Seven Dwarfs* (1937), which became the second highest-earning film of the 1940s.

TOP 10
MGM FILMS OF ALL TIME

1	*Rain Man*	1988
2	*GoldenEye*	1995
3	*Tomorrow Never Dies*	1997
4	*Rocky IV*	1985
5	*Stargate*	1994
6	*Gone With the Wind*	1939
7	*The Birdcage*	1996
8	*Rocky III*	1982
9	*Poltergeist*	1982
10	*Get Shorty*	1995

Founded in 1924, Metro Goldwyn Mayer's pre-eminence was firmly established in the 1930s and 1940s with the success of films such as *The Wizard of Oz* (1939) and contracts with numerous notable stars, including Greta Garbo, Joan Crawford, Spencer Tracy, and Clark Gable.

STUDIO TOUR
Previously inaccessible to the movie-going public, Universal's decision to open its studios to organized tours has made them one of the world's foremost tourist attractions.

TOP 10

WARNER BROS FILMS OF ALL TIME

1	*Twister*	1996
2	*Batman*	1989
3	*The Bodyguard*	1992
4	*Robin Hood: Prince of Thieves*	1991
5	*The Fugitive*	1993
6	*Batman Forever*	1995
7	*Lethal Weapon 3*	1992
8	*Batman Returns*	1992
9	*Eraser*	1996
10	*Batman and Robin*	1997

It was the coming of sound that launched the newly formed Warner Brothers into its important place in cinema history, with *The Jazz Singer* (1927) its best-known early sound production. In the 1970s, following a series of takeovers, Warner Bros embarked on an era of notable success that began with *The Exorcist* in 1973 and continued with a number of films starring Clint Eastwood.

TOP 10

20TH-CENTURY FOX FILMS OF ALL TIME

1	*Independence Day*	1996
2	*Star Wars*	1977
3	*The Empire Strikes Back*	1980
4	*Home Alone*	1990
5	*Return of the Jedi*	1983
6	*Mrs. Doubtfire*	1993
7	*True Lies*	1994
8	*Die Hard: With a Vengeance*	1995
9	*Speed*	1994
10	*Home Alone 2: Lost in New York*	1992

William Fox founded a film production company in 1912. With the coming of sound he pioneered its use, especially through the medium of Fox Movietone newsreels. The company was merged with 20th-Century Pictures in 1935, and under the control of Darryl F. Zanuck and Joseph M. Schenck achieved some of its greatest successes in the 1940s.

TOP 10

COLUMBIA/TRI-STAR/SONY FILMS OF ALL TIME

1	*Men in Black*	1997
2	*Terminator 2: Judgment Day*	1991
3	*Basic Instinct*	1992
4	*Hook*	1991
5	*Close Encounters of the Third Kind*	1977/80
6	*Look Who's Talking*	1989
7	*Air Force One*	1997
8	*Ghostbusters*	1984
9	*Jerry Maguire*	1997
10	*The Fifth Element*	1997

Founded in 1924 by Harry Cohn and his brother Jack, Columbia's first major success came in 1934 with Frank Capra's *It Happened One Night*. In the 1950s Columbia's award-winning and successful films included *The Bridge on the River Kwai* (1957), *On the Waterfront* (1954), and *From Here to Eternity* (1953).

TOP 10

MCA/UNIVERSAL FILMS OF ALL TIME

1	*Jurassic Park*	1993
2	*E.T.: the Extra-Terrestrial*	1982
3	*The Lost World: Jurassic Park*	1997
4	*Jaws*	1975
5	*The Flintstones*	1994
6	*Back to the Future*	1985
7	*Apollo 13*	1995
8	*Schindler's List*	1993
9	*Liar Liar*	1997
10	*Casper*	1995

Universal Pictures was founded in 1912 by Carl Laemmle, who soon developed it into the world's largest film studio. However, despite a handful of worthy and successful productions, such as *All Quiet on the Western Front* (1930), Universal went through a financially precarious period in the 1930s. In 1962 it was sold to MCA, which developed its strengths as a TV production company and inaugurated the organized studio tours.

SNAP FACTS

- William Fox, the colourful founder of 20th-Century Fox, was forced to sell out to a syndicate of bankers in 1930. He later went bankrupt and served time in Pennsylvania Penitentiary for allegedly bribing a judge.

- Jack L. Warner, the most powerful of the four Warner Brothers, began his career singing to entertain the audience during intermissions in the family nickelodeon in Newcastle, Pennsylvania.

- In the first Disney sound animation, *Steamboat Willie* (1928), Walt Disney himself recorded the squeaky voice of Mickey Mouse.

OUT-TAKES

TOP 10

CINEMA-GOING COUNTRIES

	Country	Annual attendance per inhabitant
1	Lebanon	35.3
2	China	12.3
3	Georgia	5.6
4	India	5.0
5	Iceland	4.5
6=	Australia	3.9
=	New Zealand	3.9
=	USA	3.9
9	Monaco	3.7
10	Canada	2.8
	UK	*2.0*

It is not the country with the most cinemas or the highest total number of visits to the cinema per year that records the highest rate of cinema-going per person, since the inhabitants of Lebanon record an annual average of more than 35 visits a year. This compares with an average of just two visits a year in the UK.

Source: UNESCO

TOP 10

FILM-GOING COUNTRIES

	Country	Total annual attendance
1	China	14,428,400,000
2	India	4,297,500,000
3	USA	981,900,000
4	Russia	140,100,000
5	Japan	130,700,000
6	France	130,100,000
7	Germany	124,500,000
8	UK	114,600,000
9	Lebanon	99,200,000
10	Australia	69,000,000

Source: UNESCO

TOP 10

YEARS WITH MOST CINEMA VISITS IN THE US, 1946–97

	Year	No. of films released	Admissions
1	1946	400	4,067,300,000
2	1947	426	3,664,400,000
3	1948	444	3,422,700,000
4	1949	490	3,168,500,000
5	1950	483	3,017,500,000
6	1951	433	2,840,100,000
7	1952	389	2,777,700,000
8	1953	404	2,630,600,000
9	1954	369	2,270,400,000
10	1955	319	2,072,300,000

From 1956, admissions continued to decline until 1963, when there was a slight increase. In 1971, the totals reached an all time low of 820,300,000. Since 1991, admissions have increased each year, reaching 1,387,700,000 in 1997.

Source: Motion Picture Association of America, Inc.

TOP 10

FILM-PRODUCING COUNTRIES

	Country	Average no. of films produced per annum (1991–96)
1	India	851
2	USA	569
3	Japan	252
4	Russia	192
5	France	143
6	China	137
7	Italy	107
8	South Korea	80
9	Turkey	71
10	UK	65

Source: Screen Digest

TOP 10

FILMS WITH THE MOST EXTRAS

	Film/country/year	Extras
1	*Gandhi*, UK, 1982	300,000
2	*Kolberg*, Germany, 1945	187,000
3	*Monster Wang-magwi*, South Korea, 1967	157,000
4	*War and Peace*, USSR, 1967	120,000
5	*Ilya Muromets*, USSR, 1956	106,000
6	*Tonko*, Japan, 1988	100,000
7	*The War of Independence*, Romania, 1912	80,000
8	*Around the World in 80 Days*, USA, 1956	68,894
9=	*Intolerance*, USA, 1916	60,000
=	*Dny Zrady*, Czechoslovakia, 1972	60,000

CINEMA GIANT
India's insatiable demand for films has resulted in its film output outstripping even that of Hollywood.

TOP 10

MOST EXPENSIVE ITEMS OF FILM MEMORABILIA EVER SOLD AT AUCTION

	Item/sale	Price (£)*
1	Vivien Leigh's Oscar for *Gone with the Wind*, Sotheby's, New York, 15 December 1993 ($562,500)	380,743
2	Clark Gable's Oscar for *It Happened One Night*, Christie's, Los Angeles, 15 December 1996 ($607,500)	364,500
3	Poster for *The Mummy*, 1932, Sotheby's, New York, 1 March 1997 ($453,500)	252,109
4	James Bond's Aston Martin DB5 from *Goldfinger*, Sotheby's, New York, 28 June 1986 ($275,000)	179,793
5	Clark Gable's personal script for *Gone with the Wind*, Christie's, Los Angeles, 15 December 1996 ($244,500)	146,700
6	"Rosebud" sled from *Citizen Kane*, Christie's, Los Angeles, 15 December 1996 ($233,500)	140,000
7	Herman J. Mankiewicz's scripts for *Citizen Kane and the American*, Christie's, New York, 21 June 1989 ($231,000)	139,157
8	Dorothy's ruby slippers from *The Wizard of Oz*, Christie's, New York, 21 June 1988 ($165,000)	104,430
9	Piano from the Paris scene in *Casablanca*, Sotheby's, New York, 16 December 1988 ($154,000)	97,469
10	Charlie Chaplin's hat and cane, Christie's, London, 11 December 1987 (resold at Christie's, London, 17 December 1993, for £55,000)	82,500

* *$/£ conversion at rate then prevailing*

RUBY SLIPPERS WORN BY JUDY GARLAND

TOP 10

COUNTRIES WITH THE MOST CINEMA SCREENS PER MILLION

	Country	Cinema screens per million
1	Belarus	414.9
2	Sweden	137.8
3	USA	105.9
4	Latvia	101.7
5	Norway	91.5
6	Iceland	86.3
7	France	80.0
8	Czech Republic	79.3
9	New Zealand	73.7
10	Switzerland	71.2

Source: Screen Digest

TOP 10

LONGEST FILMS EVER SCREENED

	Title	Country	Year	Duration hrs	mins
1	*The Longest and Most Meaningless Movie in the World*	UK	1970	48	0
2	*The Burning of the Red Lotus Temple*	China	1928–31	27	0
3	****	USA	1967	25	0
4	*Heimat*	West Germany	1984	15	40
5	*Berlin Alexanderplatz*	West Germany/Italy	1980	15	21
6	*The Journey*	Sweden	1987	14	33
7	*The Old Testament*	Italy	1922	13	0
8	*Comment Yukong déplace les montagnes*	France	1976	12	43
9	*Out 1: Noli me Tangere*	France	1971	12	40
10	*Ningen No Joken (The Human Condition)*	Japan	1958–60	9	29

TOP 10

COUNTRIES WITH THE MOST CINEMAS

	Country	No. of cinemas
1	USA	23,662
2	Ukraine	14,960
3	India	8,975
4	China	4,639
5	France	4,365
6	Italy	3,816
7	Germany	3,814
8	Belarus	3,780
9	Uzbekistan	2,365
10	Spain	2,090
	UK	*2,019*

Source: UNESCO

ON THE RADIO

GOING FOR A SPIN
The universal appeal of popular music of all types means that radio stations that play it dominate the world's airwaves.

TOP 10
RADIO STATIONS IN THE UK IN 1997

	Station	Listener hours*		Station	Listener hours*
1	BBC Radio 2	107,589,000	6	Capital Radio#	38,576,000
2	BBC Radio 4	86,281,000	7	BBC Radio 5 Live	29,769,000
3	BBC Radio 1	82,116,000	8	Classic FM	28,391,000
4	EMAP#	66,022,000	9	Virgin Radio#	27,627,000
5	GWR Group#	49,334,000	10	Atlantic 252	15,839,000

* *Total number of hours spent by all adults (over 15) listening to the station in an average week*

\# *Split frequency stations; listener hours are totals for all frequencies*

TOP 10
RADIO-OWNING COUNTRIES

	Country	Radio sets per 1,000 population
1	USA	2,093
2	UK	1,433
3	Australia	1,304
4	Canada	1,053
5	Denmark	1,034
6	South Korea	1,024
7	Monaco	1,019
8	Finland	1,008
9	New Zealand	997
10	Germany	944

The top eight countries in this list have at least one radio per person. In addition, many small island communities in the world have very high numbers of radios for their small populations to enable them to maintain regular contact with the outside world. In Bermuda there are 1,285 per 1,000 population (or 1.3 per person), in Gibraltar 1,300 per 1,000 population, and in Guam there are 1,407 radios per 1,000 population. The world record however is still held by the US, with over two radio sets per inhabitant.

Source: UNESCO

TOP 10
BESTSELLING BBC RADIO COLLECTION DRAMA TITLES

1	*Lord of the Rings*
2	*Talking Heads*
3	*The HitchHiker's Guide to the Galaxy*
4	*The Adventures of Sherlock Holmes Volume 1*
5	*Murder on the Orient Express*
6	*Spoonface Steinberg*
7	*The Secret Diary of Adrian Mole aged 13¾*
8	*Lake Wobegon Days*
9	*Woman's Hour Short Stories Volume 1*
10	*The Hobbit*

TOP 10
BBC RADIO 1 PROGRAMMES

1	*The Radio 1 Breakfast Show*
2	*Dave Pearce – Drivetime*
3	*Simon Mayo*
4	*Mark Radcliffe*
5	*Jo Whiley*
6	*The Top 40*
7	*The Evening Session with Steve Lamacq*
8	*Mark Goodier (Saturday)*
9	*Mark Goodier (Sunday)*
10	*Pete Tong – Essential Selection*

THE 10

FIRST SONY RADIO AWARDS

Year	Gold award	Personality/ Broadcaster of the Year
1983	Frank Muir, Denis Norden	Brian Johnston, Sue MacGregor
1984	David Jacobs	Brian Matthew, Margaret Howard
1985	British Forces Broadcasting Service	Jimmy Young
1986	John Timpson	Douglas Cameron
1987	*The Archers*	Derek Jameson
1988	Gerald Mansell	Alan Freeman
1989	Tony Blackburn	Sue Lawley
1990	Roy Hudd	Chris Tarrant
1991	Charlie Gillett	James Naughtie
1992	Sir James Savile	Danny Baker

The electronics company Sony has sponsored the British radio awards that bear its name since 1983. They are presented to "celebrate the quality, creativity, and excellence of those whose work brings enjoyment to millions of listeners".

TOP 10

RADIO FORMATS IN THE US

	Format	Share (percent)*
1	News/talk	16.5
2	Adult Contemporary	14.4
3	Country	10.3
4	Top 40	8.2
5	Urban	7.7
6	Album Rock	6.8
7	Spanish	6.2
8	Oldies	5.9
9	Classic Rock	4.7
10	Modern Rock	4.2

* *Of all radio listening during an average week, 6 am to midnight, autumn 1996, for listeners aged 12 plus*

Source: Copyright 1998 The Arbitron Company. May not be quoted or reproduced without the prior written permission of Arbitron

TOP 10

LONGEST-RUNNING PROGRAMMES ON BBC RADIO

	Programme	First broadcast
1	*The Week's Good Cause*	24 Jan 1926
2	*Choral Evensong*	7 Oct 1926
3	*Daily Service*	2 Jan 1928 *
4	*The Week in Westminster*	6 Nov 1929
5	*Sunday Half Hour*	14 Jul 1940
6	*Desert Island Discs*	29 Jan 1942
7	*Saturday Night Theatre*	3 Apr 1943
8	*Composer of the Week* (originally *This Week's Composer*)	2 Aug 1943
9	*Letter From America* (originally *American Letter*)	24 Mar 1946
10	*From Our Own Correspondent*	4 Oct 1946

* *Experimental broadcast; national transmission began December 1929*

In addition to these 10 long-running programmes, a further six that started in the 1940s are still on the air: *Woman's Hour* (first broadcast 7 October 1946 – although the BBC's London station 2LO had previously first broadcast a programme with this name on 2 May 1923), *Down Your Way* (29 December 1946), *Round Britain Quiz* (2 November 1947), *Any Questions?* (12 October 1948), *Book at Bedtime* (6 August 1949), and *Morning Story* (17 October 1949). *Gardeners' Question Time* was first broadcast on 9 April 1947 as *How Does Your Garden Grow?* Its name was changed in 1950. A pilot for *The Archers* was broadcast in the Midland region for a one-week trial beginning on 29 May 1950, but the serial began its national run on 1 January 1951.

TOP 10

BESTSELLING RADIO COLLECTION COMEDY TITLES

1	*Round the Horne*
2	*Hancock's Half Hour 1*
3	*The Goon Show: "Moriarty where are you?"*
4	*The Navy Lark: "Laughs Ahoy Landlubbers"*
5	*Knowing Me, Knowing You*
6	*Fawlty Towers*
7	*Blackadder Goes Forth*
8	*Yes Minister 1*
9	*I'm Sorry I Haven't a Clue*
10	*Dad's Army*

TOP TELEVISION

TELEVISION
It has been calculated that the average person in the UK will spend two years of their life watching TV.

TOP 10

CHANNEL 5 AUDIENCES, 1997*

	Programme	Date	Audience
1	Live Sport (England vs. Poland)	31 May	4,500,000
2	Speed (film)	15 Sep	3,600,000
3	This is 5	30 Mar	2,490,000
4	Deadly Summer	30 Nov	1,750,000
5	Family Affairs	30 Mar	1,720,000
6	Beyond Fear	30 Mar	1,700,000
7	The Sweeney	13 Oct	1,500,000
8	The Making of Spiceworld: the Movie	24 Dec	1,320,000
9	Mind to Kill	8 Nov	1,270,000
10	Camilla (documentary)	6 Jul	1,250,000

* Channel 5 commenced broadcasting on 30 March 1997

TOP 10 BESTSELLING BBC TV PROGRAMMES
(Programme type/no. of countries sold to)

❶ *The Living Planet* (Natural History, 82) ❷ *Flight of the Condor* (Natural History, 75) ❸ *Animal Olympian* (Natural History, 67) ❹= *The Six Wives of Henry Vlll* (Drama, 66), *The Onedin Line* (Drama, 66), *Supersense* (Natural History, 66) ❼ *The Impossible Bird* (Natural History, 63) ❽ *Tender is the Night* (Drama, 62) ❾ *Ascent of Man,* (Documentary, 62) ❿ *Faulty Towers,* (Comedy, 60)

TOP 10

LONGEST-RUNNING PROGRAMMES ON BRITISH TELEVISION

	Programme	First shown		Programme	First shown
1	Panorama	11 Nov 1953	6	Coronation Street	9 Dec 1960
2	What the Papers Say	5 Nov 1956	7	Songs of Praise	1 Oct 1961
3	The Sky at Night	24 Apr 1957	8	Top of the Pops	1 Jan 1964
4	Grandstand	11 Oct 1958	9	Horizon	2 May 1964
5	Blue Peter	16 Oct 1958	10	Match of the Day	22 Aug 1964

Only programmes appearing every year since their first screenings are listed; all are BBC programmes except *Coronation Street*. Several other BBC programmes, such as *The Good Old Days (1953-83)*, ran for many years but are now defunct. *The Sky at Night* has the additional distinction of having had the same presenter, Patrick Moore, since its first programme.

TOP 10

BBC 2 AUDIENCES, 1997

	Programme	Date	Audience
1	Have I Got News For You?*	18/19 Apr	9,110,000
2	Red Dwarf*	7/9 Feb	8,190,000
3	Shooting Stars*	22/25 Dec	6,910,000
4	Changing Rooms	22 Sep	6,900,000
5	The Antiques Show	28 Apr	6,720,000
6	Wimbledon (Henman/Krajcek)	1 Jul	6,590,000
7	Willy Wonka and the Chocolate Factory (film)	1 Jan	6,070,000
8	The Simpsons*	22/2 Dec	6,060,000
9	Ice Mummies	13 Feb	5,710,000
10	Snooker	5 May	5,650,000

* Aggregate audience

TOP 10

ITV AUDIENCES, 1997

	Programme*	Date	Audience
1	Heartbeat	16 Nov	18,400,000
2	A Touch of Frost	16 Feb	18,200,000
3	Coronation Street	17 Nov	18,000,000
4	It'll Be Alright on the Night 8	4 Jan	14,900,000
5	Emmerdale	20 Feb	14,200,000
6	The Bill	17 Jan	14,200,000
7	London's Burning	2 Feb	14,100,000
8	Police, Camera, Action!	7 Jan	13,700,000
9	Midsomer Murders: Killing Badgers Draft	23 Mar	13,500,000
10	Peak Practice	18 Feb	13,100,000

* The highest-rated episode only of series shown

TOP 10

CHANNEL 4 AUDIENCES, 1997

	Programme*	Date	Audience
1	Four Weddings and a Funeral (film)	28 Apr	7,324,000
2	Friends	10 Oct	6,040,000
3	Brookside	07 Apr	5,508,000
4	Cutting Edge	20 Jan	5,198,000
5	Dark Skies	13 Jan	5,099,000
6	Secret Lives	28 Jan	4,918,000
7	The Shawshank Redemption (film)	16 Nov	4,917,000
8	E.R.	2 Apr	4,792,000
9	Melissa	12 May	4,748,000
10	Trainspotting (film)	26 Nov	4,557,000

* The highest-rated episode only of series shown

THE 10
FIRST COUNTRIES TO HAVE TELEVISION*

	Country	Year
1	UK	1936
2	USA	1939
3	USSR	1939
4	France	1948
5	Brazil	1950
6	Cuba	1950
7	Mexico	1950
8	Argentina	1951
9	Denmark	1951
10	Netherlands	1951

* High-definition regular public broadcasting service

TOP 10
TV-WATCHING COUNTRIES IN THE WORLD

	Country	Average daily viewing time (minutes)
1	USA	239
2 =	Italy	216
=	Turkey	216
4	UK	215
5	Spain	214
6	Hungary	213
7	Japan	205
8	Greece	202
9	Canada	192
10	Argentina	191

Source: Screen Digest/Eurodata TV

TOP 10
TV-OWNING COUNTRIES IN THE WORLD

	Country	TVs in use
1	China	250,000,000
2	USA	215,000,000
3	Japan	85,500,000
4	Russia	56,000,000
5	India	47,000,000
6	Germany	46,000,000
7	Brazil	35,000,000
8	France	34,250,000
9	UK	26,000,000
10	Italy	25,500,000

Source: UNESCO

TOP 10
BBC 1 AUDIENCES, 1997

	Programme*	Date	Audience
1	Eastenders#	17/20 Apr	23,340,000
2	Funeral of Diana, Princess of Wales	6 Sep	19,290,000
3	Casualty	22 Feb	16,420,000
4	Men Behaving Badly	25 Dec	16,340,000
5	They Think It's All Over#	25/27 Dec	16,260,000
6	One Foot in the Xmas Grave	25 Dec	15,750,000
7	Before they were Famous	31 Mar	15,350,000
8	The Grand National	7 Apr	15,160,000
9	Procession to Westminster Abbey Funeral of Diana, Princess of Wales	6 Sep	14,780,000
10	The National Lottery Live	15 Mar	13,610,000

* The highest-rated episode only of series shown

Aggregate audience

TOP 10
TV AUDIENCES OF ALL TIME IN THE UK

	Programme	Date	Audience
1	Royal Wedding of HRH Prince Charles to Lady Diana Spencer	29 Jul 1981	39,000,000
2	Brazil vs. England 1970 World Cup	10 Jun 1970	32,500,000
3 =	England vs. West Germany 1966 World Cup Final	30 Jul 1966	32,000,000
=	Chelsea vs. Leeds Cup Final Replay	28 Apr 1970	32,000,000
5	Funeral of Diana, Princess of Wales	6 Sep 1997	31,000,000
6	EastEnders Christmas episode	26 Dec 1987	30,000,000
7	Morecambe and Wise Christmas Show	25 Dec 1977	28,000,000
8 =	World Heavyweight Boxing Championship: Joe Frazier vs. Cassius Clay	8 Mar 1971	27,000,000
=	Dallas	22 Nov 1980	27,000,000
10	Only Fools and Horses	29 Dec 1996	24,350,000

TOP 10
MOST CABLED AREAS IN THE UK

	Area	Homes connected		Area	Homes connected
1	Birmingham	118,046	6	Tyneside	42,558
2	Black Country	73,575	7	Thames East North	38,626
3	Avon	59,702	8	Greater London East	37,286
4	Portsmouth	48,795	9	Leeds	35,935
5	Edinburgh	43,064	10	Stockton-on-Tees	34,186

184 TOP VIDEO

THEN & NOW

TOP 10 COUNTRIES WITH THE MOST VIDEO RECORDERS

	1987			1997	
Country	VCRs			VCRs	Country
USA	52,565,000	**1**		86,825,000	USA
Japan	22,771,000	**2**		40,000,000	China
UK	11,830,000	**3**		34,309,000	Japan
Germany	11,531,000	**4**		26,328,000	Germany
France	6,935,000	**5**		18,848,000	UK
Canada	5,926,000	**6**		15,488,000	Brazil
Australia	3,787,000	**7**		15,483,000	France
Spain	3,619,000	**8**		13,161,000	Italy
Brazil	3,200,000	**9**		10,315,000	Russia
Italy	2,843,000	**10**		8,540,000	Mexico

Source: Screen Digest

- The terms "video recording" and "videotape" were first used in the early 1950s – but only among TV professionals.
- The first domestic video cassette recorders were sold in 1974, but the cost of both machines and tapes was prohibitively expensive.
- The VHS (Video Home System) was launched in 1976 in the US and 1978 in Europe.
- The abbreviation VCR (Video Cassette Recorder) was first used in the UK and US in 1971.
- By 1980, there were an estimated 7,687,000 homes with video recorders; by 1996, the global figure was put at 400,976,000 – more than a 50-fold increase.

SNAP FACT

TOP 10

VIDEO CONSUMERS IN EUROPE

	Country	Spending per video household ($)		
		Rental	**Purchase**	**Total**
1	Iceland	241.4	37.9	279.3
2	Ireland	116.3	36.8	153.1
3	Denmark	51.3	64.6	115.9
4	UK	40.7	66.6	107.3
5	Norway	65.1	41.9	107.0
6	France	14.0	82.3	96.3
7	Belgium	23.9	49.1	73.0
8	Sweden	40.0	31.3	71.2
9	Luxembourg	22.3	45.3	67.6
10	Switzerland	21.7	45.3	67.0
	EU average	*23.1*	*44.4*	*67.5*
	Western Europe average	*23.6*	*44.3*	*68.0*

Source: Screen Digest

TOP 10

BESTSELLING SPORTS/FITNESS VIDEOS OF 1997 IN THE UK

1	*Murray's Magic Moments*
2	*Jeremy Clarkson – Apocalypse Clarkson*
3	*Nick Hancock's Football Hell*
4	*Rapid Results with Beverly Callard*
5	*Rosemary Conley's New Body by Design*
6	*Living with Lions*
7	*Alistair McGowan's Football Backchat*
8	*Mr. Motivator – 10-minute Blt*
9	*Barbara Currie – Age-free Body*
10	*Manchester United – End of Season*

Source: CIN

TOP 10

BESTSELLING MUSIC VIDEOS OF 1997 IN THE UK

	Video	Artist(s)
1	*Spice – The Official Video, Volume 1*	The Spice Girls
2	*Lord of the Dance*	Michael Flatley
3	*Heathcliff*	Cliff Richard and cast
4	*Girl Power! – Live in Istanbul*	The Spice Girls
5	*Something Else*	Boyzone
6	*My Way*	Frank Sinatra
7	*The Gospel Show – Live from the Point*	Daniel O'Donnell
8	*History on Film – Volume II*	Michael Jackson
9	*Backstreet's Back ... Behind the Scenes*	Backstreet Boys
10	*Dream Cast – Les Miserables in Concert*	Live cast recording

Source: CIN

TOP 10
RENTED VIDEOS THAT SPENT LONGEST AT NO. 1

Title/year	Weeks at No. 1
1 Raiders of the Lost Ark (1983)	14
2 First Blood (1983)	11
3 Police Academy (1985)	13
4= An Officer and a Gentleman (1984)	9
= Tightrope (1985)*	9
= Se7en (1996)	9
7= Trading Places (1984–85)	8
= The Goonies (1986)	8
= Aliens (1987)	8
= Big Trouble in Little China (1987)	8

* Tightrope's tenure at the top was split into two runs of six weeks and three weeks

Long chart-topping residencies were easier to achieve in the less crowded and competitive video rental market of the early 1980s. Over a decade on, a movie that can hold no. 1 for a full month is special indeed, such is the urgency with which recent box office successes now transfer to the home viewing market.

Source: MRIB

TOP 10
MOST RENTED VIDEOS OF ALL TIME IN THE UK*

1	Four Weddings and a Funeral
2	Dirty Dancing
3	Basic Instinct
4	Crocodile Dundee
5	Sister Act
6	Home Alone
7	Forrest Gump
8	Ghost
9	Speed
10	Braveheart

* To 31 December 1997

Following its international box office success, the British comedy Four Weddings and a Funeral was a consistently huge UK renter on video at the tail-end of 1994 and through much of the following year. It wrests the all-time champion slot from the long-resident Dirty Dancing. Recent major renters Speed and Braveheart attain all-time Top 10 status for the first time.

Source: MRIB

TOP 10
MOST-PURCHASED VIDEO CATEGORIES IN THE UK

Category	Per cent of total sales
1 Feature films	40.5
2 Children's entertainment	26.5
3 TV shows	12.0
4 Music	8.5
5 Live comedy	6.5
6 Sport (excluding football)	1.8
7 Fitness	1.5
8= Football	1.2
= Miscellaneous	1.2
10 Reality video	0.3

Based on an analysis of 1995's UK high street video sales, it is clear that the biggest proportion of people who buy tapes do so in order to own copies of feature films and, to a lesser extent, favourite TV programmes.

TOP 10
MOST RENTED FILMS ON VIDEO IN THE UK, 1997

1	Independence Day
2	Star Wars – Trilogy
3	101 Dalmatians
4	Matilda
5	Evita
6	Batman and Robin
7	The English Patient
8	Trainspotting
9	Stargate
10	Jumanji

Source: CIN

TOP 10
MOST RENTED VIDEOS OF 1997 IN THE UK

Video	Approx. rentals
1 The Rock	3,002,058
2 Ransom	2,833,891
3 Independence Day	2,723,080
4 Twister	2,711,001
5 Mission: Impossible	2,704,272
6 The Nutty Professor	2,576,725
7 Jerry Maguire	2,074,554
8 Eraser	1,986,320
9 Phenomenon	1,968,791
10 Sleepers	1,773,426

Source: MRIB

TOP 10
BESTSELLING CHILDREN'S VIDEOS OF 1997 IN THE UK

1	The Hunchback of Notre Dame
2	Oliver and Company
3	Teletubbies – Here Come the Teletubbies
4	Teletubbies – Dance with the Teletubbies
5	Space Jam
6	Cinderella
7	The Many Adventures of Winnie the Pooh
8	The Black Cauldron
9	Beauty and the Beast Enchanted Christmas
10	Toy Story

Source: CIN

THE COMMERCIAL WORLD

TOP 10

EMPLOYERS IN THE UK

	Employer	Employees
1	Unilever plc	308,000
2	HM Forces	221,000
3	Police Service	207,000
4	The Post Office	180,910
5	BAT Industries plc	173,475
6	J. Sainsbury plc	154,661
7	British Telecommunications plc	148,900
8	Tesco plc	135,037
9	BTR plc	125,065
10	HSBC Holdings plc	109,093

TOP 10

OCCUPATIONS IN THE UK 100 YEARS AGO*

	Job sector	Employees
1	Agriculture	2,262,454
2	Domestic service	2,199,517
3	Conveyance (road, rail, canal, etc)	1,497,629
4	Textile manufacturing	1,462,001
5	Clothing makers and dealers	1,395,795
6	Metals, machines, and implements	1,175,715
7	Mines and quarries	943,880
8	Food	865,777
9	General labourers	583,365
10	Commercial clerks	439,972

* *At the turn of the century, there were 18,261,146 employees in the UK labour force.*

The 1900 US Census provides a snapshot of the bygone occupations of a century ago, enumerating professions that today have relatively few members, among them:

596,000 carpenters
280,000 laundresses
220,000 blacksmiths
134,000 tailors
102,000 shoemakers
42,000 porters
37,000 stonecutters
25,000 millers
8,000 bootblacks.

SNAP FACT

TOP 10

CATEGORIES OF CONSUMER SPENDING IN THE UK

	Category	Av. weekly household (£)	Expenditure as % of total
1	Food	55.15	17.8
2	Housing	49.10	15.9
3	Motoring expenditure	41.20	13.3
4	Leisure services	33.95	11.0
5	Household goods	26.74	8.7
6	Clothing and footwear	18.27	5.9
7	Household services	16.36	5.3
8	Leisure goods	15.17	4.9
9	Fuel and power	13.35	4.3
10	Alcoholic drink	12.41	4.0

Average weekly household expenditure on all commodities and services in UK in 1996/97 was £309.07, with the largest category of expenditure being on food.

TOP 10

DUTY-FREE SHOPS IN THE WORLD

1	London Heathrow Airport (UK)
2	Honolulu Airport (Hawaii, USA)
3	Silja Ferries (Finland)
4	Hong Kong Airport (China)
5	Singapore Changi Airport (Singapore)
6	Amsterdam Schiphol Airport (Netherlands)
7	Paris Charles De Gaulle Airport (France)
8	Viking Line Ferries (Finland)
9	Frankfurt Airport (Germany)
10	Manila Airport (Philippines)

In 1996, total global duty- and tax-free sales were worth $21,000,000. Sales of several of those outlets featured in the Top 10 are confidential, but industry insiders have ranked them and place them in the range of more than $250,000,000 at the bottom of the list to over $500,000,000 at the top.

TOP 10

OCCUPATIONS IN THE UK

	Job sector	Employees
1	Manufacturing	4,106,000
2	Wholesale and retail (including motor)	3,930,000
3	Real estate, renting, and business activities	2,929,000
4	Health and social work	2,566,000
5	Education	1,852,000
6	Public administration and defence	1,362,000
7	Transport, storage, and communication	1,328,000
8	Hotels and restaurants	1,307,000
9	Financial intermediation	1,031,000
10	Other community, social, and personal service activities	992,000

There were 28,700,000 people in the labour force in the UK in spring 1997, compared to a peak of 28,900,000 in spring 1990. Over the last 20 years there has been a shift among employees away from manufacturing towards the service sector.

PORT TO PORT
Although service industries have become increasingly significant in recent years, the import and export of goods remains the driving force of international trade.

TOP 10

COUNTRIES WITH THE MOST WORKERS

	Country	Labour force
1	China	709,000,000
2	India	398,000,000
3	USA	133,000,000
4	Indonesia	89,000,000
5	Russia	77,000,000
6	Japan	66,000,000
7	Brazil	71,000,000
8	Bangladesh	60,000,000
9	Pakistan	46,000,000
10	Nigeria	44,000,000
	UK	*29,000,000*

As defined by the International Labour Organization, the "labour force" includes people between the ages of 15 and 64.

Source: World Bank

TOP 10

SUPERMARKET GROUPS* IN THE UK

	Group	Sales (£) #
1	Tesco	13,034,000,000
2	J. Sainsbury†	10,852,000,000
3	Asda	6,883,000,000
4	Safeway★	6,590,000,000
5	Somerfields◆	3,201,000,000
6	Somerfield/Gateway◆	3,011,000,000
7	William Morrison	2,176,000,000
8	Waitrose (John Lewis Partnership)	1,461,000,000
9	Iceland	1,427,000,000
10	Aldi	632,000,000

* *Excluding Co-ops and "mixed goods" retailers, such as Marks and Spencer*

Excluding VAT

† *Excluding Savacentre*

★ *Including Presto*

◆ *Merged in 1998*

Based on The Retail Rankings (1998) published by Corporate Intelligence on Retailing

PATENTS & INVENTIONS

TOP 10

COUNTRIES THAT REGISTER THE MOST TRADEMARKS

	Country	Trademarks registered (1995)
1	Japan	144,911
2	China	91,866
3	USA	85,557
4	Spain	69,642
5	France	60,712
6	Argentina	37,743
7	UK	33,400
8	Mexico	29,954
9	South Korea	29,807
10	Brazil	25,330

This list includes all trademarks (product names that are thereby legally protected) and service marks (which apply to company and other names applied to services rather than products) that were actually registered in 1995. More applications are filed than granted, as many are rejected, for example for being too similar to one that already exists.

Source: World Intellectual Property Organization

POLAROID CAMERA INVENTED BY EDWIN H. LAND

TOP 10

MOST PROLIFIC PATENTEES IN THE US

	Patentee	No. of patents*
1	Thomas A. Edison	1,093
2	Francis H. Richards	619
3	Edwin Herbert Land	533
4=	Marvin Camras	500
=	Jerome H. Lemelson	500
6	Elihu Thomson	444
7	Charles E. Scribner	374
8	Philo Taylor Farnsworth	300
9	Lee de Forest	300
10	Luther Childs Crowell	293

* *Minimum number credited to each inventor*

THE 10

FIRST TRADEMARKS ISSUED IN THE US

	Issued to	Invention or discovery
1	Averill Chemical-Paint Company	Liquid paint
2	J. B. Baldy and Co	Mustard
3	Ellis Branson	Retail coal
4	Tracy Coit	Fish
5	William Lanfair Ellis and Co	Oyster packing
6	Evans, Clow, Dalzell and Co	Wrought-iron pipe
7	W. E. Garrett and Sons	Snuff
8	William G. Hamilton	Car wheel
9	John K. Hogg	Soap
10	Abraham P. Olzendam	Woollen hose

All of these trademarks were registered on the same day, 25 October 1870, and are distinguished in the ranking only by the trademark numbers assigned to them.

THE 10

FIRST PATENTS IN THE UK

	Patentee	Patent	Date
1	Nicholas Hillyard	Engraving and printing the king's head on documents	5 May 1617
2	John Gason	Locks, mills, and other river and canal improvements	1 July 1617
3	John Miller and John Jasper Wolfen	Oil for suits of armour	3 November 1617
4	Robert Crumpe	Tunnels and pumps	9 January 1618
5	Aaron Rathburne and Roger Burges	Making maps of English cities	11 March 1618
6	John Gilbert	River dredger	16 July 1618
7	Clement Dawbeney	Water-powered engine for making nails	11 December 1618
8	Thomas Murray	Sword blades	11 January 1619
9	Thomas Wildgoose and David Ramsey	Ploughs, pumps, and ship engines	17 January 1619
10	Abram Baker	Smalt (glass) manufacture	16 February 1619

TOP 10

CATEGORIES OF PATENTS IN THE UK

	Category	Number*
1	Machine elements	744
2	Measuring and testing	506
3	Telecommunications	504
4	Civil engineering and building	472
5	Conveyancing, packing, load handling, hoisting, and storing	420
6	Electric circuit elements and magnets	386
7	Metal working	336
8	Transport	329
9	Calculating, counting, checking, signalling, and data-handling	326
10	Furniture and household articles	318

* *Based on number of patents granted in a year*

TOP 10

COUNTRIES THAT REGISTER THE MOST PATENTS

	Country	Patents registered (1995)
1	Japan	101,676
2	USA	101,419
3	Germany	56,633
4	France	55,681
5	UK	48,350
6	Italy	29,896
7	Russia	25,633
8	Netherlands	23,444
9	Sweden	20,816
10	Switzerland	20,345

EDISON LIGHT BULB
Thomas Alva Edison (1847–1931) is the most prolific inventor of all time. His filament light bulb dates from 1879.

THE 10

FIRST PATENTS IN THE US

	Patentee	Patent	Date
1	Samuel Hopkins	Making pot and pearl ash	31 July 1790
2	Joseph S. Sampson	Candle making	6 August 1790
3	Oliver Evans	Flour and meal making	18 December 1790
4=	Francis Bailey	Punches for type	29 January 1791
=	Aaron Putnam	Improvement in distilling	29 January 1791
6	John Stone	Driving piles	10 March 1791
7=	Samuel Mullikin	Threshing machine	11 March 1791
=	Samuel Mullikin	Breaking hemp	11 March 1791
=	Samuel Mullikin	Polishing marble	11 March 1791
=	Samuel Mullikin	Raising nap on cloth	11 March 1791

THE 10

FIRST WOMEN PATENTEES IN THE US

	Patentee	Patent	Date
1	Mary Kies	Straw weaving with silk or thread	5 May 1809
2	Mary Brush	Corset	21 July 1815
3	Sophia Usher	Carbonated liquid	11 September 1819
4	Julia Planton	Foot stove	4 November 1822
5	Lucy Burnap	Weaving grass hats	16 February 1823
6	Diana H. Tuttle	Accelerating spinning-wheel heads	17 May 1824
7	Catharine Elliot	Manufacturing moccasins	26 January 1825
8	Phoebe Collier	Sawing wheel-fellies (rims)	20 May 1826
9	Elizabeth H. Buckley	Sheet-iron shovel	28 February 1828
10	Henrietta Cooper	Whitening leghorn straw	12 November 1828

PAPER CLIP PIONEER

Norwegian inventor Johan Vaaler devised the paper clip in 1899. Because Norway had no patent law in force at the time, he had to patent it in Germany in 1900, and his US Patent was granted in 1901. There are, in fact, earlier claimants (such as that of Matthew Schooley, who applied for a paper clip patent in the US in 1896, and the "gem" clip, which is similar to the type still in use, was being sold in 1899), but Vaaler is widely considered the originator of the paper clip as we know it. To commemorate his achievement a giant paper clip measuring 7 m/23 ft and weighing 602 kg/1,328 lb was unveiled near Oslo in 1989.

100 YEARS AGO • YEARS AGO • YEARS AGO • YEARS AGO

COMMUNICATION MATTERS

TOP 10

BESTSELLING BRITISH COMMEMORATIVE STAMPS

	Issue	Date
1	Nature conservation	May 1986
2	British butterflies	May 1981
3	RSPCA	Jan 1990
4	Flowers	Mar 1979
5	Shire horses	Jul 1978
6	Birds	Jan 1980
7	Dogs	Feb 1979
8	Birds/RSPB Centenary	Jan 1989
9	Queen Mother's 80th birthday	Aug 1980
10	Wedding of Prince Charles and Lady Diana Spencer	Jul 1981

THE 10

FIRST COUNTRIES AND CITIES TO ISSUE POSTAGE STAMPS

	Country	Stamps issued			Country	Stamps issued
1	Great Britain	1840		6	Basle, Switzerland	1845
2	New York City, USA	1842		7	USA	1847
3	Zurich, Switzerland	1843		8	Mauritius	1847
4	Brazil	1843		9	Bermuda	1848
5	Geneva, Switzerland	1843		10	France	1849

TOP 10

COUNTRIES WITH THE MOST POST OFFICES

	Country	Post offices*
1	India	280,181
2	China	113,622
3	Russia	44,669
4	USA	38,212
5	Turkey	24,860
6	Japan	24,625
7	UK	19,128
8	France	17,069
9	Ukraine	16,421
10	Germany	16,172

1996 or latest year available

TOP 10 COUNTRIES WITH THE HIGHEST RATIO OF CELLULAR MOBILE PHONE USERS
(Subscribers per 1,000)
❶ Norway (296.1) ❷ Finland (292.4)
❸ Sweden (281.4) ❹ Denmark (248.6)
❺ Australia (245.5) ❻ USA (161.9)
❼ Singapore (147.5) ❽ Japan (143.2)
❾ New Zealand (131.3)
❿ UK (122.5)
World (23.4)
Source: Siemens AG

TOP 10

COUNTRIES WITH THE MOST TELEPHONES PER PERSON

	Country	Telephones per 100 inhabitants
1	Sweden	68.41
2	Switzerland	64.40
3	USA	63.66
4	Denmark	62.03
5	Luxembourg	57.56
6	Norway	56.49
7	Iceland	56.46
8	France	55.91
9	Germany	55.76
10	Finland	55.75
	UK	52.11

Source: Siemens AG

TOP 10

COUNTRIES SENDING THE MOST LETTERS PER PERSON

	Country	Average*
1	Vatican	9,545
2	USA	689
3	Liechtenstein	573
4	Norway	525
5	Sweden	503
6	Netherlands	420
7	France	416
8	Finland	379
9	Canada	360
10	Denmark	335
	UK	312

* Number of letters posted per person in 1996, or latest year available

The remarkable anomaly of the Vatican, it must be surmised, is a statistical oddity resulting from the large numbers of official missives dispatched from the Holy See, and does not represent personal letter writing on a massive scale by its small resident population – an average of 26 letters a day per inhabitant, all passing through the Holy See's 31 postboxes.

TOP 10

COUNTRIES SENDING AND RECEIVING THE MOST LETTERS (INTERNATIONAL)

	Country	Items of mail handled per annum*
1	USA	1,658,350,000
2	UK	1,343,230,603
3	Germany	1,060,000,000
4	France	847,932,677
5	Saudi Arabia	626,146,000
6	Belgium	446,502,826
7	Nigeria	444,874,000
8	Japan	413,745,000
9	Australia	412,205,582
10	Italy	347,299,000

1996 or latest year available

Source: Universal Postal Union

COLLECTING THE MAIL
Domestic and international postal services have been developed during the past 150 years. Despite the recent burgeoning of alternative electronic methods, traditional or "snail mail" remains an important means of communication.

TOP 10

COUNTRIES SENDING AND RECEIVING THE MOST LETTERS (DOMESTIC)

	Country	Items of mail handled per annum*
1	USA	182,660,700,000
2	Japan	24,971,279,000
3	France	23,913,644,000
4	UK	17,296,000,000
5	Germany	16,638,000,000
6	India	13,462,073,000
7	Canada	10,714,615,000
8	China	7,722,465,000
9	Italy	6,236,985,000
10	Russia	6,079,300,000

1996 or latest year available

Source: Universal Postal Union

TOP 10

COUNTRIES WITH THE MOST INTERNET USERS

	Country	Percentage of population	Internet users*			Country	Percentage of population	Internet users*
1	USA	23	62,000,000		6	Sweden	22	1,900,000
2	Japan	7	8,840,000		7	India	0.16	1,500,000
3	Canada	27	8,000,000		8	Norway	32	1,400,000
4	UK	10	6,000,000		9	Taiwan	6	1,260,000
5	Germany	7	5,800,000		10	Australia	7	1,210,000
						World total	1.9	112,750,000

Estimates from various surveys, March 1998

TOP 10

OLDEST PILLAR BOXES IN DAILY USE IN THE UK

	Location	Year
1=	Union Street, St. Peter Port, Guernsey	1853
=	Barnes Cross, Bishops Caundle, Dorset	1853
3=	Mount Pleasant/College Road, Framlingham, Suffolk	1856
=	Double Street, Framlingham, Suffolk	1856
=	Market Place, Banbury, Oxfordshire	1856
=	Mudeford Green, Christchurch, Dorset	1856
=	Cornwallis/Victoria Road, Milford-on-Sea, Hampshire	1856
=	Eastgate, Warwick	1856
=	Westgate, Warwick	1856
=	High Street, Eton, Berkshire	1856

The introduction of the Penny Post in 1840 soon led to a demand from the public for roadside posting boxes, which already existed in Belgium and France.

THE BIRTH OF RADIO TELEGRAPHY

Guglielmo Marconi (1874–1937) began his studies of radio transmission in his native Italy in the early 1890s, but soon moved his operations to England where he established the Wireless Telegraph Company. There, on 27 March 1899, he succeeded in transmitting the first-ever international radio signals, from a wireless station at South Foreland, Kent, to one at Wimereux, near Boulogne, France, about 51 km/32 miles away. By 1901 Marconi had developed his system to such an extent that on 12 December he was able to transmit the first-ever transatlantic radio signal (the letter "S" in Morse code) from Poldhu, Cornwall, to St. Johns, Newfoundland, Canada.

100 YEARS AGO • YEARS AGO • YEARS AGO

FUEL & POWER

TOP 10

ENERGY CONSUMERS IN THE WORLD

	Country	Oil	Gas	Coal	Nuclear	HEP	Total
				Energy consumption 1996*			
1	USA	833.0	569.2	516.0	183.3	28.8	2,130.3
2	China	172.5	15.9	666.0	3.7	15.9	874.0
3	Russia	128.0	317.0	119.0	28.1	13.2	605.3
4	Japan	269.9	59.5	88.3	76.8	7.4	501.9
5	Germany	137.4	75.2	88.9	41.7	1.8	345.0
6	India	78.7	19.5	140.3	2.1	6.0	246.6
7	France	91.0	29.0	14.7	102.8	6.0	243.5
8	UK	83.7	76.7	44.9	24.5	0.3	230.1
9	Canada	79.5	66.4	23.1	23.9	30.3	223.2
10	South Korea	101.4	12.2	31.6	19.1	0.4	164.7
	World total	3,312.8	1,971.6	2,257.0	621.3	218.1	8,380.8

* Millions of tonnes of oil equivalent

Source: BP Statistical Review of World Energy 1997

TOP 10

OIL CONSUMERS IN THE WORLD

	Country	Consumption 1996 (tonnes)		Country	Consumption 1996 (tonnes)
1	USA	833,000,000	6	South Korea	101,400,000
2	Japan	269,900,000	7	Italy	94,100,000
3	China	172,500,000	8	France	91,000,000
4	Germany	137,400,000	9	UK	83,700,000
5	Russia	128,000,000	10	Canada	79,500,000

Source: BP Statistical Review of World Energy 1997

ATOMIC WORDS

While we may think of nuclear energy as a modern concept, it is a century since the words "neutron" and "radium" first appeared in print. Neutron (derived from the word neutral) was first suggested as a name in a scientific paper, although applied to a different concept, since the existence of the particle that is now called a neutron was not discovered until 33 years later. Radium (from radius, a ray), was described and named in *Chemical News* of 6 January 1899, after the researches of the previous year by Pierre and Marie Curie first implied the existence of the element. They shared the Nobel Physics Prize in 1903 and in 1911 Marie Curie was awarded the Chemistry Prize for her discoveries of radium and polonium.

TOP 10

HYDROELECTRIC ENERGY CONSUMERS IN THE WORLD

	Country	Consumption 1996 (tonnes of oil equivalent)
1	Canada	30,300,000
2	USA	28,800,000
3	Brazil	22,700,000
4	China	15,900,000
5	Russia	13,200,000
6	Norway	8,900,000
7	Japan	7,400,000
8=	France	6,000,000
=	India	6,000,000
10	Venezuela	4,600,000
	World total	218,100,000

Tonnes of oil equivalent is the amount of oil that would be required to produce the same amount of energy. 1,000,000 tonnes of oil is equivalent to approximately 12,000,000,000 kilowatt hours of electricity.

Source: BP Statistical Review of World Energy 1997

TOP 10

NATURAL GAS CONSUMERS IN THE WORLD

	Country	Consumption 1996 billion m³	billion ft³
1	USA	632.4	22,333.0
2	Russia	352.2	12,437.8
3	UK	85.2	3,008.8
4	Germany	83.6	2,952.3
5	Ukraine	78.2	2,761.6
6	Canada	73.7	2,602.7
7	Japan	66.1	2,334.3
8	Italy	52.1	1,839.9
9	Uzbekistan	44.4	1,568.0
10	Netherlands	41.7	1,472.6
	World total	2,190.6	77,360.2

Source: BP Statistical Review of World Energy 1997

NORTH SEA OIL
A high proportion of the oil consumed by Norway and the UK has been extracted by North Sea production platforms since 1972.

TOP 10
ELECTRICITY PRODUCERS IN THE WORLD

	Country	Production kW/hr
1	USA	3,145,892,000,000
2	Russia	956,587,000,000
3	Japan	906,705,000,000
4	China	839,453,000,000
5	Canada	527,316,000,000
6	Germany	525,721,000,000
7	France	471,448,000,000
8	India	356,519,000,000
9	UK	323,029,000,000
10	Brazil	251,484,000,000

The Top 10 electricity-consuming countries are virtually synonymous with these producers, since relatively little electricity is transmitted across national boundaries. Electricity production has burgeoned phenomenally in the post-war era.

TOP 10
COUNTRIES WITH THE LARGEST CRUDE OIL RESERVES

	Country	Reserves (tonnes)		Country	Reserves (tonnes)
1	Saudi Arabia	35,800,000,000	6	Venezuela	9,300,000,000
2	Iraq	15,100,000,000	7	Mexico	7,000,000,000
3	Kuwait	13,300,000,000	8	Russia	6,700,000,000
4	United Arab Emirates	12,600,000,000	9	Libya	3,900,000,000
5	Iran	12,700,000,000	10	USA	3,700,000,000
	UK	*600,000,000*		*World total*	*140,900,000,000*

Source: BP Statistical Review of World Energy 1997

TOP 10
COUNTRIES PRODUCING THE MOST ELECTRICITY FROM NUCLEAR SOURCES

	Country	Nuclear power stations in operation	Nuclear per cent of total	Output (megawatt-hours)
1	USA	110	21.9	100,685
2	France	57	77.4	59,948
3	Japan	53	34.0	42,369
4	Germany	20	30.3	22,282
5	Russia	29	13.1	19,843
6	Canada	21	16.0	14,902
7	Ukraine	16	43.8	13,765
8	UK	35	26.0	12,928
9	Sweden	12	52.4	10,040
10	South Korea	11	35.8	9,120
	World total	*442*	—	*350,964*

Source: International Atomic Energy Agency

TOP 10
COAL CONSUMERS IN THE WORLD

	Country	Consumption 1997 (tonnes of oil equivalent)
1	China	666,000,000
2	USA	516,000,000
3	India	140,300,000
4	Russia	119,000,000
5	Germany	88,900,000
6	Japan	88,300,000
7	South Africa	81,700,000
8	Poland	72,000,000
9	UK	44,900,000
10	Australia	42,900,000

Source: BP Statistical Review of World Energy 1997

SAVE THE PLANET

SAVE THE CAN
The recycling of aluminium and steel cans has become increasingly common: in the US alone, more than 170 million drinks cans and 13 million steel cans are recovered every day.

THEN & NOW

TOP 10 MOST COMMON TYPES OF LITTER IN THE UK

Litter	1989		1996	Litter
Cigarette ends		**1**		Chewing gum
Sweet wrappers		**2**		Cigarette ends
Matches		**3**		Matches
Bits of paper		**4**		Bits of paper
Tickets and stickers		**5**		Sweet wrappers
Other litter (all materials)		**6**		Glass fragments
Ring pulls		**7**		Plastic fragments
Cigarette wrapping		**8**		Tin foil
Other paper items		**9**		Chewing gum wrappers
Plastic fragments		**10**		Tickets

A survey carried out by the Tidy Britain Group, which counted the number of items in each category in typical samplings of litter deposited in Britain's streets, parks, and other public areas in 1989, was repeated in 1993 and 1996. The ten most common types of litter made up 98 per cent of all the litter found, and cigarette butts were found at over 90 per cent of the sites examined. There were far fewer sweet wrappers found in 1996 than in previous years, but one significant new type of litter was lottery tickets.

TOP 10

COMPONENTS OF HOUSEHOLD WASTE IN THE UK*

	Material	Percentage by weight
1	Food waste	19.8
2	Garden waste	11.2
3	Newspaper	9.7
4	DIY waste (eg bricks, rubble)	7.1
5	Loose paper	7.0
6	Glass bottles	5.4
7	Card packaging	5.3
8	Magazines	5.0
9	Plastic bags and other film	4.4
10	Nappies	4.3

* *Based on a West Midlands survey of wheeled bins, Autumn 1997*

These figures are based on a survey carried out as part of a "Slim Your Bin" campaign by the UK charity Going for Green. Their aim is to show people how to cut down on the amount of rubbish they throw away, encouraging them to plan their food purchases, compost their garden waste, and recycle waste paper, bottles, cans, clothes, and plastic waste.

TOP 10

ENVIRONMENTAL CONCERNS IN THE UK

	Issue	Percentage of people concerned
1=	Air pollution	49
=	Exhaust fumes from cars/lorries	49
3	Too much traffic	48
4	Pollution of rivers/streams/water	46
5	Pollution of seas/waste disposal at sea	44
6	Litter in streets/countryside	42
7	Pollution of beaches/coastline	41
8=	Nuclear waste	39
=	Toxic/chemical waste/toxic dumping	39
10	Destruction of rainforests/deforestation	36

MORI, the market research organization, carried out a survey of 1,874 adults in 1997, asking them which environment and conservation issues concerned them most. Pollution is clearly the Number 1 concern, including air pollution, rivers, sea, beaches, industrial pollution, and especially pollution caused by traffic. When considering the environment, most people think about issues close to home, whereas global issues, such as deforestation, global warming, and destruction of the ozone layer come much further down the list.

Source: MORI

HOUSEHOLD WASTE
*Increasingly, packaging is
being designed to be
fully recyclable.*

T O P 1 0

CARBON DIOXIDE EMITTERS
IN THE WORLD

	Country	CO_2 emissions (tonnes per head p.a.)
1	United Arab Emirates	30.78
2	USA	19.42
3	Singapore	19.05
4	Norway	16.85
5	Australia	16.12
6	Canada	14.66
7	Saudi Arabia	13.92
8=	Kazakhstan	13.19
=	Trinidad and Tobago	13.19
10	Russia	12.09

CO_2 emissions derive from three principal sources – fossil fuel burning, cement manufacturing, and gas flaring. Since World War II, increasing industrialization in many countries has resulted in huge increases in carbon output, a trend that most countries are now actively attempting to reverse. The US remains the worst offender in total, with 5,156,190 tonnes of CO_2 released in 1995.

Source: Carbon Dioxide Information Analysis Center

T O P 1 0

SULPHUR DIOXIDE EMITTERS
IN THE WORLD

	Country	Annual SO_2 emissions per head		
		kg	lb	oz
1	Czech Republic	149.4	329	6
2	Former Yugoslavia	138.2	304	11
3	Bulgaria	116.8	257	8
4	Canada	104.0	229	4
5	Hungary	81.4	179	7
6=	Romania	79.2	174	10
=	USA	79.2	174	10
8	Poland	71.1	156	12
9	Slovakia	70.0	154	5
10	Belarus	57.5	126	12

Source: World Resources Institute

T O P 1 0

DEFORESTING COUNTRIES
IN THE WORLD

	Country	Average annual forest loss 1990–95 (sq km)
1	Brazil	25,540
2	Indonesia	10,840
3	Dem. Rep. of Congo	7,400
4	Bolivia	5,810
5	Mexico	5,080
6	Venezuela	5,030
7	Malaysia	4,000
8	Myanmar (Burma)	3,870
9	Sudan	3,530
10	Thailand	3,290

While Brazil tops the list of countries with the highest amount of forest loss, the actual rate of deforestation is only 0.5 per cent per annum. Other countries are losing a much higher proportion of their total forest cover as the following list shows:

	Country	Annual rate of forest loss (per cent)
1	Lebanon	7.8
2	Jamaica	7.2
3	Afghanistan	6.8
4	Comoros	5.6
5	Philippines	3.5
6	Haiti	3.4
7	El Salvador	3.3
8=	Costa Rica	3.0
=	Sierra Leone	3.0
10	Pakistan	2.9

Source: Food and Agriculture Organization of the United Nations

THE BIRTH OF THE "BIOSPHERE"

In an issue of the journal *International Geography* published in 1899, Scottish geographer and meteorologist Hugh Robert Mill (1861–1950) introduced the word "biosphere". He divided the globe into four parts, the lithosphere (earth), hydrosphere (oceans), atmosphere, and biosphere, and defined the latter as the portion that is occupied by living things – a narrow band of earth, sea, and sky in which life is possible. This concept has been developed by environmentalists, and the name was then applied to the Biosphere, a structure erected in the United States in Arizona to conduct experiments in global warming and other environmental changes that threaten life on Earth.

YEARS AGO • YEARS AGO • YEARS AGO • YEARS AGO
100

THE WORLD'S RICHEST

THEN & NOW

TOP 10 HIGHEST-EARNING ACTORS IN THE WORLD

1987

	Actor	Income ($)
1=	William H. Cosby Jr.	57,000,000
=	Eddie Murphy	27,000,000
3	Sylvester Stallone	21,000,000
4	Arnold Schwarzenegger	18,000,000
5=	Tom Selleck	11,000,000
=	Jack Nicholson	11,000,000
7=	Paul Hogan	10,000,000
=	Steve Martin	10,000,000
9	Michael J. Fox	9,000,000

1997

	Actor	Income ($)
1=	Harrison Ford	47,000,000
=	Tim Allen	47,000,000
3	Mel Gibson	42,000,000
4	John Travolta	39,000,000
5	Roseanne	34,000,000
6	Eddie Murphy	24,000,000
7	Robin Williams	23,000,000
8	Arnold Schwarzenegger	22,000,000
9	Michael Douglas	21,000,000

Based on *Forbes* magazine's survey of top entertainers' income, in 1987 William H. Cosby was No. 1 in the list of all entertainers (including pop stars, professional sportsmen and others). The comparative survey for 1997 calculated Cosby's income as $18,000,000. Meanwhile, during the past decade, actors with the audience magnetism of Arnold Schwarzenegger and Harrison Ford have been able to command $20,000,000 or more per movie, while percentage earnings can add further sums, although their actual estimated income fluctuates according to whether they have appeared in a recent successful film.

Source: Forbes magazine

TOP 10

RICHEST RULERS IN THE WORLD*

	Ruler	Country/ in power since	Estimated wealth ($)
1	Sultan Hassanal Bolkiah	Brunei, 1967	38,000,000,000
2	King Fahd Bin Abdulaziz Alsaud	Saudi Arabia, 1982	20,000,000,000
3	President Suharto	Indonesia, 1967	16,000,000,000
4	Sheikh Jaber Al-Ahmed Al-Jaber Al-Sabah	Kuwait, 1977	15,000,000,000
5	Sheikh Zayed Bin Sultan Al Nahyan	United Arab Emirates, 1966	10,000,000,000
6	President Saddam Hussein	Iraq, 1979	5,000,000,000
7	Queen Beatrix#	Netherlands, 1980	4,700,000,000
8	Prime Minister Rafik al-Hariri	Lebanon, 1992	3,000,000,000
9	King Bhumibol Adulyadej	Thailand, 1946	1,800,000,000
10	President Fidel Castro	Cuba, 1959	1,400,000,000

* *As of 28 July 1997*

Jointly with her mother, Princess Juliana

According to analysts at *Forbes* magazine, Queen Elizabeth II's personal fortune is $350,000,000. She also has further property, art treasures, and jewellery worth a total of $16,000,000,000, but is considered their custodian, holding them in trust for the nation.

Source: Forbes magazine

TOP 10

HIGHEST-EARNING SINGERS IN THE WORLD

	Singer(s)	1996–97 income ($)
1	Beatles	98,000,000
2	Rolling Stones	68,000,000
3	Celine Dion	65,000,000
4	David Bowie	63,000,000
5	Sting	57,000,000
6=	Garth Brooks	55,000,000
=	Michael Jackson	55,000,000
8	Kiss	48,000,000
9=	Gloria Estefan	47,000,000
=	Spice Girls	47,000,000

Even though the Beatles no longer exist as a group, they continue to earn huge revenue from their recordings. The Rolling Stones typify the huge income generated by major rock tours: their Voodoo Lounge tour made $300,000,000, while Microsoft paid $4,000,000 to use their song Start Me Up to promote Windows95. The Spice Girls are newcomers to this highly volatile list.

Source: Forbes magazine

TOP 10

CITIES WITH MOST *FORBES* 400 MEMBERS

	City	Members
1	New York, New York	38
2	San Francisco, California	27
3	Los Angeles, California	12
4=	Boston, Massachusetts	9
=	Fort Worth, Texas	9
6=	Beverly Hills, California	8
=	Chicago, Illinois	8
=	Dallas, Texas	8
9=	Atlanta, Georgia	5
=	Greenwich, Connecticut	5

TOP 10
COMPUTER FORTUNES IN THE US

	Name	Company	Wealth ($)
1	Bill Gates	Microsoft	38,660,000,000
2	Paul Allen	Microsoft	14,770,000,000
3	Steve Ballmer	Microsoft	8,210,000,000
4	Larry Ellison	Oracle	8,200,000,000
5	Gordon Moore	Intel	7,970,000,000
6	Michael Dell	Dell	4,660,000,000
7	William Hewlett	Hewlett-Packard	4,200,000,000
8	Ted Waitt	Gateway 2000	2,830,000,000
9	David Duffield	Peoplesoft	1,730,000,000
10	Charles B. Wang	Computer Associates	1,200,000,000

The 10 individuals in this Top 10 list, together with Robert Galvin of Motorola ($1,100,000,000), represent the élite group of American computer billionaires, although the industry has additionally produced innumerable multi-millionaires.

Source: Forbes *magazine*

TOP 10
CLOTHING FORTUNES IN THE US

	Name	Company	Wealth ($)
1	Philip Hampson Knight	Nike	5,400,000,000
2	Peter E. Haas Sr.	Levi Strauss	2,400,000,000
3	Ralph Lauren	Ralph Lauren	1,800,000,000
4	Leslie Herbert Wexner	The Limited	1,600,000,000
5	Richard N. Goldman	Levi Strauss	1,300,000,000
6	Jim Jannard	Oakley Sunglasses	1,000,000,000
7	Peter E. Haas Jr.	Levi Strauss	970,000,000
8	Sidney Kimmel	Jones Apparel	960,000,000
9 =	Frances Koshland Geballe	Levi Strauss	900,000,000
=	Evelyn Danzig Haas	Levi Strauss	900,000,000

Heirs of jeans pioneer Levi Strauss (1830–1902) comprise half this Top 10 list, with further more distant members of the family just outside along with major shareholders in contemporary fashion companies such as Reebok and The Gap.

Source: Forbes *magazine*

TOP 10
HIGHEST-EARNING ENTERTAINERS IN THE WORLD*

	Entertainer	Profession	1996–97 income ($)
1	Steven Spielberg	Film producer/director	313,000,000
2	George Lucas	Film producer/director	241,000,000
3	Oprah Winfrey	TV host/producer	201,000,000
4	Michael Crichton	Novelist/screenwriter	102,000,000
5	Jerry Seinfeld	TV performer	94,000,000
6	David Copperfield	Illusionist	85,000,000
7	Stephen King	Novelist/screenwriter	84,000,000
8	John Grisham	Novelist/screenwriter	66,000,000
9	Siegfried and Roy	Illusionists	58,000,000
10 =	Michael Flatley	Dancer	54,000,000
=	Ron Howard and Brian Grazer	Entertainers	54,000,000

* Other than actors and pop stars

Source: Forbes *magazine*

TOP 10
FOOD AND CANDY FORTUNES IN THE US

	Name	Company	Wealth ($)
1 =	Forrest Edward Mars Sr.	Mars	3,300,000,000
=	Forrest Edward Mars Jr.	Mars	3,300,000,000
=	John Franklyn Mars	Mars	3,300,000,000
=	Jacqueline Mars Vogel	Mars	3,300,000,000
5	Mary Alice Dorrance Malone	Campbell Soup	2,800,000,000
6 =	Bennett Dorrance	Campbell Soup	2,600,000,000
=	William Wrigley	Wrigley gum	2,600,000,000
8	Joan Beverly Kroc	McDonalds	2,100,000,000
9	Dorrance Hill Hamilton	Campbell Soup	1,800,000,000
10	Hope Hill Van Beuren	Campbell Soup	1,600,000,000

Source: Forbes *magazine*

SNAP FACTS

- The first reference to a millionaire in print appears in British author and Prime Minister Benjamin Disraeli's novel *Vivian Grey* (1826).

- $1,000,000 in $1 bills would weigh one tonne. Placed in a pile, it would be 110 m/360 ft high – as tall as 60 average adults standing on top of each other.

DIAMONDS & GOLD

TOP 10
GOLD-PRODUCING COUNTRIES

	Country	Production 1996 (tonnes)
1	South Africa	494.6
2	USA	329.3
3	Australia	288.8
4	Canada	163.9
5	China	144.6
6	Russia	130.0
7	Indonesia	921
8	Uzbekistan	71.0
9	Peru	64.8
10	Brazil	64.2

TOP 10
COUNTRIES MAKING GOLD JEWELLERY

	Country	Gold used in 1996 (tonnes)
1	Italy	439.0
2	India	427.8
3	China	184.0
4	Saudi Arabia and Yemen	159.3
5	USA	152.4
6	Turkey	140.7
7	Indonesia	132.0
8	Taiwan	91.0
9	Malaysia	79.5
10	Hong Kong	79.0

TOP 10
LARGEST UNCUT DIAMONDS

	Diamond	Carats
1	Cullinan	3,106.00

Measuring approximately 10 x 6.5 x 5 cm/ 4 x 2½ x 2 in, and weighing 621 gm/1 lb 6 oz, the Cullinan was unearthed in 1905. Bought by the Transvaal Government for £150,000, it was presented to King Edward VII. The King decided to have it cut, and the most important of the separate gems are now among the British Crown Jewels.

	Diamond	Carats
2	Braganza	1,680.00

All trace of this enormous stone has been lost.

	Diamond	Carats
3	Excelsior	995.20

Cut by the celebrated Amsterdam firm of Asscher in 1903, the Excelsior produced 21 superb stones, which were sold mainly through Tiffany's of New York.

	Diamond	Carats
4	Star of Sierra Leone	968.80

Found in Sierra Leone on St. Valentine's Day, 1972, the uncut diamond weighed 225 g/8 oz and measured 6.5 x 4 cm/2½ x 1½ in.

	Diamond	Carats
5	Zale Corporation "Golden Giant"	890.00

Its origin is so shrouded in mystery that it is not even known which country it came from.

	Diamond	Carats
6	Great Mogul	787.50

When found in 1650 in the Gani Mine, India, this diamond was presented to Shah Jehan, the builder of the Taj Mahal. After Nadir Shah conquered Delhi in 1739, it entered the Persian treasury and apparently vanished from history.

	Diamond	Carats
7	Woyie River	770.00

Found in 1945 beside the river in Sierra Leone, whose name it now bears, it was cut into 30 stones. The largest of these, known as Victory and weighing 31.35 carats, was auctioned at Christie's, New York, in 1984 for $880,000.

	Diamond	Carats
8	Presidente Vargas	726.60

Discovered in the Antonio River, Brazil, in 1938, it was named after the then President.

	Diamond	Carats
9	Jonker	726.00

In 1934 Jacobus Jonker found this massive diamond after it had been exposed by a heavy storm. Acquired by Harry Winston, it was exhibited in the American Museum of Natural History and attracted enormous crowds.

	Diamond	Carats
10	Reitz	650.80

Like the Excelsior, the Reitz was found in the Jagersfontein Mine in South Africa in 1895.

TOP 10
DIAMOND-PRODUCING COUNTRIES

	Country	Production per annum (carats)
1	Australia	41,000,000
2	Dem. Rep. of Congo	16,500,000
3	Botswana	14,700,000
4	Russia	11,500,000
5	South Africa	9,800,000
6	Brazil	2,000,000
7	Namibia	1,100,000
8 =	Angola	1,000,000
=	China	1,000,000
10	Ghana	700,000
	World total	*100,850,000*

TOP 10
LARGEST POLISHED GEM DIAMONDS

	Diamond/last known whereabouts or owner	Carats
1	Golden Jubilee (King of Thailand)	545.67
2	Great Star of Africa/Cullinan I (British Crown Jewels)	530.20
3	Incomparable/Zale (sold in New York, 1988)	407.48
4	Second Star of Africa/Cullinan II (British Crown Jewels)	317.40
5	Centenary (De Beers)	273.85
6	Jubilee (Paul-Louis Weiller)	245.35
7	De Beers (sold in Geneva, 1982)	234.50
8	Red Cross (sold in Geneva, 1973)	205.07
9	Black Star of Africa (unknown)	202.00
10	Anon (unknown)	200.00

WORKING IN A GOLD MINE
South African gold mines have long been the world's No. 1 source of gold, producing almost a quarter of the world's total annual output of almost 2,300 tonnes.

T O P 1 0

COUNTRIES HOLDING GOLD RESERVES

	Country	Gold reserves, 1998 (Troy ounces)	(tonnes)
1	USA	261,710,000	8,140
2	Germany	95,180,000	2,960
3	Switzerland	83,280,000	2,590
4	France	81,890,000	2,547
5	Italy	66,670,000	2,073
6	Netherlands	27,070,000	841
7	Japan	24,230,000	753
8	UK	18,420,000	572
9	Portugal	16,070,000	499
10	Spain	15,630,000	486

Gold and precious stones have been measured in Troy, or Fine, ounces since medieval times. A Troy ounce is equivalent to 31.103 gm, and a tonne of gold is 32,151 ounces. Gold has a density of 19.3 gm per cm^3, so another way of looking at, say, the USA's gold reserves is to consider that it would occupy the volume of a cube with sides 7.5 m/25 ft long.

Source: International Monetary Fund

T O P 1 0

MOST EXPENSIVE SINGLE DIAMONDS SOLD AT AUCTION

	Diamond	Sale	Price ($)
1	Pear-shaped 100.10-carat "D" Flawless	Sotheby's, Geneva, 17 May 1995	16,548,750 (SF19,958,500)
2	The Mouawad Splendor, pear-shaped 11-sided 101.84-carat diamond	Sotheby's, Geneva, 14 November 1990	12,760,000 (SF15,950,000)
3	Rectangular-cut 100.36-carat diamond	Sotheby's, Geneva, 17 November 1993	11,882,333 (SF17,823,500)
4	Fancy blue emerald-cut diamond ring, 20.17 carats	Sotheby's, New York, 18 October 1994	9,902,500
5	Unnamed pear-shaped 85.91-carat pendant	Sotheby's, New York, 19 April 1988	9,130,000
6	Rectangular-cut fancy deep-blue diamond ring, 13.49 carats	Christie's, New York, 13 April 1995	7,482,500
7	Rectangular-cut 52.59-carat diamond ring	Christie's, New York, 20 April 1988	7,480,000
8	Fancy pink rectangular-cut diamond, 19.66 carats	Christie's, Geneva, 17 November 1994	7,421,318 (SF9,573,500)
9	The Jeddah Bride, rectangular-cut 80.02-carat diamond	Sotheby's, New York, 24 October 1991	7,150,000
10	The Agra Diamond, fancy light pink cushion-shaped 32.24-carat diamond	Christie's, London, 20 June 1990	6,959,700 (£4,070,000)

TOP 10 GOLD MANUFACTURERS IN THE WORLD
(Tonnes of gold used in fabrication, 1996)
❶ India (454.8) ❷ Italy (449.8) ❸ USA (245.5)
❹ China (197.9) ❺ Japan (187.5) ❻ Saudi Arabia and Yemen (162.3) ❼ Turkey (157.6) ❽ Indonesia (132.0)
❾ Taiwan (99.0) ❿ Hong Kong (83.9)

THE WEALTH OF NATIONS

TOP 10
RICHEST COUNTRIES IN THE WORLD

	Country	GDP per capita ($)
1	Liechtenstein	39,833
2	Switzerland	37,179
3	Japan	34,629
4	Luxembourg	29,857
5	Norway	28,104
6	Denmark	26,477
7	Germany	25,860
8	Austria	25,578
9	Belgium	24,949
10	Monaco	24,605
	USA	*26,037*
	UK	*18,913*

GDP (Gross Domestic Product) is the total value of all the goods and services that are produced annually within a country. (Gross National Product, GNP, also includes income from overseas.)

Source: United Nations

TOP 10
COUNTRIES WITH THE FASTEST-GROWING ECONOMIES

	Country	Average annual growth in GNP per capita 1970–95 (%)
1	South Korea	10.0
2	Botswana	7.3
3	China	6.9
4	Malta	6.1
5=	Cape Verde	5.7
=	Singapore	5.7
7=	Bhutan	5.5
=	Cyprus	5.5
9=	St. Kitts and Nevis	5.2
=	Thailand	5.2
	UK	*1.8*
	USA	*1.7*

Source: World Bank

THE 10
POOREST COUNTRIES IN THE WORLD

	Country	GDP per capita ($)
1	Sudan	36
2	São Tome and Principe	49
2	Mozambique	77
4=	Eritrea	96
=	Ethiopia	96
6	Dem. Rep. of Congo	117
7	Somalia	119
8	Tajikistan	122
9	Cambodia	130
10	Guinea-Bissau	131

Source: United Nations

THE 10
COUNTRIES WITH THE FASTEST-SHRINKING ECONOMIES

	Country	Average annual growth in GNP per capita 1970–95 (%)
1	Qatar	-5.9
2	Nicaragua	-5.3
3	Libya	-4.8
4	Dem. Rep. of Congo	-4.0
5	Kuwait	-3.5
6	Liberia	-3.0
7	Gabon	-2.8
8	Saudi Arabia	-2.9
9=	Guyana	-2.6
=	Niger	-2.6
=	Zambia	-2.6

These are countries where over the last 25 years people have on average become poorer each year. For example, at the top of the list, in Qatar people's incomes have dropped by 5.9 per cent per year.

Source: World Bank

THE 10
COUNTRIES MOST IN DEBT

	Country	Total external debt ($)
1	Mexico	165,743,000,000
2	Brazil	159,139,000,000
3	Russia	120,461,000,000
4	China	118,090,000,000
5	Indonesia	107,831,000,000
6	India	93,766,000,000
7	Argentina	89,747,000,000
8	Turkey	73,592,000,000
9	Thailand	56,789,000,000
10	Poland	42,291,000,000

The World Bank's annual debt calculations estimated the total indebtedness (including "official" debt, which is guaranteed by governments, and "private" debt which is not) of low and middle income countries at $2,177,000,000,000 in 1996, nearly double the figure for 1986, when total debt was estimated to be $1,132,400,000,000.

Source: World Bank

TOP 10
BRITISH AID RECIPIENTS

	Country	Bilateral aid from the UK (£)
1	India	90,100,000
2	Zambia	48,500,000
3	Bangladesh	48,200,000
4	Uganda	42,800,000
5	Indonesia	35,600,000
6	Pakistan	33,600,000
7	Russia	33,100,000
8	China	30,300,000
9	Malawi	30,200,000
10	Zimbabwe	29,100,000

The total gross official development assistance given by Britain in 1996 was £2,122,000,000. This includes bilateral aid, given by Britain direct to a developing country, as well as contributions to multilateral organizations' aid budgets, such as the European Union and United Nations

T O P 1 0

NOTES AND COINS IN CIRCULATION IN THE US*

	Unit	Value in circulation ($)
1	$100 bill	291,581,249,700
2	$20 bill	87,953,394,480
3	$50 bill	48,240,047,000
4	$10 bill	14,201,043,010
5	$1 bill	8,718,482,681
6	$5 bill	7,845,149,655
7	$2 bill	1,128,405,494
8	quarter	271,170,000
9	dime	178,581,000
10	nickel	42,086,000

* As of 31 December 1997

As well as the denominations in the Top 10, there are 288,192 $500 bills (value $144,096,000), 167,289 $1,000 bills ($167,289,000), 351 $5,000 bills ($1,755,000), and 345 $10,000 bills ($3,450,000), along with 13,123,260,000 cents ($13,123,260,000) in circulation.

Sources: Bureau of Engraving & Printing (bills)/US Mint (coins)

T O P 1 0

NOTES AND COINS IN CIRCULATION IN THE UK

	Unit	Value in circulation (£)
1	£20 note	9,559,000,000
2	£10 note	5,915,000,000
3	£50 note	3,273,000,000
4	£1 coin	1,142,000,000
5	£5 note	1,047,000,000
6	20p coin	337,400,000
7	50p coin	290,500,000
8	5p coin	160,800,000
9	10p coin	146,400,000
10	2p coin	92,180,000

The total value of notes in circulation as of December 1997 was £22,011,000,000 – the equivalent of a pile of £5 notes 440 km/ 273 miles high – and the total number of new notes issued in 1997 was a staggering 1,316,000,000. In addition to the notes and coins that appear in this list there are also 56,000,000 £1 notes which are still legal tender in Scotland, and 7,496,000,000 1p coins (worth £74,960,000).

T O P 1 0

COUNTRIES WITH THE HIGHEST INFLATION

	Country	Annual inflation rate (%)
1	Dem. Rep. of Congo	658.8
2	Venezuela	99.9
3=	Turkey	80.3
=	Ukraine	80.3
5	Belarus	52.7
6	Guinea Bissau	50.7
7	Russia	47.6
8	Mongolia	45.8
9	Mozambique	45.0
10	Zambia	43.9
	UK	2.4
	USA	2.9
	World	7.5

Source: International Monetary Fund

T O P 1 0

COUNTRIES IN WHICH IT IS EASIEST TO BE A MILLIONAIRE

	Country/ currency unit	Value of 1,000,000 units £	$
1	Ukraine, Karbovanets	3.62	5.52
2	Turkey, Lira	7.37	11.44
3	Dem. Rep. of Congo	12.82	19.90
4	Angola, Kwanza	20.13	31.25
5	Guinea-Bissau, Peso	35.47	55.07
6	Belarus, Rouble	37.24	57.82
7	Mozambique, Metical	57.43	89.16
8	Vietnam, Dông	58.06	90.14
9	Russia, Rouble	119.23	185.10
10	Afghanistan, Afghani	134.69	209.11

With an exchange rate running at an average of 275,869.6 Ukrainian Karbovanets to the £ (428,287.55 to the $), total assets of just £3.62/$5.62 will qualify a person as a Ukrainian millionaire.

T O P 1 0

COUNTRIES WITH MOST CURRENCY IN CIRCULATION 100 YEARS AGO

	Country	Currency in circulation 100 years ago (£) gold	silver	paper	Total
1	France	178,000,000	150,000,000	115,000,000	443,000,000
2	USA	141,000,000	87,000,000	208,000,000	436,000,000
3	Germany	122,000,000	45,000,000	71,000,000	238,000,000
4	India	10,000,000	170,000,000	12,000,000	192,000,000
5	Russia	39,000,000	14,000,000	123,000,000	176,000,000
6	UK	102,000,000	22,000,000	39,000,000	163,000,000
7	China	–	150,000,000	–	150,000,000
8	Austria	8,000,000	19,000,000	76,000,000	103,000,000
9	Italy	22,000,000	11,000,000	57,000,000	90,000,000
10	Spain	19,000,000	24,000,000	30,000,000	73,000,000

It is interesting to consider that there are now individuals in these countries who, on paper at least, own more than the entire country's money supply in the late 1890s. Today there is in excess of $1,000,000,000,000 in circulation in the US.

FOOD FOR THOUGHT

TOP 10

FOOD AND DRINK ITEMS CONSUMED IN THE UK*

	Product	Average consumption per capita per annum		
		kg	lb	oz
1	Milk, cream, and cheese	113.3	249	12
2	Vegetables (other than potatoes)	61.1	134	11
3	Meat	49.1	108	4
4	Potatoes	41.9	92	6
5	Bread	39.1	86	3
6	Fruit and nuts	39.0	86	0
7	Biscuits, cakes, cereals, etc.	22.7	50	0
8	Fruit juices	13.4	29	9
9	Butter, oils, and fats	11.8	26	0
10	Sugar and honey	9.6	21	3

Excluding beer and other alcoholic drinks

The National Food Survey, on which this list is partly based, revealed that a number of changes in the eating habits of the British people has taken place during the 1980s and 1990s, in line with increasing awareness of "healthy diets".

TOP 10

CALORIE-CONSUMING COUNTRIES IN THE WORLD

	Country	Average daily consumption per capita
1	Cyprus	3,708
2	Denmark	3,704
3	Portugal	3,639
4	Ireland	3,638
5	USA	3,603
6	Turkey	3,593
7	France	3,588
8	Greece	3,561
9	Belgium/Luxembourg	3,530
10	Italy	3,458
	UK	*3,149*
	World average	*2,712*

The calorie requirement of the average man is 2,700 and of a woman 2,500. Inactive people need less, and those engaged in heavy labour need more.

Source: Food and Agriculture Organization of the United Nations

TOP 10 CHEESE-PRODUCING COUNTRIES IN THE WORLD

(Tonnes per annum)

❶ USA (3,471,000) ❷ France (1,591,850)
❸ Germany (1,420,450) ❹ Italy (918,999)
❺ Netherlands (680,076) ❻ Russia
(476,881) ❼ Argentina (405,000) ❽ UK
(354,000) ❾ Poland (351,170)
❿ Egypt (348,750)

Source: Food and Agriculture Organization of the United Nations

THE CREATION OF THE CROISSANT

In 1899 William Morrow Chambers published *Bohemian Paris of Today*, which contained the first known reference in English to a croissant. The croissant first came into being when, in 1683, the Austrian capital Vienna was besieged by Turks. The city's bakers heard the invaders tunnelling beneath the walls at night and so thwarted the attack. As a result, they were allowed to make rolls in a crescent-shape, imitating the emblem on the Turkish flag. Known as *kipfels*, they became popular in the Austrian-Habsburg Empire. When Austrian princess Marie-Antoinette married the French dauphin in 1770, her bakers brought *kipfels* to France, where they became known as croissants.

YEARS AGO • 100 • YEARS AGO

TOP 10

BUTTER-PRODUCING COUNTRIES IN THE WORLD

	Country	Tonnes per annum*
1	India	1,300,000
2	USA	582,750
3	Germany	486,188
4	France	454,000
5	Russia	419,488
6	Pakistan	372,674
7	New Zealand	265,333
8	Poland	162,000
9	Ireland	142,400
10	Australia	134,936
	UK	*127,000*

*Including ghee

Source: Food and Agriculture Organization of the United Nations

Source: Food and Agriculture Organization of the United Nations

TOP 10
SUGAR-CONSUMING COUNTRIES IN THE WORLD

	Country	kg per capita per annum
1	Swaziland	65.80
2	Belize	57.70
3	Israel	57.01
4	Réunion	54.51
5	Costa Rica	51.87
6	New Zealand	49.76
7	Barbados	49.26
8	Brazil	47.73
9	Trinidad and Tobago	46.48
10	Malaysia	46.21
	UK	*32.52*
	USA	*29.38*

TOP 10
MEAT-EATING COUNTRIES IN THE WORLD

	Country	Consumption per capita per annum kg	lb	oz
1	USA	118.4	261	0
2	New Zealand	117.6	259	4
3	Australia	108.5	239	4
4	Cyprus	107.0	235	14
5	Uruguay	104.5	230	6
6	Austria	104.0	229	4
7	Saint Lucia	100.9	222	7
8	Denmark	99.5	219	5
9	Spain	95.8	211	3
10	Canada	95.7	210	15
	UK	*45.1*	*108*	*4*

Figures from the Meat and Livestock Commission show a huge range of meat consumption in countries around the world, ranging from the Number 1 meat consumer, the US, at 118.4 kg/216 lb per person per year, to very poor countries such as India, where it is estimated that meat consumption may be as little as 3.4 kg/7½ lb per person per year. In general, meat is an expensive food and in poor countries is saved for special occasions, therefore the richer the country, the more likely it is to have a high meat consumption. However, in recent years, health scares relating to meat, "healthy eating" concerns in many Western countries, and the rise in the number of vegetarians have all contributed to deliberate declines in consumption.

TOP 10
HOTTEST CHILLIES

	Type of chilli	Scoville units
1	Datil, Habanero, Scotch Bonnet	100,000–350,000
2	Chiltepin, Santaka, Thai	50,000–100,000
3	Aji, Cayenne, Piquin, Tabasco	30,000–50,000
4	De Arbol	15,000–30,000
5	Serrano, Yellow Wax	5,000–15,000
6	Chipolte, Jalapeno, Mirasol	2,500–5,000
7	Cascabel, Sandia, Rocotillo	1,500–2,500
8	Ancho, Espanola, Pasilla, Poblano	1,000–1,500
9	Anaheim, New Mexico	500–1,000
10	Cherry, Peperoncini	100–500

Hot peppers contain substances called capsaicinoids which determine how "hot" they are. In 1912 Wilbur Scoville pioneered a test that allowed him to measure the heat of each type of chilli – a "Scoville" unit.

TOP 10 FISH-CONSUMING COUNTRIES IN THE WORLD
(Average consumption per capita per annum)

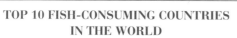

❶ Japan (66.9 kg/147 lb 8 oz) ❷ Norway (45.0 kg/99 lb 3 oz)
❸ Portugal (43.0 kg/94 lb 13 oz) ❹= Spain (30.0 kg/66 lb 2 oz),
Sweden (30.0 kg/66 lb 2 oz) ❻ Belgium (19.0 kg/41 lb 14 oz)
❼= Germany (14.0 kg/30 lb 14 oz), Italy (14.0 kg/30 lb 14 oz),
Netherlands (14.0 kg/30 lb 14 oz), Poland (14.0 kg/30 lb 14 oz)

CANDY IS DANDY

SWEET-CONSUMING COUNTRIES IN THE WORLD

	Country	chocolate kg	chocolate lb	other sweets kg	other sweets lb	total kg	total lb
1	Denmark	7	15	10	22	17	37
2	Ireland	8	18	6	13	14	31
3=	UK	8	18	5	11	13	29
=	Switzerland	10	22	3	7	13	29
=	Germany	7	16	6	13	13	29
6=	Austria	8	17	3	7	11	24
=	Belgium/Luxembourg	6	13	5	11	11	24
=	Netherlands	5	11	6	13	11	24
=	Australia	5	11	6	13	11	24
10	USA	5	11	5	11	10	22

Consumption per capita (per annum)

CANDY BRANDS IN THE US

	Brand	Market share (%)
1	Reese's Peanut Butter Cup	5.0
2	Snickers Original	4.8
3	M&M's Plain	3.5
4	M&M's Peanut	3.2
5	Hershey's Kit Kat	2.4
6=	Hershey Kisses Milk	2.3
=	Nestlé Butterfinger	2.3
8	Hershey's Milk Chocolate and Nougats Regular	2.1
9	Life Savers Original "Fruit Juicers"	2.0
10	Milky Way Original	2.0

HARRODS' BESTSELLING CHOCOLATES

1	Harrods Own Traditional English Chocolates
2	Harrods Own Swiss Chocolates
3	Harrods Own Belgian Chocolates
4	Harrods Own Handmade Truffles
5	Harrods Truffle Collection
6	Harrods Belgian Fresh Cream Chocolates
7	Leysieffer
8	Godiva
9	Nuehaus
10	Leonidas

COCOA-CONSUMING COUNTRIES IN THE WORLD

	Country	Total cocoa consumption (tonnes)
1	USA	544,100
2	Germany	244,700
3	UK	184,000
4	France	156,500
5	Russian Federation	143,900
6	Japan	112,700
7	Brazil	100,700
8	Italy	85,400
9	Belgium/Luxembourg	62,100
10	Spain	60,200

Cocoa is the principal ingredient of chocolate, and its consumption is therefore closely linked to the production of chocolate in each consuming country. Like coffee, the consumption of chocolate tends to occur mainly in the Western world and in relatively affluent countries. Since some of these Top 10 consuming nations also have large populations, the figures for cocoa consumption per capita present a somewhat different picture, being dominated by those countries with a long-established tradition of manufacturing high-quality chocolate products:

	Country	Consumption per capita kg	lb	oz
1	Belgium/ Luxembourg	5.900	13	0
2	Iceland	4.444	9	13
3	Switzerland	3.491	7	11
4	UK	3.145	6	15
5	Denmark	3.122	6	14
6	Austria	3.071	6	12
7	Germany	2.997	6	10
8	Norway	2.771	6	2
9	Malta	2.711	6	0
10	France	2.692	5	15

TOP 10
CHOCOLATE BRANDS IN THE UK

1	Cadbury's Dairy Milk
2	Kit Kat
3	Mars
4	Galaxy
5	Cadbury's Roses
6	Twix
7	Maltesers
8	Snickers
9	Quality Street
10	Aero

Per-brand sales figures are confidential, but it is said that UK sales of chocolate bars were worth a total of £1,500,000,000 in 1997.

TOP 10
OLDEST-ESTABLISHED BRITISH CHOCOLATE PRODUCTS

	Product	Year introduced
1	Fry's Chocolate Cream	1866
2	Cadbury's Dairy Milk	1905
3	Cadbury's Bournville	1908
4	Fry's Turkish Delight	1914
5	Cadbury's Milk Tray	1915
6	Cadbury's Creme Egg	1920
7 =	Cadbury's Fruit and Nut	1921
=	Terry's 1767 Bitter Bar	1921
9	Terry's Neapolitan	1922
10	Terry's Spartan	1923

TOP 10
SWEET BRANDS IN THE UK

1	Wrigley's Extra
2	Rowntree Polo
3	Trebor Extra Strong Mints
4	Wrigley's Orbit
5	Trebor Softmints
6	Maynards Wine Gums
7	Rowntree Fruit Pastilles
8	Mars Opal Fruits
9	Werthers Original
10	Leaf Chewit

TOP 10
FRUIT SWEETS IN THE UK

1	Maynards Wine-Gums
2	Rowntree Fruit Pastilles
3	Mars Opal Fruits
4	Leaf Chewits
5	Bassett's Jelly Babies
6	Mars Skittles
7	Fruit-ella
8	Rowntree Fruit Gums
9	Maynards Justfruits
10	Rowntree Jellytots

TOP 10
ICE CREAM-CONSUMING COUNTRIES IN THE WORLD

	Country	Production per capita litres	pints
1	USA	26.58	46.78
2	Finland	21.67	38.13
3	Denmark	19.75	34.76
4	Australia	18.55	32.64
5	Canada	16.60	29.22
6	Sweden	16.39	28.84
7	Norway	15.97	28.10
8	Belgium/Luxembourg	14.30	25.16
9	UK	12.48	21.96
10	New Zealand	12.43	21.87

Global statistics for ice cream consumption are hard to come by, but this list presents recent and reliable International Ice Cream Association estimates for per capita production of ice cream and related products (frozen yoghurt, sherbert, water ices, etc.). Since only small amounts of such products are exported, consumption figures can be presumed to be similar.

Source : International Dairy Foods Association

FAMILY BUSINESS

Cadbury Brothers, the British confectionery manufacturer, became a limited company in 1899. John Cadbury had started making drinking cocoa and chocolate as early as 1831. His firm received a royal warrant from Queen Victoria to supply confectionery to the palace in 1853, a role Cadbury has fulfilled ever since. Its most famous product, Cadbury's Dairy Milk, was developed in 1905. In 1969, Cadbury merged with the soft-drinks company Schweppes, but the multinational conglomerate remained under the control of descendants of John Cadbury, making it one of the largest and oldest family-run firms in the world.

YEARS AGO • YEARS AGO • 100 • YEARS AGO • YEARS AGO

ALCOHOLIC BEVERAGES

THEN & NOW

TOP 10 WINE-DRINKING COUNTRIES IN THE WORLD

1987 Country	Litres per capita p.a.		Litres per capita p.a.	1997 Country
France	75.1	**1**	60.6	Portugal
Italy	66.0	**2**	60.0	France
Portugal	64.3	**3**	58.0	Luxembourg
Luxembourg	58.5	**4**	55.0	Italy
Argentina	58.1	**5**	43.3	Switzerland
Switzerland	49.5	**6**	42.3	Argentina
Spain	46.0	**7**	34.0	Greece
Chile	34.2	**8**	32.0	Uruguay
Austria	33.9	**9**	31.5	Austria
Greece	31.8	**10**	30.3	Spain
UK	*11.0*		*13.1*	*UK*
USA	*9.1*		*7.3*	*USA*

While consumption of wine has become more popular in the UK over the last 25 years, it still does not make it into the Top 10 or even Top 20 wine-drinking countries in the world (its rank in 1997 is 25th). Between 1970 and 1997 wine consumption in the UK increased by over 350 per cent. In contrast, in France, one of the world's top wine-drinking and wine-producing countries, people have been drinking less. Wine consumption per person per year peaked at 127.3 litres in 1963, and has dropped steadily over the last 35 years to 60 litres today.

TOP 10

MOST EXPENSIVE BOTTLES OF WINE EVER SOLD AT AUCTION

	Wine/sale	Price (£)
1	Château Lafite 1787, Christie's, London, 5 Dec 1985	105,000
2	Château d'Yquem 1784, Christie's, London, 4 Dec 1986	39,600
3	Château Mouton Rothschild 1945 (jeroboam – equivalent to 4 bottles), Christie's, Geneva, 14 May 1995 (S.Fr 68,200)	36,277
4	Château Lafite Rothschild 1832 (double magnum), International Wine Auctions, London, 9 Apr 1988	24,000
5	Château Pétrus 1945 (jeroboam), Sotheby's, New York, 16 Sep 1995 ($37,375)	23,360
6	Château Mouton Rothschild 1986 (Nebuchadnezzar – equivalent to 20 bottles), Sotheby's, New York, 22 April 1995 ($36,800)	22,870
7	Château Lafite 1806, Sotheby's, Geneva, 13 Nov 1988 (S.Fr 57,200)	21,700
8	Cheval-blanc 1947 (Imperial – equivalent to eight bottles), Christie's, London, 1 Dec 1994	21,450
9=	Château Mouton Rothschild 1985 (Nebuchadnezzar), Sotheby's, Los Angeles, 12 Oct 1996 ($33,350)	21,209
=	Château Mouton Rothschild 1989 (Nebuchadnezzar), Sotheby's, Los Angeles, 12 Oct 1996 ($33,350)	21,209

TOP 10

ALCOHOL-CONSUMING COUNTRIES IN THE WORLD

	Country	Annual consumption per capita (100 per cent alcohol) litres	pints
1	Luxembourg	11.8	20.8
2	Portugal	11.2	19.7
3	France	11.1	19.5
4	Czech Republic	10.1	17.8
5	Denmark	10.0	17.6
6=	Austria	9.8	17.2
=	Germany	9.8	17.2
8	Hungary	9.5	16.7
9=	Spain	9.3	16.4
=	Switzerland	9.3	16.4
	USA	*6.6*	*11.6*

T O P 1 0
CHAMPAGNE IMPORTERS IN THE WORLD

	Country	Bottles imported (1997)		Country	Bottles imported (1997)
1	UK	22,262,972	6	Italy	6,685,582
2	Germany	19,457,909	7	Japan	2,508,842
3	USA	15,496,393	8	Netherlands	2,259,330
4	Belgium	7,948,022	9	Spain	1,244,250
5	Switzerland	6,841,842	10	Australia	1,231,596

T O P 1 0
SPIRIT BRANDS IN THE UK

	Brand	Estimated annual sales (£)		Brand	Estimated annual sales (£)
1	Bell's Extra Special	over 128,000,000	=	Bacardi	55–60,000,000
2=	Famous Grouse	85–90,000,000	7	Grant's Scotch	40–45,000,000
=	Gordon's Gin	85–90,000,000	8=	Bailey's Cream Liqueur	35–40,000,000
4	Smirnoff Red Label	80–85,000,000	=	Claymore	35–40,000,000
5=	Teacher's	55–60,000,000	10	Martell VS	30–35,000,000

T O P 1 0
SPIRIT-DRINKING COUNTRIES IN THE WORLD

	Country	Annual consumption per capita (100 per cent alcohol) litres	pints
1	Russia	5.3	9.3
2=	Romania	4.0	7.0
=	Slovak Republic	4.0	7.0
4	Cyprus	3.4	6.0
5	Poland	3.3	5.8
6=	China	3.0	5.3
=	Hungary	3.0	5.3
8	Greece	2.7	4.8
9	Bulgaria	2.5	4.4
10=	France	2.4	4.2
=	Spain	2.4	4.2

T O P 1 0
CONSUMERS OF SCOTCH WHISKY IN THE WORLD

	Country	Annual sales (£)	Annual sales (litres)
1	USA	273,020,000	33,730,000
2	France	230,260,000	36,640,000
3	Spain	183,200,000	23,550,000
4	South Korea	128,900,000	11,440,000
5	Japan	128,860,000	10,910,000
6	Germany	98,260,000	10,250,000
7	Greece	92,090,000	8,960,000
8	Thailand	76,340,000	9,000,000
9	Taiwan	72,310,000	2,620,000
10	Italy	59,020,000	6,650,000

Source: The Scotch Whisky Association

T O P 1 0
BEER-DRINKING COUNTRIES IN THE WORLD

	Country	Annual consumption per capita litres	pints
1	Czech Republic	160.0	281.6
2	Ireland	142.5	250.8
3	Germany	134.5	236.7
4	Denmark	117.6	207.0
5	Austria	116.0	204.1
6	Luxembourg	109.0	191.8
7	UK	102.3	180.0
8	Belgium	102.0	179.5
9	Australia	95.4	167.9
10	New Zealand	93.9	165.2

Despite being the world's leading producer of beer, the US is ranked in 13th position as a consumer. Many people in Africa drink a lot of beer, but as bottled beer is often very expensive, many Africans tend to consume home-made beers. These figures are hence excluded from national statistics.

SOFT DRINKS

T O P 1 0

BOTTLED WATER BRANDS PRODUCED IN THE UK

1	Evian
2	Highland Spring
3	Volvic
4	Buxton
5	Strathmore
6	Aqua-Pura
7	Caledonian (Sainsbury's own brand)
8	Mountain Spring (Tesco's own brand)
9	Chiltern Hills
10	Ballygowan

Source: Zenith International

T O P 1 0

SOFT DRINKS IN THE UK

	Drink/ advertising spend (£)	Annual sales (£)*
1	Coca-Cola 26,169,500	over 542,000,000
2	Pepsi 8,558,200	180–185,000,000
3	Robinsons 3,300,900	160–165,000,000
4	Ribena 909,100	130–135,000,000
5	Lucozade 7,021,100	105–110,000,000
6	Tango 6,584,300	100–105,000,000
7	Irn-Bru 367,300	55–60,000,000
8=	Del Monte 519,900	50–55,000,000
=	Lilt 3,034,200	50–55,000,000
=	Schweppes Mixers 17,800	50–55,000,000

* *Estimated range*

Source: Marketing

T O P 1 0

CONSUMERS OF COCA-COLA AROUND THE WORLD

	Country	Daily consumption (servings)
1	China	1,244,000,000
2	India	960,000,000
3	USA	272,000,000
4	Indonesia	203,000,000
5	Brazil	163,000,000
6	Russia	148,000,000
7	Japan	126,000,000
8	Mexico	94,000,000
9	Germany	82,000,000
10	Philippines	71,000,000

After heading this list for 110 years, the US has plummeted dramatically into third place as the two most populous countries, China and India, have adopted the world's bestselling non-alcoholic drink in a big way.

Source: Coca-Cola

T O P 1 0

TEA-DRINKING COUNTRIES

	Country	Consumption per capita p.a.		
		kg	lb oz	cups*
1	Irish Republic	3.17	7 0	1,395
2	Kuwait	2.66	5 14	1,170
3	UK	2.46	5 7	1,082
4	Qatar	2.00	4 7	880
5	Turkey	1.93	4 4	849
6	Syria	1.44	3 3	634
7	Bahrain	1.37	3 0	603
8	Sri Lanka	1.29	2 14	568
9=	New Zealand	1.23	2 11	541
=	Morocco	1.23	2 11	541
	USA	*0.34*	*0 12*	*150*

* *Based on 440 cups per kg/2 lb 3 oz*

Notwithstanding the UK's traditional passion for tea, its consumption has consistently lagged behind that of Ireland during recent years. In the same period, Qatar's tea consumption has dropped from its former world record of 3.97 kg/8 lb 12 oz (1,747 cups) per head. Within Europe, consumption varies enormously from the current world-leading Irish figure down to just 0.08 kg/3 oz (35 cups) per person in Italy. In the rest of the world, Thailand's consumption of tea, at 0.01 kg/0.4 oz (four cups) per person, is one of the lowest.

Source: International Tea Committee

COKE IN BOTTLES

The first Coca-Cola was served in Jacob's Pharmacy, a drug store in Atlanta, Georgia, on 8 May 1886, the creation of pharmacist Dr. John Styth Pemberton (1831–88). Although it was an instant success, attempts at bottling it proved short lived, and in its early years it was generally sold from soda fountains. Benjamin F. Thomas and Joseph B. Whitehead of Chattanooga, Tennessee, acquired bottling rights, incorporating the Coca-Cola Bottling Company on 9 December 1899 and selling the drink at five cents a bottle. Within 20 years there were more than 1,000 bottling plants across the US, part of a major franchising operating that has since spread worldwide.

100 YEARS AGO

TOP 10

HOT DRINKS IN THE UK

	Drink	Type	Annual sales (£)*
1	Nescafé	Instant coffee	over 248,000,000
2	Tetley	Tea	115–120,000,000
3	PG Tips	Tea	110–115,000,000
4	Gold Blend	Instant coffee	80–85,000,000
5	Kenco	Instant coffee	60–65,000,000
6	Typhoo	Tea	50–55,000,000
7	Maxwell House	Instant coffee	45–50,000,000
8	Horlicks	Malt drink	35–40,000,000
9=	Twinings	Tea	20–25,000,000
=	Yorkshire	Tea	20–25,000,000

* *Estimated range*

Despite being a nation of tea drinkers, half the entrants in this list are coffee brands. Newcomers include Twinings and Yorkshire tea, indicating that the premium tea brands are increasing in popularity, even if the total amount of tea consumed remains similar.

Source: Marketing

TOP 10

COFFEE-DRINKING COUNTRIES

	Country	Consumption per capita p.a.			
		kg	lb	oz	cups*
1	Finland	10.56	23	4	1,584
2	Denmark	9.91	21	14	1,487
3	Netherlands	9.85	21	11	1,478
4	Norway	9.77	21	9	1,466
5	Sweden	8.78	19	6	1,317
6	Austria	7.86	17	5	1,179
7	Switzerland	7.82	17	4	1,173
8	Germany	7.16	15	13	1,074
9	Belgium/Luxembourg	6.64	14	10	996
10	France	5.69	12	8	854
	USA	*4.64*	*10*	*4*	*696*
	UK	*2.43*	*5*	*6*	*365*

* *Based on 150 cups per kg/2 lb 3 oz*

Levels of coffee consumption have remained quite similar in most countries in the 1990s, with the exception of Belgium/ Luxembourg, where annual coffee consumption has doubled since 1991.

Source: International Coffee Organization

TOP 10

MILK-DRINKING COUNTRIES IN THE WORLD

	Country*	Consumption per capita p.a.	
		litres	pints
1	Ireland	155.6	273.9
2	Finland	153.4	270.0
3	Iceland	152.2	267.9
4	Norway	150.1	264.2
5	Ukraine	134.3	236.4
6	Luxembourg	130.1	229.0
7	UK	127.1	223.7
8	Sweden	125.5	220.9
9	Australia	111.4	196.1
10	USA	104.9	184.6

* *Those reporting to the International Dairy Federation only*

Source: National Dairy Council

TAKING TEA
The world is divided between countries with a tradition of tea-drinking and those where it is rarely consumed.

TRANSPORT & TOURISM

---

210 ROAD TRANSPORT

---

212 LAND SPEED RECORDS **214** ON THE RIGHT TRACK

---

216 WATER TRANSPORT   **218** PIONEERS OF FLIGHT

220 AIR TRAVEL   **222** TOURISM

TOP 10

COUNTRIES PRODUCING THE MOST MOTOR VEHICLES

	Country	Cars	Commercial vehicles	Total
1	USA	6,083,227	5,715,678	11,798,905
2	Japan	7,863,763	2,482,023	10,345,786
3	Germany	4,539,583	303,326	4,842,909
4	France	3,147,622	442,965	3,590,587
5	South Korea	2,264,709	548,005	2,812,714
6	Spain	2,213,102	199,207	2,412,309
7	Canada	1,279,312	1,117,731	2,397,043
8	UK	1,686,134	238,263	1,924,397
9	Brazil	1,466,900	345,700	1,812,600
10	Italy	1,317,995	227,370	1,545,365
	World	*37,318,281*	*14,194,882*	*51,513,163*

Source: American Automobile Manufacturers' Association

TOP 10

VEHICLE-OWNING COUNTRIES IN THE WORLD

	Country	Cars	Commercial vehicles	Total
1	USA	134,981,000	65,465,000	200,446,000
2	Japan	44,680,000	22,173,463	66,853,463
3	Germany	40,499,442	3,061,874	43,561,316
4	Italy	30,000,000	2,806,500	32,806,500
5	France	25,100,000	5,195,000	30,295,000
6	UK	24,306,781	3,635,176	27,941,957
7	Russia	13,638,600	9,856,000	23,494,600
8	Spain	14,212,259	3,071,621	17,283,880
9	Canada	13,182,996	3,484,616	16,667,612
10	Brazil	12,000,000	3,160,689	15,160,689
	World	*477,010,289*	*169,748,819*	*646,759,108*

Almost three-quarters of the world's vehicles are registered in the Top 10 countries. Of these, some 233,810,745 are in Europe, and 232,607,90 in North and Central America.

Source: American Automobile Manufacturers' Association

T O P 1 0

COUNTRIES WITH THE LONGEST ROAD NETWORKS

	Country	Length km	miles
1	USA	6,261,154	3,890,500
2	India	2,009,600	1,248,707
3	Brazil	1,939,000	1,204,839
4	France	1,512,700	939,948
5	Japan	1,144,360	711,072
6	China	1,117,000	694,072
7	Canada	1,021,000	634,420
8	Russia	948,000	589,060
9	Australia	895,030	556,146
10	Germany	639,800	397,553
	UK	*388,831*	*241,608*

T O P 1 0

BESTSELLING CARS OF ALL TIME

	Model	Year first produced	Estimated no. made
1	Volkswagen Beetle	1937*	21,220,000
2	Toyota Corolla	1963	20,000,000
3	Ford Model T	1908	16,536,075
4	Volkswagen Golf	1974	14,800,000
5	Lada Riva	1970	13,500,000
6	Ford Escort/ Orion	1967	12,000,000
7	Nissan Sunny/ Pulsar	1966	10,200,000
8	Mazda 323	1977	9,500,000
9	Renault 4	1961	8,100,000
10	Honda Civic	1972	8,000,000

* Still produced in Mexico and Brazil

Estimates of manufacturers' output of their bestselling models vary from the vague to the unusually precise. With 15,007,033 produced in the US, and the rest in Canada and the UK, between 1908 and 1927.

T H E 1 0

FIRST COUNTRIES TO MAKE SEAT BELTS COMPULSORY

	Country	Introduced		Country	Introduced
1	Czechoslovakia	Jan 1969	7	Puerto Rico	Jan 1974
2	Côte d'Ivoire	Jan 1970	8	Spain	Oct 1974
3	Japan	Dec 1971	9	Sweden	Jan 1975
4	Australia	Jan 1972	10=	Netherlands	Jun 1975
5=	Brazil	Jun 1972	=	Belgium	Jun 1975
=	New Zealand	Jun 1972	=	Luxembourg	Jun 1975

Seat belts, long in use in aircraft, were not designed for use in private cars until the 1950s. Ford was the first manufacturer in Europe to fit anchorage-points, and belts were first fitted as standard equipment in Swedish Volvos from 1959. They were optional extras in most cars until the 1970s, when they were fitted to all models.

T H E N & N O W

TOP 10 BESTSELLING CARS IN THE UK

1987 Model	Sales		Sales	1997 Model
Ford Escort	178,001	1	119,471	Ford Fiesta
Ford Fiesta	153,453	2	113,522	Ford Escort
Ford Sierra	139,878	3	107,239	Ford Mondeo
Austin/MG Metro	108,223	4	93,778	Vauxhall Vectra
Vauxhall Cavalier	98,490	5	89,537	Vauxhall Astra
Vauxhall Astra	88,637	6	79,898	Vauxhall Corsa
Ford Orion	69,252	7	66,888	Peugeot 306
Austin/MG Montego	58,238	8	62,365	Rover 200
Rover 200	50,254	9	61,913	Rover 400
Peugeot 205	49,127	10	58,033	Renault Clio

PRODUCTION LINE
By applying mass-production methods to its Model T, Ford established a world record for sales that was unbroken for over 50 years.

LAND SPEED RECORDS

THRUST SCC

TOP 10

FASTEST PRODUCTION CARS IN THE WORLD

	Model*	Max speed# km/h	mph
1	Lamborghini Diablo Roadster	335	208
2	Ferrari F50	325	202
3	Lister Storm GTL	322	200
4	Aston Martin V8 Vantage	298	185
5	Porsche 911 Turbo 4	291	181
6	Chrysler Viper GTS	285	177
7=	Marcos 4.6 Spyder†	274	170
=	TVR Cerbera	274	170
=	Lotus Esprit V8-GT	274	170
10	Maserati Ghibli Cup	272	169

* *Fastest of each manufacturer*

\# *May vary according to specification changes to meet national legal requirements*

† *Other models are capable of the same speed.*

THE 10

LATEST HOLDERS OF THE LAND SPEED RECORD

	Driver/car	Location	Date	Max speed km/h	mph
1	Andy Green (UK), *Thrust SSC*	Black Rock Desert, USA	15 Oct 1997	1,227.99	763.04
2	Richard Noble (UK), *Thrust 2*	Black Rock Desert, USA	4 Oct 1983	1,013.47	633.47
3	Gary Gabelich (USA), *The Blue Flame*	Bonneville Salt Flats, USA	23 Oct 1970	995.85	622.41
4	Craig Breedlove (USA), *Spirit of America – Sonic 1*	Bonneville Salt Flats, USA	15 Nov 1965	960.96	600.60
5	Art Arfons (USA), *Green Monster*	Bonneville Salt Flats, USA	7 Nov 1965	922.48	576.55
6	Craig Breedlove (USA), *Spirit of America – Sonic 1*	Bonneville Salt Flats, USA	2 Nov 1965	888.76	555.48
7	Art Arfons (USA), *Green Monster*	Bonneville Salt Flats, USA	27 Oct 1964	958.73	536.71
8	Craig Breedlove (USA), *Spirit of America*	Bonneville Salt Flats, USA	15 Oct 1964	842.04	526.28
9	Craig Breedlove (USA), *Spirit of America*	Bonneville Salt Flats, USA	13 Oct 1964	749.95	468.72
10	Art Arfons (USA), *Spirit of America*	Bonneville Salt Flats, USA	5 Oct 1964	694.43	434.02

TOP 10

WORLD LAND SPEED RECORDS HELD BY MALCOLM AND DONALD CAMPBELL

	Driver/date	Max speed km/h	mph
1	Malcolm Campbell, 25 Sept 1924	233.85	146.16
2	Malcolm Campbell, 21 Jul 1925	241.21	150.76
3	Malcolm Campbell, 4 Feb 1927	279.80	174.88
4	Malcolm Campbell, 19 Feb 1928	331.12	206.95
5	Malcolm Campbell, 5 Feb 1931	393.74	246.09
6	Sir Malcolm Campbell,* 24 Feb 1932	406.35	253.97
7	Sir Malcolm Campbell, 22 Feb 1933	435.93	272.46
8	Sir Malcolm Campbell, 7 Mar 1935	442.91	276.82
9	Sir Malcolm Campbell, 3 Sept 1935	480.20	301.13
10	Donald Campbell, 17 Jul 1964	644.96	403.10

* *Knighted 1931*

On 16 September 1947, British driver John Cobb achieved a speed of 630.72 km/h/ 394.20 mph in his Railton Mobil Special, at Bonneville Salt Flats, USA. His record stood for 16 years until 1963, since when it has been successively broken. In the 50 years since Cobb gained the land speed record, it has almost doubled.

T H E 1 0

LATEST HOLDERS OF THE MOTORCYCLE SPEED RECORD

Rider/ motorcycle/year	Max speed km/h	mph
1 Dave Campos, Twin 91 cu in/1,491 *cc* Ruxton Harley-Davidson *Easyriders*, 1990	518.45	322.15
2 Donald A. Vesco, Twin 1,016 cc Kawasaki *Lightning Bolt*, 1978	512.73	318.60
3 Donald A. Vesco, 1,496 cc Yamaha *Silver Bird*, 1975	487.50	302.93
4 Calvin Rayborn, 1,480 cc Harley-Davidson, 1970	426.40	264.96
5 Calvin Rayborn, 1,480 cc Harley-Davidson, 1970	410.37	254.99
6 Donald A. Vesco, 700 cc Yamaha, 1970	405.25	251.82
7 Robert Leppan, 1298 cc Triumph, 1966	395.27	245.62
8 William A. Johnson, 667 cc Triumph, 1962	361.40	224.57
9 Wilhelm Herz, 499 cc NSU, 1956	338.08	210.08
10 Russell Wright, 998 cc Vincent HRD, 1955	297.64	184.95

All the records listed here were achieved at the Bonneville Salt Flats, USA, with the exception of No. 10, which was attained at Christchurch, New Zealand.

THE FIRST TO TOP 100 KM PER HOUR

All the early attempts to establish and break the world land speed record were undertaken in Europe under the auspices of the Automobile Club de France. The first few years were dominated by rivalry between two men, Frenchman Comte Gaston de Chasseloup Laubat and Belgian Camille Jenatzy, each of whom alternately held the record on three separate occasions. It was Jenatzy who first broke the psychologically significant 100 km/h (62 mph) barrier. He did so over a 2-km course at Achères, France, on 29 April 1899 in his electrically powered vehicle, La Jamais Contente ("The Never Satisfied"), achieving a speed of 105.87 km/h (65.79 mph).

YEARS AGO • YEARS AGO • 100 • YEARS AGO • YEARS AGO

T H E 1 0

FIRST HOLDERS OF THE MOTORCYCLE SPEED RECORD

	Rider	Motorcycle	Location	Year	Max speed km/h	mph
1	Ernest Walker	994 cc Indian	Daytona Beach, USA	1920	167.67	104.19
2	Claude F. Temple	996 cc British Azani	Brooklands, UK	1923	174.58	108.48
3	Herbert Le Vack	867 cc Brough Superior	Arpajon, France	1924	191.59	118.05
4	Claude F. Temple	996 cc OEC Temple	Arpajon, France	1926	191.59	119.05
5	Oliver M. Baldwin	996 cc Zenith JAP	Arpajon, France	1928	200.56	124.62
6	Herbert Le Vack	995 cc Brough	Arpajon, France	1929	207.33	128.33
7	Joseph S. Wright	994 cc OEC Temple	Arpajon, France	1930	220.99	137.32
8	Ernst Henne	735 cc BMW	Ingolstadt, Germany	1930	221.54	137.66
9	Joseph S. Wright	995 cc OEC Temple JAP	Cork, Ireland	1930	242.50	150.68
10	Ernst Henne	735 cc BMW	Tat, Hungary	1932	244.40	151.86

THE 10 FIRST HOLDERS OF THE LAND SPEED RECORD
(Car/date/speed)

❶ Gaston de Chasseloup-Laubat (Jeantaud, 18 Dec 1898, 62.78 km/h/39.24 mph) ❷ Camille Jenatzy (Jenatzy, 17 Jan 1899, 66.27 km/h/41.420 mph) ❸ Gaston de Chasseloup-Laubat (Jeantaud, 17 Jan 1899, 69.90 km/h/43.69 mph) ❹ Camille Jenatzy (Jenatzy, 27 Jan 1899, 79.37 km/h/49.92 mph) ❺ Gaston de Chasseloup-Laubat (Jeantaud, 4 Mar 1899, 92.16 km/h/57.60 mph) ❻ Camille Jenatzy (Jenatzy, 29 Apr 1899, 105.87 km/h/65.79 mph) ❼ Léon Serpollet (Serpollet, 13 Apr 1902, 120.09 km/h/75.06 mph) ❽ William Vanderbilt (Mors, 5 Aug 1902, 121.72 km/h/76.08 mph) ❾ Henri Fournier (Mors, 5 Nov 1902, 122.56 km/h/76.60 mph) ❿ M. Augières (Mors, 17 Nov 1902, 123.40 km/h/77.13 mph)

ELECTRIC POWER
La Jamais Contente, *a torpedo-shaped electric car driven by Camille Jenatzy, broke the world land speed record three times at Achères, in Paris on 29 April 1899.*

ON THE RIGHT TRACK

T H E   1 0

FIRST COUNTRIES WITH RAILWAYS

	Country	First railway established
1	UK	27 September 1825
2	France	7 November 1829
3	USA	24 May 1830
4	Ireland	17 December 1834
5	Belgium	5 May 1835
6	Germany	7 December 1835
7	Canada	21 July 1836
8	Russia	30 October 1837
9	Austria	6 January 1838
10	Netherlands	24 September 1839

Although there were earlier horse-drawn railways, the Stockton and Darlington Railway in the north of England inaugurated the world's first steam service. At first, some of the countries listed here offered only limited services over short distances, but their opening dates mark the generally accepted beginning of each country's steam railway system.

GOING UNDERGROUND
London's Metropolitan Railway, the world's first underground service, opened on 10 January 1863. The wide-gauge track (2.134 m/7 ft) seen here at Bellmouth, Praed Street, was used in its early years.

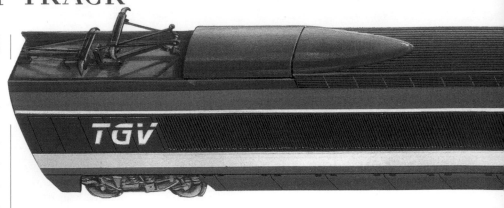

T O P   1 0

LONGEST UNDERGROUND RAILWAY NETWORKS IN THE WORLD

	Location	Opened	Stations	Total track length km	miles
1	London, UK	1863	270	401	251
2	New York, USA	1904	469	398	249
3	Paris, France*	1900	432	323	202
4	Tokyo, Japan#	1927	250	289	181
5	Moscow, Russia	1935	150	244	153
6	Mexico City, Mexico	1969	154	178	112
7	Chicago, USA	1943	145	173	108
8	Copenhagen, Denmark†	1934	79	170	106
9	Berlin, Germany	1902	135	167	104
10	Seoul, Korea	1974	130	165	103

* *Metro + RER*

\# *Through-running extensions raise total to 683 km/391 miles, with 502 stations*

† *Only partly undergound*

T O P   1 0

OLDEST UNDERGROUND RAILWAY NETWORKS IN THE WORLD

	City	Opened
1	London	1863
2	Budapest	1896
3	Glasgow	1896
4	Boston	1897
5	Paris	1900
6	Berlin	1902
7	New York	1904
8	Philadelphia	1907
9	Hamburg	1912
10	Buenos Aires	1913

TRAIN A GRANDE VITESSE
The French TGV (Train à Grande Vitesse, or high-speed train) began service between Paris and Lyons in 1981. Its former world record scheduled speed is now exceeded by even faster "bullet trains" in service in Japan.

TOP 10
LONGEST RAIL NETWORKS IN THE WORLD

	Location	Total rail length km	miles
1	USA	240,000	149,129
2	Russia	154,000	95,691
3	Canada	70,176	43,605
4	India	62,462	38,812
5	China	58,399	36,287
6	Germany	43,966	27,319
7	Australia	38,563	23,962
8	Argentina	37,910	23,556
9	France	33,891	21,059
10	Brazil	27,418	17,037

Although remaining at the head of this list, US rail mileage has declined considerably since its 1916 peak of 408,773 km/ 254,000 miles. The total of all world networks is today reckoned to be some 1,201,337 km/746,476 miles.

TOP 10
BUSIEST RAILWAY STATIONS IN THE UK

1	Euston	6	Liverpool Street
2	Kings Cross	7	Reading
3	Paddington	8	Edinburgh
4	Waterloo	9	Manchester Piccadilly
5	Victoria	10	Gatwick

The Top 10 stations are ranked according to their total revenue earned, which ranges from approximately £50,000,000 per annum for Euston, down to £19,000,000 for Gatwick. The number of annual journeys made varies between 5,440,873 for Euston to 2,568,888 in the case of Gatwick. Victoria handles the most travellers – 7,601,581 per annum.

TOP 10
FASTEST RAIL JOURNEYS IN THE WORLD*

	Journey	Train	Distance km	Speed km/h
1	Hiroshima–Kokura, Japan	Nozomi 503/508	192.0	261.8
2	Lille–Roissy, France	TGV 538/9	203.4	254.3
3	Madrid–Seville, Spain	AVE 9616/9617	470.5	209.1
4	Würzburg–Fulda, Germany	ICE	93.2	199.7
5	London–York, UK	Scottish Pullman	303.3	180.2
6	Hässleholm–Alvesta, Sweden	X2000	98.0	168.0
7	Rome–Florence, Italy	10 Pendolini	261.0	164.9
8	Baltimore–Wilmington, USA	Metroliner 110	110.1	157.3
9	Salo–Karjaa, Finland	S220 132	53.1	151.7
10	Toronto–Dorval, Canada	Metropolis	519.5	141.0

* *Fastest journey for each country; all those in the Top 10 have other similarly or equally fast services*

The fastest international journeys are those between Paris, France, and Mons, Belgium on 4 Thalys, a journey of 281.6 km/174.98 miles at an average speed of 211.2 km/h/131.23 mph.

TOP 10
BUSIEST RAIL NETWORKS IN THE WORLD

	Country	Passenger/ km per annum	miles per annum*
1	Japan	396,332,000,000	246,269,000,000
2	China	354,700,000,000	219,965,000,000
3	India	319,400,000,000	198,500,000,000
4	Russia	191,900,000,000	119,200,000,000
5	Ukraine	75,900,000,000	47,200,000,000
6	France	58,380,000,000	36,276,000,000
7	Germany	58,003,000,000	36,041,000,000
8	Egypt	47,992,000,000	29,821,000,000
9	Italy	47,100,000,000	29,270,000,000
10	South Korea	30,216,000,000	18,775,000,000
	UK	*28,656,000,000*	*17,806,000,000*
	USA	*21,144,000,000*	*13,138,000,000*

* *Number of passengers multiplied by distance carried*

WATER TRANSPORT

TOP 10
BUSIEST PORTS IN THE WORLD

	Port	Location	Goods handled p.a. (tonnes)
1	Rotterdam	Netherlands	350,000,000
2	Singapore	Singapore	290,000,000
3	Chiba	Japan	173,700,000
4	Kobe	Japan	171,000,000
5	Hong Kong	Hong Kong	147,200,000
6	Houston	USA	142,000,000
7	Shanghai	China	139,600,000
8	Nagoya	Japan	137,300,000
9	Yokohama	Japan	128,300,000
10	Antwerp	Belgium	109,500,000

The only other world port handling more than 100,000,000 tonnes is Kawasaki, Japan (105,100,000 tonnes per annum).

TOP 10
LARGEST OIL TANKERS IN THE WORLD

	Tanker	Year built	Country of origin	Gross tonnage*	Deadweight tonnage#
1	*Jahre Viking*	1979	Japan	260,851	564,763
2	*Sea Giant*	1979	France	261,862	555,051
3	*Kapetan Giannis*	1977	Japan	247,160	516,895
4	*Kapetan Michalis*	1977	Japan	247,160	516,423
5	*Sea World*	1978	Sweden	237,768	491,120
6	*Nissei Maru*	1975	Japan	238,517	484,276
7	*Stena King*	1978	Taiwan	218,593	457,927
8	*Stena Queen*	1977	Taiwan	218,593	457,841
9	*Kapetan Panagiotis*	1977	Japan	218,447	457,062
10	*Kapetan Giorgis*	1976	Japan	218,447	456,368

* The weight of the ship when empty

The total weight of the vessel, including its cargo, crew, passengers and supplies

·Source: Lloyds Register of Shipping, MIPG/PPMS

TOP 10
LONGEST SHIP CANALS IN THE WORLD

	Canal/location/opened	Length km	miles
1	St. Lawrence Seaway, Canada/USA 1959	304	189
2	Main-Danube, Germany, 1992	171	106
3	Suez, Egypt, 1869	162	101
4=	Albert, Belgium, 1939	129	80
=	Moscow-Volga, Russia, 1937	129	80
6	Kiel, Germany, 1895	99	62
7	Trollhätte, Sweden, 1916	87	54
8	Alphonse XIII, Spain, 1926	85	53
9	Panama, Panama, 1914	82	51
10	Houston, USA, 1914	81	50

TOP 10
LONGEST CRUISE SHIPS IN THE WORLD

	Ship/year built/country of origin	Length m	ft in
1	*Norway* (formerly *France*), 1961, France	315.53	1,035 2
2	*United States**, 1952, USA	301.76	990 0
3=	*Disney Magic*, 1998, Italy	294.00	964 7
=	*Disney Wonder*, 1998, Italy	294.00	964 7
5	*Queen Elizabeth 2*, 1969, UK	293.53	963 0
6	*Grand Princess*, 1998, Italy	285.00	935 0
7	*Enchantment of the Seas*, 1997, Finland	279.60	917 4
8	*Grandeur of the Seas*, 1996, Finland	279.10	915 8
9	*Vision of the Seas*, 1998, France	279.00	915 4
10	*Rhapsody of the Seas*, 1997, France	278.94	915 2

* Currently undergoing conversion to cruise ship

Source: Lloyds Register of Shipping, MIPG/PPMS

SUPERCRUISER

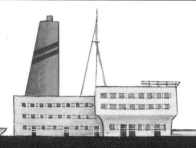

T O P   1 0

SHIPPING COUNTRIES IN THE WORLD

	Country	Ships	Total gross tonnage
1	Panama	6,188	91,128,000,000
2	Liberia	1,697	60,058,000,000
3	Bahamas	1,221	25,523,000,000
4	Greece	1,641	25,288,000,000
5	Cyprus	1,650	23,653,000,000
6	Malta	1,378	22,984,000,000
7	Norway	715	19,780,000,000
8	Singapore	1,656	18,875,000,000
9	Japan	9,310	18,516,000,000
10	China	3,175	16,339,000,000
	USA	5,260	11,789,000,000
	UK*	1,424	3,486,000,000

* Excluding Isle of Man, Channel Islands, and dependant territories

Source: Lloyds Register of Shipping, MIPG/PPMS

T O P   1 0

LONGEST CANALS IN THE UK

	Canal	Length km	miles
1	Grand Union (main line)	220.5	137
2	Leeds and Liverpool	204.4	127
3	Trent and Mersey	149.7	93
4	Kennet and Avon	139.2	86.5
5	Oxford	123.9	77
6	Shropshire Union	107.0	66.5
7	Caledonian	96.6	60
8	Staffordshire and Worcestershire	74.2	46.1
9	Llangollen	74.0	46
10	Lancaster	68.4	42.5

T O P   1 0

LARGEST CRUISE SHIPS IN THE WORLD

	Ship	Built year	country	Passenger capacity	Gross tonnage
1	*Grand Princess*	1998	Italy	3,300	104,000
2	*Carnival Triumph*	1998	Italy	3,300	101,672
3	*Carnival Destiny*	1996	Italy	3,336	101,353
4=	*Disney Wonder*	1998	Italy	2,500	85,000
=	*Disney Magic*	1998	Italy	2,500	85,000
6	*Rhapsody of the Seas*	1997	France	2,416	78,491
7=	*Dawn Princess*	1997	Italy	1,950	77,441
=	*Sun Princess*	1995	Italy	2,272	77,441
9=	*Galaxy*	1996	Germany	1,896	76,522
=	*Mercury*	1997	Germany	1,896	76,522

While the day of the passenger liner may be over, that of the cruise liner has dawned, with ever-larger vessels joining the world's cruise line fleets in the 1990s. By 2002, this list will be completely altered again as a further four vessels of more than 100,000 tonnes are completed. Three identical ships currently under construction in Finland will head the new millennium's Top 10, with a massive leap to a size of 142,000 tonnes each, and passenger capacities of almost 4,000.

Source: Lloyds Register of Shipping, MIPG/PPMS

THE WORLD'S BIGGEST LINER

The *Great Eastern*, launched in 1858 and scrapped in 1887, was the largest ship in the world until 1899, when the *Oceanic* was launched. Built by Harland and Wolff of Belfast, who were later to construct the ill-fated *Titanic*, the ship was operated by the White Star company. The *Oceanic* measured an impressive 215 m/704 ft long and 21 m/68 ft wide, and had a displacement of 17,551 tonnes. Plying between the UK and New York, the liner, which carried 1,710 passengers, was considered the most luxurious afloat. At the outbreak of the First World War, the ship was converted into a cruiser but within weeks, on 8 September 1914, it was was wrecked in dense fog off Foula, Shetland Islands; fortunately, the crew was rescued.

100 YEARS AGO · YEARS AGO · YEARS AGO

PIONEERS OF FLIGHT

MONTGOLFIER BALLOON
Although designed and built by the Mongolfiers, the first ever balloon flight was made by three other men (see list right).

T H E   1 0

FIRST ROCKET AND JET AIRCRAFT

	Aircraft/country	First flight
1	Heinkel He 176*, Germany	20 Jun 1939
2	Heinkel He 178, Germany	27 Aug 1939
3	DFS 194*, Germany	Aug 1940#
4	Caproni-Campini N-1#, Italy	28 Aug 1940
5	Heinkel He 280V-1, Germany	2 Apr 1941
6	Gloster E.28/39, UK	15 May 1941
7	Messerschmitt Me 163 Komet*, Germany	13 Aug 1941
8	Messerschmitt Me 262V-3, Germany	18 Jul 1942
9	Bell XP-59A Airacomet, USA	1 Oct 1942
10	Gloster Meteor F Mk 1, UK	5 Mar 1943

* *Rocket-powered*
\# *Precise date unknown*

T H E   1 0

FIRST MANNED BALLOON FLIGHTS*

	Balloonists/incident	Date
1	The Montgolfier brothers	21 November 1783

The Montgolfier brothers, Joseph and Etienne, tested their first unmanned hot-air balloon in the French town of Annonay on 5 June 1783. On 21 November 1783 François Laurent, Marquis d'Arlandes, and Jean François Pilâtre de Rozier took off from the Bois de Boulogne, Paris, in a Montgolfier hot-air balloon. This first-ever manned flight covered a distance of about 9 km/5½ miles in 23 minutes, landing safely near Gentilly.

2	Jacques Alexandre César Charles and Nicholas-Louis Robert	1 December 1783

Watched by a crowd of 400,000, Jacques Alexandre César Charles and Nicholas-Louis Robert made the first-ever flight in a hydrogen balloon. They took off from the Tuileries, Paris, and travelled about 43 km/27 miles north to Nesle in a time of about two hours. Charles then took off again alone, thus becoming the first solo flier.

3	Pilâtre de Rozier	19 January 1784

La Flesselle, a gigantic 40-m/131-ft high Montgolfier hot-air balloon named after its sponsor, the local Governor, ascended from Lyons piloted by Pilâtre de Rozier with Joseph Montgolfier, Prince Charles de Ligne, and the Comtes de La Porte d'Anglefort, de Dampierre, and de Laurencin – as well as the first ever aerial stowaway, a young man called Fontaine, who leaped in as it was taking off.

4	Chevalier Paolo Andreani, Augustino, and Carlo Giuseppi Gerli	25 February 1784

The Chevalier Paolo Andreani and the brothers Augustino and Carlo Giuseppi Gerli (the builders of the balloon) made the first-ever flight outside France, at Moncuco near Milan, Italy.

5	Jean-Pierre François Blanchard	2 March 1784

Jean-Pierre François Blanchard made his first flight in a hydrogen balloon from the Champ de Mars, Paris, after experimental hops during the preceding months.

6	Mr. Rosseau	14 April 1784

Mr. Rosseau and an unnamed 10-year-old drummer boy flew from Navan to Ratoath in Ireland, the first ascent in the British Isles.

7	Guyton de Morveau	25 April 1784

Guyton de Morveau, a French chemist, and L'Abbé Bertrand flew at Dijon.

8	Bremond and Hughes Bernard Maret	8 May 1784

Bremond and Hughes Bernard Maret flew at Marseilles.

9	Brun and Comte Xavier de Maistre	12 May 1784

A 20-year-old ballooning pioneer called Brun ascended at Chambéry with the Comte Xavier de Maistre, also only 20 years of age.

10	Adorne	15 May 1784

Adorne, accompanied by an unnamed passenger, took off but crash-landed near Strasbourg.

* *Several of the balloonists listed also made subsequent flights, but in each instance only their first flights are included*

BIERIOT TYPE XI
Considered one of the great achievements of the early years of flying, Louis Biériot crossed the English Channel on 25 July 1909 at a speed of just 61 km/h/38 mph.

THE WRIGHT STUFF
Although primitive to modern eyes, the Wright brothers' biplane successfully broke endurance records during 1908, thus proving that manned flight was a practical reality.

THE 10

FIRST FLIGHTS OF MORE THAN ONE HOUR

	Pilot	Duration hr	min	sec	Date
1	Orville Wright	1	2	15.0	9 Sep 1908
2	Orville Wright	1	5	52.0	10 Sep 1908
3	Orville Wright	1	10	0.0	11 Sep 1908
4	Orville Wright	1	15	20.0	12 Sep 1908
5	Wilbur Wright	1	31	25.8	21 Sep 1908
6	Wilbur Wright	1	7	24.8	28 Sep 1908
7	Wilbur Wright*	1	4	26.0	6 Oct 1908
8	Wilbur Wright	1	9	45.4	10 Oct 1908
9	Wilbur Wright	1	54	53.4	18 Dec 1908
10	Wilbur Wright	2	20	23.2	31 Dec 1908

* *First-ever flight of more than one hour with a passenger (M.A. Fordyce)*

Following Orville Wright's first-ever flight in a heavier-than-air aircraft (at Kitty Hawk, Carolina, on 17 December 1903), he and his brother Wilbur so mastered the art of flying that they totally dominated the air for the next few years. In 1908, Orville (at Fort Meyer, near Washington, DC) and Wilbur (at the Champ d'Auvours, a military base near Le Mans) made a total of 10 flights lasting more than an hour – the last of which, on the last day of the year, actually exceeded two hours and covered a distance of 124 km/77 miles.

THE 10

FIRST TRANSATLANTIC FLIGHTS

	Aircraft	Crossing	Date
1	US Navy/Curtiss flying boat NC-4	Trepassy Harbor, Newfoundland to Lisbon, Portugal	16–27 May 1919
2	Twin Rolls-Royce-engined converted Vickers Vimy bomber	St. John's, Newfoundland to Galway, Ireland	14–15 June 1919
3	British R-34 airship	East Fortune, Scotland to Roosevelt Field, New York	2–6 July 1919
4	Fairey IIID seaplane *Santa Cruz*	Lisbon, Portugal to Recife, Brazil	30 March– 5 June 1922
5	Two Douglas seaplanes, *Chicago* and *New Orleans*	Orkneys, Scotland to Labrador, Canada	2–31 August 1924
6	*Los Angeles*, a renamed German-built ZR 3 airship	Fredrichshafen, Germany to Lakehurst, New Jersey	12–15 October 1924
7	*Plus Ultra*, a Dornier Wal twin-engined flying boat	Huelva, Spain to Recife, Brazil	22 January– 10 February 1926
8	*Santa Maria*, a Savoia-Marchetti S.55 flying boat	Cagliari, Sardinia to Recife, Brazil	8–24 February 1927
9	Dornier Wal flying boat	Lisbon, Portugal to Natal, Brazil	16–17 March 1927
10	Savoia Marchetti flying boat	Genoa, Italy to Natal, Brazil	28 April– 14 May 1927

THE FIRST TO FLY

The last year of the 19th century saw some of the first experiments in human flight. In England, US-born Samuel Franklin Cody began developing kites that were capable of lifting a person off the ground (Cody went on to become the first person to fly a powered aircraft in the UK). On 30 September 1899 at Market Harborough, UK, pioneer birdman Percy Pilcher's flying machine broke up while it was being towed into the air by horses. During the same year, in the USA, the Wright Brothers embarked on the experiments with large kites and gliders that were to lead to their later success with powered flight. The year 1899 also marks the birth of US pilot Wiley Post, who in 1933 accomplished the first solo round-the-world flight.

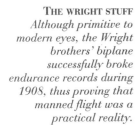

YEARS AGO • YEARS AGO • YEARS AGO • YEARS AGO • 100

AIR TRAVEL

BOEING 727-200
An enhanced version of the 727 airliner, in service since 1963, the Boeing 727-200 first flew in 1972.

COMPLAINTS AGAINST AIRLINES IN THE US

	Complaint	Total (1996)
1	Flight problems (cancellations, delays, etc.)	1,626
2	Customer service (cabin service, meals, etc.)	1,000
3	Baggage	881
4	Ticketing/boarding	857
5	Refunds	521
6	Oversales/bumping	353
7	Fares	180
8	Advertising	61
9	Tours	16
10	Smoking	13
	Total (including others not in Top 10)	5,778

The category of complaints that has undergone the most notable change is that of smoking. In 1988, 546 people complained, mostly about others smoking close by. Since the ban on smoking introduced on all US domestic flights in 1992, there are a few complaints every year from individuals who object to the prohibition.

Source: US Department of Transportation

BUSIEST AIRPORTS IN THE WORLD

	Airport/location	Passengers per annum*
1	Chicago O'Hare, Chicago, USA	66,468,000
2	Hartsfield Atlanta Int., Atlanta, USA	53,630,000
3	Dallas/Fort Worth Int., Dallas/Fort Worth, USA	52,601,000
4	London Heathrow, London, UK	51,368,000
5	Los Angeles Int., Los Angeles, USA	51,050,000
6	Frankfurt, Frankfurt, Germany	34,376,000
7	San Francisco Int., San Francisco, USA	33,965,000
8	Miami Int., Miami, USA	30,203,000
9	John F. Kennedy Int., New York, USA	28,807,000
10	Charles De Gaulle, Paris, France	28,363,000

* *International and domestic flights*

Source: International Civil Aviation Organization

BUSIEST AIRPORTS IN EUROPE

	Airport/location	Passengers per annum*
1	London Heathrow, London, UK	51,368,000
2	Frankfurt, Frankfurt, Germany	34,376,000
3	Charles de Gaulle, Paris, France	28,363,000
4	Orly, Paris, France	26,497,000
5	Schiphol, Amsterdam, Netherlands	23,069,000
6	London Gatwick, London, UK	21,045,000
7	Fiumicino, Rome, Italy	19,911,000
8	Madrid, Madrid, Spain	18,223,000
9	Palma, Mallorca, Spain	14,051,000
10	Zürich, Zürich, Switzerland	14,044,000

* *International and domestic flights*

Five further European airports – Brussels, Manchester, Milan, Munich, and Stockholm – each handled over 10,000,000 passengers per annum.

AIRCRAFT IN THE WORLD*

	Aircraft	Approximate no. in service
1	Boeing B-737	2,430
2	Douglas DC-9/MD-80	1,890
3	Boeing B-727	1,460
4	Boeing B-747	940
5	Boeing B-757	630
6	Airbus A-300/A-310	620
7	Boeing B-767	570
8	Airbus A-320	500
9	Douglas DC-10	320
10	Fokker F100	260

* *Turbo-jet airliners only; scheduled and non-scheduled carriers, excluding China and former Soviet territories*

Source: International Civil Aviation Organization

TOP 10

INTERNATIONAL FLIGHT ROUTES WITH THE MOST AIR TRAFFIC

	City A	City B	Passengers per route A to B	B to A	Total passengers
1	Hong Kong	Taipei	2,055,000	2,045,000	4,100,000
2	London	Paris	1,711,000	1,842,000	3,553,000
3	London	New York	1,322,000	1,311,000	2,633,000
4	Dublin	London	1,268,000	1,269,000	2,537,000
5	Kuala Lumpur	Singapore	1,196,000	1,119,000	2,315,000
6	Honolulu	Tokyo	1,157,000	1,137,000	2,294,000
7	Amsterdam	London	1,107,000	1,101,000	2,208,000
8	Seoul	Tokyo	1,089,000	1,081,000	2,170,000
9	Bangkok	Hong Kong	993,000	910,000	1,903,000
10	Hong Kong	Tokyo	940,000	937,000	1,877,000

Source: International Civil Aviation Authority

TOP 10

AIRLINE-USING COUNTRIES IN THE WORLD

	Country	Passenger km p.a.*
1	USA	853,389,000,000
2	UK	152,453,000,000
3	Japan	129,981,000,000
4	Australia	67,145,000,000
5	France	66,932,000,000
6	China	64,204,000,000
7	Germany	62,158,000,000
8	Russia	61,035,000,000
9	Canada	49,288,000,000
10	Netherlands	48,474,000,000

* Total distance travelled multiplied by number of passengers carried
Source: International Civil Aviation Authority

TOP 10

AIRLINES IN THE WORLD

	Airline/country	Aircraft in service	Passenger-km flown per annum*
1	United Airlines, USA	579	179,466,200,000
2	American Airlines, USA	649	165,194,200,000
3	Delta Airlines, USA	539	136,939,600,000
4	Northwest Airlines, USA	385	100,566,800,000
5	British Airways, UK	212	90,944,100,000
6	JAL, Japan	121	69,775,100,000
7	Lufthansa, Germany	269	61,600,000,000
8	USAir, USA	487	60,529,600,000
9	Continental Airlines, USA	307	57,140,000,000
10	Air France, France	137	49,519,700,000

* Total distance travelled by aircraft of these airlines multiplied by number of passengers carried

Source: International Civil Aviation Organization

TOP 10

BUSIEST INTERNATIONAL AIRPORTS IN THE WORLD

	Airport/location	International passengers per annum*
1	London Heathrow, London, UK	44,262,000
2	Frankfurt, Frankfurt, Germany	27,546,000
3	Charles de Gaulle, Paris, France	25,690,000
4	Hong Kong Int., Hong Kong, China	25,248,000
5	Schiphol, Amsterdam, Netherlands	22,943,000
6	New Tokyo International (Narita), Tokyo, Japan	20,681,000
7	Singapore International, Singapore	20,203,000
8	London Gatwick, Gatwick, UK	19,417,000
9	John F. Kennedy Int., New York, USA	15,898,000
10	Bangkok, Bangkok, Thailand	13,747,000

Other than New York's JFK, only five airports in the US handle more than 5,000,000 international passengers a year, notably Miami (13,071,000), Los Angeles (12,679,000), Chicago O'Hare (6,174,000), Honolulu (5,504,000), and San Francisco (5,238,000).

* International and domestic flights

Source: International Civil Aviation Authority

CHICAGO O'HARE AIRPORT

TOURISM

COUNTRIES EARNING THE MOST FROM TOURISM

	Country	Percentage world total	Total ($) receipts (1997)
1	USA	15.1	75,056,000,000
2	Italy	6.8	30,000,000,000
3	France	6.3	27,947,000,000
4	Spain	6.1	27,190,000,000
5	UK	4.6	20,569,000,000
6	Germany	3.7	16,418,000,000
7	Austria	2.8	12,393,000,000
8	China	2.4	12,074,000,000
9	Australia	2.1	9,324,000,000
10	Hong Kong	2.1	9,242,000,000

TOURIST COUNTRIES

	Country	Percentage world total	Visits (1997)*
1	France	10.9	66,800,000
2	USA	8.0	49,038,000
3	Spain	7.1	43,403,000
4	Italy	5.6	34,087,000
5	UK	4.2	25,960,000
6	China	3.9	23,770,000
7	Poland	3.2	19,514,000
8	Mexico	3.2	19,351,000
9	Canada	2.9	17,610,000
10	Czech Republic	2.8	17,400,000

* *International tourist arrivals, excluding one-day visitors*

Source: World Tourism Organization

STEAM RAILWAYS IN THE UK

	Railway/location	Visits (1997)
1	North Yorkshire Moors Railway	268,000
2	Severn Valley Railway, Shropshire	197,000
3	Ffestiniog Railway, Porthmadog	194,168
4	Bluebell Railway, East Sussex	175,000
5	Lakeside and Haverthwaite Railway, Cumbria	170,000
6	Snowdon Mountain Railway, Llanberis	147,981
7	West Somerset Railway, Minehead	146,883
8	Romney, Hythe, and Dymchurch Railway	136,467
9	Ravenglass and Eskdale Railway, Cumbria	135,090
10	Mid Hants Railway, New Arlesford	133,437

Source: Sightseeing Research

THE LEANING TOWER OF PISA

LEISURE PARKS AND PIERS IN THE UK

	Leisure park/ pier/location	Visits (1997)
1	Blackpool Pleasure Beach	7,800,000*
2	Palace Pier, Brighton, East Sussex	3,500,000*
3	Alton Towers, Staffordshire	2,701,945
4	Eastbourne Pier	2,300,000*
5	Pleasureland, Southport	2,100,000*
6	Chessington World of Adventures	1,750,000
7	Pleasure Beach, Great Yarmouth	1,400,000*#
8	Frontierland, Morecambe, Lancashire	1,300,000*#
9	Legoland, Windsor	1,297,818
10	Blackpool Tower	1,200,000

* *Estimated*

Free admission

Source: Sightseeing Research

WILDLIFE ATTRACTIONS IN THE UK

	Attraction/location	Visits (1997)
1	London Zoo	1,097,637
2	Chester Zoo	829,800
3	Edinburgh Zoo	548,000
4	Knowlsey Safari Park, Prescot	500,000
5	Whipsnade Wild Animal Park, Dunstable	469,946
6	Twycross Zoo, Atherstone	410,241
7	Longleat Safari Park, Wiltshire	390,000
8	Bristol Zoo	387,092
9	Colchester Zoo	354,985
10	Marwell Zoo, Hampshire	348,738

Source: Sightseeing Research

While attractions such as parks and gardens have seen a recent rise in attendances, most of Britain's major wildlife attractions have suffered a decline during the 1990s.

TOP 10
OLDEST AMUSEMENT PARKS IN THE UK

	Park/location	Year founded
1	Blackgang Chine Cliff Top Theme Park, Ventnor, Isle of Wight	1842
2	Grand Pier, Teignmouth	1865
3	Blackpool Central Pier, Blackpool	1868
4	Clacton Pier, Clacton	1871
5	Skegness Pier, Skegness	1881
6	New Walton Pier, Walton-on-Naze	1895
7	Blackpool Pleasure Beach, Blackpool	1896
8	Mumbles Pier, Mumbles	1898
9	Brighton Palace Pier, Brighton	1901
10	Britannia Pier, Great Yarmouth	1902

TOP 10
GARDENS IN THE UK

	Garden/location	Visits (1997)
1	Hampton Court Gardens, Surrey	1,200,000 *#
2	Kew Gardens, London	937,017
3	Royal Botanical Gardens, Edinburgh	899,316 #
4	Wisley Gardens, Surrey	706,619
5	Botanic Gardens, Belfast	650,000 *#
6	Tropical World, Roundhay Park, Leeds	552,252
7	Botanic Gardens, Glasgow	400,000 *#
8	Wakehurst Place, West Sussex	305,935 *#
9=	Pavilion Gardens, Buxton	300,000
=	Sir Thomas and Lady Dixon Park, Belfast	300,000 *#

Estimated   *# Free admission*

Source: Sightseeing Research

TOP 10
HISTORIC HOUSES AND MONUMENTS IN THE UK

	Property/location	Visits (1997)
1	Tower of London	2,615,170
2	Edinburgh Castle	1,238,140
3	Windsor Castle, Berkshire	1,129,629
4	Roman Baths and Pump Room, Bath	933,489
5	Warwick Castle	789,000
6	Stonehenge, Wiltshire	772,963
7	Hampton Court Palace, Surrey	643,226
8	Leeds Castle, Kent	584,670
9	Chatsworth House, Derbyshire	489,672
10	Blenheim Palace, Oxfordshire	483,489

Source: Sightseeing Research

TOP 10
TOURIST-SPENDING COUNTRIES

	Tourist country of origin	Percentage world total	Total expenditure ($) (1996)
1	Germany	13.4	50,815,000,000
2	USA	12.9	48,739,000,000
3	Japan	9.8	37,040,000,000
4	UK	6.7	24,445,000,000
5	France	4.7	17,746,000,000
6	Italy	4.1	15,516,000,000
7	Austria	3.1	11,811,000,000
8	Netherlands	3.0	11,370,000,000
9	Canada	2.9	11,090,000,000
10	Russia	2.8	10,723,000,000

In 1996 (the latest year for which comparative statistics are available), the world spent $379,129,000,000 on tourism, with the Top 10 countries (the only ones in the world spending more than $10 billion each) accounting for 63.4 per cent of the total expenditure.

Source: World Tourism Organization

TOP 10
VISITOR CENTRES IN THE UK

	Attraction/location	Visits (1997)
1	Cadbury World, Bournville	548,689
2	Old Blacksmith's Shop, Gretna Green	500,000 *
3	Chester Visitor Centre	380,000 *#
4	Giant's Causeway Visitor Centre, Bushmills	378,481 *#
5	Royal Burgh of Stirling Visitor Centre	319,550 #
6	Gatwick Skyview	263,200 *
7	Birmingham International Airport Visitor Centre	258,309
8	Cardiff Bay Visitor Centre	204,246 #
9	Denbies Wine Estate, Dorking	200,000
10	Shakespeare's Globe Exhibition, London	188,000 #

Estimated

 # Free admission

Source: Sightseeing Research

SPORTS & GAMES

TOP 10

MOST SUCCESSFUL COACHES IN AN NFL CAREER

	Coach	Games won
1	Don Shula	347
2	George Halas	324
3	Tom Landry	270
4	Curly Lambeau	229
5	Chuck Noll	209
6	Chuck Knox	193
7	Paul Brown	170
8	Bud Grant	168
9	Dan Reeves*	156
10	Marv Levy*#	154

* *Still active 1997–98 season*

\# *Announced retirement at end of 1997–98 season*

Source: National Football League

TOP 10

PLAYERS WITH THE MOST CAREER TOUCHDOWNS

	Player	Touchdowns
1	Jerry Rice*	166
2	Marcus Allen*	145
3	Jim Brown	126
4	Walter Payton	125
5	Emmitt Smith*	119
6	John Riggins	116
7	Lenny Moore	113
8	Don Hutson	105
9	Steve Largent	101
10	Franco Harris	100

* *Still active 1997–98 season*

Source: National Football League

TOP 10

MOST SUCCESSFUL TEAMS

	Team	Super Bowl games wins	losses	Pts*
1	Dallas Cowboys	5	3	13
2	San Francisco 49ers	5	0	10
3	Pittsburgh Steelers	4	1	10
4	Washington Redskins	3	2	8
5=	Green Bay Packers	3	1	7
=	Oakland/ Los Angeles Raiders	3	1	7
7	Miami Dolphins	2	3	7
8	Denver Broncos	1	4	6
9=	New York Giants	2	0	4
=	Buffalo Bills	0	4	4
=	Minnesota Vikings	0	4	4

* *Based on two points for a Super Bowl win and one for a loss; wins take precedence over losses in determining ranking*

Source: National Football League

TOP 10

LARGEST NFL STADIUMS

	Stadium/home team	Capacity
1	Pontiac Silverdrome, Detroit Lions	80,368
2	Rich Stadium, Buffalo Bills	80,091
3	Arrowhead Stadium, Kansas City Chiefs	79,101
4	Jack Cooke Stadium, Washington Redskins	78,600
5	Giants Stadium, New York Giants*	78,148
6	Mile High Stadium, Denver Broncos	76,078
7	Pro Player Stadium, Miami Dolphins	74,916
8	Houlihan's Stadium, Tampa Bay Buccaneers	74,301
9	Sun Devil Stadium, Arizona Cardinals	73,243
10	Alltell Stadium, Jacksonville Jaguars	73,000

* Seating reduced to 77,716 for New York Jets games

Source: National Football League

TOP 10

PLAYERS WITH THE MOST CAREER POINTS

	Player	Points
1	George Blanda	2,002
2	Nick Lowery	1,711
3	Jan Stenerud	1,699
4	Gary Anderson	1,681
5	Morten Andersen	1,641
6	Norm Johnson	1,558
7	Eddie Murray	1,532
8	Pat Leahy	1,470
9	Jim Turner	1,439
10	Matt Bahr	1,422

Source: National Football League

TOP 10 PLAYERS WITH THE MOST PASSING YARDS IN AN NFL CAREER
(Passing yards)
❶ Dan Marino (55,416) ❷ John Elway (48,669) ❸ Warren Moon (47,465) ❹ Fran Tarkenton (47,003) ❺ Dan Fouts (43,040) ❻ Joe Montana (40,551) ❼ Johnny Unitas (40,239) ❽ Dave Krieg (37,946) ❾ Boomer Esiason (37,920) ❿ Jim Kelly (35,467)
Source: National Football League

TOP 10

RUSHERS IN AN NFL CAREER

	Player	Total yards gained rushing
1	Walter Payton	16,726
2	Barry Sanders*	13,778
3	Eric Dickerson	13,259
4	Tony Dorsett	12,739
5	Marcus Allen*	12,243
6	Jim Brown	12,312
7	Franco Harris	12,120
8	Thurman Thomas*	11,405
9	John Riggins	11,352
10	O. J. Simpson	11,236

* Still active at end of 1997–98 season

Source: National Football League

DAN MARINO

TOP 10

POINT-SCORERS IN AN NFL SEASON

	Player	Team	Year	Points
1	Paul Hornung	Green Bay Packers	1960	176
2	Mark Moseley	Washington Redskins	1983	161
3	Gino Cappelletti	Boston Patriots	1964	155*
4	Emitt Smith	Dallas Cowboys	1995	150
5	Chip Lohmiller	Washington Redskins	1991	149
6	Gino Cappelletti	Boston Patriots	1961	147
7	Paul Hornung	Green Bay Packers	1961	146
8 =	Jim Turner	New York Jets	1968	145
=	John Kasay	Carolina Panthers	1996	145
10=	John Riggins	Washington Redskins	1983	144
=	Kevin Butler#	Chicago Bears	1985	144

* Including a two-point conversion   # The only rookie in this Top 10

ATHLETICS

T O P 1 0

HIGHEST POLE VAULTS

	Athlete/country	Year	Height m
1	Sergey Bubka, (Ukraine)	1994	6.14
2	Okkert Brits (SA)	1995	6.03
3	Igor Trandenkov (Russia)	1996	6.01
4	Rodion Gataullin (USSR)	1989	6.00
5	Lawrence Johnson (USA)	1996	5.98
6	Scott Huffman (USA)	1994	5.97
7	Joe Dial (USA)	1987	5.96
8=	Andrei Tiwontschik (Germany)	1996	5.95
=	Maxim Tarasov (Russia)	1997	5.95
10	Jean Galfione (France)	1994	5.94

If indoor world records are included, then
Sergey Bubka of the Ukraine and Rodion
Gataullin of the USSR would each make the
Top 10 twice with indoor heights of 6.15 m
(1993) and 6.02 m (1989) respectively.

CARL LEWIS
*A noted long-jumper
and one-time 100-metre
record-holder*

T O P 1 0

FASTEST WINNING TIMES FOR THE LONDON MARATHON

MEN

	Competitor/ country/year	Time hr:min:sec
1	Antonio Pinto (Portugal), 1997	2:07:55
2	Abel Anton (Spain), 1998	2:07:56
3	Steve Jones (GB), 1985	2:08:16
4	Dionicio Ceron (Mexico), 1995	2:08:30
5	Dionicio Ceron (Mexico), 1994	2:08:53
6	Douglas Wakiihuri (Kenya), 1989	2:09:03
7	Yakov Tolstikov (USSR), 1991	2:09:17
8	Hugh Jones (GB), 1982	2:09:24
9	Mike Gratton (GB), 1983	2:09:43
10	Hiromi Taniguchi (Japan), 1987	2:09:50

WOMEN

	Competitor/ country/year	Time hr:min:sec
1	Ingrid Kristiansen (Norway), 1985	2:21:06
2	Ingrid Kristiansen (Norway), 1987	2:22:48
3	Ingrid Kristiansen (Norway), 1984	2:24:26
4	Grete Waitz (Norway), 1986	2:24:54
5	Grete Waitz (Norway), 1983	2:25:29
6	Ingrid Kristiansen (Norway), 1988	2:25:41
7	Véronique Marot (GB), 1989	2:25:56
8	Rosa Mota (Portugal), 1991	2:26:14
9	Catherina McKiernan (Ireland), 1998	2:26:25
10	Wanda Panfil (Poland), 1990	2:26:31

T O P 1 0

LONGEST LONG JUMPS

	Athlete/country	Year	Dist. (m)
1	Mike Powell (USA)	1991	8.95
2	Bob Beamon (USA)	1968	8.90
3	Carl Lewis (USA)	1991	8.87
4	Robert Emmiyan (USSR)	1987	8.86
5=	Larry Myricks (US)	1988	8.74
=	Eric Walder (US)	1994	8.74

	Athlete /country	Year	Dist. (m)
7	Ivan Pedrosa (Cuba)	1995	8.71
8	K. Streete-Thompson (US)	1994	8.63
9	James Beckford (Jamaica)	1997	8.62
10	Lutz Dombrowski (East Germany)	1990	8.54

OLYMPIC RINGS
A symbol of athletic achievement for more than 100 years.

HIGHEST HIGH JUMPS

	Athlete/country/year	Height (m)
1	Javier Sotomayor (Cuba), 1993	2.45
2	Patrik Sjöberg (Sweden), 1987	2.42
3	Igor Paklin (USSR), 1985	2.41
4=	Rudolf Povarnitsyn (USSR), 1985	2.40
=	Sorin Matei (Romania), 1990	2.40
=	Charles Austin (USA), 1991	2.40
7=	Zhu Jianhua (China), 1984	2.39
=	Hollis Conway (USA), 1989	2.39
9=	Gennadi Avdeyenko (USSR), 1987	2.38
=	Sergey Malchenko (USSR), 1988	2.38
=	Dragutin Topic (Yugoslavia), 1993	2.38
=	Troy Kemp (Bahamas), 1995	2.38
=	Artur Partyka (Poland), 1996	2.38

If indoor world records are included, the following would also make the Top 10:

Carlo Thränhardt (West Germany), 1988	*2.42*
Hollis Conway (USA), 1991	*2.40*
Dietmar Mögenburg (West Germany), 1985	*2.39*
Ralph Sonn (Germany), 1991	*2.39*

FASTEST MEN ON EARTH*

	Athlete/country	Year	Time sec
1	Donovan Bailey (Canada)	1996	9.84
2	Leroy Burrell (USA)	1994	9.85
3=	Carl Lewis (USA)	1991	9.86
=	Frank Fredericks (Namibia)	1996	9.86
5	Linford Christie (GB)	1993	9.87
6	Ato Boldon (Trinidad)	1997	9.89
7	Maurice Green (USA)	1997	9.90
8	Dennis Mitchell (USA)	1996	9.91
9=	Andre Cason (UA)	1993	9.92
=	Tim Montgomery (USA)	1997	9.92
=	Jon Drummond (USA)	1997	9.92

* *Based on fastest time for the 100 metres*

FASTEST WOMEN ON EARTH*

	Athlete/country	Year	Time sec
1	Florence Griffith-Joyner (USA)	1988	10.61
2	Merlene Ottey (Jamaica)	1996	10.74
3	Evelyn Ashford (USA)	1984	10.76
4	Irina Privalova (Russia)	1994	10.77
5	Dawn Sowell (USA)	1989	10.78
6	Marlies Göhr (East Germany)	1983	10.81
7=	Gail Devers (USA)	1992	10.82
=	Gwen Torrence (USA)	1994	10.82
9=	Marita Koch (East Germany)	1983	10.83
=	Juliet Cuthbert (Jamaica)	1992	10.83

* *Based on fastest time for the 100 metres*

LONGEST-STANDING OUTDOOR WORLD RECORDS

	Event*/holder	Time/Dist. hr:min:sec	Date
1	4x1500 Metres Relay (M), W. Germany	0:14:38	17 Aug 1977
2	4x200 Metres Relay (W), E. Germany	0:01:28	9 Aug 1980
3=	25,000 Metres (M), Toshihiko Seko (Japan)	1:13:55	22 Mar 1981
=	30,000 Metres (M), Toshihiko Seko (Japan)	1:29:18	22 Mar 1981
5	1-Hour Race (W), Silvana Cruciata (Italy)	18,084m	4 May 1981
6	800 Metres (M), Sebastian Coe (GB)	0:01:41	10 Jun 1981
7	1,000 Metres (M), Sebastian Coe (GB)	0:02:12	11 Jul 1981
8	4x800 Metres Relay (M), Great Britain	0:07:03	30 Aug 1982
9	800 Metres (W), Jarmila Kratochvilová (Czechoslovakia)	0:01:53	26 Jul 1983
10	4x800 Metres Relay (W), Soviet Union	0:07:50	5 Aug 1984

* *(M) Men (W) Women*

FIRST ATHLETES TO RUN A MILE IN UNDER FOUR MINUTES

	Athlete/country	Location	Time min:sec	Date
1	Roger Bannister (GB)	Oxford	3:59.4	6 May 1954
2	John Landy (Aus)	Turku, Finland	3:57.9	21 Jun 1954
3	Laszlo Tabori (Hun)	London	3:59.0	28 May 1955
4=	Chris Chataway (GB)	London	3:59.8	28 May 1955
=	Brian Hewson (GB)	London	3:59.8	28 May 1955
6	Jim Bailey (Aus)	Los Angeles	3:58.6	5 May 1956
7	Gunnar Nielsen (Den)	Compton, USA	3:59.1	1 Jun 1956
8	Ron Delany (Ire)	Compton, USA	3:59.4	1 Jun 1956
9	Derek Ibbotson (GB)	London	3:59.4	6 Aug 1956
10	István Rózsavölgyi (Hun)	Budapest	3:59.0	26 Aug 1956

BASKETBALL

T O P 1 0

FREE THROW PERCENTAGES

	Player	Attempts	Made	Per cent
1	Mark Price	2,362	2,135	90.4
2	Rick Barry	4,243	3,818	90.0
3	Calvin Murphy	3,864	3,445	89.2
4	Scott Skiles	1,741	1,548	88.9
5	Larry Bird	4,471	3,960	88.6
6	Bill Sharman	3,559	3,143	88.3
7	Reggie Miller	5,037	4,416	87.7
8	Ricky Pierce	3,871	3,389	87.5
9	Kiki Vandeweghe	3,997	3,484	87.2
10	Jeff Malone	3,383	2,947	87.1

Source: NBA

SHAQUILLE O'NEAL

T O P 1 0

PLAYERS WITH THE MOST CAREER ASSISTS

	Player	Assists
1	John Stockton*	12,713
2	Magic Johnson	10,141
3	Oscar Robertson	9,887
4	Isiah Thomas	9,061
5	Mark Jackson*	7,538
6	Maurice Cheeks	7,392
7	Lenny Wilkens	7,211
8	Bob Cousy	6,995
9	Guy Rodgers	6,917
10	Nate Archibald	6,476

* *Still active at end of 1997–98 season*

Source: NBA

T O P 1 0

POINT-SCORERS IN AN NBA CAREER*

	Player	Total points
1	Kareem Abdul-Jabbar	38,387
2	Wilt Chamberlain	31,419
3	Michael Jordan#	29,277
4	Karl Malone#	27,782
5	Moses Malone	27,409
6	Elvin Hayes	27,313
7	Oscar Robertson	26,710
8	Dominique Wilkins	26,534
9	John Havlicek	26,395
10	Alex English	25,613

* *Regular season games only*

Still active at end of 1998 season

If points from the ABA were also considered, then Abdul Jabbar would still be No. 1, with the same total. The greatest point-scorer in NBA history, his career spanned 20 seasons before he retired at the end of the 1989 season.

Source: NBA

T O P 1 0

HIGHEST-EARNING PLAYERS IN THE NBA, 1996–97

	Player/team	Earnings ($)*
1	Michael Jordan, Chicago Bulls	30,140,000
2	Horace Grant, Orlando Magic	14,857,000
3	Reggie Miller, Indiana Pacers	11,250,000
4	Shaquille O'Neal, Los Angeles Lakers	10,714,000
5	Gary Payton, Seattle Supersonics	10,212,000
6	David Robinson, San Antonio Spurs	9,952,000
7	Juwan Howard, Washington Bullets	9,750,000
8	Hakeem Olajuwon, Houston Rockets	9,655,000
9	Alonzo Mourning, Miami Heat	9,380,000
10	Dennis Rodman, Chicago Bulls	9,000,000

* *Salary only*

T O P 1 0

POINTS SCORED IN THE WNBA

	Game	Score
1	Utah Starzz vs. Los Angeles Sparks	102–89
2	Cleveland Rockers vs. Utah Starzz	95–68
3	Sacramento Monarchs vs. Utah Starzz	93–78
4	Los Angeles Sparks vs. Sacramento Monarchs	93–73
5	Los Angeles Sparks vs. Utah Starzz	91–69
6	Cleveland Rockers vs. Los Angeles Sparks	89–85
7	Houston Comets vs. Sacramento Monarchs	89–61
8	Los Angeles Sparks vs. Sacramento Monarchs	88–77
9	Los Angeles Sparks vs. Cleveland Rockers	87–84
10	Charlotte Sting vs. New York Liberty	07–69

Source: STATS Inc.

TOP 10

BIGGEST ARENAS IN THE NBA

	Arena/location	Home team	Capacity
1	Georgia Dome, Atlanta, Georgia	Atlanta Hawks	34,821
2	The Alamodome, San Antonio, Texas	San Antonio Spurs	34,215
3	Charlotte Coliseum, Charlotte, North Carolina	Charlotte Hornets	24,042
4	United Center, Chicago, Illinois	Chicago Bulls	21,711
5	The Rose Garden, Portland, Oregon	Portland Trailblazers	21,538
6	The Palace of Auburn Hills, Auburn Hills, Michigan	Detroit Pistons	21,454
7	Gund Arena, Cleveland, Ohio	Cleveland Cavaliers	20,562
8	CoreStates Center, Philadelphia, Pennsylvania	Philadelphia 76ers	20,444
9	SkyDome, Toronto	Toronto Raptors	20,125
10	Byrne Meadowlands Arena, East Rutherford, New Jersey	New Jersey Nets	20,049

Source: The Sporting News Official NBA Guide

TOP 10

MOST SUCCESSFUL NBA COACHES

	Coach	Games won*		Coach	Games won*
1	Lenny Wilkens#	1,120	6	Jack Ramsay	864
2	Bill Fitch#	944	7	Don Nelson	851
3	Red Auerbach	938	8	Cotton Fitzsimmons	832
4	Dick Motta	936	9	Gene Shue	784
5	Pat Riley#	909	10	John MacLeod	707

* Regular season games only

 # Still active 1997–98 season

Lenny Wilkens reached his 1,000th win on 1 March 1996, when the Atlanta Hawks beat the Cleveland Cavaliers 74–68 at The Omni. Pat Riley, who as coach of the LA Lakers, the New York Knicks, and the Miami Heat between 1981 and 1998, acquired the best percentage record with 909 wins from 1,295 games, representing a 0.702 per cent success rate.

Source: NBA

TOP 10

MOST SUCCESSFUL DIVISION 1 NCAA TEAMS

	College	Division 1 wins		College	Division 1 wins
1	Kentucky	1,720	6	Temple	1,496
2	North Carolina	1,709	7	Syracuse	1,477
3	Kansas	1,665	8=	Oregon State	1,454
4	St. John's	1,554	=	Pennsylvania	1,454
5	Duke	1,548	10	Indiana	1,429

Source: NCAA/STATS Inc.

TOP 10

PLAYERS TO HAVE PLAYED MOST GAMES IN THE NBA AND ABA

	Player	Games played
1	Robert Parish	1,611
2	Kareem Abdul-Jabbar	1,560
3	Moses Malone	1,455
4	Artis Gilmore	1,329
5	Buck Williams*	1,307
6	Elvin Hayes	1,303
7	Caldwell Jones	1,299
8	John Havlicek	1,270
9	Paul Silas	1,254
10	Julius Erving	1,243

* Still active at end of 1997–98 season

The ABA (American Basketball Association) was established as a rival to the NBA (National Basketball Association) in 1968 and survived until 1976. Because many of the sport's top players "defected", their figures are still included in this list.

Source: NBA

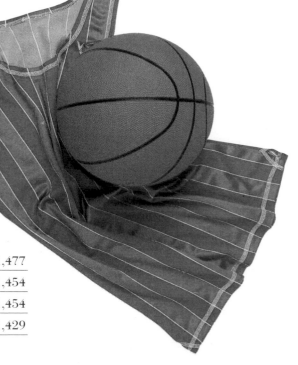

CRICKET

RUN-MAKERS OF ALL TIME IN TEST CRICKET

	Player/country	Years	Tests	Runs
1	Allan Border (Australia)	1978–92	156	11,174
2	Sunil Gavaskar (India)	1971–87	125	10,122
3	Graham Gooch (England)	1975–95	118	8,900
4	Javed Miandad (Pakistan)	1976–94	124	8,832
5	Viv Richards (West Indies)	1974–91	121	8,540
6	David Gower (England)	1978–92	117	8,231
7	Geoff Boycott (England)	1964–82	108	8,114
8	Gary Sobers (West Indies)	1954–74	93	8,032
9	Colin Cowdrey (England)	1954–75	114	7,624
10	Gordon Greenidge (West Indies)	1974–91	108	7,558

WICKET-TAKERS OF ALL TIME IN TEST CRICKET

	Player/country	Years	Tests	Wickets
1	Kapil Dev (India)	1978–94	131	434
2	Richard Hadlee (New Zealand)	1973–90	86	431
3	Ian Botham (England)	1977–92	102	383
4	Malcolm Marshall (West Indies)	1978–91	81	376
5	Courtney Walsh (West Indies)	1984–98	100	367
6	Imran Khan (Pakistan)	1971–92	88	362
7	Dennis Lillee (Australia)	1971–84	70	355
8	Wasim Akram (Pakistan)	1985–98	77	334
9	Curtley Ambrose (West Indies)	1988–98	78	330
10	Bob Willis (England)	1971–84	90	325

HIGHEST INDIVIDUAL INNINGS IN A TEST DEBUT

	Batsman	Match/venue	Year	Score
1	Reginald Foster	England vs. Australia (Sydney)	1902–04	287
2	Lawrence Rowe	West Indies vs. New Zealand (Kingston)	1971–72	214
3	Brendon Kuruppu	Sri Lanka vs. New Zealand (Colombo)	1986–87	201*
4	George Headley	West Indies vs. England (Bridgetown)	1929–30	176
5	Khalid Ibadulla	Pakistan vs. Australia (Karachi)	1964–65	166
6	Charles Bannerman	Australia vs. England (Melbourne)	1976–77	165*
7	Archie Jackson	Australia vs. England (Adelaide)	1928–29	164
8=	Javed Miandas	Pakistan vs. New Zealand (Lahore)	1976–77	163
=	Andrew Hudson	South Africa vs. West Indies (Bridgetown)	1991–92	163
10	Kepler Wessels	Australia vs. England (Brisbane)	1982–83	162

* Not out

TEST RECORD-BREAKER

In the Test Match between England and South Africa at Newlands, Cape Town, in April 1899, South African cricketer Jimmy Sinclair (1876–1913) scored 106, becoming the first-ever Test batsman to make more than half his team's total. He also became the first cricketer to score a century and take six wickets in the same Test innings, and was the first South African player to score both 50 runs and a century in a Test. Sinclair had already made a name for himself as a powerful batsman, in 1897 setting a South African record of 301 not out in a local match at Johannesburg. Playing against Australia at Cape Town in the 1902–03 Test, he scored a century in 80 minutes, the second fastest ever at that time.

PARTNERSHIPS IN TEST CRICKET

	Player/match/year	Runs
1	Sanath Jayasuriya/Roshan Mahanama, Sri Lanka vs. India, 1997–98	567
2=	Andrew Jones/Martin Crowe, New Zealand vs. Sri Lanka, 1990–91	467
=	Bill Ponsford/Don Bradman, Australia vs. England, 1934	467
4	Mudasser Nazar/Javed Miandad, Pakistan vs. India, 1982–83	451
5	Conrad Hunte/Gary Sobers, West Indies vs. Pakistan, 1957–58	446
6	Vinoo Mankad/Pankaj Roy, India vs. New Zealand, 1955–56	413
7	Peter May/Colin Cowdrey, England vs. West Indies, 1957	411
8	Sidney Barnes/Don Bradman, Australia vs. England, 1946–47	405
9	Gary Sobers/Frank Worrell, West Indies vs. England, 1959–60	399
10	Qasim Omar/Javed Miandad, Pakistan vs. Sri Lanka, 1985–86	397

Gundappa Viswanath, Yashpal Sharma, and Dilip Vengsarkar put on 415 runs for India's third wicket against England at Madras in 1981–82.

TOP 10

HIGHEST TEAM TOTALS IN TEST CRICKET

	Match (winners first)	Venue	Year	Score
1	Sri Lanka vs. India	Colombo	1997–98	952–6 dec
2	England vs. Australia	The Oval	1938	903–7 dec
3	England vs. West Indies	Kingston	1929–30	849
4	West Indies vs. Pakistan	Kingston	1957–58	790–3 dec
5	Australia vs. West Indies	Kingston	1954–55	758–8 dec
6	Australia vs. England	Lord's	1930	729–6 dec
7	Pakistan vs. England	The Oval	1987	708
8	Australia vs. England	The Oval	1934	701
9	Pakistan vs. India	Lahore	1989–90	699–5 dec
10	Australia vs. England	The Oval	1930	695

England held the record for the highest test cricket total for nearly 60 years before Sri Lanka achieved the No. 1 position last year. England went into the fourth and final Test against the Australians at the Oval in 1938 needing a win to square the series. They achieved this by a massive margin of an innings and 579 runs, still their biggest winning margin in Test Cricket. Australian bowler "Chuck" Fleetwood-Smith returned figures of 87 overs, 11 maidens, 1 wicket for 298 runs, the greatest number of runs conceded by a bowler in Test Cricket. After being padded up for a day and a half while Len Hutton piled on the runs, England No. 5 Eddie Paynter was dismissed for a duck.

TOP 10

BATSMEN WITH MOST TEST CENTURIES

	Batsman/country	Centuries
1	Sunil Gavaskar (India)	34
2	Don Bradman (Australia)	29
3	Allan Border (Australia)	27
4	Gary Sobers (West Indies)	26
5 =	Greg Chappell (Australia)	24
=	Viv Richards (West Indies)	24
7	Javed Miandad (Pakistan)	23
8 =	Walter Hammond (England)	22
=	Geoff Boycott (England)	22
=	Colin Cowdrey (England)	22

THE 10

LOWEST COMPLETED INNINGS IN TEST CRICKET

	Match (losers first)	Venue	Year	Total
1	New Zealand vs. England	Auckland	1954–55	26
2 =	South Africa vs. England	Port Elizabeth	1895–96	30
–	South Africa vs. England	Birmingham	1924	30
4	South Africa vs. England	Cape Town	1898–99	35
5 =	Australia vs. England	Birmingham	1902	36
=	South Africa vs. Australia	Melbourne	1931–32	36
7 =	Australia vs. England	Sydney	1887–88	42
=	New Zealand vs. Australia	Wellington	1945–46	42
=	India* vs. England	Lord's	1974	42
10	South Africa vs. England	Cape Town	1888–89	43

India batted one player short

THE 10

FIRST TEST CENTURIES SCORED BY ENGLISH BATSMEN

	Player/venue	Score	Date
1	W.G. Grace (The Oval)	152	6–8 Sep 1880
2	George Ulyett (Melbourne)	149	10–14 Mar 1882
3	Allan Steel (Sydney)	135*	17–21 Feb 1883
4	Allan Steel (Lord's)	148	21–23 Jul 1884
5	Walter Read (The Oval)	117	11–13 Aug 1884
6	William Barnes (Adelaide)	134	12–16 Dec 1884
7	John Briggs (Melbourne)	121	1–5 Jan 1885
8	Arthur Shrewsbury (Melbourne)	105*	21–25 Mar 1885
9	Arthur Shrewsbury (Lord's)	164	19–21 Jul 1886
10	W.G. Grace (The Oval)	170	12–14 Aug 1886

Not out

All 10 centuries were scored against Australia. W.G. Grace's two centuries were the only ones he scored in Test Cricket. Grace's total of 170 runs at the Oval in 1886 was the highest in a Test Match in England for 35 years.

TOP 10

HIGHEST INDIVIDUAL TEST INNINGS

	Player/year/match	Runs
1	Brian Lara, 1993–94, West Indies vs. England	375
2	Gary Sobers, 1957–58, West Indies vs. Pakistan	365*
3	Len Hutton, 1938, England vs. Australia	364
4	Sanath Jayasuriya, 1997–98, Sri Lanka vs. India	340
5	Hanif Mohammad, 1957–58, Pakistan vs. West Indies	337*
6	Walter Hammond, 1932–33, England vs. New Zealand	336
7	Don Bradman, 1930, Australia vs. England	334
8	Graham Gooch, 1990, England vs. India	333
9	Andrew Sandham, 1929–30, England vs. West Indies	325
10	Bobby Simpson, 1964, Australia vs. England	311

Not out

Sanath Jayasuriya is a new entry not only to this list, but also shares No. 1 status in the list of Top 10 Partnerships in Test Cricket, by a 100-run margin over the former record-holders.

GOLF

TIGER WOODS

TOP 10 MONEY WINNERS WORLDWIDE, 1997
(Winnings)

❶ Tiger Woods (US), $2,082,381 ❷ David Duval (US), $1,885,308 ❸ Ernie Els (South Africa), $1,814,029 ❹ Greg Norman (Australia), $1,720,573 ❺ Davis Love III (US), $1,635,953 ❻ Jim Furyk (US), $1,619,460 ❼ Colin Montgomerie (Scotland), $1,609,300 ❽ Justin Leonard (US), $1,587,531 ❾ Scott Hoch (US), $1,418,272 ❿ Jumbo Ozaki (Japan), $1,362,433

T O P   1 0

LOWEST WINNING SCORES IN THE US MASTERS

	Player*	Year	Score
1	Tiger Woods	1997	270
2=	Jack Nicklaus	1965	271
=	Raymond Floyd	1976	271
4=	Ben Hogan	1953	274
5=	Ben Crenshaw	1995	274
6=	Severiano Ballesteros (Spain)	1980	275
=	Fred Couples	1992	275
8=	Arnold Palmer	1964	276
=	Jack Nicklaus	1975	276
=	Tom Watson	1977	276
=	Nick Faldo (UK)	1996	276

All US players unless otherwise stated

T O P   1 0

LOWEST FOUR-ROUND SCORES IN THE BRITISH OPEN

	Player	Country	Year	Venue	Score
1	Greg Norman	Australia	1993	Sandwich	267
2=	Tom Watson	USA	1977	Turnberry	268
=	Nick Price	South Africa	1994	Turnberry	268
4=	Jack Nicklaus	USA	1977	Turnberry	269
=	Nick Faldo	UK	1993	Sandwich	269
=	Jesper Parnevik	Sweden	1994	Turnberry	269
7=	Nick Faldo	UK	1990	St. Andrews	270
=	Bernhard Langer	Germany	1993	Sandwich	270
9=	Tom Watson	USA	1980	Muirfield	271
=	Fuzzy Zoeller	USA	1994	Turnberry	271
=	Tom Lehman	USA	1996	Lytham	271

T O P   1 0

LOWEST WINNING SCORES IN THE US OPEN

	Player*	Year	Venue	Score
1=	Jack Nicklaus	1980	Baltusrol	272
=	Lee Janzen	1993	Baltusrol	272
3	David Graham (Aus)	1981	Merion	273
4=	Jack Nicklaus	1967	Baltusrol	275
=	Lee Trevino	1968	Oak Hill	275
6=	Ben Hogan	1948	Riviera	276
=	Fuzzy Zoeller	1984	Winged Foot	276
=	Ernie Els (SA)	1997	Congressional	276
9=	Jerry Pate	1976	Atlanta	277
=	Scott Simpson	1987	Olympic Club	277

All US players unless otherwise stated

THE GOLF TEE

On 12 December 1899, Dr. George F. Grant registered US Patent No. 638,920. His invention was the golf tee, the little pedestal of wood or plastic that tees the ball up at the commencement of each hole. Grant was a Boston dentist and an avid golfer. Not wishing to get his hands dirty by shaping a mound of earth or sand, as all golfers or their caddies did at that time, he came up with the invention of the tapered wooden tee peg, which had a bowled top to hold the ball in place. Although the majority of golfers now use tees, which today are most commonly made of plastic rather than wood, their use is not compulsory.

100 YEARS AGO

T O P 1 0

PLAYERS WITH THE MOST WINS ON THE US TOUR IN A CAREER

	Player*	Tour wins
1	Sam Snead	81
2	Jack Nicklaus	71
3	Ben Hogan	63
4	Arnold Palmer	60
5	Byron Nelson	52
6	Billy Casper	51
7=	Walter Hagen	40
=	Cary Midlecoff	40
9	Gene Sarazen	38
10	Lloyd Mangrum	36

* All US players

For many years Sam Snead's total of wins was held to be 84 but the PGA Tour amended his figure in 1990 after discrepancies had been found in their previous lists. They deducted 11 wins from his total but added eight others, which should have been included, for a revised total of 81. The highest-placed current member of the regular Tour is Tom Watson, in joint 11th place with 32 wins. The highest placed overseas player is Gary Player (South Africa), with 22 wins. Sam Snead, despite being the most successful golfer on the US Tour, never won the US Open. After more than 25 attempts, his best finish was 2nd on four occasions. The most successful woman on the US Women's Tour is Kathy Whitworth, with 88 Tour wins — and, like Snead, she never won the US Open.

PLAYERS TO WIN THE MOST MAJORS IN A CAREER

	Player*	Open	British Open	US Masters	PGA	Total
1	Jack Nicklaus	3	4	6	5	18
2	Walter Hagen	4	2	0	5	11
3=	Ben Hogan	1	4	2	2	9
=	Gary Player (SA)	3	1	3	2	9
5	Tom Watson	5	1	2	0	8
6=	Harry Vardon (UK)	6	1	0	0	7
=	Gene Sarazen	1	2	1	3	7
=	Bobby Jones	3	4	0	0	7
=	Sam Snead	1	0	3	3	7
=	Arnold Palmer	2	1	4	0	7

* All US players unless otherwise stated

MONEY WINNERS OF ALL TIME*

	Player#	Career winnings ($)
1	Greg Norman (Australia)	11,936,443
2	Tom Kite	10,286,177
3	Fred Couples	8,885,487
4	Nick Price (Zimbabwe)	8,869,231
5	Mark O'Meara	8,656,374
6	Davis Love III	8,509,657
7	Payne Stewart	8,465,062
8	Tom Watson	8,307,277
9	Corey Pavin	8,130,356
10	Scott Hoch	7,930,700

* To 12 January 1998

All US players unless otherwise stated

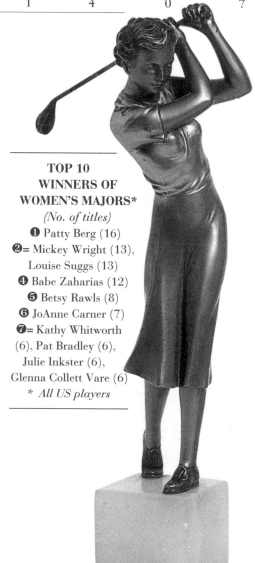

TOP 10 WINNERS OF WOMEN'S MAJORS*
(No. of titles)
❶ Patty Berg (16)
❷= Mickey Wright (13), Louise Suggs (13)
❹ Babe Zaharias (12)
❺ Betsy Rawls (8)
❻ JoAnne Carner (7)
❼= Kathy Whitworth (6), Pat Bradley (6), Julie Inkster (6), Glenna Collett Vare (6)
* All US players

SNAP FACT
● At the golf course at Richmond, Surrey, UK, on 25 May 1957, an actor holed in one from the eighth tee. Later on the same day a solicitor holed in one from the sixth tee. Both golfers were called Edward Chapman – a unique example of two holes in one on one day by two men with one name.

HORSE RACING

TOP 10

JOCKEYS IN THE GRAND NATIONAL

	Jockey*	Years	Wins
1	George Stevens	1856–70	5
2	Tom Oliver	1838–53	4
3=	Mr. Tommy Pickernell	1860–75	3
=	Mr. Tommy Beasley	1880–89	3
=	Arthur Nightingall	1890–1901	3
=	Ernie Piggott	1912–19	3
=	Mr. Jack Anthony	1911–20	3
=	Brian Fletcher	1968–74	3
9=	Mr. Alec Goodman	1852–66	2
=	John Page	1867–72	2
=	Mr. Maunsell Richardson	1873–74	2
=	Mr. Ted Wilson	1884–85	2
=	Percy Woodland	1903–13	2
=	Arthur Thompson	1948–52	2
=	Bryan Marshall	1953–54	2
=	Fred Winter	1957–62	2
=	Richard Dunwoody	1986–94	2

* Amateur riders are traditionally indicated by the prefix "Mr."

TOP 10

FASTEST-WINNING TIMES OF THE GRAND NATIONAL

	Horse	Year	Time min	sec
1	Mr. Frisk	1990	8	47.8
2	Red Rum	1973	9	01.9
3	Royal Athlete	1995	9	04.6
4	Lord Gwyllene	1997	9	05.8
5	Party Politics	1992	9	06.3
6	Grittar	1982	9	12.6
7	Maori Venture	1987	9	19.3
8	Reynoldstown	1935	9	20.0
9	Red Rum	1974	9	20.3
10	Golden Miller	1934	9	20.4

TOP 10

JOCKEYS IN THE ST. LEGER

	Jockey	Years	Wins
1	Bill Scott	1821–46	9
2=	John Jackson	1791–1822	8
=	Lester Piggott	1960–84	8
4=	Ben Smith	1803–24	6
=	Fred Archer	1877–86	6
6=	John Mangle	1780–92	5
=	Tom Challoner	1861–75	5
=	Jack Watts	1883–96	5
=	Gordon Richards	1930–44	5
10=	Bob Johnson	1812–20	4
=	Joe Childs	1918–26	4
=	Charlie Smirke	1934–54	4
=	Joe Mercer	1965–81	4
=	Pat Eddery	1986–97	4

TOP 10

JOCKEYS IN A FLAT RACING SEASON

	Jockey	Year	Wins
1	Gordon Richards	1947	269
2	Gordon Richards	1949	261
3	Gordon Richards	1933	259
4	Fred Archer	1885	246
5	Fred Archer	1884	241
6	Fred Archer	1883	232
7	Gordon Richards	1952	231
8	Fred Archer	1878	229
9	Gordon Richards	1951	227
10	Gordon Richards	1948	224

Richards rode over 200 winners in a season 12 times, while Archer did so on eight occasions. The only other men to reach double centuries are Tommy Loates (1893), Pat Eddery (1990), Michael Roberts (1992), and Frankie Dettori (1995).

TOP 10

JOCKEYS IN THE OAKS

	Jockey	Years	Wins
1	Frank Buckle	1797–1823	9
2=	Frank Butler	1843–52	6
=	Lester Piggott	1957–84	6
4=	Sam Chifney Jr.	1807–25	5
=	John Day	1828–40	5
=	George Fordham	1859–81	5
7=	Sam Chifney Sr.	1782–90	4
=	Dennis Fitzpatrick	1787–1800	4
=	Tom Cannon	1869–84	4
=	Fred Archer	1875–85	4
=	Jack Watts	1883–93	4
=	Joe Childs	1912–21	4
=	Harry Wragg	1938–46	4
=	Willie Carson	1978–90	4

TOP 10

FASTEST-WINNING TIMES OF THE EPSOM DERBY

	Horse	Year	Time min	sec
1	Lammtara	1995	2	32.31
2	Mahmoud	1936	2	33.80
3	Kahyasi	1988	2	33.84
4	Reference Point	1987	2	33.90
5	Hyperion	1933	2	34.00
6=	Windsor Lad	1934	2	34.00
=	Generous	1991	2	34.00
8	Erhabb	1994	2	34.16
9	Golden Fleece	1982	2	34.27
10	Call Boy	1927	2	34.40

Only races at Epsom are considered. Dante won the 1945 wartime substitute race at Newmarket in 2 minutes 26.6 seconds. Electronic timing was first used in 1964. Barely two seconds separate the times of the current record-holder and the 10th ranked horse in the list.

TOP 10

JOCKEYS IN THE 1,000 GUINEAS

	Jockey	Years	Wins
1	George Fordham	1859–83	7
2	Frank Buckle	1818–27	6
3 =	Jem Robinson	1824–44	5
=	John Day	1826–40	5
5 =	Jack Watts	1886–97	4
=	Fred Rickaby jr	1913–17	4
=	Charlie Elliott	1924–44	4
8 =	Bill Arnull	1817–32	3
=	Nat Flatman	1835–57	3
=	Tom Cannon	1866–84	3
=	Charlie Wood	1880–87	3
=	Dick Perryman	1926–41	3
=	Harry Wragg	1934–45	3
=	Rae Johnstone	1935–50	3
=	Gordon Richards	1942–51	3
=	Walter Swinburn	1989–93	3

TOP 10

JOCKEYS IN THE EPSOM DERBY

	Jockey	Years	Wins
1	Lester Piggott	1954–83	9
2 =	Jem Robinson	1817–36	6
=	Steve Donoghue	1915–25	6
4 =	John Arnull	1784–99	5
=	Frank Buckle	1792–1823	5
=	Bill Clift	1793–1819	5
=	Fred Archer	1877–86	5
8 =	Sam Arnull	1780–98	4
=	Tom Goodison	1809–22	4
=	Bill Scott	1832–43	4
=	Jack Watts	1887–96	4
=	Charlie Smirke	1934–58	4
=	Willie Carson	1979–94	4

Lester Piggott has been so dominant in the post-war era that he has had five more Derby winners than the second highest post-war winning jockey, Willie Carson.

TOP 10

JOCKEYS IN THE 2,000 GUINEAS

	Jockey	Years	Wins
1	Jem Robinson	1825–48	9
2	John Osborne	1857–88	6
3 =	Frank Buckle	1810–27	5
=	Charlie Elliott	1923–49	5
=	Lester Piggott	1957–92	5
6 =	John Day	1826–41	4
=	Fred Archer	1874–85	4
=	Tom Cannon	1878–89	4
=	Herbert Jones	1900–09	4
=	Willie Carson	1972–89	4

SNAP FACTS

- Although races were held at Aintree from 1829, the first Grand National, on 26 February 1839, was won by Lottery, ridden by Jem Mason.

- As well as hurdles in the early race, riders had to jump a stone wall and gallop across a ploughed field.

- Manifesto ran in the Grand National eight times, winning in 1897 and 1899.

TOP 10

JOCKEYS OF ALL TIME IN THE UK

	Jockey	Champion Jockey titles	Best season total	Career Flat winners
1	Gordon Richards	26	269	4,870
2	Lester Piggott	11	191	4,493
3	Pat Eddery	11	209	4,000
4	Willie Carson	5	182	3,828
5	Doug Smith	5	173	3,111
6	Joe Mercer	1	164	2,810
7	Fred Archer	13	246	2,748
8	Edward Hide	0	137	2,593
9	George Fordham	14	166	2,587
10	Eph Smith	0	144	2,312

When Pat Eddery rode Silver Patriarch to victory in the St. Leger at Doncaster on 13 September 1997, he became only the third member of the elite "4,000 club" – jockeys who had won more than 4,000 races during their careers. This Top 10 comprises members of this elite group together with the runners-up at that time.

TOP 10

JOCKEYS IN ENGLISH CLASSICS

	Jockey	Years	1,000 Guineas	2,000 Guineas	Derby	Oaks	St. Leger	Wins
1	Lester Piggott	1954–92	2	5	9	6	8	30
2	Frank Buckle	1792–1827	6	5	5	9	2	27
3	Jem Robinson	1817–48	5	9	6	2	2	24
4	Fred Archer	1874–86	2	4	5	4	6	21
5 =	Bill Scott	1821–46	0	3	4	3	9	19
=	Jack Watts	1883–97	4	2	4	4	5	19
7	Willie Carson	1972–94	2	4	4	4	3	17
8 =	John Day	1826–41	5	4	0	5	2	16
=	George Fordham	1859–83	7	3	1	5	0	16
10	Joe Childs	1912–33	2	2	3	4	4	15

The first of Piggott's record 30 winners was Never Say Die in the 1954 Derby. Piggott was only 19 years of age at the time. His 30th and last win to date was in the 1992 2,000 Guineas.

MOTOR RACING

TOP 10 FASTEST GRAND PRIX RACES

	1987				1997	
Circuit	Grand Prix	Speed (km/h)		Speed (km/h)	Grand Prix	Circuit
Osterreichring	Austrian	235.42	1	238.04	Italian	Monza
Silverstone	British	235.30	2	228.58	German	Hockenheim
Monza	Italian	232.64	3	210.61	Austrian	A1 Ring
Hockenheim	German	220.39	4	208.25	Japanese	Suzuka
Spa-Francorchamps	Belgian	205.68	5	206.85	British	Silverstone
Imola	San Marino	195.20	6	204.36	Australian	Albert Park
Mexico City	Mexican	193.41	7	203.85	Spanish	Jerez
Suzuka	Japanese	192.85	8	203.21	San Marino	Imola
Paul Ricard	French	188.56	9	200.65	Luxembourg	Nürburgring
Estoril	Portuguese	188.22	10	196.83	Belgian	Spa-Francorchamps

DRIVERS WITH THE MOST GRAND PRIX WINS IN A CAREER

	Driver/country	Years	Wins
1	Alain Prost (France)	1981–93	51
2	Ayrton Senna (Brazil)	1985–93	41
3	Nigel Mansell (UK)	1985–94	31
4	Jackie Stewart (UK)	1965–73	27
5=	Jim Clark (UK)	1962–68	25
=	Niki Lauda (Austria)	1974–85	25
=	Michael Schumacher (Germany)	1992–97	25
8	Juan Manuel Fangio (Argentina)	1950–57	24
9	Nelson Piquet (Brazil)	1980–91	23
10	Damon Hill (UK)	1993–96	21

TOP 10 YOUNGEST FORMULA ONE WORLD CHAMPIONS OF ALL TIME
(Country/age)

❶ Emerson Fittipaldi (Brazil, 25 yrs 9 mths) ❷ Michael Schumacher (Germany, 25 yrs 10 mths) ❸ Jacques Villeneuve (Canada, 26 yrs 5 mths) ❹ Niki Lauda (Austria, 26 yrs 7 mths) ❺ Jim Clark (UK, 27 yrs 7 mths) ❻ Jochen Rindt (Austria, 28 yrs 6 mths) ❼ Ayrton Senna (Brazil, 28 yrs 7 mths) ❽= James Hunt, Nelson Piquet (UK/Brazil, 29 yrs 2 mths) ❿ Mike Hawthorn (UK, 29 yrs 6 mths)

CONSTRUCTORS WITH THE MOST FORMULA ONE GRAND PRIX WINS

	Constructor	Years	Wins		Constructor	Years	Wins
1	Ferrari	1951–97	113	6	Benetton	1986–97	27
2	McLaren	1968–97	107	7	Tyrrell	1971–83	23
3	Williams	1979–97	103	8	BRM	1959–72	17
4	Lotus	1960–87	79	9	Cooper	1958–67	16
5	Brabham	1964–85	35	10	Renault	1979–83	15

JACQUES VILLENEUVE

MONEY-WINNERS AT THE INDIANAPOLIS 500, 1997

	Driver	Prizes ($)
1	Arie Luyendyk	1,568,150
2	Scott Goodyear	513,300
3	Jeff Ward	414,250
4	Buddy Lazier	279,250
5	Tony Stewart	345,050
6	Davey Hamilton	264,000
7	Billy Boat	259,700
8	Robbie Buhl	235,200
9	Robbie Groff	222,350
10	Fermín Vélez	216,400

Source: Indianapolis Motor Speedway

DRIVERS WITH THE MOST WINSTON CUP RACE WINS*

	Driver	Years	Wins
1	Richard Petty	1958–92	200
2	David Pearson	1960–86	105
3=	Bobby Allison	1975–88	84
=	Darrell Waltrip#	1972–98	84
5	Cale Yarborough	1957–88	83
6	Dale Earnhardt#	1975–98	71
7	Lee Petty	1949–64	55
8=	Ned Jarrett	1953–66	50
=	Junior Johnson	1953–66	50
10	Herb Thomas	1949–62	48

* *To March 31, 1998*

\# *Still driving at end of 1998 season*

The Winston Cup is a season-long series of races organized by the National Association of Stock Car Auto Racing, Inc. (NASCAR). Races, which take place over enclosed circuits such as Daytona speedway, are among the most popular motor races in the United States.

Source: NASCAR

CONSTRUCTORS WITH THE MOST FORMULA ONE WORLD TITLES

	Constructor/country	Years	Titles
1	Williams (UK)	1980–97	9
2	Ferrari (Italy)	1961–83	8
3=	Lotus (UK)	1963–78	7
=	McLaren (UK)	1974–91	7
5=	Brabham (UK)	1966–67	2
=	Cooper (UK)	1959–60	2
7=	BRM (UK)	1962	1
=	Matra (France)	1969	1
=	Tyrrell (UK)	1971	1
=	Vanwall (UK)	1958	1
=	Benetton (Italy)	1995	1

TOP 10 DRIVERS TO COMPETE IN THE MOST FORMULA ONE GRAND PRIX RACES
(Country/races)

❶ Riccardo Patrese (Italy, 256) ❷ Gerhard Berger (Austria, 210) ❸ Andrea de Cesaris (Italy, 208) ❹ Nelson Piquet (Brazil, 204) ❺ Alain Prost (France, 199) ❻ Michele Alboreto (Italy, 194) ❼ Nigel Mansell (UK, 185) ❽ Graham Hill (UK, 176) Jacques Laffite (France, 176) ❿ Niki Lauda (Italy, 171)

DRIVERS WITH THE MOST FORMULA ONE WORLD TITLES

	Driver	Country	World titles between years	Races won	World titles
1	Juan Manuel Fangio	Argentina	1951–57	24	5
2	Alain Prost	France	1985–93	51	4
3=	Jack Brabham	Australia	1959–66	14	3
=	Jackie Stewart	UK	1969–73	27	3
=	Niki Lauda	Austria	1975–84	25	3
=	Nelson Piquet	Brazil	1981–87	23	3
=	Ayrton Senna	Brazil	1988–91	41	3
8=	Alberto Ascari	Italy	1952–53	13	2
=	Jim Clark	UK	1963–65	25	2
=	Graham Hill	UK	1962–68	14	2
=	Emerson Fittipaldi	Brazil	1972–74	14	2
=	Michael Schumacher	Germany	1994–95	27	2

NASCAR MONEY-WINNERS OF ALL TIME*

	Driver	Total prizes ($)		Driver	Total prizes ($)
1	Dale Earnhardt	31,692,650	6	Darrell Waltrip	16,382,260
2	Bill Elliott	18,251,882	7	Mark Martin	15,053,967
3	Jeff Gordon	17,215,112	8	Ricky Rudd	13,803,150
4	Terry Labonte	17,135,662	9	Geoff Bodine	11,833,069
5	Rusty Wallace	16,803,870	10	Dale Jarrett	11,771,762

* *To March 31, 1998*

Source: NASCAR

RUGBY LEAGUE

TOP 10

TRY–SCORERS IN THE 1997 SUPER LEAGUE

Player/club	Tries
1 Nigel Vagana (Warrington Wolves)	17
2 = Alan Hunte (St. Helens Saints)	15
= Jason Robinson (Wigan Warriors)	15
= Tony Smith (Wigan Warriors)	15
= Paul Sterling (Leeds Rhinos)	15
= Anthony Sullivan (St. Helens Saints)	15
7 = Danny Arnold (St. Helens Saints)	14
= Phil Bergman (Paris St. Germain)	14
9 = Gary Connolly (Wigan Warriors)	13
= Andy Johnson (Wigan Warriors)	13
= James Lowes (Bradford Bulls)	13

TOP 10

SCORING TEAMS IN CHALLENGE CUP FINALS*

Team	Points
1 Wigan	406
2 Leeds	239
3 St. Helens	211
4 Widnes	158
5 Huddersfield	130
6 Warrington	129
7 Hull	128
8 Wakefield Trinity	118
9 Bradford	113
10 Halifax	110

* Including the two-stage finals during World War II

TOP 10

POINTS–SCORERS IN THE SUPER LEAGUE

Club	Total points
1 Wigan Warriors	1,585
2 St. Helens Saints	1,542
3 Bradford Bulls	1,536
4 London Broncos	1,227
5 Halifax Blue Sox	1,191
6 Leeds Rhinos	1,099
7 Warrington Wolves	1,006
8 Oldham Bears	934
9 Sheffield Eagles	914
10 Castleford Tigers	881

TOP 10

WINNERS OF THE CHALLENGE CUP

Club	Years	Wins
1 Wigan	1924–95	16
2 Leeds	1910–78	10
3 Widnes	1930–84	7
4 = Huddersfield	1913–53	6
= St. Helens	1956–96	6
6 = Wakefield Trinity	1909–63	5
= Warrington	1905–74	5
= Halifax	1903–87	5
9 = Bradford Northern	1906–49	4
= Castleford	1935–86	4

The first Challenge Cup final, then known as the Northern Union Cup, was held at Headingley, Leeds, on 24 April 1897. Batley were the first winners, beating St. Helens 10–3 in front of a crowd of 13,492. When Wigan were eliminated by Salford in 1996, it ended Wigan's eight-year run without a single defeat in the Challenge Cup. The last team to beat them before Salford was Oldham, in 1987.

TOP 10

POINTS–SCORERS IN A RUGBY LEAGUE MATCH

Player/match	Year	Pts
1 George West, Hull Kingston Rovers vs. Brookland Rovers	1905	53
2 Jim Sullivan, Wigan vs. Flimby & Fothergill	1925	44
3 Sammy Lloyd, Castleford vs. Millom	1973	43
4 Dean Marwood, Workington Town vs. Highfield	1992	42
5 = Paul Loughlin, St. Helens vs. Carlisle	1986	40
= Martin Offiah, Wigan vs. Leeds	1992	40
7 = James Lomas, Salford vs. Liverpool City	1907	39
= Major Holland, Huddersfield vs. Swinton Park Rangers	1914	39
9 = John Woods, Leigh vs. Blackpool Borough	1977	38
= Bob Beardmore, Castleford vs. Barrow	1987	38
= John Woods, Leigh vs. Ryedale-York	1992	38

TOP 10

CLUBS WITH THE MOST LANCE TODD TROPHY WINS

Club	Wins
1 Wigan	13
2 St. Helens	8
3 = Wakefield Trinity	5
= Widnes	5
5 = Bradford Northern	3
= Castleford	3
= Featherstone Rovers	3
= Warrington	3
9 Leeds	2
10 = Barrow	1
= Halifax	1
= Huddersfield	1
= Hull	1
= Hull Kingston Rovers	1
= Hunslet	1
= Leigh	1
= Workington Town	1

The Lance Todd Award is presented to the Man of the Match in the Challenge Cup final at Wembley.

RUGBY UNION

TOP 10

RUGBY UNION COUNTRIES*

1	New Zealand
2	South Africa
3	Australia
4	France
5	England
6	Western Samoa
7	Argentina
8	Italy
9	Scotland
10	Ireland

* As of 1 February 1998, as ranked by World Rugby magazine.

TOP 10

BIGGEST WINS IN THE INTERNATIONAL CHAMPIONSHIP

	Match (winners first)	Venue	Year	Score
1	England vs. Wales	Twickenham	1998	60–26
2	France vs. Scotland	Murrayhead	1998	51–16
3	Wales vs. France	Swansea	1910	49–14
4	France vs. Scotland	Paris	1997	47–20
5	England vs. Ireland	Twickenham	1997	46–6
6=	France vs. Ireland	Paris	1996	45–10
=	France vs. Ireland	Paris	1996	45–10
8	France vs. Ireland	Paris	1992	44–12
9	England vs. Scotland	Twickenham	1997	41–13
10	England vs. France	Paris	1914	39–13

This Top 10 is based on the winning team's scores, not the margin of victory, except where two nations share the highest score.

TOP 10

BIGGEST BRITISH LIONS' TEST WINS

	Opponents/venue	Test/year	Score
1	Australia, Brisbane	2nd Test 1966	31–0
2	South Africa, Pretoria	2nd Test 1974	28–9
3	South Africa, Port Elizabeth	3rd Test 1974	26–9
4=	Australia, Sydney	2nd Test 1950	24–3
=	Australia, Sydney	2nd Test 1959	24–3
6	South Africa, Johannesburg	1st Test 1955	23–22
7	South Africa, Port Elizabeth	3rd Test 1938	21–16
8	New Zealand, Wellington	2nd Test 1993	20–7
9	Australia, Brisbane	2nd Test 1989	19–12
10	Australia, Sydney	3rd Test 1989	19–18

TOP 10

INDIVIDUAL POINTS–SCORERS IN ONE WORLD CUP TOURNAMENT

	Player/country	Year	Pts
1	Grant Fox, New Zealand	1987	126
2	Gavin Hastings, Scotland	1995	104
3	Thierry Lacroix, France	1995	103
4	Andrew Mehrtens, New Zealand	1995	84
5	Michael Lynagh, Australia	1987	82
6	Rob Andrew, England	1995	70
7	Ralph Keyes, Ireland	1991	68
8	Michael Lynagh, Australia	1991	66
9	Gavin Hastings, Scotland	1987	62
10	Gavin Hastings, Scotland	1991	61

TOP 10

HIGHEST–SCORING INTERNATIONAL RUGBY UNION MATCHES, 1993–98*

	Winners/losers	Date	Score
1	Hong Kong vs. Singapore	27 Oct 1994	164–13
2	New Zealand vs. Japan	4 Jun 1995	145–17
3	Japan vs. Thailand	4 Nov 1996	141–10
4	Hong Kong vs. Taiwan	9 Nov 1996	114–12
5	South Korea vs. Malaysia	5 Nov 1996	112–5
6	Italy vs. Poland	26 May 1996	107–19
7	Italy vs. Czech Republic	18 May 1994	104–8
8	Hong Kong vs. Malaysia	3 Nov 1996	103–5
9=	Japan vs. Malaysia	26 Oct 1994	103–9
=	Argentina vs. Paraguay	24 Sep 1995	103–9

* 1 March 1993 to 28 February 1998

THE 10

FIRST PLAYERS INDUCTED INTO THE RUGBY UNION HALL OF FAME

1	Serge Blanco
2	Graham Mourie
3	Peter Dixon
4	Gareth Edwards
5	Simon Poidevin
6	Grant Fox
7	Jo Maso
8	Hugo Porta
9	Mike Gibson
10	Andy Irvine

In November 1996 Rugby News launched its own Hall of Fame and each month thereafter nominated a new inductee.

SOCCER – THE WORLD CUP

TOP 10

HIGHEST-SCORING MATCHES IN THE FINAL STAGES OF THE WORLD CUP

	Match/year	Score
1	Austria *vs.* Switzerland, 1954	7–5
2 =	Brazil *vs.* Poland, 1938	6–5
=	Hungary *vs.* W. Germany, 1954	8–3
=	Hungary *vs.* El Salvador, 1982	10–1
5	France *vs.* Paraguay, 1958	7–3
6 =	Hungary *vs.* South Korea, 1954	9–0
=	W. Germany *vs.* Turkey, 1954	7–2
=	France *vs.* W. Germany, 1958	6–3
=	Yugoslavia *vs.* Congo (Dem. Rep.), 1974	9–0
10 =	Italy *vs.* USA, 1934	7–1
=	Sweden *vs.* Cuba, 1938	8–0
=	Uruguay *vs.* Bolivia, 1950	8–0
=	England *vs.* Belgium, 1954	4–4
=	Portugal *vs.* North Korea, 1966	5–3

Hungary's 8–3 victory over West Germany in 1954 was in the Group matches, where for tactical reasons West Germany fielded six reserves. When the two teams met again in the final, West Germany won 3–2.

TOP 10

HIGHEST-SCORING WORLD CUP FINALS

	Year	Games	Goals	Average per game
1	1954	26	140	5.38
2	1938	18	84	4.66
3	1934	17	70	4.11
4	1950	22	88	4.00
5	1930	18	70	3.88
6	1958	35	126	3.60
7	1970	32	95	2.96
8	1982	52	146	2.81
9 =	1962	32	89	2.78
=	1966	32	89	2.78

TOP 10

GOAL–SCORERS IN THE FINAL STAGES OF THE WORLD CUP

	Player/country/years	Goals
1	Gerd Müller, W. Germany, 1970–74	14
2	Just Fontaine, France, 1958	13
3	Pelé, Brazil, 1958–70	12
4	Sandor Kocsis, Hungary, 1954	11
5 =	Helmut Rahn, W. Germany, 1954–58	10
=	Teófilio Cubillas, Peru, 1970–78	10
=	Grzegorz Lato, Poland, 1974–82	10
=	Gary Lineker, England, 1986–90	10
9 =	Leónidas da Silva, Brazil, 1934–38	9
=	Ademir Marques de Menezes, Brazil, 1950	9
=	Vavà, Brazil, 1958–62	9
=	Eusébio, Portugal, 1966	9
=	Uwe Seeler, W. Germany, 1958–70	9
=	Jairzinho, Brazil, 1970–74	9
=	Paolo Rossi, Italy, 1978–82	9
=	Karl-Heinz Rummenigge W. Germany, 1978–86	9

TOP 10

HIGHEST-SCORING WINS BY COUNTRIES ON THEIR DEBUT IN THE FINAL STAGES OF THE WORLD CUP

	Winners/losers	Year	Score
1	Italy *vs.* United States	1934	7-1
2	Germany *vs.* Belgium	1934	5-2
3	France *vs.* Mexico	1930	4-1
4	Hungary *vs.* Egypt	1934	4-2
5 =	Chile *vs.* Mexico	1930	3-0
=	USA *vs.* Belgium	1930	3-0
7 =	Romania *vs.* Peru	1930	3-1
=	Spain *vs.* Brazil	1934	3-1
=	Portugal *vs.* Hungary	1966	3-1
=	Tunisia *vs.* Mexico	1978	3-1

TOP 10

HOST COUNTRIES IN THE WORLD CUP

	Host	Year	Final standing
1 =	Uruguay	1930	Winners
=	Italy	1934	Winners
=	England	1966	Winners
=	West Germany	1974	Winners
=	Argentina	1978	Winners
6 =	Brazil	1950	Runners-up
=	Sweden	1958	Runners-up
8 =	Chile	1962	Third
=	Italy	1990	Third
10 =	France	1938	Last 8
=	Switzerland	1954	Last 8
=	Mexico	1970	Last 8
=	Mexico	1986	Last 8

Spain in 1982 (last 12) and the US in 1994 (last 16) are the only two host countries not to have reached the last eight.

THE 10

HIGHEST-SCORING DEFEATS BY COUNTRIES ON THEIR DEBUT IN THE FINAL STAGES OF THE WORLD CUP

	Losers/winners	Year	Score
1	South Korea *vs.* Hungary	1954	0-9
2	Dutch East Indies *vs.* Hungary	1938	0-6
3	Poland *vs.* Brazil	1938	5-6
4	New Zealand *vs.* Scotland	1982	2-5
5	Bolivia *vs.* Yugoslavia	1930	0-4
6 =	Mexico *vs.* France	1930	1-4
=	Turkey *vs.* W. Germany	1954	1-4
8	Egypt *vs.* Hungary	1934	2-4
9 =	Belgium *vs.* USA	1930	0-3
=	El Salvador *vs.* Belgium	1930	0-3
=	Iran *vs.* Holland	1978	0-3
=	North Korea *vs.* Soviet Union	1966	0-3
=	Paraguay *vs.* USA	1950	0-3

THE 10
COUNTRIES WITH THE MOST PLAYERS SENT OFF IN THE FINAL STAGES OF THE WORLD CUP

Country	Dismissals
1= Argentina	7
= Brazil	7
3 Uruguay	6
4= Czechoslovakia	4
= Germany/W. Germany	4
= Hungary	4
7 Yugoslavia	3
8= Cameroon	2
= Chile	2
= Holland	2
= Italy	2
= Soviet Union	2

A total of 60 players have received their marching orders in the final stages of the World Cup since 1930. The South American nations account for 23 of them.

THE 10
LEAST SUCCESSFUL COUNTRIES IN THE WORLD CUP

	Country	Tournaments	Matches played	won
1	Bulgaria	5	16	0
2	South Korea	4	11	0
3=	El Salvador	2	6	0
=	Bolivia	3	6	0
5	Republic of Ireland	1	5	0
6	Egypt	2	4	0
7=	Canada	1	3	0
=	Greece	1	3	0
=	Haiti	1	3	0
=	Iraq	1	3	0
=	New Zealand	1	3	0
=	United Arab Emirates	1	3	0
=	Congo (Dem. Rep.)	1	3	0

TOP 10
COUNTRIES THAT HAVE PLAYED THE MOST MATCHES IN THE FINAL STAGES OF THE WORLD CUP

	Country	Tournaments	Matches played
1=	Brazil	15	73
=	Germany/W. Germany	13	73
3	Italy	13	61
4	Argentina	11	52
5	England	9	41
6=	Uruguay	9	37
=	Spain	9	37
=	Sweden	9	37
9=	France	9	34
=	USSR/Russia	8	34

WORLD CUP 1994
The 1994 World Cup was held in the United States, playing to packed stadiums. The final, in which Brazil beat Italy, was the first to be decided on penalties.

WORLD TENNIS

MARTINA HINGIS

TOP 10

WINNERS OF WOMEN'S GRAND SLAM SINGLES TITLES

	Player/country	A	F	W	US	Total
1	Margaret Court (Australia)	11	5	3	5	24
2	Steffi Graf (Germany)	4	5	7	5	21
3	Helen Wills-Moody (USA)	0	4	8	7	19
4=	Chris Evert-Lloyd	2	7	3	6	18
=	Martina Navratilova (Czechoslovakia/USA)	3	2	9	4	18
6	Billie Jean King (USA)	1	1	6	4	12
7=	Maureen Connolly (USA)	1	2	3	3	9
=	Monica Seles (Yugoslavia/USA)	4	3	0	2	9
9=	Suzanne Lenglen (France)	0	2	6	0	8
=	Molla Mallory (USA)	0	0	0	8	8

A = Australian Open; F = French Open; W = Wimbledon; US = US Open

TOP 10 FEMALE PLAYERS IN THE WORLD*

❶ Martina Hingis ❷ Jana Novotna
❸ Lindsay Davenport ❹ Amanda Coetzer
❺ Monica Seles ❻ Iva Majoli ❼ Mary Pierce
❽ Arantxa Sanchez Vicario ❾ Irina Spirlea
❿ Nathalie Tauziat
* According to WTA rankings 18 January 1998

TOP 10

WINNERS OF MEN'S GRAND SLAM SINGLES TITLES

	Player/nationality	A	F	W	US	Total
1	Roy Emerson (Aus)	6	2	2	2	12
2=	Bjorn Borg (Swe)	0	6	5	0	11
=	Rod Laver (Aus)	3	2	4	2	11
4	Pete Sampras (USA)	2	0	4	4	10
5=	Jimmy Connors (USA)	1	0	2	5	8
=	Ivan Lendl (Cze)	2	3	0	3	8
=	Fred Perry (GB)	1	1	3	3	8
=	Ken Rosewall (Aus)	4	2	0	2	8
9=	René Lacoste (Fra)	0	3	2	2	7
=	William Larned (USA)	0	0	0	7	7
=	John McEnroe (USA)	0	0	3	4	7
=	John Newcombe (Aus)	2	0	3	2	7
=	William Renshaw (GB)	0	0	7	0	7
=	Richard Sears (USA)	0	0	0	7	7
=	Mats Wilander (Swe)	3	3	0	1	7

A = Australian Open; F = French Open; W = Wimbledon; US = US Open

TOP 10

SHORTEST MEN'S SINGLES FINALS AT WIMBLEDON

Match	Year	Set scores	Total games
1= William Renshaw vs. John Hartley	1881	6–0 6–1 6–1	20
= Fred Perry vs. Gottfried von Cramm	1936	6–1 6–1 6–0	20
3= William Johnston vs. Frank Hunter	1923	6–0 6–3 6–1	22
= Donald Budge vs. Bunny Austin	1938	6–1 6–0 6–3	22
= John McEnroe vs. Jimmy Connors	1984	6–1 6–1 6–2	22
6= Lew Hoad vs. Ashley Cooper	1957	6–2 6–1 6–2	23
= Rod Laver vs. Martin Mulligan	1962	6–2 6–2 6–1	23
= John Newcombe vs. Wilhem Bungert	1967	6–3 6–1 6–1	23
9= Ellsworth Vines vs. Bunny Austin	1932	6–4 6–2 6–0	24
= Jack Kramer vs. Tom Brown	1947	6–1 6–3 6–2	24
= Jimmy Connors vs. Ken Rosewall	1974	6–1 6–1 6–4	24
= John McEnroe vs. Chris Lewis	1983	6–2 6–2 6–2	24

TOP 10

PLAYERS WITH THE MOST US SINGLES TITLES

	Player*	Years	Titles
1	Molla Mallory (*née* Bjurstedt)	1915–26	8
2 =	Richard Sears	1881–87	7
=	William Larned	1901–11	7
=	Bill Tilden	1920–29	7
=	Helen Wills-Moody	1923–31	7
=	Margaret Court (*née* Smith)(Aus)#	1962–70	7
7	Chris Evert-Lloyd	1975–82	6
8 =	Jimmy Connors	1974–83	5
=	Steffi Graf (Ger)	1988-96	5
10 =	Robert Wrenn	1893–97	4
=	Elisabeth Moore	1896–1905	4
=	Hazel Wightman (*née* Hotchkiss)	1909–19	4
=	Helen Jacobs	1932–35	4
=	Alice Marble	1936–40	4
=	Pauline Betz	1942–46	4
=	Maria Bueno (Bra)	1959–66	4
=	Billie Jean King (*née* Moffitt)	1967–74	4
=	John McEnroe	1979–84	4
=	Martina Navratilova	1983–87	4
=	Pete Sampras	1990–96	4

* All players are from the US unless otherwise stated.

\# Includes two wins in Amateur Championships of 1968 and 1969 which were held alongside the Open Championship

Organized lawn tennis started in the United States following the formation of the USLTA on 21 May 1881, and on 31 August that year the first national championships got under way on the courts of the Newport, Rhode Island, Casino. There were no stands, all the courts being simply roped off to prevent spectators wandering across them during play. The men's singles and doubles were the only events contested, with competitors playing in a wide variety of attire, including coloured blazers and cravats.

TOP 10

SHORTEST WOMEN'S SINGLES FINALS AT WIMBLEDON

	Match/year	Set scores	Total games
1	Dorothea Lambert Chambers *vs.* Dora Boothby, 1911	6–0 6–0	12
2 =	Doris Hart *vs.* Shirley Fry, 1951	6–1 6–0	13
=	Billie Jean King *vs.* Evonne Cawley, 1975	6–0 6–1	13
4 =	Lottie Dod *vs.* Blanche Bingley, 1887	6–2 6–0	14
=	Lottie Dod *vs.* Blanche Hillyard, 1892	6–1 6–1	14
=	Blanche Hillyard *vs.* Lucy Austin, 1894	6–1 6–1	14
=	Suzanne Lenglen *vs.* Elizabeth Ryan, 1921	6–2 6–0	14
=	Suzanne Lenglen *vs.* Molla Mallory, 1922	6–2 6–0	14
=	Suzanne Lenglen *vs.* Joan Fry, 1925	6–2 6–0	14
=	Alice Marble *vs.* Kay Stammers, 1939	6–2 6–0	14

TOP 10

DAVIS CUP-WINNING TEAMS

	Country	Wins
1	United States	31
2	Australia	20
3	France	8
4 =	Sweden	6
=	Australasia	6
6	British Isles	5
7	Great Britain	4
8	West Germany	2
9 =	Germany	1
=	Czechoslovakia	1
=	Italy	1
=	South Africa	1

PETE SAMPRAS

TOP 10

MALE PLAYERS IN THE WORLD*

	Player	Country
1	Pete Sampras	USA
2	Patrick Rafter	Australia
3	Michael Chang	USA
4	Jonas Bjorkman	Sweden
5	Yevgeny Kafelnikov	Russia
6	Greg Rusedski	GB
7	Petr Korda	Czech Republic
8	Marcelo Rios	Chile
9	Carlos Moya	Spain
10	Thomas Muster	Austria

* According to ATP rankings as of 18 January 1998

WINTER SPORTS

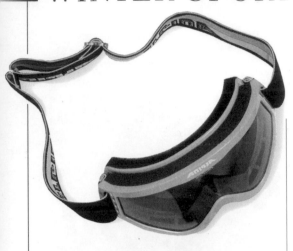

FASTEST-WINNING TIMES OF THE IDITAROD DOG SLED RACE

	Winner/year	Day	Time hr	min	sec
1	Doug Swingley, 1995	9	2	42	19
2	Jeff King, 1996	9	5	43	19
3	Jeff King, 1998	9	5	52	26
4	Martin Buser, 1997	9	8	30	45
5	Martin Buser, 1994	10	13	2	39
6	Jeff King, 1993	10	15	38	15
7	Martin Buser, 1992	10	19	17	15
8	Susan Butcher, 1990	11	1	53	28
9	Susan Butcher, 1987	11	2	5	13
10	Joe Runyan, 1989	11	5	24	34

The race, which has been held annually since 1973, stretches from Anchorage to Nome, Alaska, covering 1,864 km/ 1,158 miles. Iditarod is a deserted mining village along the route, and the race commemorates an emergency operation in 1925 to get medical supplies to Nome following a diphtheria epidemic.

Source: Iditarod Trail Committee

ALPINE SKIING WORLD CUP TITLES – MEN

	Name/country	Years	Titles
1	Marc Girardelli (Luxembourg)	1985–93	5
2=	Gustavo Thoeni (Italy)	1971–75	4
=	Pirmin Zurbriggen (Switzerland)	1984–90	4
4=	Ingemar Stenmark (Sweden)	1976–78	3
=	Phil Mahre (USA)	1981–83	3
6=	Jean Claude Killy (France)	1967–68	2
=	Karl Schranz (Austria)	1969–70	2
8=	Piero Gross (Italy)	1974	1
=	Peter Lüscher (Switzerland)	1979	1
=	Andreas Wenzel (Leichtenstein)	1980	1
=	Paul Accola (Switzerland)	1992	1
=	Kjetil Andre Aamodt (Norway)	1994	1
=	Alberto Tomba (Italy)	1995	1
=	Lasse Kjus (Norway)	1996	1
=	Luc Alphand (France)	1997	1
=	Hermann Maier (Austria)	1998	1

ALPINE SKIING WORLD CUP TITLES – WOMEN

	Name/country	Years	Titles
1	Annemarie Moser-Pröll (Austria)	1971–79	6
2=	Vreni Schneider (Switzerland)	1989–95	3
=	Petra Kronberger (Austria)	1990–92	3
4=	Nancy Greene (Canada)	1967–68	2
=	Hanni Wenzel (Liechtenstein)	1978–80	2
=	Erika Hess (Switzerland)	1982–84	2
=	Michela Figini (Switzerland)	1985–88	2
=	Maria Walliser (Switzerland)	1986–87	2
=	Kajta Seizinger (Germany)	1996–98	2
10=	Gertrude Gabl (Austria)	1969	1
=	Michèle Jacot (France)	1970	1
=	Rosi Mittermeier (West Germany)	1976	1
=	Lise-Marie Morerod (Switzerland)	1977	1
=	Marie-Thérèse Nadig (Switzerland)	1981	1
=	Tamara McKinney (USA)	1983	1
=	Anita Wachter (Austria)	1993	1
=	Pernilla Wiberg (Sweden)	1997	1

DOWNHILL RACER
Ski races have been held since the last century, but have developed as major Olympic and World events in the 20th century along with the international growth of interest in the sport.

TOP 10

WORLD AND OLYMPIC FIGURE SKATING TITLES – MEN

	Skater/country	Years	Titles
1	Ulrich Salchow (Sweden)	1901–11	11
2	Karl Schäfer (Austria)	1930–36	9
3	Dick Button (USA)	1948–52	7
4	Gillis Grafstrom (Sweden)	1920–29	6
5 =	Hayes Jenkins (USA)	1953–56	5
=	Scott Hamilton (USA)	1981–84	5
7 =	Willy Bockl (Austria)	1925–28	4
=	David Jenkins (USA)	1957–60	4
=	Ondrej Nepela (Czechoslovakia)	1971–73	4
=	Kurt Browning (Can)	1989–93	4

TOP 10

WORLD AND OLYMPIC FIGURE SKATING TITLES – WOMEN

	Skater/country	Years	Titles
1	Sonja Henie (Norway)	1927–36	13
2 =	Carol Heiss (USA)	1956–60	6
=	Herma Planck Szabo (Austria)	1922–26	6
=	Katarina Witt (East Germany)	1984–88	6
5 =	Lily Kronberger (Hungary)	1908–11	4
=	Sjoukje Dijkstra (Netherlands)	1962–64	4
=	Peggy Fleming (USA)	1966–68	4
8 =	Meray Horvath (Hungary)	1912–14	3
=	Tenley Albright (USA)	1953–56	3
=	Annett Poetzsch (East Gemany)	1978–80	3
=	Beatrix Schuba (Austria)	1971–72	3
=	Barbara Ann Scott (Canada)	1947–48	3
=	Kristi Yamaguchi (USA)	1991–92	3
=	Madge Sayers (UK)	1906–08	3

TOP 10

OLYMPIC FIGURE SKATING COUNTRIES

	Country	G	S	B	Total
1 =	USSR/CIS/Russia	20	14	6	40
=	USA	12	13	15	40
3	Austria	7	9	4	20
4	Canada	2	8	8	18
5	UK	5	3	7	15
6	France	2	2	7	11
7 =	Sweden	5	3	2	10
=	Germany/West Germany	4	3	3	10
=	East Germany	3	3	4	10
10 =	Norway	3	2	1	6
=	Hungary	0	2	4	6

TOP 10

WINNERS OF WORLD ICE DANCE TITLES

	Skater/country	Years	Titles
1 =	Alexsandr Gorshkov (USSR)	1970–76	6
=	Lyudmila Pakhomova (USSR)	1970–76	6
3 =	Lawrence Demmy (UK)	1951–55	5
=	Jean Westwood (UK)	1951–55	5
5 =	Courtney Jones (UK)	1957–60	4
=	Eva Romanova (Czechoslovakia)	1962–65	4
=	Pavel Roman (Czechoslovakia)	1963–65	4
=	Diane Towler (UK)	1966–69	4
=	Bernard Ford (UK)	1966–69	4
=	Jayne Torvill (UK)	1981–84	4
=	Christopher Dean (UK)	1981–84	4
=	Natalya Bestemianova (USSR)	1985–88	4
=	Andrei Bukin (USSR)	1985–88	4
=	Oksana Gritschuk (Rus)	1994–97	4
=	Yevgeniy Platov (Rus)	1994–97	4

TOP 10 OLYMPIC BOBSLEIGHING NATIONS
(Total number of medals)

❶ Switzerland (26) ❷ Germany/West Germany (17) ❸ USA (14) ❹ East Germany (13) ❺ Italy (11) ❻ UK (4) ❼= Austria (3), USSR (3) ❾= Canada (2), Belgium (2)

TOP 10

WINTER OLYMPIC MEDAL-WINNING COUNTRIES

	Country	G	S	B	Total
1	Russia/USSR	108	77	74	259
2	Norway	83	87	69	239
3	USA	59	58	43	160
4	Germany/West Germany	57	52	45	154
5	Austria	39	53	53	145
6	Finland	38	49	48	135
7	East Germany	39	36	35	110
8	Sweden	39	28	35	102
9	Switzerland	29	31	32	92
10	Canada	25	26	28	79
	UK	*7*	*4*	*13*	*24*

THIS SPORTING LIFE

TOP 10

FILMS WITH SPORTING THEMES

	Film/year	Sport
1	*Days of Thunder* (1990)	Stock car racing
2	*Rocky IV* (1985)	Boxing
3	*Rocky III* (1982)	Boxing
4	*Rocky* (1976)	' Boxing
5	*A League of Their Own* (1992)	Baseball
6	*Rocky II* (1979)	Boxing
7	*Tin Cup* (1996)	Golf
8	*White Men Can't Jump* (1992)	Basketball
9	*Cool Running* (1993)	Bobsleighing
10	*Field of Dreams* (1989)	Baseball

Led by superstar Sylvester Stallone's *Rocky* series, the boxing ring, a natural source of drama and thrills, dominates Hollywood's most successful sports-based epics. Baseball is a popular follow-up, both in the films in this Top 10 and others just outside.

RECORD-BREAKER
Although eclipsed by higher earners since, Chariots of Fire (1973) was once the most successful sporting film of all time.

TOP 10

MOST DANGEROUS AMATEUR SPORTS

	Sport	Risk factor*
1	Powerboat racing	15
2	Ocean yacht racing	10
3	Cave diving	7
4	Potholing	6
5=	Drag racing	5
=	Karting	5
7=	Microlyte	4
=	Hang gliding	3
=	Motor racing	3
=	Mountaineering	3

* *Risk factor refers to the premium insurance companies place on insuring someone for that activity – the higher the risk factor, the higher the premium.*

People are frequently injured playing such sports as football and rugby, but as large numbers participate and the percentage injured is relatively small, the risk is considered slight. With certain sports, the level at which individuals participate can greatly affect the level of danger involved: for example, mountaineering can be a fairly safe sport if confined to lower mountains.

Source: General Accident

TOP 10

MOST COMMON SPORTING INJURIES

	Common name	Medical term
1	Bruise	Soft tissue contusion
2	Sprained ankle	Sprain of the lateral ligament
3	Sprained knee	Sprain of the medial collateral ligament
4	Low back strain	Lumbar joint dysfunction
5	Hamstring tear	Muscle tear of the hamstring
6	Jumper's knee	Patella tendinitis
7	Achilles tendinitis	Tendinitis of the Achilles tendon
8	Shin splints	Medial periostitis of the tibia
9	Tennis elbow	Lateral epicondylitis
10	Shoulder strain	Rotator cuff tendinitis

TOP 10

CATEGORIES OF ATHLETES WITH THE LARGEST HEARTS*

1	*Tour de France* cyclists
2	Marathon runners
3	Rowers
4	Boxers
5	Sprint cyclists
6	Middle-distance runners
7	Weightlifters
8	Swimmers
9	Sprinters
10	Decathletes

* *Based on average medical measurements*

The heart of a person who engages regularly in a demanding sport enlarges according to the level of strenuousness.

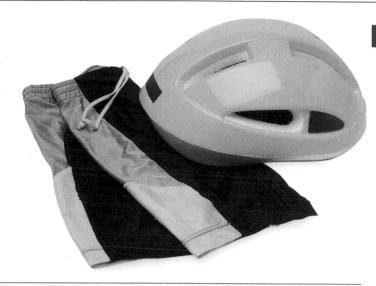

TOP 10

PARTICIPATION SPORTS, GAMES, AND PHYSICAL ACTIVITIES IN THE UK

	Activity	Percentage participating 1996*
1	Walking	44.5
2	Swimming	14.8
3	Keep fit/yoga	12.3
4	Cue sports	11.3
5	Cycling	11.0
6	Weight training	5.6
7	Football	4.8
8	Golf	4.7
9	Running, jogging, etc.	4.5
10	Weightlifting	1.3

* Based on the percentage of people over age 16 participating in each activity in the four weeks before the interview

In the last 10 years, walking, keep fit/yoga, cycling, and weight training have become much more popular, while activities such as snooker and darts have fallen in popularity. A total of 45.6 per cent of those interviewed said they had been involved in at least one sporting or physical activity other than walking in the previous four weeks.

TOP 10

SPECTATOR SPORTS IN THE UK

	Sport	Percentage of adults who paid to watch in 1995
1	Football	13.1
2	Cricket	4.5
3 =	Horse racing	3.8
=	Rugby Union	3.8
5	Motor racing	3.3
6	Greyhound racing	2.5
7	Stock car racing	2.5
8	Rugby league	2.4
9	Motor cycle racing	2.1
10	Tennis	1.8

Source: The Sports Council

TOP 10

HIGHEST-EARNING SPORTSMEN IN THE WORLD*

	Name/sport	endorsements#	Income 1997 ($) salary	total
1	Michael Jordan, Basketball	47,000,000	31,300,000	78,300,000
2	Evander Holyfield, Boxing	1,300,000	53,000,000	54,300,000
3	Oscar De La Hoya, Boxing	1,000,000	37,000,000	38,000,000
4	Michael Shumacher (Ger), Motor racing	10,000,000	25,000,000	35,000,000
5	Mike Tyson, Boxing	—	27,000,000	27,000,000
6	Tiger Woods, Golf	24,000,000	2,100,000	26,100,000
7	Shaquille O'Neal, Basketball	12,500,000	12,900,000	25,400,000
8	Dale Earnhardt, Stock car racing	15,500,000	3,600,000	19,100,000
9	Joe Sakic, Ice Hockey	100,000	17,800,000	17,900,000
10	Grant Hill, Basketball	12,000,000	5,000,000	17,000,000

* All sportsmen are from the US unless otherwise stated
# Sponsorship and royalty income from endorsed sporting products.

Used by permission of Forbes Magazine

TOP 10

SPORTING EVENTS WITH THE LARGEST TV AUDIENCES IN THE UK, 1997

	Event	Channel	Audience
1	Grand National	BBC1	12,000,000
2 =	FA Cup Final (Chelsea vs. Middlesborough)	BBC1	11,100,000
=	Champions League Live (Manchester United vs. Porto)	ITV	11,100,000
4	Champions League Live (Manchester United vs. B. Dortmund)	ITV	10,800,000
5 =	The European Match (Porto vs. Manchester United)	ITV	10,300,000
=	Champions League Live (B. Dortmund vs. Manchester United)	ITV	10,300,000
7	Road to Wembley (Manchester United vs. Spurs)	BBC1	10,200,000
8	Match of the Day (Chelsea vs. Liverpool)	BBC1	10,000,000
9	Champions League Live (Manchester United vs. Feyenoord)	ITV	9,900,000
10	Champions League Live (Feyenoord vs. Manchester United)	ITV	9,700,000

TOYS & GAMES

TOP 10
MOST EXPENSIVE TEDDY BEARS SOLD AT AUCTION IN THE UK

Bear/sale	Price (£)*
1 "Teddy Girl", Christie's, London, 5 Dec 1994	110,000
2 "Happy", a dual-plush Steiff teddy bear, 1926, Sotheby's, London, 19 Sep 1989	55,000
3 "Elliot", a blue Steiff bear, 1908, Christie's, London, 6 Dec 1993	49,500
4 "Teddy Edward", a golden mohair teddy bear, Christie's, London, 9 Dec 1996	34,500
5 Black Steiff teddy bear, c.1912, Sotheby's, London, 18 May 1990	24,200
6 Steiff teddy bear, c.1905, Christie's, London, 8 Dec 1997	23,000
7 "Albert", a Steiff teddy bear c.1910, Christie's, London, 9 Dec 1996	18,400
8 "Theodore", a miniature Steiff teddy bear, 9 cm/3½ in tall, c.1948, Christie's, London, 11 Dec 1995	14,625
9= "Black Jack", a black Steiff teddy bear, Christie's, London, 22 May 1997	13,800
= Cinnamon Steiff teddy bear, c.1905, Christie's, London, 23 May 1997	13,800

* Prices include buyer's premium

TOP 10
LEISURE ACTIVITIES AMONG ADULTS IN THE UK

	Activity	Percentage * participating
1	Watching television	99
2	Visiting/entertaining	96
3	Listening to the radio	88
4	Listening to records/tapes/CDs	78
5=	Reading books	65
=	Visiting a pub	65
7	Meal in a restaurant (not fast food)	62
8	Gardening	49
9	Drive for pleasure	47
10	Walking	45

* Based on percentage of people over 16 participating in each activity in the three months prior to interview for leisure activities outside of the home, or in the four weeks prior to interview for leisure activities in the home

Watching television continues to be the most popular leisure activity at home in the UK, with listening to music and the radio also very popular. The most common activity outside the home is visiting a pub, although this varies in different parts of the country.

TOP 10
MOST EXPENSIVE DOLLS SOLD AT AUCTION IN THE UK

	Doll/sale	Price (£)
1	Kämmer and Reinhardt doll, Sotheby's, London, 8 Feb 1994	188,500
2	Kämmer and Reinhardt bisque character doll, German, c.1909, Sotheby's, London, 17 October 1996 (previously sold at Sotheby's, London, 16 Feb 1989 for £90,200)	108,200
3	Kämmer and Reinhardt bisque character doll, German, c.1909, Sotheby's, London, 17 Oct 1996	91,700
4	William and Mary wooden doll, English, c.1690, Sotheby's, London, 24 Mar 1987	67,000
5	Albert Marque bisque character doll, Sotheby's, London, 17 Oct 1996	71,900
6	Wooden doll, Charles II, 17th century, Christie's, London, 18 May 1989	67,000
7	Albert Marque bisque character doll, Sotheby's, London, 17 Oct 1996	58,700
8=	Albert Marque bisque character doll, Christie's, London, 23 May 1997	56,500
=	Mulatto pressed bisque swivel-head Madagascar doll, Sotheby's, London, 17 Oct 1996	56,500
10	Shellacked pressed bisque swivel-head doll, Sotheby's, London, 17 Oct 1996	45,500

BARBIE
The basic Barbie doll, dressed in just a bikini, sells for a mere £5.99 while the most expensive, a collector's item, retails for around £600

MOST EXPENSIVE TOYS EVER SOLD AT AUCTION IN THE UK*

	Toy/sale	Price (£)
1	*Titania's Palace*, a doll's house with 2,000 items of furniture, Christie's, London, 10 Jan 1978	135,000
2	Hornby 00-gauge train set#, Christie's, London, 27 Nov 1992	80,178
3	Russian carousel (tinplate ferris wheel), *c.*1904, Sotheby's, London, 10 Feb 1993	62,500
4=	Tinplate carousel by Märklin, *c.*1910, Sotheby's, London, 23 Jan 1992	47,300
=	Set of Märklin horse-drawn fire appliances, *c.*1902, Sotheby's, London, 23 Jan 1992	47,300
6	*Augusta Victoria*, a tinplate 4-volt electric ocean liner, by Märklin, Christie's, London, 21 May 1992	41,800
7	*Maine*, a tinplate clockwork battleship, by Märklin, *c.*1904, Sotheby's, London, 1989	39,600
8	Märklin gauge-I locomotive Christie's, London, 23 May 1997	35,200
9	*Pierrot serenading the moon*, a clockwork musical automaton, by G. Vichy, Christie's, London, 1991	31,900
10	*Emily*, a tinplate clockwork paddleboat, by Märklin, *c.*1902 Sotheby's, London, 1989	28,600

* *Excluding dolls and teddy bears*

\# *The largest ever sold at auction*

TREASURE HOUSE
Dolls' houses and their miniature contents are highly prized among collectors and often attain substantial prices at auction.

UK TOYS AND GAMES, 1997*

	Product	Manufacturer
1	Talking Whizz Kid Power Mouse	V Tech Electronics
2	Action Man Moonraker	Hasbro (UK) Ltd
3	Monopoly	Waddingtons Games Ltd
4	Teletubbies figures	Martin Yaffe Int.
5	Tamagotchi	Bandai
6	Jenga	MB/Parker
7	Pre-Computer Prestige	V Tech Electronics
8	Action Man Super Biker	Hasbro (UK) Ltd
9	Sky Diver Action Man	Hasbro (UK) Ltd
10	Pre-Computer Unlimited	V Tech Electronics

* *Ranked by value of retail sales*

Source: NPD Group Worldwide

BESTSELLING COMPUTER GAMES AT W. H. SMITH

1	Fifa 98 Road to World Cup
2	Croc
3	Wallace and Gromit Cracking
4	Tomb Raider
5	Champ Manager
6	Theme Hospital
7	Final Fantasy
8	Grand Theft Auto
9	Toca Touring Car Championship
10	Monopoly

BESTSELLING BOARD GAMES AT W. H. SMITH

1	Jenga
2	Goosebumps One Day at Horrorland
3	Scrabble
4	Monopoly
5	Boggle
6	Star Wars Monopoly
7	Articulate
8	Rummikub
9	Uno Stacko
10	Taboo

INDEX

ACKNOWLEDGMENTS

Special thanks – as always – to Caroline Ash, and to Dafydd Rees, who has taken responsibility for the music lists and contributed many US-related lists. Thanks also to Luke Crampton, Jackie Lane, and Ian Morrison, and to the late Barry Lazell, who contributed his expertise to most of the previous editions of *The Top 10 of Everything*, and who is greatly missed. Thanks also to the individuals, organizations, and publications listed below who kindly supplied information to enable me to prepare many of the lists.

Richard Braddish, Steve Butler, Sharron Clarke, Kaylee Coxall, Dr. Stephen Durham, Christopher Forbes, Russell E. Gough, Max Hanna, Peter Harland, William Hartston, Duncan Hislop, Tony Hutson, Alan Jeffreys, Robert Lamb, Anthony Lipmann, Dr. Benjamin Lucas, Dr. Jacqueline Mitton, Tim O'Brien, Tim O'Donovan, Mark Rathbone, Adrian Room, Rocky Stockman, MBE, James Taylor, Tony Waltham, Arthur H. Waltz

Academy of Motion Picture Arts and Sciences, American Automobile Manufacturers Association, American Correctional Association, American Forestry Association, American Library Association, *Amusement Business*, *Annual Abstract of Statistics*, Arbitron, Art Sales Index, ASH, Associated Press, Audit Bureau of Circulations, Automobile Association, BAFTA, BBC Worldwide Television, *Billboard*, BMI, *The Bookseller*, Book Trust, Bookwatch Ltd., BPI, *BP Statistical Review of World Energy*, Brit Awards, British Airports Authority, British Astronomical Society, British Broadcasting Corporation, British Library, British Rate & Data, Bureau of Federal Prisons, Bureau of Justice Statistics, Cadbury Schweppes Group, Cameron Mackintosh Ltd., *Campaign*, Carbon Dioxide Information Analysis Center, Central Intelligence Agency, Channel 5, Channel Four Television, Channel Swimming Association, Charities Aid Foundation, Christian Research Association, Christie's, CIN, Civil Aviation Authority, *Classical Music*, Coca-Cola, Corporate Intelligence Ltd., Countryside Commission, Cremation Society, *Crime in the United States*, *Criminal Statistics England & Wales*, Death Penalty Information Center, Department of the Army, Corps of Engineers, Department of Health, Department of Trade and Industry, Department of Transport, Diamond Information Centre, Eurodata TV, Euromonitor, Federal Bureau of Investigation, Feste Catalogue Index Database/Alan Somerset, *Flight International*, Food and Agriculture Organization of the United Nations, *Forbes Magazine*, Ford Motor Company Ltd., Friends of the Earth, General Accident, Generation AB, Geological Museum, London, Going for Green, Gold Fields Mineral Services Ltd., Governing Council of the Cat Fancy, Harrods Ltd., Haymarket Publishing, Health and Safety Executive, Higher Education Statistics Agency, Home Accident Surveillance System (HASS), Home Office, Iditarod Trail Committee, Independent Television, Indianapolis 500, Information Resources, Inc., Institute of Sports Medicine, International Atomic Energy Agency, International Civil Aviation Organization, International Cocoa Organization, International Coffee Organization, International Dairy Foods Association, International Ice Cream Association, International Tea Committee, International Union for the Conservation of Nature, International Union of Geological Sciences Commission on Comparative Planetology, *International Water Power and Dam Construction Handbook*, Interpol, ITV Network Centre, Kennel Club, Library Association, Lloyds Register of Shipping/MIPG/PPMS, London Regional Transport, London Transport Lost Property, *Marketing*, *Melody Maker*, Meteorological Office, MORI, Motor Vehicle Manufacturers Association, MRIB, NASA, National Association for Stock Car Auto Racing (NASCAR), National Basketball Association (NBA), National Dairy Council, National Football League (NFL), National Grid Company plc, National Piers Society, NCAA, *New Musical Express*, Niagara Falls Museum, Nobel Foundation, Northern Lighthouse Board, NPD Group Worldwide, Nua Ltd., Office of National Statistics, Ordnance Survey, *Oxford English Dictionary*, Patent Office, *Petfood Industry Magazine*, Pet Food Institute, Phobics Society, *Playbill*, Popular Music Database, Produktschap voor Gedistilleerde Dranken, Professional Golf Association (PGA), Public Lending Right, Public Library Association, Pullman Power Products Corporation, *Railway Gazette International*, RAJAR, Really Useful Group, *Record Collector*, Recording Industry Association of America (RIAA), Registrar General, Relate National Marriage Guidance, Royal Aeronautical Society, Royal College of Music, Royal Mail, Royal Mint, Royal Opera House, Royal Society for the Prevention of Cruelty to Animals, Royal Society for the Protection of Birds, Royal Society of Arts, Royal Television Society, Science Museum, London, Scotch Whisky Association, *Screen Digest*, Shakespeare Birthplace Trust, Siemens AG, Sightseeing Research, W. H. Smith Ltd., Sony UK Ltd., Sotheby's, *Spaceflight*, Spink & Son Ltd., *Sporting News*, Sports Council, *Statistical Abstract of the United States*, STATS Inc., Taylors of Loughborough, *Theatre World*, Tidy Britain Group, *Time*, *The Times*, Trebor Bassett Ltd., Trinity House, UNESCO, *Uniform Crime Statistics*, United Nations, Universal Postal Union, University of Westminster, *USA Today*, US Board on Geographic Names, US Bureau of the Census, USCOLD, US Department of Justice, US Geological Survey, US Immigration and Naturalization Service, US Social Security Administration, *Variety*, World Bank, World Health Organization, World Resources Institute, World Tourism Organization, Zenith International.

PICTURE CREDITS

t=top , c=centre, a=above, b=below, l=left, r=right
© Academy & Motion Picture Arts & Services ® 167tl
Allsport USA/Brian Bahr 228tc /Dave Cannon 245tr /Mark Thompson 236bl
BFI/United International Pictures 148br
Camera Press/N. Diaye 111br
Christie's Images 179tr
Corbis/Bettmann/Everett 70tl, 162t /UPI 163bl
Ecoscene 43br
Mary Evans Picture Library 71br, 126bc, 211br
Ronald Grant Archive 177bl, 177tr, 177tl
Susan Greenhill 6tl
Hulton Getty 56r, 84tr, 219tc
Image Bank 127tr
Liaison 74tr
London Transport Museum 214bl
National Maritime Museum 44cr
National Motor Museum, Beaulieu 82bc, 210tl Novosti 13tl
Paramount/Courtesy Kobal 149tr
Redferns/David Redfern 180tl
Rex Features 92tl, 105bl, 113tl, 123bc, 128tl, 131bl, 134tl, 136tl, 137bc, 140tr, 159ca, 159cb, 161bl, 164tl, 176bl, 212tl, 220tl, 243tr, 246bl /Jim Graham 145tr /B. Heinrich 169br /Iwasa 94br /Kevin Kolczyn 232tl / Raddaiz 168tr /Tim Rooke 49br, 242tl /Sipa Press 112tr, 139tr, 241b /Richard Sowersby 108tl /Bob Strong 19br /Pierre Suu 130tl / John Webster 85br
Royal Geographical Society 58bl
Science & Society Picture Library 189bl
Science Museum 218bl
Science Photo Library/Nasa 11tl
Frank Spooner Pictures 22b, 40bl, 48tr, 81tc, 89bl, 115tr, 120br, 132cc, 133tr, 135br, 142bl, 143bc, 157tl, 158bl, 160tr, 172tr, 174bl, 175tc, 225br, 226bl, 226tr /Joe Baker 142tr /Alain Benainous 152tl /Liaison 14bl /Singh Spooner 178bl
Sporting Pictures (UK) Ltd 244br
Tony Stone Images 87tl /Ben Edwards 97tr /Bill Heinsohn 194tr /Arnulf Husmo 193tl /Peter Pearson 107bc /Dave Saunder 199tl /Jack Vearey 199br /Baron Wolman 187bc / Herbert Zetti 155bl
Topham Picturepoint 72br, 146tr
Universal/Courtesy Kobal 148tl
Zefa Pictures 25tr, 63bl, 100bc, 109br

Every effort has been made to trace the copyright holders and we apologize in advance for any unintentional omissions. We would be pleased to insert the appropriate acknowledgments in any subsequent edition of this publication.

ILLUSTRATIONS

Richard Bonson, Mick Loates, Eric Thomas, Richard Ward, John Woodcock

INDEX

Patricia Coward

PUBLISHER'S ACKNOWLEDGMENTS

Dorling Kindersley would like to thank Chris Gordon and Jason Little for administrative and DTP assistance.

PACKAGER'S ACKNOWLEDGMENTS

GLS would like to thank Terry Burrows, Michael Downey, Christian Kepps, and Angela Wilkes for additional editorial assistance, and Dave Farrow for additional design assistance.